F
TRA
MW01688567

## ST. JOHN'S RIVER

Rose M. Wilson

# FLORIDA

## TRAVEL SMART®

**Rose M. Wilson**
**David J. Wilson**

John Muir Publications
A Division of Avalon Travel Publishing

John Muir Publications
A Division of Avalon Travel Publishing
5855 Beaudry Street
Emeryville, CA 94608



Printed in the United States of America
First edition. First printing March 2000

ISSN:1524-3915
ISBN: 1-56261-444-4

Editors: Dianna Delling, Nancy Gillan
Production: Marie J.T. Vigil
Design: Marie J.T. Vigil
Cover Design: Janine Lehmann, Marie J.T. Vigil
Typesetting: Kathleen Sparkes, White Hart Design
Map Style Development: American Custom Maps—Jemez Springs, NM USA
Map Illustrator: Michael Hermann, Kathleen Sparkes
Printer: Publishers Press
Front cover photos: *small*—© Dusty Willison/International Stock (Miami, FL)
*large*—© Andre Jenny/International Stock (Tampa, FL)
Back cover photo: © Mary McCulley/International Stock

Distributed to the book trade by
Publishers Group West
Berkeley, California

# *FLORIDA TRAVEL•SMART:* A GUIDE THAT GUIDES

Most guidebooks are primarily directories, providing information but very little help in making choices—you have to guess how to make the most of your time and money. *Florida Travel•Smart* is different: By highlighting the very best of Florida it acts like a personal tour guide rather than a directory.

## TAKE THE STRESS OUT OF TRAVEL

Sometimes traveling causes more stress than it relieves. Sorting through information, figuring out the best routes, determining what to see and where to eat and stay, scheduling each day in order to get the most out of your time—all of this can make a vacation feel daunting rather than fun. Relax. We've done a lot of the legwork for you. This book will help you plan a trip that suits *you*—whatever your time frame, budget, and interests.

## SEE THE BEST OF THE STATE

Authors David and Rose Wilson have lived in Florida for 13 years. They have hand-picked every listing in this book, and they give you an insider's perspective on what makes each one worthwhile. So while you'll find many of the big tourist attractions listed here, you'll also find lots of smaller, lesser-known treasures, such as the Florida International Museum in St. Petersburg or the quirky Fred Bear Museum in Gainesville.

In selecting the restaurants and accommodations for this book, the authors sought out unusual spots with local flavor. While in some areas of Florida chains are unavoidable, wherever possible the authors direct you to one-of-a-kind places. We also know that you want a range of options: One day you may crave fresh, local seafood at an upscale restaurant, while the next day you would be just as happy (as would your wallet) with authentic, inexpensive Cuban cuisine. Most of the restaurants and accommodations listed here are moderately priced, but the authors also include budget and splurge options, depending on the destination.

## CREATE THE TRIP YOU WANT

We all have different travel styles. Some people like spontaneous weekend jaunts, while others plan longer, more leisurely trips. You may want to cover as much ground as possible, no matter how much time you have. Or maybe you prefer to focus your trip on one part of the state or on some special interest, such as history, nature, or art. We've taken these differences into account.

Though the individual chapters stand on their own, they are organized in a geographically logical sequence, so that you could conceivably fly into Jacksonville, drive chapter by chapter to each destination in the book, and end up close to where you started. Of course, you don't have to follow that sequence, but it's there if you want a complete picture of Florida.

Each destination chapter offers ways of prioritizing when time is limited: In the Perfect Day section, the authors suggest what to do if you have only one day to spend in the area. Also, every Sightseeing Highlight is rated, from one to four stars: ★★★★—or "must see" sights first, followed by ★★★ sights, then ★★ sights, and finally ★—or "see if you have spare time" sights. At the end of each sight listing is a time recommendation in parentheses. User-friendly maps help you locate the sights, restaurants, and lodging of your choice.

And if you're in it for the ride, so to speak, you'll want to check out the Scenic Routes described at the end of several chapters. They take you through some of the most scenic parts of Florida.

In addition to these special features, the appendix has other useful travel tools:

- The Planning Map and Mileage Chart help you determine your own route and calculate travel time.
- The Special Interest Tours show you how to design your trip around any of six favorite interests.
- The Calendar of Events provides an at-a-glance view of when and where major events occur throughout the state.
- The Resource Guide tells you where to go for more information about national and state parks, individual cities and counties, local bed-and-breakfasts, and more.

## HAPPY TRAVELS

With this book in hand, you have many reliable recommendations and travel tools at your fingertips. Use it to make the most of your trip. And have a great time!

# WHY VISIT FLORIDA?

From families pursuing activity-packed summer vacations to nature lovers exploring the huge subtropical wilderness of the Everglades, more than 40 million visitors annually cross the border into the Sunshine State. Florida's expansive coastline supports nearly every type of water activity, from surfing on the Atlantic beaches to world-record fishing in the Gulf of Mexico. Plentiful shellfish make shell collecting a popular pastime, and thousands of lakes, rivers, and canals support river floating, waterskiing, tubing, canoeing, snorkeling, and diving. Parks and forests offer more than 2,000 miles of hiking and bicycling trails. And paddocks and training tracks around Ocala are home to a growing thoroughbred industry that has produced six Kentucky Derby champions, including 1978's Triple Crown winner, Affirmed.

Winter visitors include avid baseball fans who fill the sports stadiums of their favorite teams—20 of the 28 major-league clubs—for spring-training games. Golf is played year-round, with more than 1,000 courses offering public play. Other sports of every description, from lawn bowling and croquet to recreational hiking and canoeing or kayaking, have cadres of devoted participants. Arts and shopping venues are abundant, and some offer spectacular architecture as well as unsurpassed quality. There is, of course, an incredible selection of family amusements and theme parks, particularly in Central Florida. But family-oriented activites are not confined to the Orlando region.

From the excitement of the Daytona International Speedway to the quiet of an Everglades sawgrass marsh, Florida offers something for everyone. Indeed, diversity is one of the state's finest assets.

## LAY OF THE LAND

You won't need an oxygen tank to climb Florida's highest point—it's only 345 feet above sea level, on a hilltop near Lakewood in the Panhandle. Essentially, Florida is a flat, peninsular pancake, barely higher than the surrounding waters of the Atlantic Ocean and the Gulf of Mexico. True, there are some lovely sections of the state where the terrain rolls into small hills; perhaps these seem so attractive to Floridians because they provide at least some minor relief from the true horizontal.

Water is what Florida is all about: The state boasts around 1,200 miles of coastline, more than 2,275 miles of tidal shoreline, and 663 miles of beaches. Among the more than 7,700 lakes is one of the nation's largest, the 700-square-mile Lake Okeechobee. With this much water you'd expect to find islands, and you will: The state has about 4,500 of them.

While Florida's geographical features are duplicated in one way or another in other parts of the country, there is nothing else anywhere like the Everglades, that vast, bird-filled area of mangrove swamps, sawgrass prairies, and subtropical jungle that defines the state between Lake Okeechobee and Florida Bay. To appreciate the size of the Everglades, consider that 1.5-million-acre Everglades National Park encompasses only one-seventh of the treeless "river of grass." In the past, humans struggled to survive here. Now the passion is to preserve the uniqueness of the Everglades and the wildlife it spawns and shelters for future generations.

## FLORA AND FAUNA

In a state with nearly a hundred state parks, two national parks, three national forests, two national seashores, and more than a dozen wildlife refuges, it's not surprising that Florida wildlife is most commonly of the type that lives or feeds near water.

The huge, colorful, live coral reef along the Florida Keys harbors an amazing variety of fish and other sea life. Angelfish, butterfly fish, parrot fish, sea cucumbers, shrimp, crabs, sea fans, anemones, and marine worms all thrive in these waters. Clinging to much of the rest of Florida's shoreline, limestone reefs are home to grouper, snapper, mackerel, cobia, amberjack, and many other species. Oysters, crabs, and shrimp proliferate in the fertile, sheltered estuaries where the rivers meet the sea, feeding in the mangroves, salt marshes, and sea grass. Mullet are plentiful, entertaining—they're most likely the fish you'll see and hear leaping clear of the water and landing with a splash at sunset—and a major food source for sea trout, redfish, tarpon, catfish, and black drum, as well as the multitude of Florida shorebirds and waders.

Dense clusters of red, black, and white mangroves cover the coastal areas. Mangrove thickets offer such substantial protection from the elements that boat owners shelter their craft in the midst of mangrove islands during hurricane threats. As the mangroves' leaves decay and die, they become food for the animals living within their complex root systems, making them an ideal spot for fish breeding. Unfortunately, the same conditions make them equally attractive to mosquitoes, and these bloodsucking insects can be a serious problem in Florida, particularly when winter temperatures aren't low enough to kill off the population.

If the state is widely known for any particular sea creature, it is undoubtedly the manatee, that bulbous, gentle gray creature found almost exclusively in Florida waters. In winter you can see them in the Crystal and Homosassa Rivers and in other warm, shallow waters, especially along Fort Myers and Sanibel Island on the west coast, along the St. Johns River, and at Blue Spring State Park in Orange City.

Florida is a nesting ground for loggerhead and other sea turtles that come ashore to lay their eggs. But it's a risky business. The hatchlings are lucky if they find the sea before either eggs or young turtles are eaten by raccoons. Spotting a dolphin is common enough, though not a guaranteed treat. Along the west coast, watch for them moving north just off the Gulf of Mexico shoreline at dusk. You have a far better chance of seeing an alligator sunning itself or floating, motionless, just breaking the water's surface. They can be found on the golf courses, in every lake, along the banks of the state's rivers, and practically everywhere you tread in the Everglades. Gators generally cause little harm—except to small mammals—but they don't take kindly to teasing.

There must be 10 birds for every tree in Florida. From songbirds to wading birds to birds of prey, the state's bird population is enormous and supremely varied. Bird-watching is a popular pastime throughout the state. Enclaves of magnificent, black frigate birds, roseate spoonbills, and flamingos thrive in the millions of acres of pines, hammocks, and mangroves. White ibis, great egrets, tricolored herons, purple gallinules, gulls, pelicans, anhingas, and cormorants are easy to find. Inland nature preserves are likely places for spotting sandhill cranes, wood storks, bald eagles, hawks, and owls.

Bobcats may often be spotted around Everglades National Park, and the few remaining Florida panthers (there may be about 40) live in the more forested areas, but you're unlikely to see any. Instead, look for tiny, bright-green tree frogs, often found in the center of red, water-filled bromeliads. Watch where you're walking: blue-tailed skinks, lizards of every description, and green or brownish anoles, which can change colors to blend in with their environment, rush and leap about in the undergrowth and in both tall and short grass. It's not uncommon for visitors to become just a bit spooked with all the animal activity going on around them. All these little creatures are harmless and quite useful as they lie in wait for moths and roaches.

It's not for nothing that Ponce de León named this land for his homeland's "Feast of Flowers." Florida has long been known for its lush, abundant native plant life. Some locals say that in Florida you can spit on the ground and it'll grow. Jungle-like forests of mahogany hammocks, strangler figs, sawgrass, sea dunes, slash and longleaf pine forests, and live oaks and cypress trees draped with Spanish moss are typical scenic backdrops. The climate is so conducive to successful landscaping that formal gardens are common. Ornamental gardens foster such blooming flowers as azaleas, camellias, magnolias, orchids, and bougainvillea. A Florida garden during spring, when the azaleas are in full bloom, is a sight not to be missed.

## HISTORY

A thousand years ago, the Timucuan people inhabited the northern sections of what is now Florida, the Apalachees lived in the west, and the ferocious Calusas lived in the Everglades. Interspersed were smaller groups such as the Tequestas, who tried to mind their own business on little pockets of coastline. The Native Americans left only small traces of their civilizations, so most of Florida's known recorded history stems from the spring of 1513, when Spanish explorer Juan Ponce de León landed at or near present-day St. Augustine and pronounced it Spanish territory. He called it "Florida" in honor of Spain's Easter holiday, *Pascua Florida*, the Feast of Flowers.

*Florida became the 27th state in 1845. It seceded from the Union at the start of the Civil War, in which it played only a minor role.*

Soon, Hernando de Soto arrived to explore and map the territory. He made it from Tampa Bay to Tallahassee, and then into other southern states until he died along the Mississippi River. In 1565 Pedro Menendez de Aviles landed near where Ponce de León had first come ashore, and established St. Augustine, the first permanent European settlement in the United States.

After 200 years of sporadic fighting between Spain, France, and England, Spain ceded Florida to England in return for Cuba. That arrangement held until after the American Revolution, during which Spain regained the territory, only to sell it to the United States in 1821 after Andrew Jackson's raids into northern Florida had provoked the First Seminole War. The Seminoles were not a tribe, but rather a collection of Creek and other southeastern tribes who had been forced southward as the colonies expanded.

The disastrous Second Seminole War, begun in 1835 by then-President Jackson, eventually resulted in the defeat of the Indians, most of whom were shipped to Indian Territory in what is now Oklahoma. Some disappeared into the Everglades, and the Seminoles and Miccosukees live there still.

For good or ill, Florida is what it is today because of the efforts of two railroad tycoons, Henry Flagler and Henry Plant, who raced each other down the state establishing luxury accommodations for rich visitors from the north. They left behind magnificent buildings that serve today as museums (Flagler's Whitehall in Palm Beach; Plant's Moorish-style Henry B. Plant Museum on the University of Tampa campus) or hotels. Well-known figures began to build "winter cottages" in Florida. A rare photo shows *Uncle Tom's Cabin* author Harriet Beecher Stowe relaxing with her family near Jacksonville in about 1873.

As news of Florida's subtropical climate spread, land speculators arrived, and then more-ordinary tourists. Everyone from Henry Ford to Ransom E. Olds (the Oldsmobile founder also left his name behind in Oldsmar, on Tampa Bay) got in on the land rush. It was boom time all over the state until the fantasy burst in 1926.

Despite a sometimes uneven economy, there really haven't been any bad times in Florida since World War II. The nature of South Florida changed with the arrival of huge numbers of Cubans in the 1960s. And as air-conditioning became universal and mosquito control programs began to take effect, the numbers of northern retirees began to swell until, in the late 1980s, a thousand new residents a day were setting up households in the state. Today, with a population of more than 15 million, Florida ranks fourth among the states, but that number is swelled each year by more than 40 million visitors from all over the world. Huge numbers of them head straight for Central Florida, to the great theme parks of Walt Disney World and Universal Studios.

Today Florida faces significant problems because its population is growing so rapidly, and the debates over how to develop wisely are endless. Nevertheless, great wild areas have been put aside, and though many of the sights people come to see are man-made wonders, you don't have to wander far off the concrete highways to find the natural state.

## CULTURES

Native Americans have been living in Florida's Panhandle for perhaps 12,000 years, according to evidence found near Fort Walton Beach and other settlement sites. And archeological evidence indicates that about 2,500 years ago at least some of these groups had developed agricultural societies. What remains of native culture in Florida today is that of the Seminoles and Miccosukees, whose *chickees* (palm-thatched roof shelters) dot various beaches and tourist attractions. Recorded history began with the Spanish conquerors and explorers, and the names of places throughout Florida reflect their influence.

The major threads of Florida culture today, however, stem from much more recent times. Whip-cracking "Crackers," who tilled the soil and whipped their oxen, lent their name to Florida's style of homes with wide porches for rocking chairs and open walkways to catch a breeze in the constant fight against the heat. Unprotected work in the fields gave the Crackers red necks, but as both a noun and an adjective the term "redneck" has come to be used in a derogatory manner, implying a kind of rural, Neanderthal ignorance in everything from politics to religion.

Today in Florida you are likely to experience a sometimes confusing weave of Southern, Northern, and Hispanic cultures. It would be logical to believe that Florida is part of the South, but that's largely a physical rather than a cultural condition. With some exceptions, only in the Panhandle west of Tallahassee do vestiges of the gracious South remain. This is where you will find most of Florida's stately mansions, sweeping lawns, and unhurried outdoor garden parties.

In Miami and other areas of the southeast, and also in Central Florida, you will find strong Cuban, Puerto Rican, Latin American, and South American influences. This extends to far more than the cuisine, which is a delightful mix of Spanish, Mexican, and Caribbean flavors. Particularly in Miami, you should be prepared for Spanish everywhere. Street signs and billboards may have Spanish first, English second, or vice versa. Even such a standard American food as the lowly hot dog is likely to be entered as *perros calientes* on display boards, street carts, and menus. And as you approach the heart of the Spanish district, Little Havana and Calle Ocho (S.W. Eighth Street), English may disappear altogether. This amounts to culture shock for some visitors, but if you're not Hispanic you might see it as a way of getting a close-up look at another culture without having to buy an overseas flight.

Most everywhere else around the state, you'll hear accents from New York, Boston, Chicago, and elsewhere mixed with a touch of Southern drawl among permanent residents, young and old. About 37 percent of Floridians were born in the state. All other residents are from somewhere else, creating Florida's own melting pot. Add the hundreds of thousands of "snowbirds"—Canadians and northern U.S. residents who come to Florida each winter for six months of ice-free roads and relatively balmy temperatures—and you begin to get a sense of the nuances that define Florida culture today.

## THE ARTS

Not so very long ago, the Florida arts scene was a cheap target for retirees who took to writing letters to the editor complaining that the main disadvantage of spending winters in Florida was the fact that it coincided with the performing arts season in their "real" (northern) home city or state. If that was ever true, it certainly is not today. Superb, visually stunning performing-arts halls exist around the state, from magnificent Kravis Center for the Performing Arts in West Palm Beach to glittering Broward Center for the Performing Arts in Fort Lauderdale; from the purple Van Wezel Performing Arts Center in Sarasota to Ruth Eckerd Hall in Clearwater and the Tampa Bay Performing Arts Center in Tampa. These halls are major stops for world touring orchestras, top-ranked traveling Broadway shows, and solo artists. The Florida Orchestra in Tampa Bay and the Florida Philharmonic Orchestra in West Palm Beach are major arts institutions, as are professional theater companies in Sarasota, St. Petersburg, and Miami.

While it seems that every town with a population of 500 has its own museum these days, several art and science museums in Florida rank among the finest anywhere in the country. The largely undiscovered Appleton Museum of Art in Ocala is itself a visual treat, with mesmerizing displays of European and Asian art. The Norton Museum of Art in West Palm Beach has one of the country's finest European and American art collections, while the John and Mable Ringling Museum of Art in Sarasota displays what is said to be the world's largest collection of Baroque, Italian, and Flemish Renaissance paintings. The world's largest single collection of Salvador Dalí works is in St. Petersburg, just a few blocks from the Florida International Museum, whose blockbuster "Treasures of the Czars" and "Titanic" exhibits wowed visitors from around the world.

In short, the state has long since made up any artistic deficits it may have carried. Whether your taste runs to music from Mahler or Madonna, or the artwork of Albrecht Dürer or Andy Warhol, you'll find first-rate examples in Florida.

## CUISINE

Culinary rages come and go, but after you try some of the best "Floribbean" cuisine the state has to offer, you may join others in hoping that this is one fad that hangs around for awhile. The piquant flavors brought out by the tart, spicy, citrus elements are uncommonly good and when the ideal combination is attained, the natural sweetness of the fruits offers a taste unlike any other. Floribbean conch chowder is a staple in the southern reaches of the Keys.

As you would expect, Cuban and Spanish dining options are legion in Florida, especially in areas with high concentrations of Hispanic residents. Plantains, rice and beans, roast pork, or chicken with yellow rice are typical dishes. Hot sauce is always available, but keep in mind that Spanish food is not spicy and shouldn't be lumped in with Mexican cuisine, which is also well represented throughout the state.

For the most part, for true Southern cooking you'll have to head for the Panhandle. There the Deep South influence brings you breakfasts of steaming grits and biscuits with sausage gravy, fried catfish and hushpuppies, or fried green tomatoes and fried okra for dinner.

Despite Florida's preeminence as a cattle-producing state, the fruits of the sea probably constitute the most common category on the average menu, whether in a barefoot beach bar or an upscale restaurant. Firm, sweet-tasting native redfish is a specialty, and grouper, mullet, and amberjack are prevalent throughout the state, served fried, baked, broiled, or blackened. If you're in Apalachicola or Cedar Key, opt for the local oysters—they're among the best anywhere. November through May is the season for stone-crab claws, prized for their sweet meat and the relative ease of getting to it.

The fruits of the soil are celebrated throughout Florida. Strawberries, tomatoes, watermelon, and citrus fruits are inviting in season. If you see greenish Key lime pie, reject it. Real Key lime pie is light yellow, made from the juice of tiny, extra-tart Key limes. February and March are strawberry-picking months, and that's when Plant City holds its annual Strawberry Festival. Watch the newspapers if you like to pick your own fruits and vegetables—the classifieds run farm listings under the heading "Good Things to Eat," and the fresh strawberries from the farms in Central Florida along I-4 and southeast of Tampa are to die for. Blueberries do well in Florida, too; Ocala holds a Blueberry Festival in late spring every year.

## OUTDOOR ACTIVITIES

Water, of course, is at the heart of a huge portion of the state's outdoor activities: diving, snorkeling, windsurfing, parasailing, kayaking, boating, canoeing, waterskiing, swimming, and shelling, for example. And then there's sunbathing. Lying on a chaise out in the backyard doesn't count—you must be near the water to truly sunbathe, preferably at the beach, and Florida is home to 663 miles of some of the finest beaches in the world.

More than 4,000 sunken ships lie beneath the coastal waters that surround the Florida peninsula, rusting bait for scuba divers and snorkelers in such places as the Florida Keys National Marine Sanctuary, John Pennekamp National Park, and the reefs off Boynton Beach. Cave divers love to explore the springs and underwater caverns of central and north Florida. Boaters can easily find ramps into lakes and rivers, and bait-and-tackle shops are everywhere near the best fishing holes (which can be very large, indeed, in this state).

Uncongested waters along the coast challenge deep-sea anglers. (For detailed information on boating and a *Florida Boater's Guide*, call the Florida Marine Patrol, 904/488-5600.) The "World's Luckiest Fishing Village," the Panhandle town of Destin, owes its well-deserved reputation to the close proximity of deep Gulf of Mexico waters—100-foot depths are accessible within a few miles of shore. Destin holds a month-long fishing rodeo every October. In the Keys, Islamorada has reached near-legendary status among fishermen. Throughout the state, there are enough piers, jetties, bridges, and just plain accessible shoreline to make renting a fishing boat unnecessary. Fishing piers along the coastline offer top-notch fishing for as many as 600 species, many of which, when not eating each other, feed on the barnacles attached to the pilings, just waiting for a hook to descend.

The flat terrain of central and north central Florida is perfect for soaring and gliding, hot-air ballooning, and skydiving. Tennis facilities are available at most resorts, and most cities and towns have free tennis courts. Florida has more golf courses than any other state—1,200 in all. And though it was once thought that Florida's golf courses were all level and uninteresting, that's no longer the case: The game's best course designers have taken care of the terrain problem, and the top-rated courses now have moguls and hills and something they call "Florida waste" (not sand, not fairway, just gravel and scrub: stay out of it).

Serious hikers can tackle the Florida Trail, a well-marked hiking path that links one end of the state to the other (for a copy of the *Florida Trails* booklet, call the Florida Department of Natural Resources, 850/488-3701), and there are plenty of shorter hikes in state preserves and forests.

# PLANNING YOUR TRIP

Before you set out on your trip, you'll need to do some planning. Use this chapter in conjunction with the tools in the appendix to answer some basic questions. First of all, when are you going? You may already have specific dates in mind; if not, various factors will probably influence your timing. Either way, you'll want to know about local events, the weather, and other seasonal considerations. This chapter discusses all of that, while the Calendar of Events in the appendix provides a month-by-month view of major area events.

How much should you expect to spend on your trip? This chapter addresses various regional factors you'll want to consider in estimating your travel expenses. How will you get around? Check out the section on local transportation. If you decide to travel by car, the Planning Map and Mileage Chart in the appendix can help you figure out exact routes and driving times, while the Special Interest Tours provide several focused itineraries. The chapter concludes with some reading recommendations, both fiction and nonfiction, to give you various perspectives on Florida. If you want specific information about individual cities or counties, use the Resource Guide in the appendix.

## WHEN TO GO

Let's be blunt here. Don't come to Florida in February or March unless you want to join the largest crowds at the theme parks and the heaviest traffic on the state's highways. These are the months when Florida is filled with winter residents and visitors, baseball spring-training fans and, in certain towns, college kids on Spring Break. If you have great latitude in choosing the time to visit, try for May or September. The roads are more open, the beaches much less crowded, and the theme park lines less aggravating.

No matter when you come, you can expect to see the sun. A lot. It's not for nothing that Florida is nicknamed the Sunshine State. There is hardly ever a gray day in the peninsular part of Florida, a boast dramatized by a St. Petersburg newspaper that promised to give out free papers on any day that the sun didn't shine. The largest number of days it ever had to give away papers in one year is four.

While visitors often can't see the seasons passing, residents can feel subtle shifts in temperature as spring settles into a long, hot, wet summer that can and often does last through October. If you visit during summer, often the obvious choice for families with children, you should be aware that summer is the rainy season. Torrential downpours lasting an hour or two occur almost daily, commonly in late afternoon. These storms are often accompanied by violent lightning, which can be more of a hazard in the flat Florida landscape than elsewhere. Several people are killed by lightning each year, so take commonsense precautions whether you're on the golf course or visiting theme parks.

December, January, and February are the coolest months, but in the state's subtropical central portion the temperatures seldom dip into the 30s. If they do, it's only for a day or two. It hardly ever gets that cold in southern Florida, however, where you'll find the bulk of the state's citrus growers. The northern regions have a more temperate climate. It's not terribly unusual to find subfreezing winter temperatures in Tallahassee, and sometimes snow falls south of the Georgia–Alabama line.

Ideally, travel in Florida in the "shoulder" spring or fall seasons, when daytime temperatures are warm but not extreme and the evenings are only a bit cooler. Visiting between July and November has its own potential hazard, because this is hurricane season. However, as terrible as they can be, there is usually ample warning and plenty of time to move away from the coasts to inland locations.

## HOW MUCH WILL IT COST?

You don't need a fat bankroll to visit Florida, but your journey will be more enjoyable if you can at least taste some of the high life the state has to offer. If possible, budget accordingly. Save where you can so you can splurge on a few luxurious nights or meals at historic resorts you would otherwise only read about.

If, like most Florida visitors, you are at least partially drawn by the Orlando area theme parks, be prepared to spend, and big. Disney's parks charge more than $45 a day for adults and only slightly less for children, so a family of four is going to drop at least $200 on a visit to *one* park by the time a few refreshments and drinks are factored in. Add even modest accommodations in nearby Kissimmee and a meal or two, and that's $350 to $400 for one 24-hour period. Now, Disney has four parks, Universal has two, and there's SeaWorld and Arabian Knights and King Henry's Feast and Medieval Times and . . . visit several and you'll be facing a staggering sum. Similar costs may be expected for visits to Busch Gardens in Tampa and Cypress Gardens in Winter Haven.

Don't let figures like that put you off, however. There are many other wonderful places in Florida, where beaches cost nothing more than the occasional parking fee, fascinating natural preserves and state parks cost just a few dollars for a car full of people, and the nearly constant sunshine is free. A stroll down the great streets in Miami Beach, Bal Harbour, or even along what is perhaps the costliest shopping street in the nation, Palm Beach's Worth Avenue, need cost you nothing but leisure time, and you'll have fascinating architecture to admire even as the ever-watchful store clerk catches you shaking your head over the $500 price tag on a short-sleeve shirt.

You can count on spending more or less depending on where you visit. Spending the night, eating at really good restaurants, and enjoying the highlights in places like Palm Beach, Boca Raton, and Miami Beach along the east coast, for example, will cost a considerable amount. The same can be said for the Naples and Sarasota areas on the Gulf of Mexico coast. On the other hand, moderately priced motels and inexpensive restaurants abound in Jacksonville, Tallahassee, Central Florida towns, and the Gulf of Mexico coast from Tampa Bay north.

One way to cut expenses is to travel in the low season—summer and sometimes late spring and early fall. Florida is relatively empty in summer, with the "snowbirds" having flown back north, preferring to take a winter getaway. Hotels drop their prices like stones just to keep their rooms filled. A room at The Breakers in Palm Beach that will cost you a minimum of $350 a night in December can be had for about $175 in June. And those kinds of savings apply nearly everywhere. It might be enough of a break to persuade you to check in at the Amelia Island Plantation or the Marriott at Sawgrass Resort to try their famous golf courses. You won't find such off-season deals at most of the high-end restaurants, but local newspapers often advertise two-for-one specials at many perfectly good eateries during summer months. Discounts are widely available for most attractions (pick up discount-coupon brochures in most hotels and at nearly every visitors center) but not for the Disney parks.

A central point to remember when visiting Florida is that this is a state designed for visitors. Accommodations and meals are available in every price range, and since there is considerable competition for your business, you're likely to do well regardless of your spending level. Tourism as an industry would fail if visitors only came once, so everyone in the hospitality and attraction business in Florida wants your goodwill. They want you to come back again.

## ORIENTATION AND TRANSPORTATION

If you can follow an interstate highway, you can get just about anywhere in Florida. I-10 crosses Florida's panhandle from Pensacola to Jacksonville; I-95 hugs the Atlantic coastline from the Georgia border to Miami; and I-75 generally draws a line paralleling the Gulf of Mexico coastline until it cuts straight across the state through the Everglades to Miami. I-4 bisects the state from Tampa to Daytona, and Florida's Turnpike, a toll road, provides a north–south crossover speedway from I-75 near Ocala to the east coast, all the way to Florida City.

The chapters of this book are arranged in an order that takes you south along the east coast, north along the west coast and then up into the Panhandle. But you don't have to stay on the interstates to approximate that scheme. U.S. 1 (called Federal Highway in many towns and cities) will take you from Jacksonville to the tip of Key West, and SR A1A is the coastal roadway beside the Atlantic beaches. U.S. 41 and then U.S. 19 will take you from Miami to Perry, at the eastern edge of the Panhandle, and U.S. 98 carries on to Pensacola. Direct routes across the interior of the state are harder to find, but U.S. 27 will lead you down the middle of Florida from Perry to Miami, and SR 60 crosses east to west, from Vero Beach to Clearwater Beach.

It's worth noting that Floridians tend to drive very fast, a practice aided by the fact that highways are generally in very good condition, and that they're flat and straight. Aside from the rare sinkhole that can develop suddenly (and can be large enough to swallow a small car), road hazards are mostly presented by impatient drivers. As a visitor, you may not always be certain where you are going and you may be driving more slowly than residents. If so, stay in the right lanes and let the SUVs roar on by. It's good policy, and it's much safer than presenting a rolling roadblock when the speed limit is 70 and everyone's traveling at 75 to 80 mph.

A final note on speed: Remember the Hollywood film in which stereotypical Southern police set up speed traps to raise money for the town picnic?

That's actually happened in the towns of Waldo, Starke, and Lawtey, along U.S. 301 northeast of Gainesville. Avoiding a ticket means dropping from 55 mph to a 30-mph crawl through those towns on four- and six-lane highways. If you don't, the boys in blue will get you.

If you prefer to fly, you'll find airports in every major city and in many smaller cities, too. The Tampa and Orlando airports are usually rated among the finest in the nation, but you can also easily fly to West Palm Beach, Fort Lauderdale, Miami, Sarasota, Fort Myers, Jacksonville, and Tallahassee on major carriers.

Train aficionados might want to take Amtrak down the country's East Coast to Tampa or Miami, or from the West Coast all the way to Jacksonville. Amtrak also operates a car–train service along the East Coast. For a price, they'll load your car on the train and you can ride the rails until you get to Winter Park, north of Orlando.

## RECOMMENDED READING

Florida's history and the colorful characters who built the state (or tried to tear it down) are the subjects of innumerable books. Perhaps one of the best ways to get the flavor of the state is to pick up a book or two by Al Burt, who for more than 20 years was a roving columnist for the *Miami Herald*.

Burt's collection of odd and memorable stories about life in Florida, *Becalmed in the Mullet Latitudes* (Southeastern Printing Co., Inc., 1983), takes you into the nation's smallest post office, in Ochopee, and finds generations of turpentine industry Crackers near the Georgia line. It's amusing and amazing.

Immerse yourself in a more recent volume, *Al Burt's Florida: Snowbirds, Sand Castles, and Self-Rising Crackers* (University Press of Florida, 1997) for a real sense of Florida's expanding and evolving cultural scene, including an excellent evocation of the wonderful Wakulla Springs.

Douglas Whitley's *Roadside History of Florida* (Mountain Press, 1997) is an absorbing roam across the state, presenting little-known but fascinating facts. This book also reproduces some historic photographs.

For a more serious look at the state, *The New History of Florida* by Michael Gannon (University Press of Florida, 1996) is concise and beautifully written, and reads more like a novel than a textbook. Spare a few hours for railroad robber-baron Henry Flagler, too. Sidney Walter Martin's *Henry Flagler: Visionary of the Gilded Age* (Tailored Tours Publications, 1998) follows this wealthy adventurer down the state's east coast as he creates his 522-mile string of luxury hotels, farms, and entire towns on his way across the islands and the ocean to Key West.

Ferdie Pacheco used to be the "fight doctor," the ringside physician at some of the most famous heavyweight bouts of the Muhammed Ali era. Pacheco is a native of Ybor City, Tampa's ethnic enclave, and in *The Christmas Eve Cookbook with Tales of Nochebuena and Chanukah* (University Press of Florida, 1998), he and his wife, Lusita, present a wonderful collection of stories and recipes from the Cubans, Italians, Jews, and Spaniards who poured into Ybor City's collective around 1900.

An underappreciated aspect of Florida life is its ranching and the fact that Florida was as much cowboy territory as the West. In *Cracker: Florida's Enduring Cowboys* (Long Wind Publishing, 1998), photojournalist Jon Kral details where the term "Cracker" came from. By the time you finish, you'll have to look at the cover to be certain you've been reading about Florida rather than Arizona.

Much is written about the Everglades and the efforts to preserve it, but nothing surpasses the book that started that preservation effort: Marjory Stoneman Douglas's *The Everglades: River of Grass* (Pineapple Press, 50th anniversary edition, 1997).

If you like to explore on foot, go straight to *Guide to Florida Historical Walking Tours* by Roberta Sandler (Pineapple Press, 1998) for fascinating visits to Robert Frost's vacation cottage in Key West or to the architectural masterpieces and historic landmarks that dot the state.

# 1
# JACKSONVILLE

Here you are, barely into Florida and already notching up superlatives for being in the largest city (by land area) in the United States, which just happens to sit astride the country's longest north-flowing river (St. Johns, at 273 miles). The tiny river settlement of Cowford—so called because it was, in fact, a cattle crossing point—became Jacksonville in 1822, when Florida's military governor (and later U.S. president) Andrew Jackson was figuring out what to do with this land of swamp and mosquitoes. For the first part of the twentieth century, Jacksonville was Florida's leading city, a railroad terminus for eastern seaboard holidaymakers, a center for movie studios during the silent-film era, a major naval base, and later, a banking and insurance center. The naval base and a number of major banks and insurance companies are still here.

Jacksonville today is far down the list of major Florida tourist destinations. Certainly, the city's highest-rated attractions should not be passed over, but it usually happens that visitors find compelling reasons to head north or southeast of the city.

To the north, Jacksonville is graced by Amelia Island, a strip of sand 2.5 miles wide edged by 13 miles of perfect Atlantic quartz beach sand and dunes. The island is filled with saltwater marshes and huge wildlife populations that surround historic Fernandina Beach, the island's only town and, by the way, Florida's first resort. No fewer than 50 blocks of architecturally varied homes and buildings around Centre Street are listed on the National Register of Historic Places.

Past Jacksonville's swampy eastern borders, visitors migrate toward the resorts and lodgings of Ponte Vedra Beach, not just for more sun and sand but for memorable dining and some of the finest golf courses in the Southeast.

## A PERFECT DAY IN JACKSONVILLE

Wake up with the sunrise 30 miles north of Jacksonville on lovely Amelia Island before you stroll the cobblestone streets and enjoy breakfast at one of the little restaurants somewhere in Fernandina Beach's historic core. Watch the shrimpers get their boats ready at the town's marina, then wander freely around Centre Street and its tributaries. Head south to the metropolis, straight to the Cummer Gallery of Art and find a nearby coffeehouse for an early afternoon snack. Then make your way to the Karpeles Manuscript Library. In the late afternoon, head over to Jacksonville Landing. The riverside marketplace not only has shops to intrigue you but also is a staging point for water taxis that will take you across the impressively broad St. Johns River to the maritime museum historical center or to one of the area's first-rate restaurants for dinner. Get a western window seat so you can watch the sun sink into the horizon above the river.

## SIGHTSEEING HIGHLIGHTS

### ★★★★ CUMMER GALLERY OF ART

**826 Riverside Ave., Jacksonville, 904/356-6857**

Decorative and fine arts dating from 2000 B.C. form the heart of the permanent exhibit in northeast Florida's best collection of Western art. The paintings include Thomas Sully's *Portrait of a Young Lady,* as well as work by Winslow Homer and landscapes by Thomas Gainsborough. The museum houses the Wark Collection of exquisite early eighteenth-century Meissen porcelain tableware. Traveling exhibits complement the permanent collection. Some visitors come just to spend time in the magnificent formal garden, modeled after the gardens of the Villa Gamberaia in Florence.

***Details:*** *Open Tue, Thu, 10–9, Wed, Fri–Sat 10–5, Sun 2–5 (closes for two weeks every April). Admission: $5 adults, $3 children and seniors. (2–3 hours)*

# JACKSONVILLE

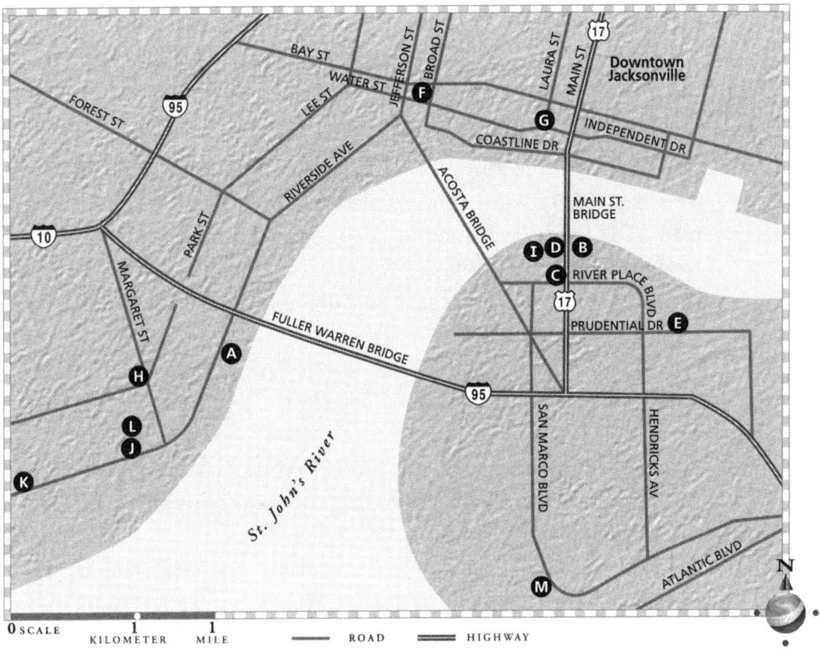


## SIGHTS

- Ⓐ Cummer Gallery of Art
- Ⓑ Jacksonville Historical Center
- Ⓒ Jacksonville Maritime Museum
- Ⓓ Museum of Science and History

## FOOD

- Ⓔ Crawdaddy's
- Ⓕ Juliette's
- Ⓖ Mozzarella's Cafe
- Ⓗ Notre Gourmet
- Ⓘ River City Brewing Company

## LODGING

- Ⓙ Cleary-Dickert House
- Ⓚ House on Cherry Street
- Ⓛ Plantation Manor Inn
- Ⓜ San Marco Point House

---

## ★★★★ KARPELES MANUSCRIPT LIBRARY

**101 W. First St., Jacksonville, 904/356-2992**

After the documents have been signed, the music written, the letters delivered and read, what happens to those scraps of paper? Some end up in wonderful places like this, a repository for one of the world's largest private holdings of historical documents. Changing exhibits may display letters from Napoleon Bonaparte or George

Washington, the Emancipation Proclamation signed by Abraham Lincoln, an international treaty, or original manuscripts of the music of Mozart or Beethoven.

***Details***: *Open daily noon–4. Free. (1 hour)*

## ★★★★ KINGSLEY PLANTATION

**11676 Palmetto Ave., Fort George Island, 904/251-3537**

This early nineteenth-century plantation, home to Florida's oldest plantation house, is named for Zephaniah Kingsley, who operated it from 1813 to 1839. Visitors will learn a great deal about slave life through exhibits and by walking around the kitchen house, barn, garden, and remains of 23 slave cabins.

***Details:*** *Located three miles west of A1A at the end of a gravel road. Open daily 9–5. Free. (1–2 hours)*

## ★★★ ALEXANDER BREST MUSEUM AND GALLERY

**2800 University Blvd. N., Arlington, Jacksonville, 904/745-7371**

Steuben glass, Bing & Grondahl porcelains, and cloisonné from the eighteenth to twentieth centuries are the core of this small but highly regarded fine and decorative arts collection on the campus of Jacksonville University. The museum also has an extensive display of hand-carved ivory.

***Details:*** *Open Mon–Fri 9–4:30, Sat noon–5. Free. (1–2 hours)*

## ★★★ JACKSONVILLE MUSEUM OF CONTEMPORARY ART

**4160 Boulevard Center Dr., Southside, Jacksonville, 904/398-8336**

Among the artists represented in the impressive permanent collection at the Museum of Contemporary Art are Ed Paschke, Sam Gilliam, Alexander Calder, and Joan Miró. The museum also features an extensive collection of pre-Columbian artifacts and rotating exhibits.

***Details:*** *Open Tue–Wed, Fri 10–4, Thu 10–10, Sat–Sun 1–5. Admission: $3 adults, $2 children and seniors. (1 hour)*

## ★★★ JACKSONVILLE ZOOLOGICAL GARDENS

**8605 Zoo Rd., Northside, Jacksonville, 904/757-4463**

The city's zoo is home to more than 800 animals which are kept in natural habitats with names like the Plains of East Africa and Birds of the Rift Valley. In the African Savannah, elevated walkways take you right past lions. A walk-through aviary featuring natural trees and a waterfall offers close-up looks at exotic birds. Boat, train, and elephant rides are available at extra cost.

**Details:** *From I-95, take Exit 124. Open daily 9–5. Admission: $6.50 adults, $4 children, $4.50 seniors. Train ride: $3 adults, $1.50 children, $2 seniors. (2–3 hours)*

## ★★ AMELIA ISLAND MUSEUM OF HISTORY

**233 S. Third St., Fernandina Beach, Amelia Island, 904/261-7378**

This small museum features artifacts that detail the island's occupation under eight different flags. The docents here are experts on the area's fascinating history; ask about guided walking tours of the historic district.

**Details:** *Open Mon–Sat 10–2. Free. (30 minutes)*

## ★★ FORT CAROLINE NATIONAL MEMORIAL

**12713 Fort Caroline Rd., Arlington, Jacksonville, 904/641-7155**

In 1564 French Protestant colonial adventurers led by René de Laudonnière established a settlement here on the St. Johns River, only to be massacred the next year by Spanish colonialists. From the visitors center, a quarter-mile walk through the oak woods leads to a model of the original fort. Inside, you'll see French and Indian artifacts and learn about the politics and religious strife of the sixteenth-century. The Ribault Monument, an obelisk a half-mile east of the fort, commemorates the colony.

**Details:** *Open daily 9–5. Free. (1 hour)*

## ★★ JACKSONVILLE MARITIME MUSEUM

**Jacksonville Landing, 904/355-9011, Southbank Riverwalk, Jacksonville, 904/398-9011**

Across the St. Johns River from each other, the two locations of this museum display its collection of model ships, photos, artifacts, and paintings related to the maritime history of the port city from 1842 through World War II.

**Details:** *Jacksonville Landing museum open Mon–Sat 11–7, Sun 1–5. Riverwalk museum open daily 11–5 except Tue 11–4, Sun 1–5. Free. (30 minutes)*

# FERNANDINA BEACH

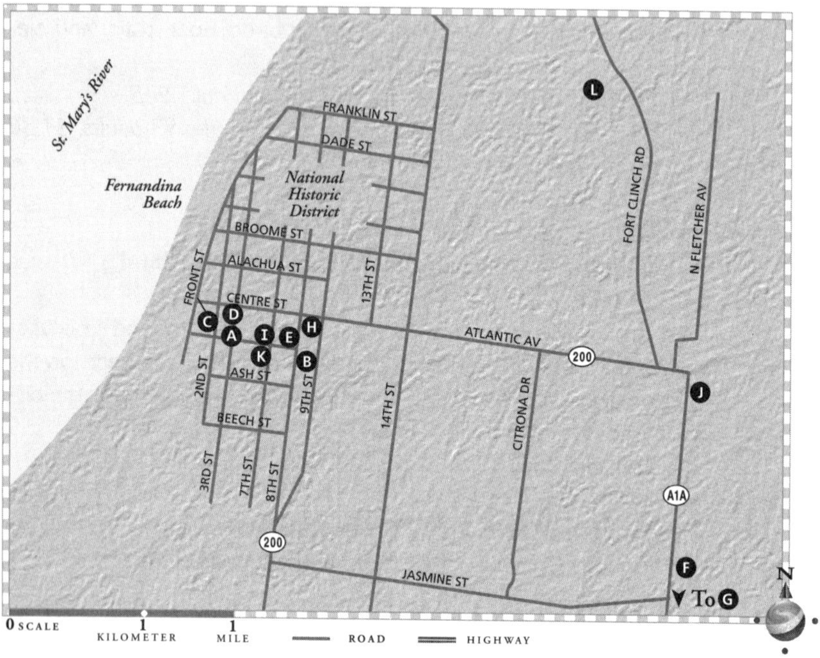


## SIGHTS

- Ⓐ Amelia Island Museum of History

## FOOD

- Ⓑ Beech Street Grill
- Ⓒ Brett's Waterway Cafe
- Ⓓ Florida House Inn
- Ⓔ Horizons

## LODGING

- Ⓕ The 1735 House
- Ⓖ Amelia Island Plantation
- Ⓗ Amelia Island Williams House
- Ⓘ Bailey House
- Ⓙ Elizabeth Point Lodge
- Ⓚ Fairbanks House

## CAMPING

- Ⓛ Fort Clinch State Park

---

### ★★ MUSEUM OF SCIENCE AND HISTORY

**1025 Museum Cir., Southbank, Jacksonville, 904/396-7062**

Permanent displays (including plenty of hands-on exhibits) include a Civil War collection and exhibits that explore the ecology of the St. Johns River and pre-Columbian Indian cultures. Physical science demonstrations are given in the science theater, and the Alexander Brest Planetarium presents multimedia shows every day.

***Details**: Open Mon–Fri 10–5, Sat 10–6, Sun 1–6. Admission: $6 adults, $4 children, $4.50 seniors. (1½–2 hours)*

### ★★ MUSEUM OF SOUTHERN HISTORY

**4304 Herschel St., Riverside, Jacksonville, 904/388-3574**

The lifestyle and culture of the Antebellum South is presented through artifacts and displays that relate medical, military, and political mores of the time. Other exhibits explore the fashions of the time.

***Details:** Open Tue–Sat 10–5. Admission: $1 adults and children. (30 minutes)*

### ★ JACKSONVILLE HISTORICAL CENTER

**100B Wharfside Way, Southbank Riverwalk, Jacksonville, 904/398-4301**

Here the city's rich history is traced through artifacts and documents from its early days as a Timucuan Indian settlement to its growth into a major port.

***Details:** Open daily noon–5. Free. (30 minutes)*

## FITNESS AND RECREATION

Want to stand on the highest point along the Atlantic coast south of Sandy Hook, New Jersey? Stop laughing long enough to go to **Fort George State Cultural Site**, Fort George Rd. E., Fort George, 904/251-2320, and climb Mount Cornelia, a 65-foot-high hill on Fort George Island that has been occupied by humans for more than 5,000 years. No telling if the various tribes and human groupings came here for the view. Modern visitors bicycle and hike along the trails under moss-draped stands of laurel and live oak.

It's invigorating to hike or ride horseback along the beach trails of the **Amelia Island State Recreation Area**, along A1A north of Little Talbot Island State Park, 904/251-2320. **Seahorse Stables**, 904/261-4878, offers guided horseback rides along the beach. **Fort Clinch State Park**, 2601 Atlantic Ave. (A1A), Fernandina Beach, 904/277-7274 (see Camping, below), offers similar opportunities; while at **Guana River State Park**, 2690 S. Ponte Vedra Blvd., Ponte Vedra Beach, 904/825-5071, nine miles of old service roads are open for hikers and mountain bikers. This park also offers boating on the Guana and Tolomato Rivers.

Golfers may be pardoned for thinking they've landed in a never-never land of wonderful courses, starting with Amelia Island's 54 holes, some of them

# JACKSONVILLE AND THE BEACHES

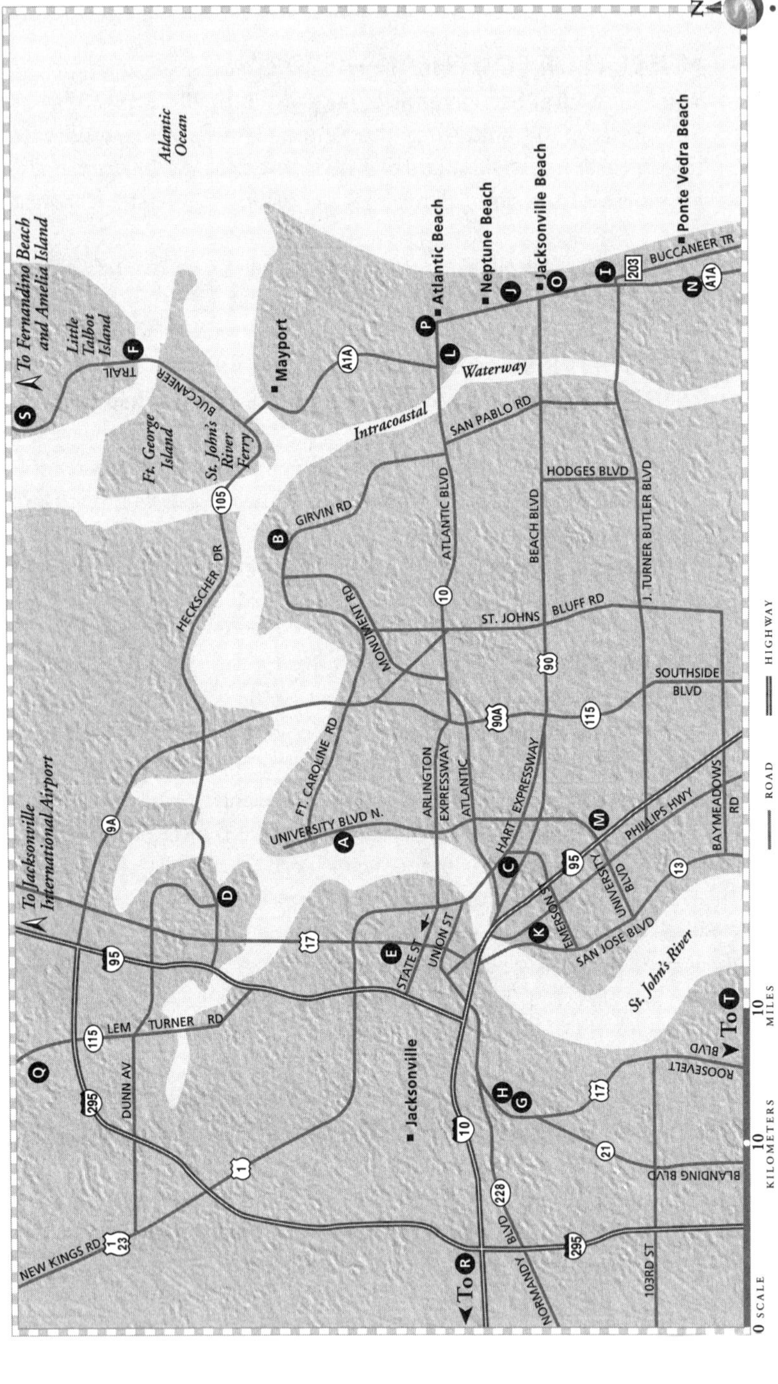

arranged in oceanside links configuration, and continuing through the six championship courses at the **Marriott at Sawgrass Resort** in Ponte Vedra Beach, 800/457-4653 or 904/285-7777. You'll have to stay at the Marriott to play these courses, but it's a good bet you won't regret it, especially if you get a tee time on the famed TPC Sawgrass Stadium Course that hosts the PGA Players Championship every year. There are many courses here, but others likely to remain in your list of great courses played are **Eagle Harbor** in Orange Park, **Queen's Harbour** in Jacksonville, and **The Ravines** in Middleburg.

The professional sports scene got a big boost when the **Jacksonville Jaguars** joined the National Football League. Sports fans can also follow professional soccer with the **Jacksonville Cyclones,** minor-league hockey with the **Jacksonville Lizard Kings**, and minor-league baseball with the Detroit Tigers' AA-affiliate **Jacksonville Suns**.

The greyhounds run at three area tracks, **Jacksonville Kennel Club**, **Orange Park Kennel Club,** and **St. Johns Greyhound Park**.

## FOOD

You don't have to spend a day's pay on dinner on Amelia Island, although you can do so quite easily. The **Beech Street Grill**, 801 Beech St., 904/277-3662, has moderately priced daily blackboard specials featuring local seafood served with herbs and homemade sauces and chutneys. Less than a block away, **Horizons**, at Eighth and Ash Streets, 904/321-2430, is for special occasions, a restaurant listed among the chosen few by area food critics. Its menu

### SIGHTS

- Ⓐ Alexander Brest Museum and Gallery
- Ⓑ Fort Caroline National Memorial
- Ⓒ Jacksonville Museum of Contemporary Art
- Ⓓ Jacksonville Zoological Gardens
- Ⓔ Karpeles Manuscript Library
- Ⓕ Kingsley Plantation
- Ⓖ Museum of Southern History

### FOOD

- Ⓗ Biscotti's
- Ⓘ Eddie's Palm Valley Crossing
- Ⓙ First Street Grille
- Ⓙ Island Grille
- Ⓚ Metro Diner
- Ⓛ Ragtime Tavern & Seafood Grill
- Ⓜ Wedge Cafe

### LODGING

- Ⓝ Marriott at Sawgrass Resort
- Ⓞ Ruby Inn by the Sea
- Ⓟ Sea Turtle Inn

### CAMPING

- Ⓠ Flamingo Lake RV Resort
- Ⓡ Hidden River Ranch
- Ⓢ Little Talbot Island State Park
- Ⓣ Whiteys Fish Camp

*Note: Items with the same letter are located in the same area.*

includes everything from salads to pastas, seafood, and poultry. **Brett's Waterway Cafe**, 1 S. Front St., 904/261-2660, which overlooks the Amelia River (Intracoastal Waterway), offers not only well-regarded seafood and aged-beef entrees but also the best dining seats from which to watch the sunset. There are many other first-rate restaurants on the island, but before you leave, stop in at the **Florida House Inn**, 22 S. Third St., 904/261-3300, for its Southern cooking served in all-you-can-eat boardinghouse style. By the way, this is the place where, in the 1880s, Cuban national hero José Martí plotted to reclaim Cuba's independence from Spain.

In Jacksonville, for seafood jambalaya, Cuban pasta, and all-around excellent casual dining, try the **River City Brewing Company**, 835 Museum Cir., Southbank, 904/398-2299, or **Crawdaddy's**, 1643 Prudential Dr., a dressy/casual seafood house with a 1920s fish-camp ambience and dining areas overlooking the St. Johns River. The **Metro Diner**, 3302 Hendricks Ave., San Marco, 904/398-3701, serves Florida blue-crab cakes and other dishes not usually associated with the average diner, while **Mozzarella's Cafe**, 2 Independent Dr., Jacksonville Landing, serves simple fare, with seating near the bank of the St. Johns River. **Juliette's**, 2345 W. Water St., 904/355-7118, in the Omni Jacksonville Hotel, is an upscale bistro for special occasions, one of the few perennials on the Top 25 list published by *Jacksonville* magazine.

For salads, sandwiches, pizza, and the coffee of your choice, go to **Biscottis**, 3556 St. Johns Ave., Avondale, 904/387-2060. **Notre Gourmet**, 1038 Park St., Riverside, 904/634-0605, specializes in Creole cuisine, and locals flock here for jerk chicken, jambalaya, gumbo, and blackened fish. For local seafood, it's hard to top the **Island Grille**, 981 N. First St., Jacksonville Beach, 904/241-1881. Try the blackened grouper with pineapple salsa, the coconut shrimp, or any of the salads or pork entrees. Not far away is the **First Street Grille**, 807 First St., Jacksonville Beach, 904/246-6555, yet another beachfront restaurant with an award-winning menu of bayou shrimp, baked oysters, shrimp Dijon, and similar fare. Inexpensive dining in a setting overlooking the Intracoastal Waterway can be found at **Eddie's Palm Valley Crossing**, 3020 Palm Valley Rd., Ponte Vedra Beach, 904/285-5028. At Atlantic Beach, stop in at the **Ragtime Tavern & Seafood Grill**, 207 Atlantic Blvd., 904/241-7877, for Cajun meals. The **Wedge Cafe**, 5711 Bowden Rd., Southpoint, 904/731-7598, is a creative sort of place featuring dishes with Floridian, Californian, and Caribbean influences.

## LODGING

Depending on your price range, you won't go wrong with any of the following accommodations.

The proud main house of **Elizabeth Point Lodge**, 98 S. Fletcher Ave., Amelia Island, 800/772-3359 or 904/277-4851, www.florida-inns.com/elizabeth.htm, sits high on the beach, its 25 moderate- to high-rate guest rooms located in and around this 1890s "Nantucket shingle"–style house. The lodge consistently wins high ratings on national lists of the best waterfront inns. Not far away, **The 1735 House**, 584 S. Fletcher Ave., 800/872-8531 or 904/261-4148, www.ameliaislandlodging.com, is a cozy, suites-only, oceanfront hotel that could also look at home on Cape Cod.

Slightly less expensive, located a few blocks from the Amelia River, **Bailey House**, 28 S. Seventh St., Fernandina Beach, 800/251-5390 or 904/261-5390, www.bailey-house.com, offers eight distinctive rooms in a turreted 1895 Queen Anne–style home. Two blocks south, **The Fairbanks House**, 227 S. Seventh Ave., 800/261-4838 or 904/277-0500, www.fairbankshouse.com, offers 12 rooms in an 1885 Italianate villa with arched piazzas and scented gardens. And steps away sits one of the oldest and one of the best inns in the nation, according to the publications that make such lists, **The Amelia Island Williams House**, 103 S. Ninth St., 800/414-9258 or 904/277-2328, www.williamshouse.com. The house dates from 1856 and is one of the very few antebellum mansions left in Florida. It is also one of the most opulent, with five working fireplaces and eight guest rooms that feature claw-foot tubs antiques dating back to the 1500s. Prices equal other accommodations on the island. No mention of lodging on Amelia Island is complete without reference to **Amelia Island Plantation**, 3000 First Coast Hwy., 800/874-6878 or 904/261-6161, www.aipfl.com, that 1,330-acre sprawling oceanside complex of 679 rooms, suites, and rentable condos surrounded by 54 holes of the most splendid golf any player could desire. The price range is huge, with special deals sometimes available in the off-season between December and March. If you can't afford to stay here, at least have breakfast at the oceanfront Amelia Inn Dining Room.

There are several alternatives to the large number of chain motels in Jacksonville. Among the nicest is the **House on Cherry Street**, 1844 Cherry St., Riverside, 904/384-1999. Often listed among Florida's best bed-and-breakfast inns, this restored colonial home on the St. Johns River has four rooms with antique furnishings. In the same vicinity, the elegant **Cleary-Dickert House**, 1804 Copeland St., Riverside, 904/387-4762, offers three suites in a 1914 structure attached to an English garden. You might recognize the inn a few doors away, because the three-story, 1905 mansion with verandahs and massive Doric columns, the **Plantation Manor Inn**, 1630 Copeland St., Riverside, 904/384-4630, has been featured in the National Trust for Historic Preservation wall calendar. Moderate rates prevail at the

**San Marco Point House**, 1709 River Rd., 904/396-1448, another top-rated bed-and-breakfast known for its random, never dull, collection of artifacts.

For accommodations toward the beaches, try the **Sea Turtle Inn** at 1 Ocean Blvd., Atlantic Beach, 904/249-7402, a moderately priced resort; or check into one of the three rooms at **Ruby Inn by the Sea**, 802 Second St. S., Jacksonville Beach, 904/241-5551, www.jaxbeach.com/rubyinn, which takes its name, Ruby, from the 1884–86 name of the town.

Finally, if your wallet permits it, consider the **Marriott at Sawgrass Resort**, 1000 TPC Blvd., Ponte Vedra Beach, 800/457-4653 or 904/285-7777. As a guest at this luxury resort, you'll be able to play some of the best and best-known golf courses in the country.

## CAMPING

Good camping is limited in Florida's northeast corner. If you're west of town, try the aptly named **Hidden River Ranch** at Macclenny, 912/843-2603 (from I-10 at Glen St. Mary, drive north on SR 125 to SR 127, then north to SR 122, and turn right). The 88-acre property, adjoining the St. Mary's River and laced with walking and riding trails, offers 12 full-hookup sites as well as tent sites scattered throughout the woods. (Note: The ranch has a Georgia area code but is in fact in Florida—merely a telephone-company anomaly.)

Just south of the city, **Whiteys Fish Camp**, 2032 CR 220, Orange Park, 904/269-4198, on Swimming Pen Creek near the St. Johns River, offers full RV hookups and the usual facilities, plus a well-regarded seafood restaurant. **Flamingo Lake RV Resort**, 3640 Newcomb Rd., Jacksonville, 904/766-0672, has 98 full-hookup sites, well-kept grounds, a lakeside pavilion with grills and tables, and canoes, boats, and rental bicycles. On a sea island not too far from the city is **Little Talbot Island State Park**, 12157 Heckscher Dr., 904/251-2320, which has 40 sites, 32 with full hookups. You can surf the Atlantic and watch for rabbits, bobcats, and an endless variety of shorebirds as well as cast lines for redfish, flounder, mullet, and sheepshead.

North of the city, pull into 1,118-acre **Fort Clinch State Park**, 2601 Atlantic Ave. (A1A), Fernandina Beach, 904/277-7274, which offers 62 full-hookup sites (and has a 30-foot limit), sand dunes, Atlantic Ocean swimming, and candlelight tours of the unfinished Fort Clinch, whose construction timetable was undoubtedly slowed by the fact that it changed hands more than once during the Civil War.

## NIGHTLIFE

Jacksonville has an active music scene, beginning with the **Jacksonville Symphony Orchestra**, which plays all of its concerts at the Times-Union Center for the Performing Arts, 904/354-5547. The University of North Florida presents an extensive jazz concert series every year, while at Jacksonville Beach, an ongoing series of quartets, quintets, and chorales is presented at the St. Paul's By-The-Sea Episcopal Church, 904/249-5194. In town, the **Alhambra Dinner Theatre,** 12000 Beach Blvd., Southside, 904/641-1212, is known for presenting professional Broadway-style stage shows Tuesdays through Sundays.

## SHOPPING

With the advent of the shopping mall, it suddenly didn't matter what city you were in. A mall is a mall is a mall, with only cosmetic differences distinguishing one from another. In Jacksonville, the usual-suspect anchors may be found among the 140 stores at **The Avenues Mall**, with clones at **Regency Square Mall**, the city's first. Shopping is more adventurous at **The Jacksonville Landing**, the popular riverside marketplace that houses 65 shops, boutiques, and restaurants. A water taxi will take you across the St. Johns River to the Riverwalk parks and restaurants. Also a little different is the **Worth Antiques Gallery**, the city's largest collection of shops offering everything from European objets d'art to oriental furniture.

## Scenic Route: The Northern Islands

*In the rush to see Florida's best-known attractions, visitors often miss the natural beauty of the northeast corner of the state. A short drive—less than 40 miles—along A1A will give you a chance to absorb the essence of these picturesque islands.*

*Begin on the northern tip of* **Amelia Island** *at* **Fort Clinch State Park**, *which occupies the southern edge of Cumberland Sound, the dividing line between Georgia and Florida. The well-preserved 1847 fort guarded the sound in the Civil War and the Spanish-American War. Drive south through* **Egan Creek Marsh**, *past the 150-year-old* **Amelia Island Lighthouse** *to* **Atlantic Avenue** *(SR 200). Turn right, drive a mile west to Centre Street in* **Fernandina Beach**, *and explore the town, which President James Monroe called a "festering fleshpot" because of the smuggling and pirate activity that once went on here.*

*Drive south on Eighth Street, then go left on Jasmine Street to rejoin A1A at the ocean. Following A1A south, you'll cross the* **Nassau River** *onto* **Talbot Island**, *pass* **Kingsley Plantation** *to the bridge to* **Little Talbot Island**, *then continue over the Fort George Inlet to* **Fort George Island**. *Watch for the entrance to* **Fort Carolina National Memorial**, *and you'll end your drive at another historic spot where American soldiers battled the Spanish for the prize that was Florida.*

# 2 ST. AUGUSTINE

A 208-foot cross towers over coastal marshlands, flowing sand hills, longleaf pines, and massive oaks dripping with Spanish moss. The stainless-steel colossus marks the site of the Mission of Nombre de Dios, where the first Christian mass was celebrated in this country. This pastoral setting is the quintessence of historic St. Augustine, the nation's oldest city.

In fact, the favorite word here is "oldest," and that's the compelling reason to visit. A drive down St. Augustine's Old Route A1A today yields countless billboard invitations to visit the Oldest House, the Oldest Store Museum, the Oldest Wooden Schoolhouse, and more. Continuous European settlement in St. Augustine preceded the settlement of Jamestown by 42 years and the landing of the *Mayflower* in Plymouth by more than half a century.

Designed in the Spanish tradition, the quaint downtown is perfect for walking. Streets are laid out in a grid, converging in the central tree-studded Plaza de la Constitución, the heart of the city, where townspeople have sold their wares for centuries. Many streets within the six-block historic area are off-limits to motor vehicles, offering a sense of simplicity and peace to strolling visitors. Wooden-shuttered stucco houses draped with clinging vines and bright bougainvilleas meet the sidewalks, and, except for necessary restorations, many of the small Spanish colonial homes have changed little since they were built.

St. Augustine stands today as an engrossing tribute to the past, gracefully and quite successfully blending that historic past with a vital present.

# ST. AUGUSTINE

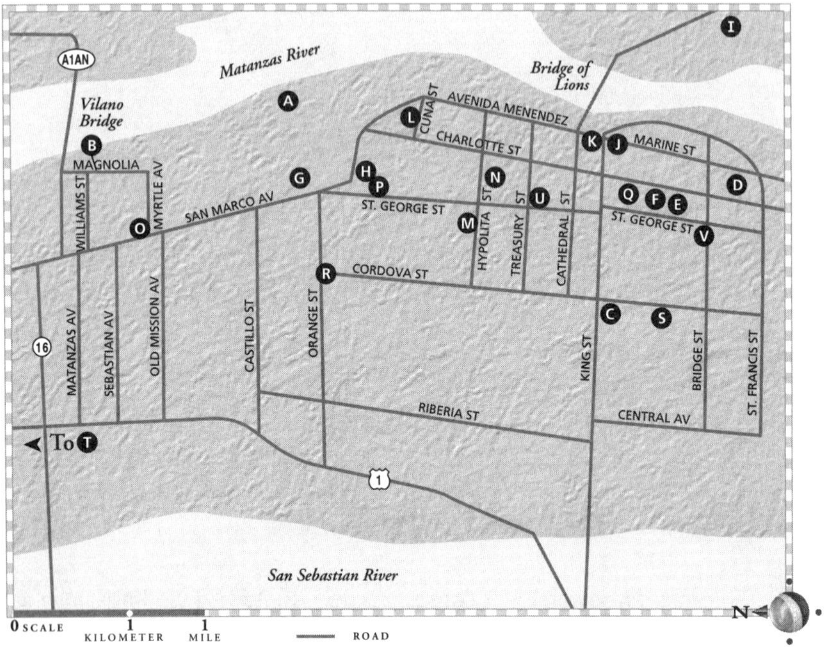


## SIGHTS

- Ⓐ Castillo de San Marcos National Monument
- Ⓑ Fountain of Youth
- Ⓒ Lightner Museum
- Ⓓ Oldest House Museum Complex
- Ⓔ Oldest Store Museum
- Ⓕ Potter's Wax Museum
- Ⓖ Ripley's Believe It Or Not! Museum
- Ⓗ Spanish Quarter Village
- Ⓘ St. Augustine Lighthouse and Museum

## FOOD

- Ⓙ AIA Ale Works
- Ⓚ Athena Restaurant
- Ⓛ Brewster's Coffeehouse
- Ⓜ Columbia Restaurant
- Ⓝ Pizza Garden
- Ⓞ Raintree Restaurant

## LODGING

- Ⓟ Carriage Way Bed & Breakfast
- Ⓠ Casa de Solana
- Ⓡ Casa de Sueños
- Ⓢ Old City House Inn and Restaurant
- Ⓣ Radisson Ponce de León Golf Resort
- Ⓤ St. Augustine Hotel
- Ⓥ St. Francis Inn

## A PERFECT DAY IN ST. AUGUSTINE

Rent a bike (or borrow one from your guest house); pick up a tall, strong coffee and some pastry from one of the downtown bakeries; and head for the waterfront to watch the boats cruising by. As the Old City wakes up, hit a few of the local used-book stores for some reading material, then take the Bridge of Lions over to St. Augustine Beach and Anastasia Island. If you like, climb the lighthouse for a look around, then find a market or sandwich shop and get some lunch for later. Explore the Anastasia State Recreation Area or, if you feel like stretching out on the sand, rent an umbrella and beach chair for the day to read, relax, and watch the resident sandpipers, gulls, terns, herons, and egrets.

## SIGHTSEEING HIGHLIGHTS

### ★★★★ CASTILLO DE SAN MARCOS NATIONAL MONUMENT

**1 S. Castillo Dr., 904/829-6506**

This symmetrical stone citadel with 12-foot-thick walls is the oldest standing masonry fort in the United States. Over the years it has withstood numerous sieges, from pirate attacks to British invasions. In 1924 the fort was designated a National Monument, but more otherworldly and ectoplasmic goings-on have earned it a listing in the National Directory of Haunted Places. Cross a drawbridge over the moat, step out into a grassy courtyard, and explore the musty turrets, interior rooms furnished to reflect the stark aspects of garrison life, powder room, and 35-foot-high ramparts, where cannons once guarded the scenic entry to the city from Matanzas Bay. Spanish soldier reenactors give demonstrations of artillery fire on weekends and holidays, in the methodical and precise methods used in centuries gone by. (As one master gunner explained, "With black powder you only make a mistake once.")

***Details:*** *At A1A and U.S. 1. Open daily 9–5. Admission: $4 adults, children free. (45 minutes)*

### ★★★★ FOUNTAIN OF YOUTH

**11 Magnolia Ave., 800/356-8222 or 904/829-3168**

Who could visit St. Augustine without sipping from the cool waters of the Fountain of Youth? Ponce de León believed drinking from this eternal spring would make "old men young again," and who knows? Maybe that's why there are so many older people living in Florida. Anyway, there's an old stone springhouse on the spot now. Brisk, crystalline spring water bubbles up from the legendary underground stream to a fountain, where a costumed guide captures it in little plastic glasses for sampling. The water is also available (from the gift shop) to take home with you. Also on the grounds are a museum, various Timucuan Indian artifacts, and a memorial to Ponce de León on the site of the ancient Indian town of Seloy. Breathe in the fragrance of the salt air; walk around the secluded archaeological park, shaded by ancient live oak trees festooned with Spanish moss; and see the centuries-old pottery, arrowheads, clay figures, and other artifacts remaining from the first St. Augustine mission and colony.

*Sightseeing at most attractions in St. Augustine is pretty much year-round, but opening and closing times can vary from high season to low, so call ahead to check on early or late hours.*

**Details:** *Open daily 9–5. Admission: $4.75 adults, $1.75 children. (45 minutes)*

## ★★★★ LIGHTNER MUSEUM

### 75 King St., 904/824-2874

Just a walk through the inner courtyard of this Spanish Renaissance-style complex will give you an idea of the elegance experienced by guests at Henry Flagler's former Alcazar Hotel. The 1889 structure is a lavish setting for Chicago magazine publisher Otto C. Lightner's ornate collections of cut and blown glass, porcelain, buttons, furniture, toys, fine and decorative art, antiques, and old musical instruments. The old resort, which once held the country's largest indoor swimming pool and other assorted amenities for the railroad magnate and his well-to-do associates, is now also the showplace home of St. Augustine's City Hall and a shopping complex. But the museum is the reason to come. You can see an alabaster model of the Taj Mahal, elaborate dolls and doll clothing, upholstered furniture, bronze sculptures, lustrous Tiffany stained-glass windows, and more in this authentic original setting.

**Details:** *Open daily 9–5. Admission: $5 adults, children free. (1–2 hours)*

## ★★★ OLDEST STORE MUSEUM

### 4 Artillery Lane, 904/829-9729

Walk through the swinging doors into the former C. F. Hamblen Store, St. Augustine's original "superstore," which began operating in the early

1800s. In Henry Flagler's heyday, around 1900, the general store provided building materials and supplies to customers along the East Coast and as far as the Bahamas. This was the hub of town, where people would shop for everything from groceries and fabric to medicines and hard goods, have spectacles fitted, get their teeth pulled, get a shave and haircut, have their horses shod, or catch up on the latest news. The collection has about 100,000 original store items, including bikes, tools, guns, household goods, pharmaceuticals, and hardware, displayed in original showcases and on the same wooden shelves used a hundred years ago. The old hanging lanterns are still used, though they've been converted to electricity. A player piano providing the musical background and the smell of the old pickle barrel cement the feeling of having stepped back in time. A collection of tin and porcelain signs, promotional items, and antique advertising art is particularly impressive.

***Details:*** *Open Mon–Sat 9–5, Sun 10–5. Admission: $5 adults, $1.50 children. (1 hour)*

## ★★★ SPANISH QUARTER VILLAGE

**29 St. George St., 904/825-6830**

Behind the walls of this restored 1740 Spanish colonial village, guides clad in period britches and bonnets offer a living history lesson as they reenact daily activities of early settlers and soldiers in authentically furnished homes from several centuries. Take the guided tour if there's one going when you arrive; otherwise you can wander about to explore the area on your own. Staff members cheerfully explain what they're doing and why things were done that way as they go about their potting, woodworking, spinning, weaving, blacksmithing, candle-dipping, and tavern keeping. If you visit in June, you'll see reenactors parading down St. George Street daily as part of the month-long "Celebration of Centuries."

***Details:*** *Open daily 9–5. Admission: $6 adults, $3.75 children. (1 hour)*

## ★★ OLDEST HOUSE MUSEUM COMPLEX

**14 St. Francis St., 904/824-2872**

The complex of buildings around the Gonzalez-Alvarez House covers more than 400 years of St. Augustine history, including the Museum of Florida's Army, Historical Society Research Library, Oldest House, Spanish kitchens, and lovely ornamental gardens. The Oldest House itself, a National Historic Landmark, has excellent historical exhibits on its structure, restoration, and residents over the years, and on St. Augustine history, including the sixteenth-century British occupation of the city. Outside in the arcade, look for four terra-cotta statues, circa 1893, cast for the Chicago World's Fair. They pay tribute to the four seasons.

***Details:*** *South of the Plaza. Open daily 9–5. Admission: $5 adults, $3 children. (1 hour)*

### ★★ POTTER'S WAX MUSEUM
**17 King St., 904/829-9056**

The first wax museum in the United States, Potter's is tops for authentic costuming and striking sets. More than 200 famous people from the past and present include religious leaders, artists, authors, musicians, presidents, and explorers, from Beethoven to Whoopi Goldberg. Of particular interest here are some of the most prominent players in St. Augustine's history, like Don Juan Ponce de León; Don Pedro Menendez de Aviles, who landed on the east coast with some 1,500 of his countrymen and settled St. Augustine in 1565; and British commander Sir Francis Drake, who moved in and burned the city in 1586.

***Details:*** *Open daily 9–5 (summer 9–9). Admission: $5.95 adults, $2.75 children. (1 hour)*

### ★★ RIPLEY'S BELIEVE IT OR NOT! MUSEUM
**19 San Marco Ave., 904/824-1606**

Ripley's is a continual source of amusement for those with an affinity for the weird. Its strange exhibits delight the child in all of us, particularly those who grew up reading the syndicated series in the Sunday comics. Visitors can see a scale model of the Eiffel Tower, constructed entirely of toothpicks; a two-headed calf; shrunken heads; rusty-looking dungeons of torture and their haggard denizens; a totally disorienting room constructed to fool the brain with its false perspectives; and (with the help of a powerful magnifying-glass setup) the Lord's Prayer in full, engraved on the head of a pin by a prison inmate (convicted of forgery!).

***Details:*** *Open daily 9–9. Admission: $8.95 adults, $4.95 children. (1–2 hours)*

### ★ ST. AUGUSTINE LIGHTHOUSE AND MUSEUM
**81 Lighthouse Ave., on Anastasia Island, 904/829-0745**

Florida's first official lighthouse was completed in 1824. The 161-foot

**DATIL—A LITTLE DAB'LL DO YA**

Closely related to the fiery habañeros found throughout the Caribbean, and comparable in both flavor and scorching heat level, datil peppers are known to flourish only in St. Augustine. Perhaps the plant was brought here by Minorcan settlers in the mid-1700s, or it may have come with Spanish sailors via the Central American trade routes in the eighteenth and nineteenth centuries. The locally grown peppers, originally used in a savory, hellishly hot sauce created by restaurant owner Chris Way at Barnacle Bill's Seafood House, are now grown here and sold under the Dat'l Do-It product line, with names like Hellish Relish, Devil Drops, Test Tube Babies, and Minorcan Mustard.

black-and-white candy-striped tower's powerful beam flashes every 30 seconds. It's a good place to bring children over seven years old, who can climb the 219 spiral stairs for a fantastic view of Matanzas Bay and St. Augustine's distinctive skyline. The museum at its base has maritime and nautical artifacts, and there's a beach and picnic area here, too.

***Details:*** *On A1A, Anastasia Island. Open daily, museum 9:30–5, tower 10–4:30. Admission: Tower and museum, $5 adults, $2 children; museum only, $2 adults, children free. (1 hour)*

## FITNESS AND RECREATION

Pari-mutuel greyhound racing with full-card simulcast wagering can be found at **St. John's Greyhound Park**, U.S. 1 and Race Track Rd., 904/824-2779. The **St. Augustine Speedway**, 904/825-2886, features five divisions of stock-car racing.

Both fresh- and saltwater fishing are excellent. Catches are likely to be catfish, speckled trout, and largemouth bass, and major tournaments are held year-round. The **Anastasia State Recreation Area**, 904/461-2033, offers 18 miles of recreational possibilities, including excellent camping, hiking, nature trails, and fishing. Boat charters and water-sports equipment rentals are available, and canoeing, kayaking, waterskiing, and parasailing are popular.

The area is renowned for golf, from the still-expanding **World Golf**

# GREATER ST. AUGUSTINE

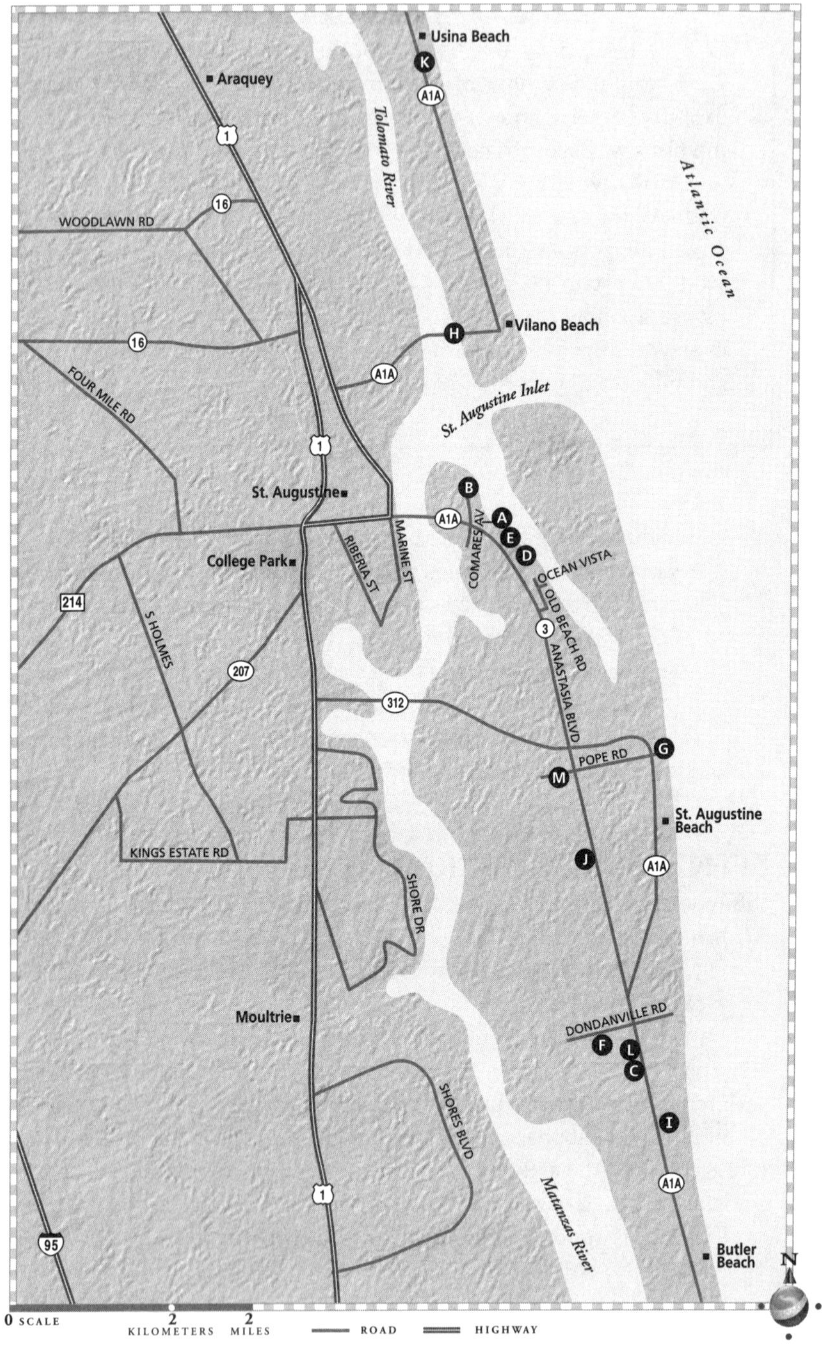

**Village**, 800/948-4746, with its Hall of Fame museum and three championship courses, to excellent public courses with challenging layouts and plenty of water and sand. For more information, call **Florida's First Coast of Golf**, 800/555-0807.

## FOOD

Old World Spanish and Cuban cuisine is the draw at the **Columbia Restaurant**, 98 St. George St., 904/824-3341, with authentic dishes like paella, black bean soup, snapper Alicante, or chicken Ybor. For elegant dining in casual environs, visit the **Raintree Restaurant**, 102 San Marco Ave., 904/824-7211, an 1879 Victorian home whose hallmark is its great desserts.

For moderate cost and fun dining, try the **AIA Ale Works**, 1 King St., 904/829-2977, for sandwiches, burgers, salads, quesadillas, and a few unusual but well-regarded microbrewed beers. In the heart of Old Town, share a drippy, New York–style pizza in a relaxed, outdoor garden atmosphere at the **Pizza Garden**, 21 Hypolita St., 904/825-4877. Also inexpensive and good is the **Athena Restaurant**, 14 Cathedral Place, 904/823-9076, a classic Greek diner, for *pastitsio*, stuffed grape leaves, and baklava.

Sit out on the porch at **Brewster's Coffeehouse**, 19 Cuna St., 904/824-9695, with a specialty coffee, beer or wine, sandwich or pastry; perhaps you'll catch a poetry reading while you're there.

On Anastasia Island, you can count on a dinnertime wait at the **Gypsy Cab Co.**, 828 Anastasia Blvd., 904/824-8244—but go anyway. This Floribbean gem is always packed with locals who favor the distinctive house salad dressing and fresh seafood or huge plates of pasta. Nearby, the waterfront **Conch House**, 57 Comares St., 904/829-8646, features Caribbean and American dishes, plus an outside deck and thatched dining hut with a

---

**FOOD**

- Ⓐ Capt. Jack's
- Ⓑ Conch House
- Ⓒ Greenstreets Restaurant
- Ⓓ Gypsy Cab Co.
- Ⓔ Lighthouse Park Restaurant
- Ⓕ Saltwater Cowboys

**LODGING**

- Ⓖ Howard Johnson Ocean Front Resort
- Ⓗ Town and Country Motel

**CAMPING**

- Ⓘ Bryn Mawr Camp Resort
- Ⓙ Cooksey's Camping Resort
- Ⓚ North Beach Camp Resort
- Ⓛ Ocean Grove RV Resort
- Ⓜ St. Augustine Beach KOA

## How to See St. Augustine

Several companies offer worthwhile narrated introductions to the sites, color, and charm of the Old City. Horse-drawn carriages are readily available and the gentle clip-clop of the horses' hooves on the cobblestone streets enhances this nostalgic, alternative way to tour the endearing city. There are other ways, too—by foot, trolley, or seafaring vessel. Try any of these:

• **A Ghostly Experience Walking Tour**, 888/461-1009. Walk with a guide in period dress on a 1½-hour nightly tour that emphasizes local folklore and ghostly experiences.

• **Colee's Sightseeing Carriage Tours**, 904/829-2818. This is the only tour that includes Aviles Street in the Old Spanish Quarter.

• **St. Augustine Historical Tours**, 800/397-4071 or 904/829-3800. Charming green-and-white open-air trolleys leave every 15 or 20 minutes from the Old Jail.

• **St. Augustine Scenic Cruise**, Municipal Marina, 4125 Coastal Hwy., 800/542-8316 or 904/824-1806. Cruise (1¼ hours) along the tranquil waters of the St. Augustine waterfront and Matanzas Bay, with narration by third- and fourth-generation captains.

• **Sightseeing Trains**, 170 San Marco Ave., 800/226-6545 or 904/829-6545. Enjoy a narrated tour, stop off at major attractions, and reboard the train later or elsewhere along the seven-mile route.

• **St. Augustine Trolley Tours**, 167 San Marco Ave., 800/397-4071 or 904/829-3800. Animated guides combine colorful anecdotes, humorous stories and historical information into a one-hour, seven-mile city tour.

• **Tours by Mary Way Jacobs**, 212D San Marco Ave., 904/829-5598. Call for tour packages, walking tours, and evening candlelight tours with a strolling minstrel.

gorgeous view of Salt Run. Pastas, burgers, seafood, and a children's menu are available at the **Lighthouse Park Restaurant,** 442 Ocean Vista Ave., 904/826-4002. There's also good family dining at the moderately priced **Capt. Jack's**, 410 Anastasia Blvd., 904/829-6846, where tasty corn fritters come with most nightly specials. Try the fried oysters, broiled seafood, or Floridian alligator tail and Key lime pie at **Saltwater Cowboys**, 299 Dondanville Rd., 904/471-2332, a turn-of-the-nineteenth-century, Old Florida fish camp, surrounded by saltwater marshes. For breakfast or lunch, **Greenstreets Restaurant**, 4320 A1A S. in Ocean Gate Shopping Plaza, 904/471-5573, offers friendly service and moderate prices, and everything is homemade from family recipes.

## LODGING

More than two dozen old homes in St. Augustine have been converted to delightful bed-and-breakfast inns. This genre of lodging often has stairs or walkways that are narrow or uneven, but staying in these places will give healthy, agile adults a closer, more intimate look at the residential parts of town.

One of the most distinctive is the pink stucco **Casa de Solana**, 21 Aviles St., 800/760-3556 or 904/824-3555, which has only four suites and a shady garden, goldfish pond, and fountain outside; bike rentals and a full breakfast in the elegant dining room are included. The **Casa de Sueños**, 20 Cordova St., 800/824-0804 or 904/824-0887, www.oldcity.com/suenos, is comfortable and moderately priced. The family-run **Old City House Inn and Restaurant**, 115 Cordova St., 800/653-4087 or 904/826-0113, has five rooms, all with private entrances. Beverages and homemade desserts are available all day at the homey Victorian **Carriage Way Bed & Breakfast**, 70 Cuna St., 800/908-9832 or 904/829-2467, which offers good value and comfortable rooms, several of which have verandahs.

Also reasonable, and perfect for a romantic getaway (ask for the Balcony Room) is the cozy, Old World Spanish–style **St. Francis Inn**, 279 St. George St., 800/824-6062 or 904/824-6068, www.stfrancisinn.com. There's a two-bedroom cottage, rooms, suites, fireplaces, whirlpool tubs, free bicycle rentals, and a fish pond and brick courtyard outside. The inexpensive and pleasant **St. Augustine Hostel**, 32 Treasury St., 904/808-1999, offers a library and bike rentals.

Chains include the ideally located **Howard Johnson Ocean Front Resort**, 300 A1A Beach Blvd., 800/752-4037 or 904/471-2575, with full kitchens and access to Anastasia State Park's beach on one side and the county fishing pier on the other. Just north of downtown, golfers in plus-fours would feel right at home in the eye-popping Old Florida setting surrounding the **Radisson Ponce de Leon Golf Resort**, 4000 U.S. 1 N., 800/228-2821 or 904/824-2821, which has tennis, croquet, a gourmet restaurant, and a challenging Donald Ross–designed golf course edged by scenic marshlands and the Intracoastal Waterway.

Families will be comfortable at the **Town and Country Motel,** 110 Vilano Beach Rd., 904-824-5078, which has 20 inexpensive poolside units, furnished kitchens, and laundry facilities.

## CAMPING

You can enjoy camping year-round at **St. Augustine Beach KOA**, 525 W. Pope Rd., 800-562-4022 or 904/471-3113, which has full hookups, tent sites, and cabins, plus boat and bike rentals; pets on leashes are welcome, and there are free daily shuttles to the historic area. Also on St. Augustine Beach, **Ocean Grove RV Resort**, 4225 A1A S., 800/342-4007 or 904/471-3414, has shady pull-through and tent sites, full hookups, a pool, hot tub, and boat ramp, plus cabins, canoes, and bikes for rent. Nearby, **Cooksey's Camping Resort**, 2795 SR 3, 904/471-3171, has 200 sites for RVs and tents, bathhouses with hot water, full hookups, miniature golf, bike trails, and both pool and lake swimming. **Bryn Mawr Camp Resort**, on the beach at 4850 Hwy. A1A S., 904/471-3353, offers full hookups, paved pull-through sites, a pool, tennis, shuffleboard, horseshoes, and fishing. The **North Beach Camp Resort**, 4125 Coastal Hwy. (A1A), 800/542-8316 or 904/824-1806, camping@aug.com, has 120 shaded sites on 60 acres of oaks and palmettos, with full hookups, tent sites, a beach, recreation area, boat rentals, and restaurants; pets are welcome.

## NIGHTLIFE

Theater buffs can call about performances at the **Limelight Theatre**, 1681 U.S. 1 S., 904/825-1164, or **St. Augustine Amphitheatre**, 1340 A1A S., 904/471-1965, where the official state play, *The Cross and Sword*, is performed from late June to early September.

**Leonard's Trade Winds Lounge**, 124 Charlotte St., 904/829-9336, downtown across from the Bridge of Lions, is St. Augustine's oldest drinking establishment. It has live entertainment nightly after 5 p.m.

For late-night drinks and entertainment, try **Scarlett O'Hara's**, 70 Hypolita St., 904/824-6535, or the **White Lion Tavern**, 20 Cuna St., 904/829-2388, which features an outdoor patio overlooking the Castillo green.

# 3 DAYTONA BEACH AND THE SPACE COAST

Hubbub. Motion. Noise. They've been part and parcel of Daytona and the Space Coast since the beginning of the century, and they show no signs of letup. With its awesome 23-mile-long beach and a side-by-side history of seaside holidaymaking and fast cars, Daytona is Florida's most famous east coast destination. It was on these hard-packed sands that automotive pioneer Henry Ford raced his roadsters in the early 1900s. The racing tradition is preserved at the Daytona International Speedway, while the beachside amusements and band shell maintain the area's reputation as the original family beach vacation icon, long before its popularity as a raucous Spring Break and Bike Week destination. And while the decibel levels intensify during Bike Week, it's nothing compared to the sound from the more than two dozen space shuttles launched from Kennedy Space Center each year.

The roar of the surf draws thousands to the east coast surfing capital of Cocoa Beach. But there's quiet, too. Vacationers in search of natural pursuits can linger along the 25-mile Canaveral National Seashore, exploring its 57,000 acres of wilderness, unspoiled barrier beaches, shallow lagoons, and dunes. And those seeking the thrill of visiting foreign ports can board the cruise ships that leave several times a week from the Port of Canaveral.

Whether you choose a day of hiking on New Smyrna Beach, reflecting on the history of motor sports at Daytona USA, or exploring the future of space travel, a vacation time spent here can be as rigorous or as calm as you like it.

# DAYTONA BEACH

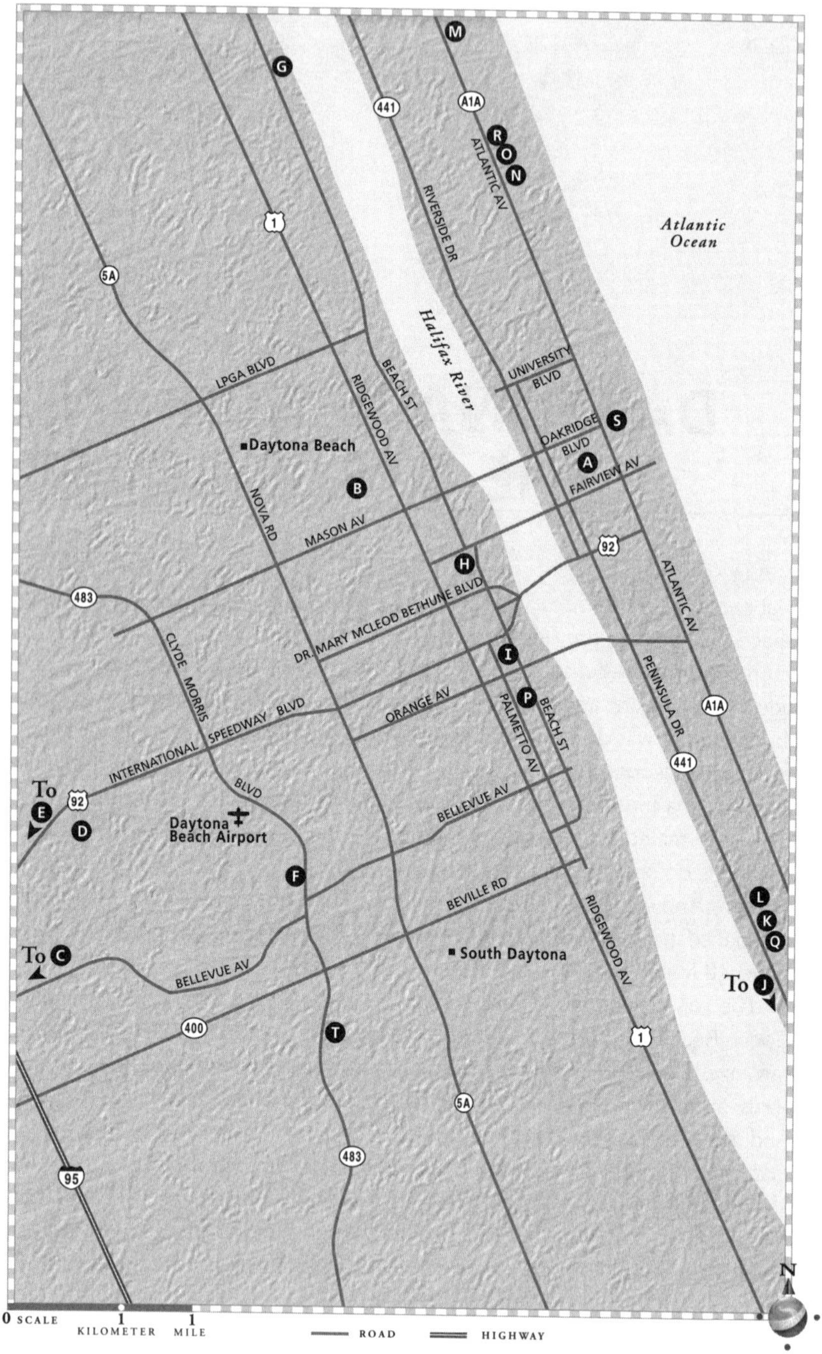

## A PERFECT DAY IN DAYTONA BEACH AND THE SPACE COAST

There's nothing like watching the sun come up on a sand dune–covered beach. The smell of the salt air is invigorating as you jog, run, or saunter at leisure along the shoreline. During nesting season, you may notice turtle tracks or even eggs in the sand; if you see a nest beneath a screen, it's probably a loggerhead turtle nest that's been covered by a park ranger or local nature lover to protect the eggs from raccoons or other predators. Spend your morning at the Space Center, where you can almost feel the heat of the engines and the 7.5 bazillion pounds of thrust as the shuttle explodes into flight in the IMAX theater. If you prefer motor-sports excitement, head instead for Daytona USA and the Speedway. For a relaxing afternoon, you can visit a microbrewery and shop at the Beach Street historic area or walk over to the Museum of Arts and Sciences. Then let Captain Jim on A Tiny Cruise Line show you the sights from the water before dinner at the historic Live Oak Inn.

## SIGHTSEEING HIGHLIGHTS

### ★★★★ DAYTONA BEACH

Daytona Beach is broad, sandy, and gorgeous. With a width of 500 feet at low tide, it's excellent for beach volleyball, building sand castles, or flying kites. If you feel energetic, it's a great place to run or jog. The sand is exceptionally hard-packed—hard enough that auto racer Sir Malcolm Campbell set a speed record of 276.8 mph here in

---

**SIGHTS**

- Ⓐ Adventure Landing
- Ⓑ Daytona Beach
- Ⓒ Daytona Flea and Farmers Market
- Ⓓ Daytona USA and Daytona International Speedway
- Ⓔ Mark Martin's Klassix Auto Museum
- Ⓕ Museum of Arts and Sciences
- Ⓖ A Tiny Cruise Line

**FOOD**

- Ⓗ Live Oak Dining Room
- Ⓘ Riverfront Brewing Company
- Ⓙ Sophie Kay's Waterfall Restaurant
- Ⓚ Steve's Venice

**LODGING**

- Ⓛ Bahama House
- Ⓜ Beachcomer Oceanfront Inn
- Ⓝ Capri Motel

**LODGING (continued)**

- Ⓞ Casa Marina Hotel
- Ⓟ Coquina Inn
- Ⓠ Daytona Beach Hilton Resort
- Ⓡ Ocean Villa Motel
- Ⓢ Thunderbird Beach Motel

**CAMPING**

- Ⓣ Daytona Beach Campground

1935. The beach hasn't been used officially as a speedway since 1959 but regulated auto traffic is still allowed, and even though the speed limit is only 10 mph, cars can appear suddenly. Parents of small children should be watchful on both sides of the shoreline; it's not just the waves that can pose a danger here.

This area is popular with tourists year-round. A honky-tonk, rowdy, beach-party scene blankets the sand, which can seem overrun with college crowds, especially during Spring Break (chug-a-lug!). The Boardwalk area includes an open-air band shell, amusements, arcades, souvenir shops, a clock tower, and Oceanfront Park. You can walk out nearly a quarter of a mile into the Atlantic on Hurricane Floyd–shortened Ocean Pier, or ride the gondola skyride for a bird's-eye view of the oceanfront.

***Details:*** *For current information about beach conditions, traffic, and activities, contact the Volusia County Beach Hotline, 904/239-7873 or check out www.volusia.org/beaches.*

## ★★★★ DAYTONA USA AND DAYTONA INTERNATIONAL SPEEDWAY

**1801 W. International Speedway Blvd., Daytona Beach, 904/254-2700, 904/947-6800, or 904/253-7223, www/daytonausa.com**

This is the ultimate motor-sports theme park, with a fascinating combination of high-tech exhibits and hands-on interaction. Visitors can see original photos of the record-setting speed runs on the beach, interview famous racers on video, and experience a knock-your-socks-off surround-sound presentation. You can even help change a tire, racing the clock as part of a team pit-stop competition, and design and test your own race cars. Don't pass up the 30-minute Speedway Tour on an open-air tram that circles the 2.5-mile Daytona International Speedway racetrack, infield, pit, and garage areas. You'll learn about the choreography involved in a 15- or 20-second pit stop and get a firsthand look at what the 31-degree banking on the first turn really amounts to—it's a lot steeper than it looks on TV.

***Details:*** *Open daily 9–7. Daytona USA admission: $10 adults, $5 children, $8 seniors; Speedway tour: $5. (2–3 hours)*

## ★★★★ KENNEDY SPACE CENTER

**SR 405, Titusville, 800/872-1969 or 321/452-2121, www.kscvisitor.com**

**WATCHING A LAUNCH**

Want to watch a NASA launch? When skies are clear you can see the shuttle (or rocket) trail from across the state, but you can get a better look if you're on the Space Coast. Unless you work for NASA, don't expect to get too close to the launch pad. If you're willing to battle some horrendous traffic and head out at least four hours before take-off time, though, you can get a prime viewing spot.

Your best bets are inland along U.S. Highway 1 in Titusville, and along A1A and the Atlantic Ocean in Cape Canaveral and Cocoa Beach. (The Cocoa Beach Pier is a great spot.) A lucky few—those who hold $10 tickets, purchased several days in advance at the Kennedy Space Center complex—are allowed inside the secured area along the NASA Causeway, about six miles from the launch pad, to watch. And for an additional fee, the U.S. Astronaut Hall of Fame has rooftop viewing and extended hours during launches, when NASA updates are broadcast over the sound system.

You can't confirm a takeoff in advance; all are subject to weather and operational requirements. Delays are not uncommon, so dress accordingly for the temperature, and be prepared for sun or rain. Bring your camera or videocam, as well as sunscreen, insect repellent, and binoculars.

For updated launch information, call NASA at 407/867-4636 or the Kennedy Space Center Visitor Complex at 321/452-2121.

Get an inkling of an understanding of space-travel technology as you stand dwarfed beneath a real *Saturn V* moon rocket, longer than a football field. Kennedy Space Center and Cape Canaveral Air Force Station are headquarters for the country's space operations. The spacecraft that carried Neil Armstrong and Edwin "Buzz" Aldrin, the first men to walk on the moon, was launched here, as were the *Atlantis, Challenger, Columbia, Discovery*, and *Endeavour* shuttles. Multimedia displays include the Rocket Garden, a collection of retired spacecraft (and spare parts), a moon rock, and two IMAX theaters, which show a tour of the Russian Space Station *Mir* and live-action NASA footage taken by astronauts in space. The thunderous sound system lets you feel like you're standing on the launch pad during the launch. And as if the huge-screen format weren't enough, there's a 3-D movie that takes viewers on an interplanetary quest for water, flying through the mountain passes and valleys of Mars!

Also on the complex grounds is the 42-foot-tall Astronauts Memorial (Space Mirror). This rotating, black-granite monument is engraved with the names of the seven astronauts killed in the 1986 *Challenger* space-shuttle disaster.

***Details:*** *Located 11 miles east of I-95. Open daily 9 a.m.–dusk. Combo (Mission Pass, bus tour, and two IMAX movies) admission: $25.72 adults, $19.90 children. Bus tours only: $14 adults, $10 children. IMAX theater admission: $7.50 adults, $5.50 children. (half-day minimum)*

## ★★★ CANAVERAL NATIONAL SEASHORE

**Along A1A, New Smyrna Beach, 321/428-3384**

Canaveral's long, wind-burnished beach stretches across 24 miles of pristine, deserted wilderness along the sparkling, dark-blue Atlantic. The sand here on the East Coast is coarser, yellower, and easier to sink into than the sugary white sand of the Gulf Coast beaches. Maybe you've been feeling a little stressed lately? A day of fishing, bird-watching, or just walking along the shore couldn't be more enjoyable anywhere else. If you have binoculars, a water bottle, a fishing pole, and some sunscreen, you'll be all set.

Gulls screech territorial rights, and ghost crabs skitter for their holes as you approach. Pelicans dive-bomb for fish, and tiny sanderlings race through the froth of receding waves, looking for the small clams and tiny coquinas burrowing frantically at the edge of the tidal wash. Some 23 species of migratory birds pass through here in winter, and another 300 species live here year-round, as do various mammals, fish, amphibians, and reptiles. Tropical sea grapes, beach berries, saw palmettos, and yucca plants wave in the breeze among the dunes. Offshore, you may spot a school of dolphins or an occasional shark or whale. On a cool winter's day, you can't beat this walk at the seashore for mental, physical, and spiritual rejuvenation.

***Details:*** *Park open daily 6–6 (6–8 in summer); visitor center open daily, 9-4:30. (1 hour minimum)*

## ★★★ MUSEUM OF ARTS AND SCIENCES

**1040 Museum Blvd., Daytona Beach, 904/255-0285, www.moas.org**

The scenic Tuscawilla Preserve is the home of this excellent museum. It's right near the historic district and is continually expanding an already impressive permanent collection. You can't miss the amazing, 13-foot-tall skeleton of a 130,000-year-old giant ground sloth, which was found in South Daytona. The Cuban gallery includes modern art and artifacts from the private collection of Fidel Castro's predecessor, General Fulgencio Batista. There's also a wing dedicated to the history of African American Floridians and a compelling African art collection of carvings and masks.

**Details:** *Open Tue–Fri 9–4, Sat–Sun noon–5. Admission: $4.50 adults, $1.50 children. (1½ hours)*

## ★★★ RON JON SURF SHOP OF FLORIDA

**4151 N. Atlantic Ave., Cocoa Beach, 321/799-8888**

This is the original, the granddaddy of all Florida surf shops, advertised on billboards across the state. A landmark since 1963 here in the surfing capital of the east coast, Ron Jon's carries all kinds of beach and surf apparel, and most people leave the store with at least one of its famous T-shirts. Beach bikes, surfboards, and body boards are available for rent, and the Cocoa Beach Visitor Center is inside.

**Details:** *Open daily, 24 hours. (15 minutes–1 hour)*

## ★★★ U.S. ASTRONAUT HALL OF FAME

**6225 Vectorspace Blvd., Titusville, 321/269-6100, www.astronauts.org**

Video footage, personal memorabilia, and one-of-a-kind artifacts offer a tribute to America's astronauts and their historic space missions. Outside the main building, you can sit in the cargo bay of a full-scale space-shuttle replica with a thundering 3-D sound system. You'll see a multiscreen video and feel like you're part of a rumbling, roaring launch into space. Inside the building, simulators enable you to experience zero gravity, rendezvous with the space station *Mir*, feel the pull of 4 G's in the G-force simulator, and then bank, soar, and barrel-roll in full-throttle aerial aerobatic maneuvers. U.S. Space Camp programs held here consist of five days of activities, including classroom instruction, propulsion exercises, astronaut training on simulators, and a simulated space-shuttle mission.

**Details:** *Located ¼ mile east of U.S. 1 on SR 405, just west of Kennedy Space Center. Open daily 9–5; longer in summer. Admission: $13.95 adults, $9.95 children. (2–3 hours)*

### ★★ ADVENTURE LANDING

**Ocean Walk Village, 601 Earl St., Daytona Beach, 877/845-9255, www.adventurelanding.com**

This new Caribbean-themed, wet-or-dry waterpark/entertainment center is a five-acre tangle of tubes, tunnels, and towers. The signature water attraction, a one- or two-person high-energy thrill, features open and tunnel sliding through six waterfalls on a 560-foot-long tube river ride. Other stars are an exhilarating 75-foot-high, totally enclosed slide—a 400-foot looping, twisting run through pitch-blackness—and a half-million gallon wave pool with three- to four-foot waves. Younger children can't get enough of the three-story interactive Treehouse, with 12 levels and more than 250 nozzles to spray, squirt, and surprise them. Dry park activities include a unique inline bobsledding-type adventure that loops through back-to-back 360-degree tunnels, high-bank walls, and exhilarating acceleration drops. Three nine-hole mini-golf courses, a 110-game arcade of fantasy games, redemption games, and driving simulators, and a quarter-mile racetrack with single- or double-seat go-carts, hairpin turns, bridges, and underpasses offer a variety of activities, priced individually.

***Details:*** *Open daily 10 a.m.–midnight (waterpark open seasonally 10–8). Waterpark admission: $19.95 (all day), go-carts $6, mini-golf $6. (1 hour minimum)*

### ★★ A TINY CRUISE LINE

**425 S. Beach St., 904/226-2343, Daytona Beach, www.visitdaytona.com/tinycruise**

*Fancy*, an 1890s-style, family-run fantail launch, offers visitors a riverside window into the history of old Daytona. On this leisurely Halifax River excursion, Captain Jim entertains you with stories and historic details as you glide, just yards from the shoreline, past yachts, beautiful riverfront estates, islands, and wading birds. Midday tours stop briefly at a river park, and you can bring your own lunch and enjoy it here. At sunset, soft music sets the mood for drifting along the river. Have the perfect cassette? Bring it along. Jim's very accommodating, and the kids can steer the boat if they ask.

***Details:*** *Boards from Halifax Harbor Marina. Open daily; times vary. Admission: $8.71–$13.90 depending on cruise. (1–2 hours)*

### ★★ DAYTONA FLEA AND FARMERS MARKET

**2987 Bellevue Ave., Daytona Beach, 904/252-1999**

**SHIP AHOY**

**Port Canaveral**, a large, modern cruise-ship terminal in Cape Canaveral (800/767-8226), hosts a number of cruise lines, to the tune of a million passengers a year. Ships depart four days a week for the Bahamas and Key West; call Cape Canaveral Cruise Line, 321/783-4052 or Premier Cruises, 800/327-7113 for information. Short, four-hour gaming cruises sail daily; call Sterling Casino Lines, 321/783-2212 or SunCruz Casino, 321/783-2770.

Call it a flea *world*. This huge flea market, housed in a giant building just a mile west of the Speedway, has 40 acres of bargains. Up to 1,000 vendors in three miles of vending space offer goods ranging from cheap sunglasses and T-shirts to Ray-Bans, Waterford crystal, upscale clothing, fine jewelry, antiques, and collectibles. An air-conditioned wing called the Corner Shops, a large produce section, nine snack bars, and two sit-down restaurants offer respite if you get too hot or tired. And if all the dealing makes you a bit too enthusiastic, you'll find an ATM machine on the premises. Many merchants take charge cards, too.

***Details:*** *Located at U.S. 92 and I-95. Open Fri–Sun 8–5. Admission: Free. (2 hours minimum)*

## ★★ MARK MARTIN'S KLASSIX AUTO MUSEUM

**2909 W. International Speedway Blvd., Daytona Beach, 800/881-8975 or 904/252-3800**

Great period sets and scenery add to the overall quality and nostalgic ambience of this vintage auto museum, which chronicles the role of the automobile and its various subcultures in American history. There's an extensive Harley-Davidson motorcycle exhibit, gleaming examples of just about every Corvette ever made, lots of motorsports memorabilia, a virtual race-car simulator, and a 1950s-style soda fountain/ice-cream emporium where you can share a banana split or chocolate soda.

***Details:*** *Open daily 9–6 (varies seasonally). Admission: $10 adults, $5 children, $8 seniors. (1 1/2 hours)*

# GREATER DAYTONA

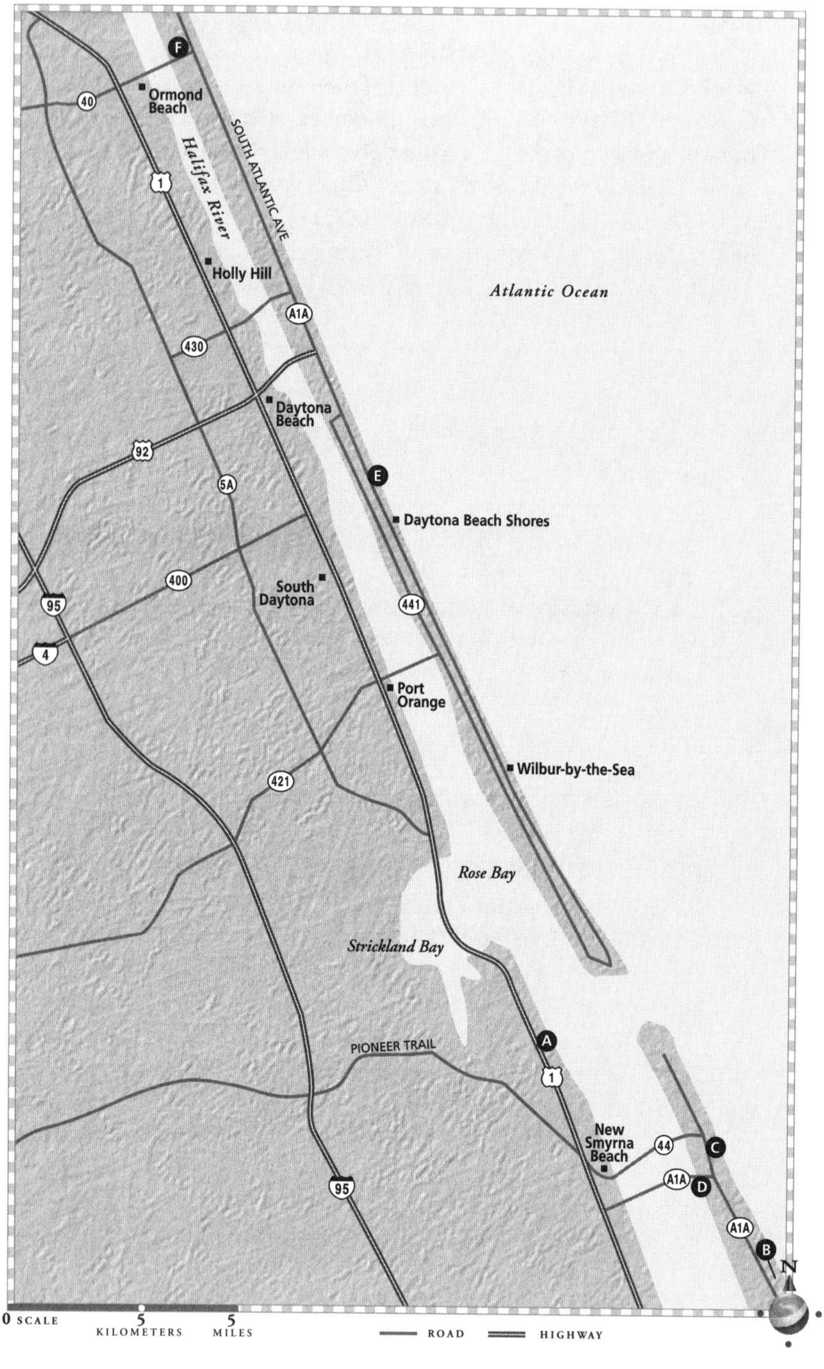

★★ **VALIANT AIR COMMAND WARBIRD AIR MUSEUM**
**Space Coast Regional Airport, 6600 Tico Rd., Titusville, 321/268-1941**

Visualize and explore the history of flight in the United States as you examine these historic military aircraft from World Wars I and II, plus Korea and Vietnam. Aviation buffs will appreciate this collection of memorabilia and artifacts, including model planes, uniforms, aircraft controls, and a flight simulator.

***Details:*** *Open daily 10–6. Admission: $7.50 adults, $4 children. (1–2 hours)*

## FITNESS AND RECREATION

The Daytona Beach area offers excellent ocean fishing. Marlin, sailfish, dolphin, king mackerel, wahoo, tuna, grouper, red snapper, and amberjack are all caught locally. Offshore charters and party boats depart daily, particularly from around Ponce Inlet on the southern tip of Daytona Beach Shores.

Scenic waterways include three canoe trails in the **Florida Recreational Trail System**. Jet Skis, windsurfers, sailboards, and powerboats are available for rental year-round, and parasailing is also offered. Diving and snorkeling are popular; a number of shipwrecks, including the nineteenth-century Spanish–American War gun-running liberty ship, the *Mindanao*, are waiting to be explored.

A variety of golf courses suits every level of play. One of the most satisfying is the Rees Jones–designed **LPGA International** in Daytona Beach, 904/274-3880, with tee boxes positioned to give even high-handicappers a respectable round. **Golf Daytona Beach**, 800/881-7065 or 904/239-7065, www.golf-daytona.com, a program that packages golf and lodging, offers free greens fees if you rent a cart and play after noon.

---

### FOOD

- Ⓐ Franco's Italian and Seafood Grille
- Ⓑ JB's Fish Camp
- Ⓒ Riverview Charlie's

### LODGING

- Ⓒ Riverview Hotel

### CAMPING

- Ⓓ New Smyrna Beach KOA Kampground
- Ⓔ Nova Family Campground
- Ⓕ Ocean Village Camper Resort

*Note: Items with the same letter are located in the same area.*

Just west of the Speedway, greyhound-racing fans flock to the **Daytona Beach Kennel Club**, 904/252-6484, year-round. Horseback riding is available at **Shenandoah Stables**, 904/257-1444 in Daytona Beach. And go-cart aficionados will enjoy the action at **Speed Park MotorSports Thrill Park** in Daytona Beach, 904/253-3278.

The three-deck, 550-passenger ***SunCruz Casino*** ship, 904/322-9000 at Ponce Inlet, or 888/765-5711 at the Cove at Port Canaveral, offers full Las Vegas–style casino gaming cruises.

The boys of summer are no strangers to the area. The **Florida Marlins** hold major-league spring training from February through March at the Space Coast Stadium in Viera, 321/633-9200.

## FOOD

Restaurants on the East Coast range from fast food to buffets to gourmet dining. In Daytona Beach's Beach Street historic area, the **Riverfront Brewing Company**, 230 S. Beach St., 904/248-2722, is an acclaimed microbrewery with a full menu and handcrafted beers. South of downtown, across from the Halifax Harbour Marina on Daytona Beach Shores, the **Live Oak Inn Dining Room**, 448 S. Beach St., 904/252-4667, offers health-conscious meals in a historic country inn. Just south, for informal candlelight Italian dining nightly in an Old World supper-club setting, try **Steve's Venice**, 2616 S. Atlantic Ave., 904/761-2444. South of there, dine in the modestly elegant ambience of **Sophie Kay's Waterfall Restaurant**, 3516 S. Atlantic Ave., Daytona Beach Shores, 904/756-4444; make reservations for dinner or Sunday lunch, since the fine American and continental dishes make this a locals' favorite.

**JB's Fish Camp**, 859 Pompano Ave., New Smyrna Beach, on the Indian River, 904/427-5747, is great for casual dining in a large shack with screened windows, and you can watch the kitchen staff bringing in the fresh-caught local oysters and plump, fresh river clams. Also in New Smyrna, **Franco's Italian and Seafood Grille**, 1610 S. Dixie Frwy., 904/423-3600, is informal, with inexpensive "early bird" specials, pastas, roasted duck, and wood-fired pizza. In the Riverview Hotel, **Riverview Charlie's**, 101 Flagler Ave., 904/428-1865, offers an expansive view of the Intracoastal Waterway and excellent lunch, dinner, or Sunday brunch.

For a friendly atmosphere and waterfront dining on the Indian River in Titusville, try **Paul's Smokehouse Restaurant and Lounge**, 3665 S. Washington Ave., 321/267-3663. Paul's is known for its prime rib, seafood, and barbecue; there's a casual decor of early American memorabilia and a special children's menu.

In Cocoa Beach, for elegant, semiformal continental dining, visit the **Mango Tree**, 118 N. Atlantic Ave., 321/799-0513; food presentation is exquisite, service is meticulous, and live swans in an indoor pond complement the tropical garden atmosphere. **Yen Yen Chinese**, 2 N. Atlantic Ave., 321/783-9512, is outstanding for casual dining, while the family-owned **Bernard's Surf**, 2 S. Atlantic Ave., 321/783-2401, is another good choice, with a personable staff serving aged steaks and ocean-fresh seafood.

## LODGING

The Daytona Beach area has a tremendous selection of lodging options in the low to moderate price range, as well as some luxurious accommodations in the larger chains. If you favor a B&B, stay in the Historic District at the **Coquina Inn**, 544 S. Palmetto Ave., Daytona Beach, 800/727-0678 or 904/254-4969, which serves a full gourmet breakfast and has a charming picket-bordered second-floor porch. Families will be comfortable at the **Beachcomer Oceanfront Inn**, 2000 N. Atlantic Ave., Daytona Beach, 800/245-3575 or 904/252-8513, with a kiddie pool and shuffleboard. Further south, the **Thunderbird Beach Motel**, 500 N. Atlantic Ave., 800/234-6543 or 904/253-2562, is inexpensive, clean, comfortable, and close to everything.

Three well-maintained and reasonable motel/apartment facilities on Daytona Beach share heated pools and a 60-foot water slide that's a big hit with kids. The **Ocean Villa Motel**, 828 N. Atlantic Ave., Daytona Beach, 800/225-3691 or 904/252-4644, www.sunviking.com/oceanvilla, has a picturesque oceanfront setting and beachside pool. The **Capri Motel**, also oceanside at 832 N. Atlantic, 800/874-1820 or 904/252-2555, has a kiddie pool and game room. Across the street, the **Casa Marina Hotel**, 837 N. Atlantic Ave., 800/225-3691 or 904/252-4644, offers fully equipped kitchens and microwaves. Farther south, in Daytona Beach Shores, the **Bahama House**, 2001 S. Atlantic Ave., 904/248-2001, right on the beach, has bright, spacious apartments with private balconies and a free cocktail hour daily. Rooms are large and luxurious at the newly renovated **Daytona Beach Hilton Resort**, 2637 S. Atlantic Ave., 800/525-7350 or 904/767-7350.

At the east end of the North Causeway Bridge, the **Riverview Hotel**, 103 Flagler Ave., New Smyrna Beach, 904/428-5858, is a historic country bed-and-breakfast inn with three floors (but no elevator). Two of the 18 rooms date to 1886; the dining room has a lovely 1930s-style ambience.

The chains are your best bet in Titusville. Try the **Best Western Space Shuttle Inn**, 3455 Cheney Hwy. (SR 50 at I-95), 321/269-9100; **Ramada Inn Kennedy Space Center**, 3500 Cheney Hwy., 321/269-5510; or **Days**

# THE SPACE COAST

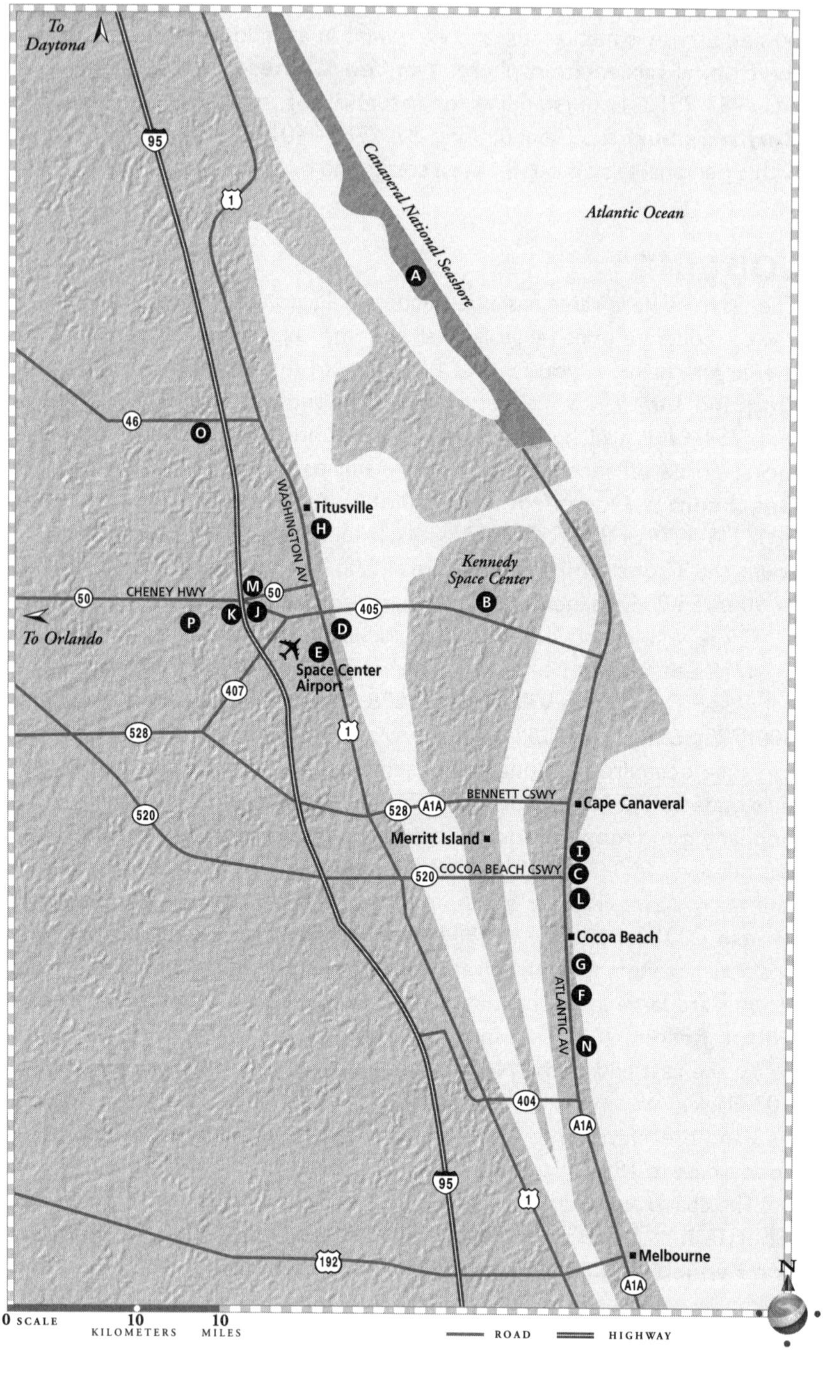

**Inn Kennedy Space Center**, 3755 Cheney Hwy., 321/269-4480, to stay within easy viewing of the shuttle launches.

In Cocoa Beach, the inexpensive **Luna Sea Bed & Breakfast Motel,** 3185 N. Atlantic Ave., 800/586-2732 or 321/783-0500, across the street from the beach, is fairly large for a B&B. Some rooms have kitchens; continental breakfast includes homemade muffins, bagels, and flavored cream cheese. A bit higher but still a good value is **Sea Esta Villas**, 686 S. Atlantic Ave., 321/783-1739.

## CAMPING

Coastal camping, picnicking, nature walks, and fishing can provide endless hours of enjoyment. The following locations are all open year-round.

Near the Daytona Speedway, pull into the **Ocean Village Camper Resort**, 2162 Ocean Shore Blvd., Ormond Beach, 904/441-1808, which has tent sites, full hookups, trailer rentals, a game room, RV supply shop, and tiki huts on a lighted beach. There are shaded pull-throughs, tent sites, a game room, rec hall, and separate adult and kiddie pools at the **Nova Family Campground**, 1190 Herbert St., Port Orange, Daytona, 904/767-0095. You'll find a heated pool, horseshoes, a playground, shuffleboard, and a friendly staff at the **Daytona Beach Campground**, 4601 Clyde Morris Blvd., Daytona Beach, 904/761-2663, plus full hookups, paved pads, pull-throughs, and tent sites. Just south of Daytona, the **New Smyrna Beach KOA Kampground**, 1300 Old Mission Rd., 800/562-1244 or 904/427-3581, has pull-throughs, full hookups, tent sites, a pool, and a mini-golf course.

In Titusville, the **Great Outdoors RV/Golf Resort**, 135 Plantation Dr., Titusville, 800/621-2267 or 321/269-5004, www.tgoresort.com, offers a

---

### SIGHTS

- **A** Canaveral National Seashore
- **B** Kennedy Space Center
- **C** Ron Jon Surf Shop of Florida
- **D** U.S. Astronaut Hall of Fame
- **E** Valiant Air Command Warbird Air Museum

### FOOD

- **F** Bernard's Surf
- **G** Mango Tree
- **H** Paul's Smokehouse Restaurant and Lounge
- **I** Yen Yen Chinese

### LODGING

- **J** Best Western Space Shuttle Inn
- **K** Days Inn Kennedy Space Center

### LODGING *(continued)*

- **L** Luna Sea Bed & Breakfast Motel
- **M** Ramada Inn Kennedy Space Center
- **N** Sea Esta Villas

### CAMPING

- **O** Cape Kennedy KOA Kampground
- **P** Great Outdoors RV/Golf Resort

3,000-acre nature-lovers' park, stocked fishing, a par-71 golf course, RV service center, paved streets and pads, full hookups, cabins, and five bathhouses. Closest to the Space Center, the **Cape Kennedy KOA Kampground**, 4513 W. Main St., Mims (Titusville), 800/562-3365 or 321/269-7361, has large, shady pull-throughs and full hookups, cabins, a rec room, and adult clubhouse; tent sites have water and electricity.

## NIGHTLIFE

On Ormond Beach, the **Rockin' Ranch**, 801 S. Nova Rd., 904/673-0904, has a large dance floor and is popular with boot-scootin' locals for national and local country acts. **Daytona Opry**, 2400 S. Ridgewood Ave., South Daytona, 888/333-6779 or 904/756-6779, offers nightly two-hour family productions of country, bluegrass, gospel, popular, rock 'n' roll, and variety shows.

Believe it or not, Daytona Beach is the summer home of the **London Symphony Orchestra**, which performs at Peabody Auditorium, 904/257-7790. Theatergoers can call the **Daytona Playhouse**, 100 Jessamine Blvd., Daytona Beach, 904/255-2431, which has staged shows from September through June for more than 40 years. The **Seaside Music Theater**, 904/252-6200, a professional music theater with a full pit orchestra, puts on summer shows at the Daytona Beach Community College Theater and winter productions at Ormond Beach Performing Arts Center.

**Teauila's Hawaii Supper Club**, on the top floor of the Ramada Oceanfront Resort, 2700 N. Atlantic Ave., Daytona Beach, 904/672-3770, offers a luau with native Hawaiian hula and fire dancers, great comedy, and an all-you-can-eat feast, including coconut mahi-mahi, roast pork, and Polynesian dishes.

In the Cocoa Beach area, call the **Brevard Cultural Alliance**'s 24-hour arts line at 321/690-6819 for what's happening while you're in town.

# 4 DISNEY WORLD, UNIVERSAL STUDIOS, AND SEAWORLD

From early morning 'til the small hours of the next, man-made excitement rules in the theme-park heaven between Lake Buena Vista and Orlando. And it's not limited to within the parks: Even the electrical poles along I-4 have mouse ears.

The always-keen competition for the tourist market has heated up in recent years, causing Disney to add an animal park, SeaWorld to build adventure rides, and Universal Studios to design an entertainment complex and dueling roller coasters. Building development plans of each of the big three show no signs of letup. Choices for the visitor with only a few days here are enough to cause theme-park fatigue even before you buy your tickets.

Generally, from Labor Day to early December (except Thanksgiving weekend) and again throughout January, park attendance is at its lightest, especially in the morning. The most crowded times are when school is out, especially from Christmas to New Year's. All the parks, especially Disney, have special holiday promotions, at which times attendance skyrockets. Families who take summer vacations generally do so in June and July, but by August the numbers start to drop. Trouble is, particularly for those with very young children or older people who can't take the heat, midday activities can be just too much. So plan accordingly: If you come in summer, get an early start and be back poolside at your hotel or move to one of the waterparks when the pavement starts to melt around you.

# DISNEY WORLD RESORT

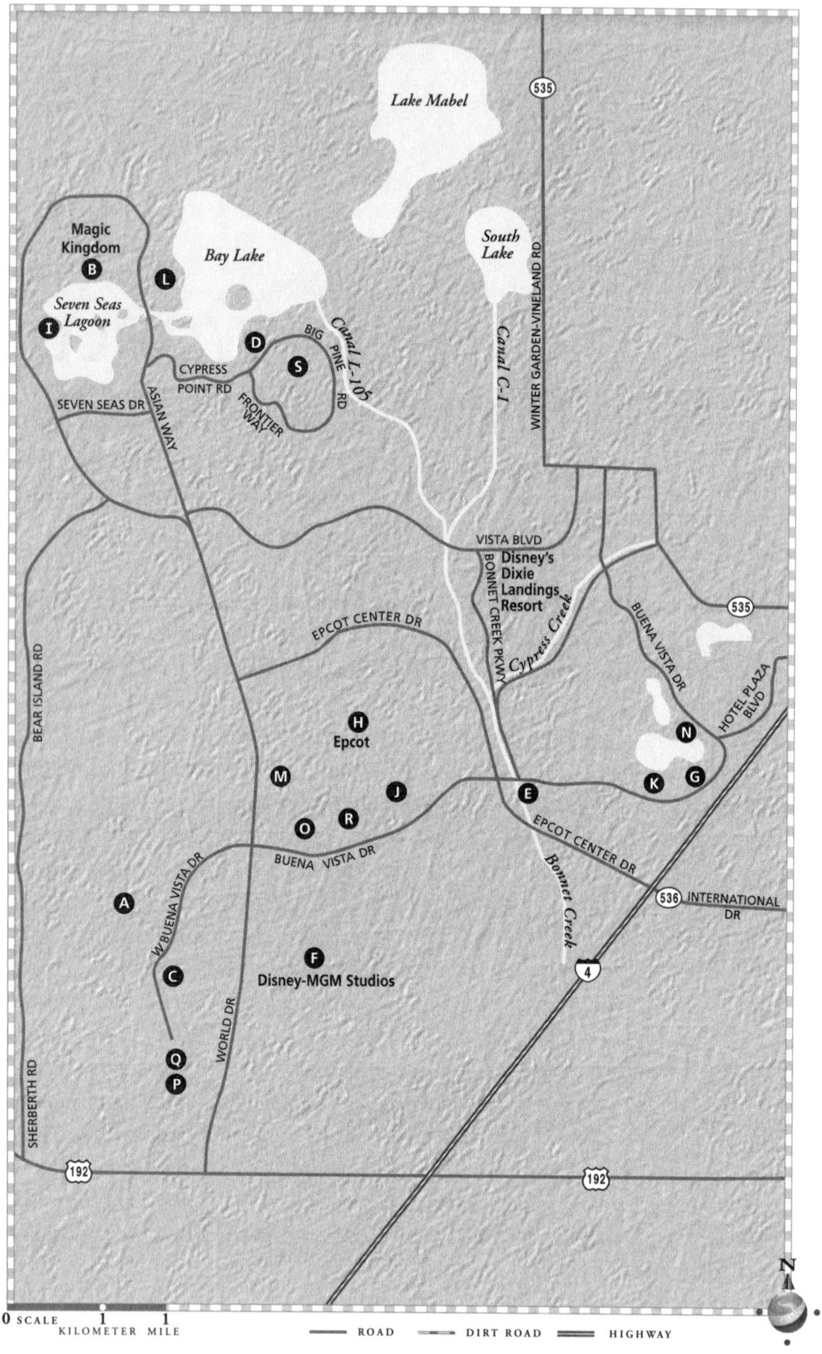

## A PERFECT DAY IN THE WORLD OF DISNEY

You've got to get up early for this one. Determine your first-choice park—seeing any one of them in depth will be more satisfying than trying to run between two or more. The kids will love a Disney character breakfast; otherwise, grab a bite and just head for the park. (If you're visiting a Disney park, call the day before for official opening time and arrive 45 minutes before that: They always open 30 minutes or so before official opening, and you can get a head start on the rides before the crowds arrive.) If this isn't your only day in town, take a mid-afternoon break back at your hotel pool, then return to the park refreshed at 5 or so, when the crowds start to thin out. Otherwise, explore the attraction's nooks and crannies to your heart's content. Unwind at the Legos playground and have dinner at Downtown Disney, then get over to Pleasure Island for some pub-hopping, or return to your hotel, hit the hot tub, and trade foot-and-leg massages before falling exhausted into bed.

## SIGHTSEEING HIGHLIGHTS

### ★★★★ DISNEY'S MAGIC KINGDOM

**WDW Resort, Lake Buena Vista, 407/824-4321, www.disneyworld.com**

---

### SIGHTS

- Ⓐ Disney's Animal Kingdom
- Ⓑ Disney's Magic Kingdom
- Ⓒ Disney's Water Parks–Blizzard Beach
- Ⓓ Disney's Water Parks–River Country
- Ⓔ Disney's Water Parks–Typhoon Lagoon
- Ⓕ Disney–MGM Studios
- Ⓖ Downtown Disney
- Ⓗ Epcot

### FOOD

- Ⓘ 1900 Park Fare
- Ⓙ Alfredo's
- Ⓚ Bongos Cuban Cafe
- Ⓛ California Grill
- Ⓛ Chef Mickey's Buffet
- Ⓜ Dolphin Fountain & Snack Shop
- Ⓝ Fulton's Crab House
- Ⓞ Harry's Safari Grille and Bar
- Ⓞ Palio Fine Italian Bistro
- Ⓝ Portobello Yacht Club
- Ⓚ Rainforest Cafe
- Ⓜ Tubbi's Buffeteria
- Ⓘ Victoria & Albert's
- Ⓚ Wolfgang Puck Express

### LODGING

- Ⓟ Disney's All-Star Music Resort
- Ⓠ Disney's All-Star Sports Resort
- Ⓡ Disney's Boardwalk
- Ⓜ Walt Disney World Dolphin
- Ⓞ Walt Disney World Swan

### CAMPING

- Ⓢ Disney's Fort Wilderness Resort & Campgrounds

*Note: Items with the same letter are located in the same place.*

Walt Disney himself might have imagined it, but few others could have predicted when it opened in 1971 that Walt Disney World's Magic Kingdom would become the single most-visited tourist destination in the world. Indeed, it welcomes nearly 40 million people each year. The primary thoroughfare, **Main Street U.S.A.**, is a recreation of a late-nineteenth-century street, with an old drugstore, a silent movie theater, cafés, shops, and horse-drawn streetcars. From here, roads run out like spokes from a hub to the park's six other "lands"—**Tomorrowland, Adventureland, Fantasyland, Frontierland, Liberty Square, and Mickey's Toontown**—each featuring its own themed shops, dining, and entertainment. Daily shows and attractions include bands, parades, and lively theatrical productions on several outdoor stages. **Cinderella's Castle**, at the center of the park, is visible from throughout the park and makes a convenient meeting place if your group decides to split up.

Among other top attractions in the Magic Kingdom: the thrilling coaster ride through the blackness of outer space in **Space Mountain** (try this ride first thing to beat the crowds); the special effects–filled **Big Thunder Mountain Railroad**; and the spooky but fun **Haunted Mansion**.

To find your way about the huge park, pick up a Magic Kingdom guidebook at the City Hall information center, where you'll also find a schedule of daily events.

***Details:*** *Open daily at about 9 a.m. (hours vary seasonally). Admission: $46 adults, $37 children. Parking $5. (full day minimum)*

## ★★★★ EPCOT

**WDW Resort, Lake Buena Vista, 407/939-7704, www.disneyworld.com**

More educational and mentally stimulating than heart-stopping, Epcot emphasizes the delight of discovery. The park is divided into two distinct areas, Future World and the World Showcase.

In **Future World**, scads of high-tech toys and hands-on exhibits let you see for yourself how and why things work the way they do. Attractions combine science and technology with the wonders of the natural world. If you stop first at the Spaceship Earth dome, you can pick up a schedule of events; then *run* to the computer terminals if you want a dinner reservation at any of the restaurants in the park's World Showcase.

The huge **Innoventions Building** has all the latest technological and communications devices set up for hands-on demonstrations. One of Epcot's newest rides, **Test Track**, lets you experience the thrill of pushing a test car to its limits as it turns, climbs, and maneuvers on a track at up to 65 mph. In the **House of the Future**, you'll see the latest developments in home, health, and fitness.

In the **World Showcase**, a large lagoon is circled by "villages" representing countries from around the world, including Mexico, Japan, Morocco, China, Norway, France, the United Kingdom, and the United States. Each village is staffed by bilingual Disney cast members, and each has shops, restaurants, music, and rides and attractions, including giant, 360-degree movie screens, puppet shows, dancers, and musicians. (The films in China and France are particularly memorable.) A nightly IllumiNations fireworks and laser show takes place over the lagoon.

*Tickets for all attractions in this chapter can be bought online in advance through the websites, so you can receive them by mail and save waiting in at least one line. Multi-day and multi-park passes offer substantial savings over the daily rates.*

Those who tire easily can board a shuttle that makes a continual loop around the World Showcase; a ferry docks at several points around the lagoon. If you've purchased multi-day passes, take the eight-mile monorail circuit that connects Epcot with the Magic Kingdom and parking lots.

***Details:*** *Open daily at 9 a.m.; closing hours vary seasonally. Admission: $46 adults, $37 children. Parking $5. (full day)*

## ★★★★ SEAWORLD ADVENTURE PARK

**7007 SeaWorld Dr., 800/327-2424 or 407/363-2200, www.seaworld.com**

SeaWorld, in an effort to broaden its appeal, has added some adventure rides to its long-successful mix of marine exhibits. Now you can head for the new **Journey to Atlantis** adventure and thrill ride, where you'll travel on a "water-coaster" and high-speed rails through the mysterious Lost City. Expect plenty of splashing and special effects. Elsewhere, a gondola-like "jetcopter" lets you soar through danger above the **Wild Arctic** base station, overlooking polar bears, beluga whales, and walruses. You'll see why this attraction won the Exhibit of the Year award from the American Zoo and Aquarium Association when it opened in 1996.

Pay attention when choosing your seat at the Killer Whales show—if the seats in the covered stadium are wet, consider how they might have gotten that way. (The grace and beauty of the park's mascot, the 25-foot, five-ton Shamu, and "baby" Namu are enough to bring tears to your eyes, but that's not how.)

You can feed a dolphin or touch a velvety stingray at the **Key West** exhibit. At **Pacific Point Preserve**, the park has recreated the rugged beaches and grottos of the northern Pacific coast. California sea lions, harbor seals, and fur seals cavort on the rocks and in the water. You can buy a few fish to feed these playful creatures (they're seasoned beggars).

If you've never seen a Florida manatee, now's your chance. In the manatee exhibit, you can watch these gentle, endangered giants from above and below the water in a lush lagoon, and learn about the efforts to protect them from extinction.

Perhaps the most amazing exhibit, as impressive as any of the best aquariums anywhere, is in **Terrors of the Deep**. Eels, lionfish, puffers, sleek barracuda, and toothy sharks swim over and around you, just inches away, as you walk through the world's largest underwater acrylic tunnel.

As an Anheuser-Busch–owned property, SeaWorld also features a Clydesdale Hamlet where you can see the company's colossal horses and relax over a cold brew in a hospitality center.

SeaWorld's educational program offers three 60-minute tours at additional charge (you'll need to call in advance to reserve space). You'll see polar bears and penguins on the **Polar Expedition** tour, shadow a bird specialist to feed and monitor the avian life on the **Bird's Eye View** tour, or learn more about one of humankind's most feared predatory creatures on the **Sharks** tour.

***Details:*** *Open daily at 9 a.m.; closing hours vary seasonally. Admission: $46 adults, $37 children. Parking $5. (5–8 hours)*

## ★★★ DISNEY–MGM STUDIOS

**Lake Buena Vista, 407/939-7704, www.disneyworld.com**

This movie-based theme park features the sets and characters of MGM's best-loved movies. If you stop first at the Crossroads of the World booth as you enter to pick up a map, and the Production Information window to find out what's in production, you can be part of an audience while you visit. The old hotel set in the **Twilight Zone Tower of Terror** ride is super-realistic, complete with overhanging vines and peeling paint outside and a musty-smelling library inside. But the ride isn't for the faint-hearted. Due to an "elevator failure," you'll free-fall nearly 13 stories—let's just say it'll get your attention. The **Indiana Jones and the Temple of Doom** stunt show is full of surprises and action. You can experience a blast into outer space on **Star Tours**, a *Star Wars* thrill ride. Mulan and her friends parade down Hollywood Boulevard, and various interactive shows give you an inside, sometimes hands-on look at movie production.

***Details:*** *Open daily 7–6. Admission: $46 adults, $37 children. Parking $6. (full day)*

## ★★★ DOWNTOWN DISNEY

**Lake Buena Vista, 407/828-3800, www.DowntownDisney.com**

The 120-acre Downtown Disney—which includes the **West Side**, **Marketplace**, and **Pleasure Island** areas—is the ever-evolving entertainment complex at Disney World. You can while away several hours—at no charge—in this metropolis of restaurants, clubs, and shops. Cigar, memorabilia, candy, New Age, and magnet shops welcome browsers and buyers alike, and there's an enormous Virgin Music store with 300 CD listening stations. Under the rusty old water tower at the edge of the **House of Blues Voodoo Garden**, you can dine in Mississippi Delta ambience or catch an evening concert. The **DisneyQuest** family interactive center offers five levels of computer-based entertainment, and the world-famous, Montreal-based circus **Cirque du Soleil** now performs here. Towering dinosaurs, aliens, and a spaceship, all built entirely from Lego bricks, stand outside the **Lego Imagination Center**. Inside, remarkable Lego constructions, from planes and trains to people and animals, offer inspiration and motivation to purchase the endless variety of Lego kits and materials sold here.

***Details:*** *Open daily. Free, except Pleasure Island $19.61 in the evening. Individual venues charge for concerts and shows.*

## ★★★ UNIVERSAL STUDIOS FLORIDA

**1000 Universal Studios Plaza, Orlando, 800/224-3838 or 407/363-8000, www.usf.com**

If you've seen the Universal Studios "Ride the Movies" ad campaign, you may feel a tinge of disappointment: you won't really experience the full, high-soaring drama of ET's midnight ride on a solitary bicycle under a full moon here. That said, a visit to Universal is a great day of adventure, not just for movie buffs, but for everybody who's ever heard of *King Kong*, *Jaws*, or *E.T., The Extra Terrestrial*. In particular, the **Kongfrontation** ride, with another killer set, this one replicating a New York subway, is extremely realistic and captivating as your elevated train crosses paths with the furious, howling, growling primate. On the **Back to the Future** ride, you'll board a time machine. The voice of wacky inventor Doc Brown (Christopher Lloyd) narrates while your vehicle lurches and rumbles through both past and future, following the movie plot lines. Also, don't miss the 3-D format movie ***Terminator 2.***

Behind-the-scenes TV- and movie-making are demonstrated at **Nickelodeon Studios**; the ***Hercules and Xena*** **show; Alfred Hitchcock:The Art of Making Movies;** ***The Lost World: Jurassic Park***; and the **Gory, Gruesome, and Grotesque Horror Makeup Show**. There's also a **Wild West** stunt show complete with blazing guns and Western-style props, a feisty old Ma Barker type and her not-too-bright sons, people falling through burning buildings, and that sort of thing.

For youngsters, America's favorite purple dinosaur, Barney, is here, as are a number of live-animal screen actors, including Babe, Benji, Lassie, and Mr. Ed. On the **Funtastic World of Hanna-Barbera** ride, you board a spaceship for a cleverly designed insider's look at the world of cartoons. And those who enjoyed the broad slapstick comedy of Michael Keaton's character in the movie won't want to miss the jokes and rock band of creepy deadbeats at **Beetlejuice's Graveyard** musical revue.

Outside on the streets, the **Hollywood Boulevard** movie set includes a replica of the tall, cast-concrete Kress store on California's Hollywood Boulevard. You can admire the hot rods and listen to the a cappella singing group out in front of Mel's Drive-In (from *American Graffiti*), or sit down and have a slice of pizza at Louie's Italian Restaurant (from *The Godfather*).

***Details:*** *Open daily at 9 a.m.; closing hours vary seasonally. Admission: $46 adults; $37 children. Parking $6. (full day)*

## ★★★ UNIVERSAL STUDIOS ISLANDS OF ADVENTURE

**1000 Universal Studios Plaza, Orlando, 800/224-3838 or 407/363-8000, www.usf.com**

Islands of Adventure is the area's newest theme park, combining the power of imagination with state-of-the-art technology. Myths, legends, and superheroes from the best-loved stories of all time will find a home here. Attractions include **Dr. Seuss at Seuss Landing**; the prehistoric world of **Jurassic Park**; **Comic Strip Lane** and the homes of Dennis the Menace, Blondie and Dagwood, and more; **Marvel Super Hero Island**, an explosive city caught in the battle between good and evil; and incredible **Spiderman** 3-D ride exploding with realistic high-tech effects. So here's to the cat in your hat.

***Details:*** *Open daily at 9 a.m.; closing hours vary seasonally. Admission: $46 adults; $37 children. Parking $6. (full day)*

## ★★★ WET 'N WILD

**6200 International Dr., Orlando, 800/992-9453 or 407/351-1800, www.wetnwild.com**

If you've left a cooler climate and are feeling a bit . . . *warm*, this always-busy Universal Studios–owned waterpark is for you. How daring you are will determine which of the thrill rides you'll enjoy most. Try the **Bubba Tub**, a six-story water slide in which the whole family can ride together in one tub; or the **Black Hole**, in which you plummet 500 feet in pitch-blackness (in this one you're on your own). An extensive children's area has mini-versions of the adult rides. The park offers heated pools in cooler weather, plus lockers, lifeguards, changing facilities, and food concessions. Those on tight budgets or special diets may want to bring their own food and picnic at the edge of a lake.

***Details:*** *Exit 30A off I-4. Open daily; hours vary seasonally. Admission: $28.95 adults, $22.95 children. Parking $5. (half-day minimum)*

## ★★ DISNEY'S ANIMAL KINGDOM

**Lake Buena Vista, 407/939-7704, www.disneyworld.com**

At the center of Disney's newest theme park stands the 14-story **Tree of Life**, its mighty trunk decorated with zebras, wildcats, spiders—more than 300 types of animals in all. You can circle the garden for a 360-degree view, then scurry down to the **"It's Tough To Be A Bug"** auditorium and don 3-D glasses for a riotous, multisensory look at life in the insect world. The **Kilimanjaro Safari** ride draws long lines fast, and by mid-morning the wildlife viewing can be sparse, so make your way to this attraction early in the day for your best chance at seeing the animals that live in this authentic-looking African savannah.

Frankly, Disney's Animal Kingdom is fine, but it just doesn't live up to the hype. If you want to see lots of wild animals up close, this won't be the place. There are more people dressed in animal costumes than there are real animals here. For value and animal sightings, Busch Gardens in Tampa (see Chapter 13, Tampa Bay) or the older, smaller, and far-less-expensive Central Florida Zoo in Sanford (see Chapter 5, Greater Orlando) are more satisfying.

***Details:*** *Open daily 7–6. Admission: $46 adults, $37 children. Parking $5. (6 hours minimum)*

## ★★ DISNEY'S WATER PARKS—WDW RESORT

**Lake Buena Vista, 407/560-9283, www.disneyworld.com**

Youngsters will have a ball at any of these three parks brimming with cool, watery fun. The water at all three is heated during winter, making them appropriate on all but the coldest days.

**Typhoon Lagoon**, 407/560-4073, recreates a tropical paradise with a huge body-surfing lagoon and thrill rides ranging from winding water slides to white-water rafting and tube rides. **River Country**, 407/824-2760, in the Fort Wilderness Resort and Campground, offers a nostalgic day by the ol' swimmin' hole, with rustic rope swings, flume rides, more water slides, a pool, and a sandy beach (in Central Florida!). The premise at **Blizzard Beach**, 407/560-3400, is that a winter ski resort has fallen victim to a rapid meltdown. The realistic-looking snowdrifts and ski lifts can be disconcerting in the heat of summer, but the exhilarating water rides, slides, flumes, rafting, and tube runs offer a cool respite from the Florida sun.

***Details:*** *All three parks open daily 10 a.m.–dusk. Typhoon Lagoon admission: $26.45 adults, $20.65 children. River Country admission: $16.91 adults, $13.25 children. Blizzard Beach admission: $26.45 adults, $20.67 children. (half-day minimum)*

## ★★ UNIVERSAL STUDIOS CITYWALK

**1000 Universal Studios Plaza, Orlando, 800/224-3838 or 407/363-8000, www.usf.com**

Brilliantly colored 10-story towers, contemporary free-form sculptures, and a two-tiered promenade encircle a four-acre harbor at this eclectic complex of retail stores, restaurants, and entertainment venues, each with a distinctive culture. On the roster are **Bob Marley—A Tribute to Freedom**, an authentic replica of the Reggae King's home in Kingston, Jamaica; **City Jazz**, a daytime musical-educational center housing the **Thelonious Monk Institute of Jazz** and an evening jivin' joint; the **Latin Quarter**, where you can dine and shop amid the driving rhythms and decor from all 21 Latin American countries; a 20-screen movie theater; the **Lombard Street** shopping area; and several nightclubs (see Nightlife) and eateries (see Food). The nightspots have "open license" throughout CityWalk, so you can order cocktails to go and carry them from one club to another. Like other Universal Studios venues, CityWalk serves as a set for real TV and film production, so you may want to have a pen and autograph book handy in case you get lucky.

***Details:*** *The CityWalk area is free to the public for browsing, sightseeing, shopping, and dining. Individual clubs within the complex charge admission, depending on events.*

## FOOD

With the exception of the concessions within the parks, which are generally unimaginative and overpriced, most Disney-operated restaurants are top-shelf, portions are generous, and you'll usually be entertained one way or another while you enjoy a meal. Several venues offer Disney character breakfasts, where kids can dine on Mickey Mouse–shaped pancakes and look forward to visits from Mickey and Minnie, Goofy, Winnie the Pooh, and assorted other cartoon friends; more information is available by calling 407/939-3463.

If you're spending the day at Epcot, stop at the Earth Station computer terminals in the Starship Earth dome as soon as you enter to reserve a table for lunch or dinner at **Alfredo's** in Italy. (Forget the diet and have the buttery, original-recipe Fettuccine Alfredo!)

At Disney's Contemporary Resort, 4600 W. World Dr., Lake Buena Vista, families with children can start the day with a Disney character breakfast at **Chef Mickey's Buffet**. The **California Grill**, 407/824-1576, on the rooftop, offers a splendid view of the area and a "show kitchen," where guests can chat with the chefs.

The family-style **1900 Park Fare** in Disney's Grand Floridian Resort and Spa, 4401 Grand Floridian Way, 407/939-3463, serves a Disney character breakfast. Also at the Grand Floridian, the exclusive **Victoria & Albert's** offers a romantic, formal evening to remember. Seating at one of only 18 tables is at either 6 or 9 p.m. for a six-course prix fixe dinner (upwards of $80 per person), served by Maid Victoria and Butler Albert while a harpist plays.

At the Walt Disney World Swan, 1200 Epcot Resort Blvd., Lake Buena Vista, 407/934-3000, **Palio Fine Italian Bistro** has strolling musicians,

# DISNEY WORLD AREA

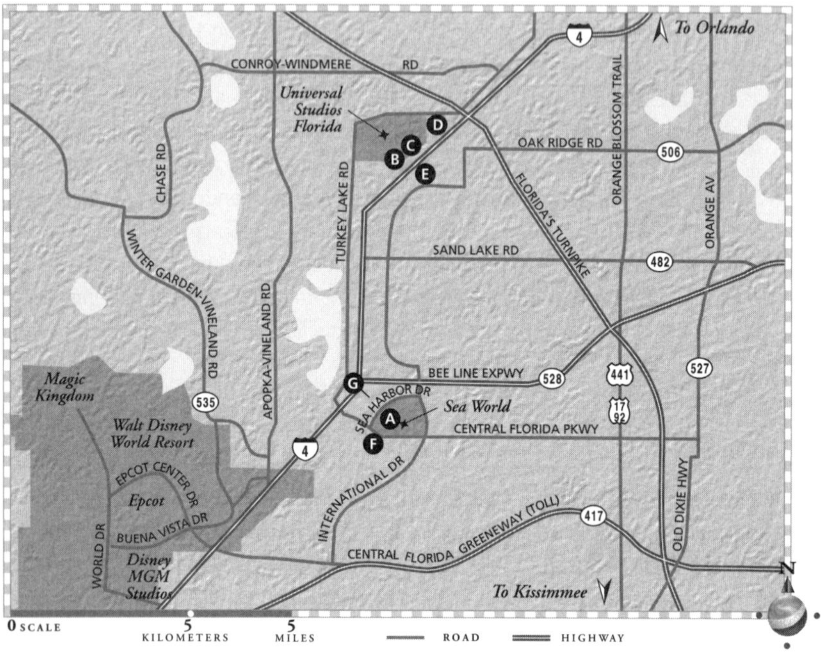


## SIGHTS

- **A** SeaWorld Adventure Park
- **B** Universal Studios CityWalk
- **C** Universal Studios Florida
- **C** Universal Studios Islands of Adventure
- **D** Wet 'n Wild

## FOOD

- **B** Emeril's
- **B** Jimmy Buffett's Margaritaville
- **B** NASCAR Cafe
- **B** NBA Restaurant
- **C** Starlite Cafe

## LODGING

- **E** Delta Orlando Resort
- **F** Hilton Grand Vacations Club
- **C** Portofino Bay Hotel
- **G** Renaissance Orlando Resort

*Note: Items with the same letter are located in the same area.*

---

moderately priced Northern Italian cuisine, wood-fired pizzas, and an extensive dessert buffet. **Harry's Safari Grille and Bar** offers an unusual wild-game menu in a casual atmosphere. For relaxed dining in the WDW Dolphin next door, 407/934-4000, hit the buffet at the 24-hour **Tubbi's Buffeteria**, or the '50s-themed **Dolphin Fountain & Snack Shop**.

You can't get a bad meal at Downtown Disney, but low-budget options are scarce. Call for reservations or expect a wait for a superb dinner at **Fulton's Crab House**, 1670 Buena Vista Dr., 407/934-2628, which specializes in fresh seafood. It's housed in a replica paddlewheel ship in the lagoon. (Try your server's recommendations on the chef's nightly specials.) Next door, the **Portobello Yacht Club**, 1650 Buena Vista Dr., 407/934-8888, offers regional Italian dishes and a respectable wine list. Thunder, lightning, talking trees, and gentle rain showers punctuate the vibrant, lively decor at the **Rainforest Cafe**, 407/827-8500. Live tropical birds, saltwater aquariums, and other natural exhibits mix with special effects and good American family dining. No reservations are taken, so go straight there and leave your name if this is your first choice.

At Downtown Disney West Side, perhaps you'll spot superstar owners Emilio and Gloria Estefan at **Bongos Cuban Cafe**, 407/828-0999, which offers savory Cuban foods and Latin music. The smells inside the famous superchef's **Wolfgang Puck Express**, 407/828-0107, are heavenly for a fast lunch or takeout; the full-price dining experience can be found a short walk away on the West Side, 407/938-9653.

At Universal Tower Resort Hotel, the **Starlite Cafe**, 407/351-2100, is inexpensive for good family dining, with a children's menu, low-volume music, pool tables, dart boards, and TVs. Universal Studios' new CityWalk complex has a number of imaginative dining options, like **Jimmy Buffett's Margaritaville**, with its cascading margarita fountain; **Emeril's**, for flamboyant master chef Emeril Lagasse; the officially sanctioned **NASCAR Cafe**, with rows of racing machines and paraphernalia from professional NASCAR drivers; and the **NBA Restaurant**, which glorifies the history and present-day action of NBA and WNBA basketball.

## LODGING

Lodging at Disney properties offers good quality and service, early admission to parks, free parking, and other advantages, but you'll pay well for them. That said, if you want to experience the secret of their success, call the **Disney Reservations Center** at 407/934-7639, or try any of the ones listed here.

Lakeside walkways offer a romantic setting for an evening stroll at the **Walt Disney World Swan** and **Dolphin**, 1500 Epcot Resorts Blvd., Lake Buena Vista, 800/227-1500 (both), 407/934-3000 (Swan) or 407/934-4000 (Dolphin), www.swandolphin.com. Five-story swan and dolphin statues rest atop the buildings so you can tell them apart. From here you can stroll through the Disney's Boardwalk entertainment district to get to Epcot, or cruise the waterways in a complimentary ferry that links the various properties within the WDW Resort.

Rates are steep at **Disney's Boardwalk**, 2101 N. Epcot Resorts Blvd., 407/939-5100, but you'll be right in the heart of the fun. Disney's lowest-priced properties, both in Lake Buena Vista, are still more costly than most off-property motels, but amenities include babysitting services, currency exchange, on-site restaurants, and shuttles to WDW parks. If this sounds good, book accommodations at **Disney's All-Star Music Resort**, 1801 W. Buena Vista Dr., 407/934-7639 or **Disney's All-Star Sports Resort**, 1701 W. Buena Vista Dr., 407/934-7639.

In Orlando's Maingate area outside Universal Studios, the **Delta Orlando Resort**, 5715 Major Blvd., 800/634-4763, has an 800-room hotel with a four-leaf clover-shaped pool plus mini-golf, tennis, sand volleyball courts, and basketball courts to give guests some exercise between running back and forth to the area attractions. Opened in summer of 1999, the **Portofino Bay Hotel** at Universal Studios Escape, 6800 Lakewood Plaza Dr., Orlando, 407/503-1000, is modeled after the world-renowned Italian seaside village of Portofino. The 750-room resort resembles a romantic Mediterannean village built around a small bay. Amenities include a world-class spa, a Roman aqueduct-style pool with a water slide, and a bocce-ball court.

Just across from SeaWorld, the **Renaissance Orlando Resort**, 6677 Sea Harbor Dr., 800/327-6677 or 407/351-5555, has a dramatic sunlit atrium at its center and extra-large guest rooms. About a mile south, at Central Florida Parkway, the **Hilton Grand Vacations Club**, 6924 Grand Vacations Way, 800/448-2736 or 407/239-0100, offers accommodations from studios to three-bedroom villas.

## CAMPING

Families and campers in tents or RVs can stay at **Disney's Fort Wilderness Resort & Campgrounds**, 4510 N. Fort Wilderness Tr., 407/934-7639. Others who want to experience the rustic wilderness can rent rooms, condos, or trailers. The 740-acre camping area offers 800 spaces with grills, electrical hookups, and paved pads, and it accepts pets. Advance reservations are a must. Amenities include tennis, a frontier-style dinner show, nightly campfires, parasailing, a petting farm, fishing, boating, horseback riding, and bicycle rentals.

## NIGHTLIFE

Party the night away at **Pleasure Island**, 407/934-7781, a must-visit for those who thrive in a crowded party atmosphere. The streets are filled with constant entertainment: musicians, shops, dining, videos, caricaturists, and more. Clubs have no drink minimums, soft drinks are inexpensive, and the "open license" lets you buy a drink from one club and consume it in the street or carry it into the next club. An entrance fee of $19.61 lets you in to all the clubs and shows, except for occasional special events. Persons under 18 are admitted with parents, but preadolescents are out of their element. You can hear tall tales of intrigue at the early-1900s **Adventurers Club**, dance to live bands on an outside stage, or listen to jazz in a 1930s speakeasy or classic rock at the three-story **Rock & Roll Beach Club**, then belt out the vocal track of your favorite tune and make a music video at **SuperStar Studios**. Plenty of high-tech special effects surround a rotating dance floor at **Mannequins Dance Palace**, and stand-up comics deliver family-suitable laughs aplenty at the **Comedy Warehouse**.

At the edge of Pleasure Island, hear rising country stars and kick your heels up at the **Wildhorse Saloon,** with a two-story setup around a good-sized dance floor. (If you come in from the side, you can get into the Wildhorse only for just a $5 cover, without paying the full Pleasure Island price.) The **House of Blues** at Downtown Disney, 407/934-2222, is a terrific concert venue featuring national acts nightly. Live reggae groups play outside in the lakeside **Voodoo Garden**, with its folk and voodoo art and juke-joint decor. Across the street, the celebrated French-Canadian circus, **Cirque du Soleil**, uses no animals, but the costumes and acrobatics are astounding.

**Disney's Boardwalk**, 407/939-5100, on the Lake Buena Vista waterfront has an active nighttime scene with its **Atlantic Dance Hall,** featuring live music from Big Band to Motown and contemporary, and the ever-popular dueling pianos at **Jellyrolls**. For quiet drinks and board games, go upstairs in the BoardWalk Inn to the **Belle Vue Room**. Sports fans can keep score at the **ESPN Club**, a high-tech family-friendly sports bar. The interior resembles the sideline of a football stadium, servers are called coaches, and each booth has a small TV—they even have TVs above the bathroom stalls!

**Universal's** newest contender in the entertainment arena is its **CityWalk** complex, 407/363-8000, with restaurants, theaters, and recreations of famous nightspots from elsewhere, including **Jimmy Buffett's Margaritaville**, **Pat O'Brien's** dueling pianos party bar, the **Motown Cafe**, and the **Latin Quarter**, with the culture, cuisine and driving dance beats of 21 Latin nations.

You can visit Hawaii without ever leaving SeaWorld at the **Aloha! Polynesian Luau**, 407/351-3600, which offers a four-course meal and two hours of authentic island entertainment. For foot-stompin' hoedown-style dinner theater, visit the **Hoop-Dee-Doo Revue**, 407/824-4321, at Disney's Fort Wilderness Resort, a country-western vaudeville show with Disney characters and all-you-can-eat country vittles.

# 5
# GREATER ORLANDO

Before the Mouse and his competitors grew up to blanket Greater Orlando with ingenious thrill rides, outdoor enthusiasts came here to experience its natural and cultural charms. Today there is diversity—and diversion—for all. There's such a range of leisure activities around Orlando that visitors will have no trouble overfilling a vacation.

Travel just north of Orlando, especially in Seminole County, and you can see what this area was like before development. Families will enjoy visiting a farm park, airboating across the surface of a lake full of alligators, or, just south of Orlando, strolling through re-created Chinese countryside.

Visitors seeking natural beauty can find it cruising or canoeing on unspoiled rivers lined with cabbage palms and longleaf pines and frequented by wild turkeys and bald eagles. Herons, ospreys, warblers, ibises, and swallows live in the brush and ferns of Central Florida's forest and marshland. Botanical gardens and secluded lakes teeming with bass are easy to find. Of course, there are plenty of smaller theme parks, amusements, and dinner theaters for those who can't get enough of this type of excitement. But, when you need a break from the hubbub, this is also a diverse area to vacation and enjoy some relaxation time with the people you came here to be with.

Note: Disney World, Universal Studios, and SeaWorld are covered in Chapter Four.

# ORLANDO NORTH/WINTER PARK AREA

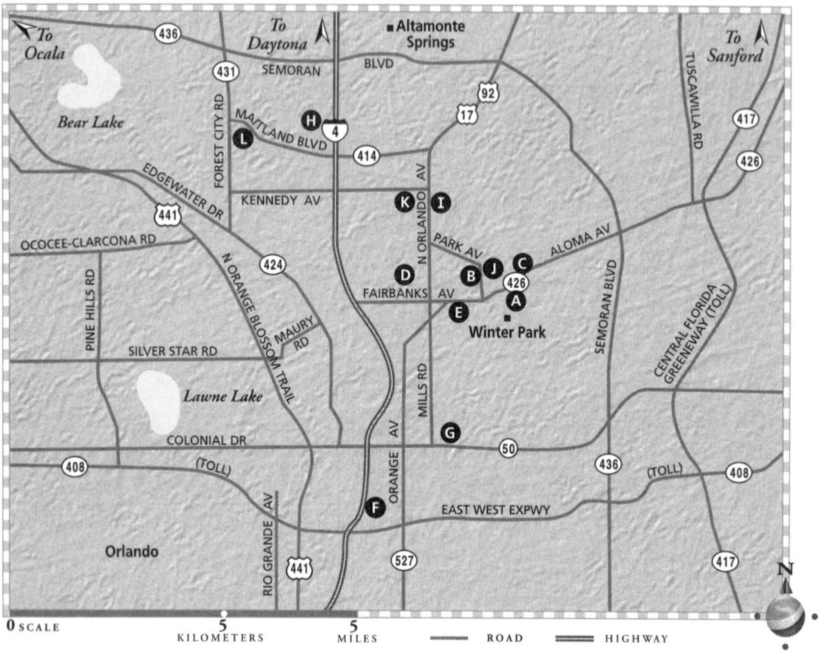


## SIGHTS

- Ⓐ Albin Polasek Museum and Sculpture Gardens
- Ⓑ Charles Hosmer Morse Museum of American Art
- Ⓒ Scenic Boat Tours
- Ⓓ Winter Park Historical Museum

## FOOD

- Ⓔ Brazilian Pavilion
- Ⓕ Crackers Seafood Restaurant
- Ⓖ La Normandie
- Ⓕ Lili Marlene's
- Ⓗ Maison y Jardin
- Ⓘ Nicole St. Pierre
- Ⓙ Park Plaza Gardens

## LODGING

- Ⓚ Thurston House

## CAMPING

- Ⓛ Orlando Green Acres RV Resort

*Note: Items with the same letter are located in the same area.*

## A PERFECT DAY IN GREATER ORLANDO

Park the car for the day and begin with a stroll through the village green in downtown Winter Park, with its colorful hanging baskets, picturesque fountains, and vibrant flower beds. Take the Scenic Boat Tour for a look at lakeside mansions and other postcard-pretty scenery. Later, walk to the Albin Polasek Museum and Sculpture Garden to view the works of this late Czech artist. Continue to the Cornell Fine Arts Museum on the Rollins College campus, stopping en route for a look at the stained-glass windows of the Knowles Memorial Chapel. Have lunch on Park Avenue and cross the railroad track to the Winter Park Historical Museum in the Farmer's Market Building. For now, pass by the shops so you can get to the Charles Hosmer Morse Museum in plenty of time before closing. Later you can browse to your heart's content. If you've a reservation, dine at Maison y Jardin tonight, or head over to Church Street Station for a meal and the evening festivities.

## GETTING AROUND GREATER ORLANDO

International Drive, the palm tree–lined boulevard stretching roughly five miles between SeaWorld and Universal Studios, requires nothing as much as patience to negotiate. You'll enjoy it most if you treat it as part of the overall sightseeing experience—there's nothing like it for the flurry of activity and sheer number of cars and pedestrians spilling into the streets. We'll also recommend some dining and lodging options along this route.

The northern half has all the tacky gift and souvenir stores, sports-team apparel, trendy eateries, and restaurants serving foods from around the world. The southern part is hotel row and includes the huge Orange County Convention Center, the Pointe Orlando complex, and more upscale shopping and attractions. A green trolley system, I-Ride, runs every 15 minutes or so, stopping at 54 marked stops along the way.

Orlando's airport is the 15th-busiest in the nation. All the major car-rental agencies and many hotels have shuttles to and from the airport, and taxi and limousine service is available. The city's economical bus system, Lynx, marks its stops with a lynx-pawprint logo.

Major highways and thoroughfares are generally well marked and provide easy access for visitors. The major east–west route crossing the state, I-4, connects Orlando with U.S. 192, Kissimmee's major thoroughfare, and continues west to Tampa and St. Petersburg or east to Daytona, the Space Coast, and Port Canaveral. If you're driving, just remember Greater Orlando is Florida's most popular tourist destination. Many people on the roads don't know where they're going, and drivers may turn or stop without warning. Be watchful, cut someone a break who needs it, and stay in the right lane if you're going slower than other traffic.

## SIGHTSEEING HIGHLIGHTS

### ★★★★ CHARLES HOSMER MORSE MUSEUM OF AMERICAN ART

**445 Park Ave. N., Winter Park, 407/645-5311 or 407/645-5324**

This spacious and architecturally lovely museum, with continually changing exhibits from its own extensive collection, features the work of such masters as Frank Lloyd Wright, George Inness, and Maxfield Parrish. The jewel in the museum's crown is the largest single collection in the country of works by Louis Comfort Tiffany. In addition to his beautiful stained-glass pieces is a large collection of his other works, including intricate, opal-encrusted jewelry and art glass, ceramics, and pottery, for which he is also celebrated, though less well-known. New to the Morse collection is the reassembled stained-glass chapel Tiffany designed for the 1893 World's Columbian Exposition in Chicago. He considered the Byzantine-Romanesque chapel, with its complex mosaics and leaded-glass windows, among his best pieces of work.

***Details:*** *Fairbanks Exit off I-4 to Park Ave. Open Tue–Sat 9:30–4, Sun 1–5. Admission: $3 adults, $1 children. (1–1½ hours)*

### ★★★★ GATORLAND

**14501 S. Orange Blossom Tr., Orlando, 800/393-5297 or 407/855-5496, www.gatorland.com**

"Bring more tourists," reads a sign in the gift shop. "The last ones were delicious!" At this old-fashioned Florida Cracker attraction, you can see more than 3,000 Florida alligators and jungle crocodiles, plus birds and other animals. (The Crackers were the Old Florida farmers, so-called for the sound made by their trademark 20-foot-long braided-buckskin whips.) Shows and exhibits here feature gator wrestling and Florida snakes. The "Jungle Crocs of the World" show demonstrates the power and ferocity of these man-eating predators. Ride around the park on the Gatorland Train, pet the llamas and deer, and hand-feed the colorful lorikeets. It's good family fun. Between shows, you can walk out on a 1,500-foot boardwalk and nature trail that winds

**ALLIGATOR AWARENESS**

If you spend any time around the lakes and woods of Central Florida, you're sure to see at least one alligator, and possibly many more. Alligators can weigh up to a half-ton and they can live as long as 120 years.

Females are fiercely protective of their young, and bulls in mating season can be totally unreasonable. Never try to feed these predators—it's against the law for a very good reason. Feeding the gators conditions them to associate people with food, which can prove fatal to both humans and their pets. Give any alligators you encounter wide berth. They can actually move quite quickly for short distances. Wild gators (the operative word here being "*wild*") will generally move away from people, but you won't be able to tell if the one staring back at you has been fed before—and may be anticipating a similar handout.

through a cypress swamp, or climb a three-story observation tower that overlooks an alligator-breeding marsh where another sign reads, "No swimming." (No problem.)

***Details:*** *On U.S. 441. Open daily 9 a.m.–dusk. Admission: $12.67 adults, $9.49 children. (half-day)*

## ★★★ ALBIN POLASEK MUSEUM AND SCULPTURE GARDENS

**633 Osceola Ave., Winter Park, 407/647-6294, www.polasek.org**

These three acres of lush gardens are filled with the classical figurative sculpture and whimsical mythological creations of Czech artist Albin Polasek. Polasek, who died in 1965, settled in Winter Park after he fled Hitler's invasion of Czechoslovakia. His bronze sculpture *Mother Crying Over World*, cast in 1942 when the world was agonizing over the events of World War II, depicts a woman kneeling in grief with her head bowed over a globe.

***Details:*** *On SR 426, east of I-4, just east of Park Ave. Open Wed–Sat 10 a.m.–noon and 1–4 p.m., Sun 1–4. Free. (1–1½ hours)*

### ★★★ KATIE'S WEKIVA RIVER LANDING

**190 Katie's Cove, Sanford, 407/628-1482**

Katie's offers canoe or kayak rentals, so you can spend a day on the wild Wekiva River, which meanders through miles of quiet waterways overhung with subtropical vegetation. A river trip offers a rare view of the real Florida that most visitors won't see. Otters, raccoons, turtles, and small alligators live in and along the river; larger gators often sun themselves on the banks, but leave them alone and you'll get along fine. If you prefer to explore the area on land, Katie's rents bicycles, and riverside camping is available in tents or rustic log cabins.

***Details:*** *I-4 to SR 46; about five miles west to Wekiva Park Dr. Hours vary seasonally. (half-day minimum)*

### ★★★ SCENIC BOAT TOURS

**312 E. Morse Blvd., Winter Park, 407/644-4056**

Shallow-draft boats (which sit high in the water and don't require deep water for navigation) piloted by knowledgeable guides tour Lake Osceola and its tributary lakes and canals around historic Winter Park. It's a totally relaxing excursion, cruising past formal gardens, sprawling oaks, lushly landscaped estates, stately mansions, and the Mediterranean-style buildings of Rollins College campus. Tropical birds feed along the lake's banks and swoop across the water's surface. This bargain-priced Winter Park tradition is just a short walk from the Park Avenue shopping area.

***Details:*** *Open daily 10–4. Admission: $6 adults, $3 children. (1 hour)*

### ★★ BOGGY CREEK AIRBOAT RIDES

**3702 Big Bass Rd., Kissimmee, 407-344-9550, www.gemserv.com/bcairboats**

These scenic airboat tours range from leisurely idle cruises to wind-in-your-face races through the wilderness of the Central Florida wetlands. They're safe and fun, with Coast Guard–approved captains and boats. If you crave an adrenaline rush, try a night tour and watch for the pairs of tiny red eyes that surround your boat in the darkness.

***Details:*** *Open daily 9–5:30. Daytime tours: $16 adults, $8 children. Nighttime tours: $25. (1–1½ hours)*

### ★★ CENTRAL FLORIDA ZOOLOGICAL PARK

**3755 N. U.S. 17-92, Sanford, 407/323-4450**

# SANFORD

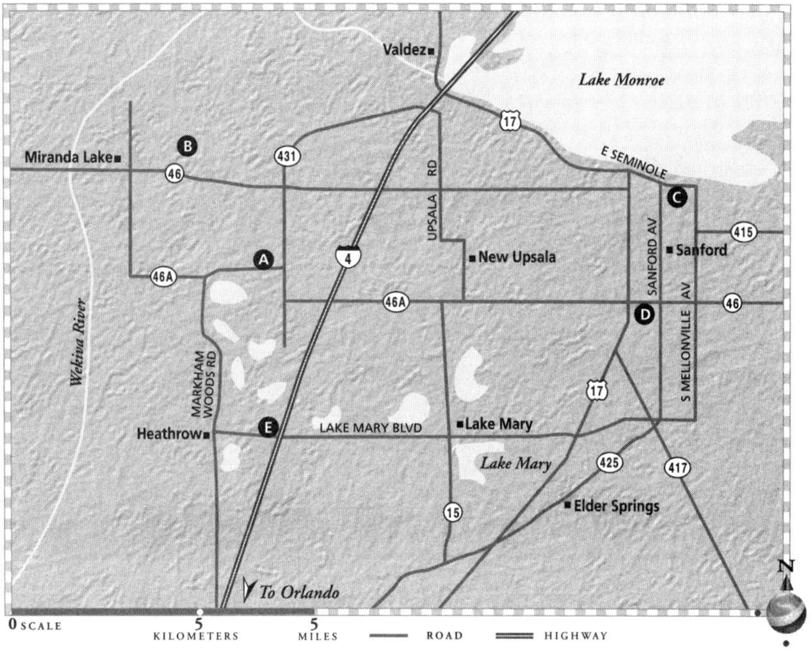


## SIGHTS

- **A** Central Florida Zoological Park
- **B** Katie's Wekiva River Landing
- **C** Rivership Romance

## LODGING

- **D** Higgins House B&B

## CAMPING

- **B** Katie's Wekiva River Landing
- **E** Twelve Oaks RV Resort

*Note: Items with the same letter are located in the same area.*

---

The bellowing and hooting of howler monkeys greet you at this pleasant zoo in a 109-acre forest of palms, cypress trees, and oaks. Look for the two-toed sloths hanging motionless from the trees. You can look through windows at animal newborns in the nursery, and children can make animal friends in the petting zoo. You're likely to see a docent strolling the grounds carrying a tiny hedgehog or screech owl or calling to Peruvian llamas or colorful macaws. The extensive herpetarium offers a fascinating and safe way to observe some of the seldom-seen reptiles and amphibians that share the Florida habitat.

***Details:*** *Open daily 9–5. Admission: $7 adults, $3 children, $4 seniors. (2–3 hours)*

## ★★ FLYING TIGERS WARBIRD RESTORATION MUSEUM

**231 N. Hoagland Blvd., Kissimmee, 407/933-1942, www.warbirdmuseum.com**

Explore hands-on displays of American warplanes, armaments, and equipment, and watch technicians and curators work on the restoration and reconstruction projects that are always under way at this military museum. Changing exhibits may include a B-17 Flying Fortress, P-51 Mustang, or P-38 Lightning. Plane rides are available in a WACO open-cockpit biplane.

***Details:*** *Seven miles east of I-4, off U.S. 192. Mon–Sat 9–6, Sun 9–5. Admission: $6 adults, $5 children/seniors. (1–2 hours)*

## ★★ GREEN MEADOWS PETTING FARM

**1368 S. Poinciana Blvd., Kissimmee, 407/846-0770**

The two-hour, hands-on tour of Green Meadows offers visitors the chance to see more than 300 gentle farm animals, milk the cows, and take a bumpy, tractor-drawn hayride. Youngsters can take a miniature train ride and a pony ride, too. Bring a picnic if you like and eat it in the shade of the oak trees—just watch out for the marauding resident peacocks. They can get aggressive and may try to steal your lunch.

***Details:*** *Open daily 9:30–4. Admission: $13 adults/children, $9 seniors. (2–3 hours)*

## ★★ RIPLEY'S BELIEVE IT OR NOT! MUSEUM

**8201 International Dr., 407-363-4418 or 407/345-0501**

Cameras and camcorders are welcome in this amazing museum of peculiar phenomena and bizarre inventions and creations from around the world. The building itself is designed to look as if it's losing its battle with a huge Florida sinkhole. Ripley's will delight those who grew up with the series in the Sunday comics—its weird relics range from a two-headed kitten to a Rolls Royce made of matchsticks.

***Details:*** *Open daily 9 a.m.–11 p.m. Admission: $9.95 adults, $6.95 children. (2 hours)*

### ★★ RIVERSHIP ROMANCE

**Monroe Harbour Marina, 433 N. Palmetto Ave., Sanford, 800/423-7401 or 407/321-5091, www.rivershipromance.com**

Bird and wildlife sightings are continuous from atop the *Rivership Romance*, a 110-foot triple-deck enclosed catamaran that offers three- and four-hour luncheon and moonlight dining/dance cruises along the picturesque St. Johns River. True romantics and ballroom dancers especially will enjoy getting out on the floor when the band starts up. Call ahead for special music and show nights. You won't go hungry on the four-hour luncheon cruise—even after both brunch and lunch, there's chilled jumbo shrimp still to come!

***Details:*** *Luncheon cruises daily at 11, $35–$45; dinner cruises, $50. (3–4 hours)*

### ★★ SPLENDID CHINA

**3000 Splendid China Blvd., Kissimmee, 800/244-6226 or 407/396-7111, www.floridasplendidchina.com**

What if they built a theme park and nobody came? The developers of this unusual park seriously misjudged Central Florida visitors' interest in Chinese history. The good news is that you'll have this nicely landscaped attraction relatively to yourself. On a stroll through this re-created Chinese countryside, you'll see detailed replicas of more than 60 famous Chinese landmarks. There are a few good acrobatic, dance, and magic shows; reasonably priced gift and art shops; craft demonstrations; and plenty of photo ops. No thrill rides or video arcades here, although you can watch uncaged exotic animals in the fine Wild Cats show (it's not hard to get good seats!) and pose for a photo beside a white tiger or a 700-pound lion.

***Details:*** *Located off U.S. 192. Open daily 9:30–7. Admission: $26.99 adults, $16.99 children. (half-day minimum)*

### ★★ WATER MANIA

**6073 W. Irlo Bronson Hwy., Kissimmee 800/527-3092 or 407/396-2626, www.watermania-florida.com**

Water Mania's naturally wooded, three-acre picnic/relaxation area comes in handy for those needing a break from the wave pool, tubes, sand volleyball, basketball, go-carts, and other slipping, sliding, and drenching water rides. Brace yourself for the 400-foot, twisting, turning Anaconda, and the Wipe-Out bodyboard/surf simulator. The kids will sleep soundly tonight.

***Details:*** *Open daily 9:30–7 (varies seasonally). Admission: $23.95 adults, $17.95 children; half price after 4 p.m. (half-day minimum)*

### ★ JUNGLELAND

**4580 W. Irlo Bronson Hwy., Kissimmee, 407/396-1012**

More than 400 rare and exotic animals from around the world—including big cats, tropical birds, primates, bears, llamas, and alligators—can be seen live at Jungleland. There's a petting zoo for the little ones, and live alligator shows are offered several times daily.

***Details:*** *Located on U.S. 192. Open daily 9–6. Admission: $9.95 adults, $6.95 children, $7.95 seniors. (2–4 hours)*

### ★ WINTER PARK HISTORICAL MUSEUM

**200 W. New England Ave., Winter Park, 407/647-8180**

Winter Park was once Central Florida's premier urban village. Housed in a restored railroad freight depot in a farmer's market, the museum chronicles local history through photos, collectibles, and memorabilia.

***Details:*** *Open Thu 11–3, Sat 9–1, Sun 1–4. Free. (30 minutes)*

## FITNESS AND RECREATION

Greater Orlando boasts some of Florida's finest golf courses, and golf-and-room packages abound. In fact, there are more than 130 courses here. Sure bets that won't disappoint you include **Falcon's Fire Golf Club** in Kissimmee, 407/239-5445, a 6,900-yard Rees Jones–designed championship course, and the Jack Nicklaus–designed **Grand Cypress Golf Club** in Orlando, 407/239-1909, which rewards accuracy above distance.

This is a big-league sports destination. Area teams include the NBA's minor league **Orlando Magic**; arena football's **Orlando Predators**; ice hockey's **Orlando Solar Bears**; the **Orlando Rays**, AA minor-league affiliate of the Tampa Bay Devil Rays; and the **Houston Astros** in spring training, 407-933-6500. The Women's Professional Fastpitch Softball team, the **Wahoos**, is here; as are the **Jackals**, a franchise of the Roller Hockey International League. Pro soccer fans can follow the **Orlando Sun Dogs**.

Ballooning, soaring, and sightseeing flights are available for a bird's-eye view of the attractions below. Call **Blue Ridge Balloons**, 407/894-5040; **Orange Blossom Balloons**, 407/239-7677; or **Air Florida Charter**, 407/888-4114.

Fans of pari-mutuel wagering can visit the **Orlando-Seminole Jai Alai**

SPLENDID CHINA, KISSIMMEE

Rose M. Wilson

**Fronton,** 407/339-6221, to watch this seventeenth-century Basque sport from September through January. The greyhounds run in Longwood at **Sanford-Orlando Kennel Club**, 407/831-1600; and in nearby Casselberry at **Seminole Greyhound Park**, 407/699-4510.

Canoeing, kayaking, and bike riding are popular activities at Wekiwa Springs. You can fish from the banks on Little Wekiva River (yes, there are two spellings) or, for offshore fishing, call **Cutting Loose Expeditions** in Winter Park, 800/533-4746 or 407/629-4700.

## FOOD

Finding good restaurants here is easy. The area takes pride in fulfilling the expectations of its tourist industry. Your servers will generally introduce themselves, and their imprinted name tags often have their hometowns on them, too, a handy conversation-starter.

On the south side of Orlando, visit the **Ming Court Wok & Grille**, 9188 International Dr., 407/351-9988, for regional Oriental specialties with a gourmet flair. Thai and Oriental foods are also good at the semiformal **Siam Orchid**, 7575 Republic Dr., 407/351-0821.

For a quick lunch at the Mediterranean Mercado on International Drive,

# GREATER ORLANDO/KISSIMMEE

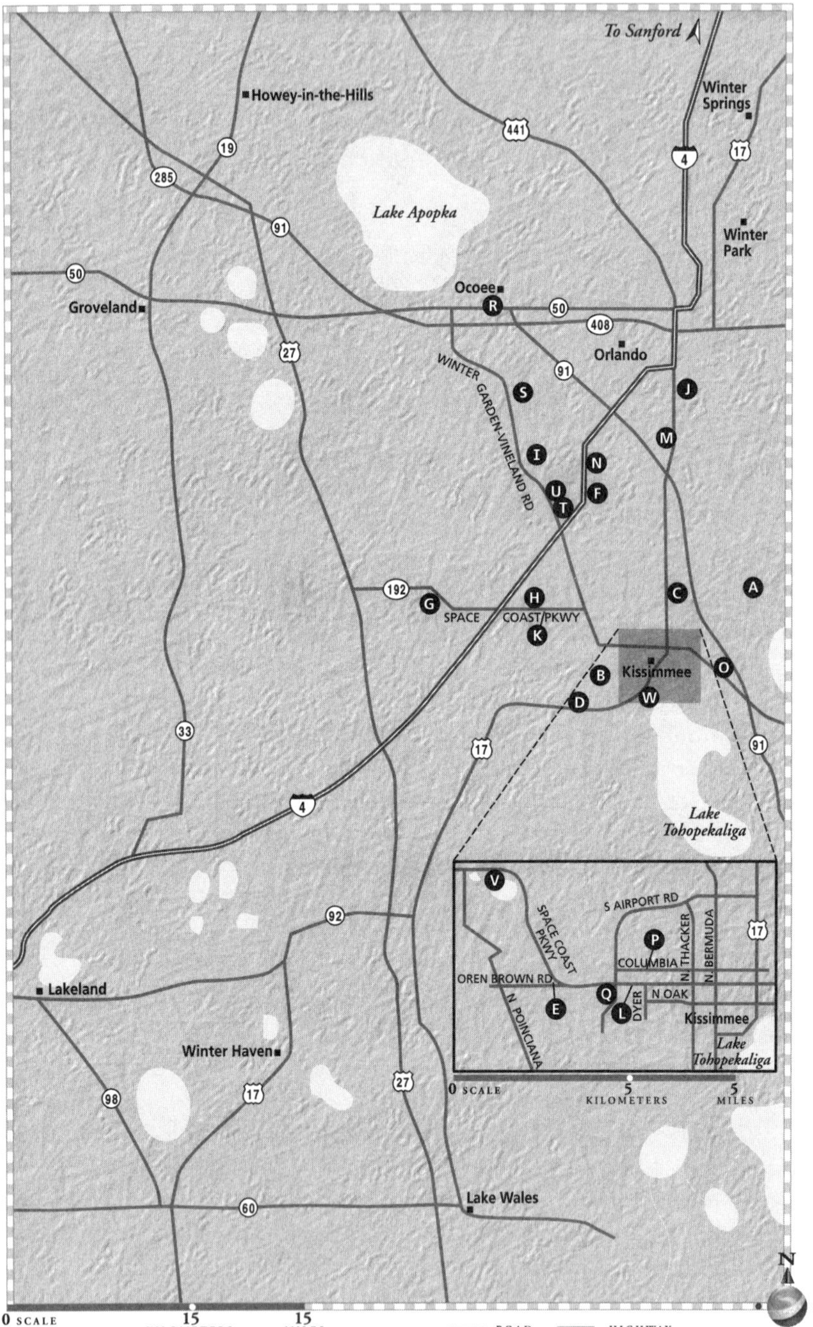

try the **Sabor Latino** in the food court, run by native Brazilians who serve up delicacies of their home country. At the Florida Mall you'll dine like royalty on such delectable delights as clay-baked flatbreads, pan-seared duck, and broiled rock grouper at the **SFA Cafe** at Saks Fifth Avenue, 407/812-4500; eat al fresco on the patio, where a soothing fountain will help you relax after a strenuous shopping expedition.

For moderately priced continental cuisine with a spectacular view of Lake Windsong, go to **Cascade** in the Hyatt Regency Grand Cypress, 1 Grand Cypress Blvd., 800/233-1234 or 407/239-1234. If you feel like splurging, try the nouvelle cuisine of **La Coquina**, in the same building.

Fine French cuisine is also available in Orlando at moderate prices. Dress is casual at **La Normandie**, 2021 E. Colonial Dr., 407/896-9976, which offers "early bird" and health-conscious choices. **Le Coq au Vin**, 4800 S. Orange Ave., is also excellent, with a relaxed, neighborhood-type atmosphere.

**Lili Marlene's** at Church Street Station, 407/422-2434, offers a romantic setting for lunch, dinner, or the generous Sunday buffet brunch. Part of the old Strand Hotel, its stained-glass transoms, burnished brass railings, oak booths salvaged from the pews of a French Catholic church, and copper gas lanterns reflect the warmth expressed in its WW II–namesake ballad. Also at Church Street, the moderately priced **Crackers Seafood Restaurant**, 407/422-2434, specializes in fresh seafood, including live Maine lobster and a raw bar.

Browsing in the shops along Park Avenue in Winter Park, you're sure to work up an appetite. Dine on award-winning continental dishes in a New Orleans–style courtyard at the **Park Plaza Gardens**, 319 Park Ave. S., 407/645-2475. For casual but authentic, gourmet-quality Brazilian steaks, fish,

---

**SIGHTS**

- A Boggy Creek Airboat Rides
- B Flying Tigers Warbird Restoration Museum
- C Gatorland
- D Green Meadows Petting Farm
- E Jungleland
- F Ripley's Believe It or Not! Museum
- G Splendid China
- H Water Mania

**FOOD**

- I Cascade
- I La Coquina
- J Le Coq au Vin
- F Ming Court Wok & Grille
- K Pacino's Italian Ristorante
- L Punjab Indian Restaurant
- F Sabor Latino
- M SFA Cafe
- N Siam Orchid

**LODGING**

- O Best Western Kissimmee
- P Condo Lodge
- Q Days Inn–Hwy. 192
- R Meadow Marsh
- F Peabody Orlando
- S PerriHouse
- T Riu Orlando
- U Sheraton Safari Hotel
- V Sun Motel
- W Unicorn Inn

*Note: Items with the same letter are located in the same area.*

**DINNER THEATERS**

Dinner shows in Orlando and Kissimmee are big business. At $35 to $40 each, meal bills for a week can add up; but it's a night's entertainment, and most include beer, wine, and soft drinks. Here are a few of the most popular:

- **American Gladiators Orlando Live!**, 5515 W. Irlo Bronson Hwy., Kissimmee, 800/228-8534.
- **Arabian Knights**, 6225 W. Irlo Bronson Hwy., Kissimmee, 407/239-9223.
- **Capone's Dinner and Show**, 4740 W. Irlo Bronson Hwy., Kissimmee, 800/220-8428 or 407/397-2378.
- **King Henry's Feast**, 8984 International Dr., Orlando, 800/883-8181 or 407/351-5151.
- **Medieval Times**, 4510 W. Irlo Bronson Hwy., Kissimmee, 800/229-8300 or 407/396-1518.
- **Pirate's Dinner Adventure**, 6400 Carrier Dr., Orlando, 800/866-2469.
- **Sleuths Mystery Dinner Theater**, 7508 Republic Dr., Orlando, 800/393-1985 or 407/363-1985.
- **Wild Bill's Wild West Extravaganza**, 5260 W. U.S. 192, Kissimmee, 800/883-8181 or 407/351-5151.

black beans, and plantains, visit the family-run **Brazilian Pavilion** at 140 W. Fairbanks Ave., 407/740-7440.

In Maitland, for elegant French/continental cuisine, including such unusual offerings as ostrich filets, visit **Nicole St. Pierre,** 1300 S. Orlando Ave., 407/647-7575, a plantation-style home in an idyllic, park-like setting.

For an especially memorable dining experience, make reservations at **Maison y Jardin**, 430 S. Wymore Rd., Altamonte Springs, 407/862-4410. If you arrive before dark, explore the formally landscaped grounds and then make your selections from a superb continental menu and wine cellar in this Mediterranean villa.

In Kissimmee, the staff at the family-owned and moderately priced **Pacino's Italian Ristorante**, 5795 W. U.S. 192, 407/396-8022, will entertain you with an animated Italian operetta while you eat. If Indian food is your passion, don't pass by the **Punjab Indian Restaurant**, 3404 W. Vine St. (E. U.S. 192), 407/354-1160.

## LODGING

No shortage here. Greater Orlando offers nearly 100,000 rooms and accommodations in every price range, from top-of-the-line luxury resorts to economy motels without pools.

To immerse yourself in an Orlando institution, make reservations at the towering **Peabody Orlando**, 9801 International Dr., 407/352-4000, a luxury hotel renowned for meticulous guest service. The Peabody is perhaps best known for its flock of resident ducks that parade through the hotel twice daily from their marble Duck Palace, near the rooftop tennis courts, into the elevator and along a red carpet to the fountain in the gleaming, marbled lobby; if you don't stay here, call for times and try to stop by for the Duck Parade.

For an enchanted evening just a few minutes from the Disney entrance in Lake Buena Vista, call the **PerriHouse**, 10417 Centurion Ct., 800/780-4830 or 407/876-4830, a romantic B&B on a rural six-acre country estate and bird sanctuary. Rooms and "birdhouse cottages" here come with customized getaway packages including chilled wine and cheese or hors d'oeuvres, fresh roses, or strawberries and cream delivered to your room. If you call when you're going out, they'll set up candles and soft music and be gone before you get back as a surprise for your magnificent other.

Kids love the huge python water slide at the pool of the **Sheraton Safari Hotel,** 12205 Apopka-Vineland Rd., 800/423-3297 or 407/239-0444, and childless adults can find quiet space by the poolside hot tub. It's just a quarter-mile from the entrance to Disney Marketplace. Across the street, the **Riu Orlando**, 8688 Palm Pkwy., 888/222-9963 or 407/239-8500, also offers good value.

In Maitland, lakefront porches, gardens, delicious complimentary breakfast, and proximity to antiquing, museums, and award-winning restaurants are good reasons to choose **Thurston House**, 851 Lake Ave., 800/843-2721 or 407/539-1911, www.thurstonhouse.com. Another cozy B&B option is the **Meadow Marsh**, 940 Tildenville School Rd., Winter Garden, 888/656-2064 or 407/656-2064, an Old Florida Victorian farmhouse with single bedrooms, suites, or a tiny private cottage.

The **Higgins House B&B**, 420 S. Oak Ave., in historic Sanford,

## CENTRAL FLORIDA

*If you don't count the world-famous Cypress Gardens, a sojourn in Central Florida is about as close as it gets to an "off the beaten track" vacation. It's a region for airboat rides, bird-watching, and exploring nature preserves. This is lake country, citrus country, and cattle country.*

*With hundreds of lakes, Central Florida is home to some of the best fishing in the state. The St. Johns River and the 35,000-acre Lake Kissimmee are especially well regarded fishing spots. Rent a houseboat and stay on the St. Johns River while you're visiting: Call* ***Holly Bluff Marina****, 800/237-5105 or 904/822-9992, or* ***Hontoon Landing****, 800/248-2474 or 904/734-2474, both in DeLand.*

*Lake Harris, in Howey-in-the-Hills, is full of bass, and the marina there offers fishing and boat rentals from a cypress-lined shore. You'll be reminded of the town's name if you stay and golf at the hilly* ***Mission Inn Golf and Tennis Resort****, 10400 CR48, 352/324-3101, particularly if you've gotten used to the flatter courses common to most of Florida.*

*The area's biggest draw is* ***Cypress Gardens****, 2641 S. Lake Summit Dr., Winter Haven, 800/282-2123 or 863/324-2111, a tropical floral and topiary paradise that's kinder and gentler than the theme parks of Orlando. The park is known for its revolutionary water-ski shows, but there are other things here to enjoy. The grounds have been laid out to resemble an 1860s riverside town, and visitors can enjoy scenic boat tours, high-energy Moscow circus acts, a champion figure skating show, musical performers, and more. Bird lovers can get acquainted with handfuls of tame, brightly colored lorikeets (which, by the way, love jewelry and belt buckles) in the aviary.*

*More serene is a visit to* ***Bok Tower Gardens****, Burns Ave., Lake Wales, 863/676-1408, a heavenly, park-like setting of gardens and woodlands. Magazine publisher Edward Bok erected a 205-foot, pink-marble carillon tower here on 157 lushly landscaped acres atop one of Florida's highest peaks, and concerts are given daily at 3 p.m. Butterflies flit through the gardenias, jasmine, azaleas, camellias and magnolias; fountains trickle; and swans and ducks float in the* *reflecting pools. If the orange groves that surround the gardens are in blossom, there's no sweeter smell nor a retreat so memorable.*

*Lovers of antiques (and who have deep pockets) may enjoy a visit to* **Chalet Suzanne**, *3800 Chalet Suzanne Dr., Lake Wales, 863/676-6011, where buckled brick walkways wind through a 70-acre Old-World estate. The inn is filled with knickknacks, stained glass, and intricate lamps from faraway places, but rooms can be tiny and the exterior is a bit ramshackle. Dinner, on the other hand, is exquisite, with candlelight and a live pianist, so as a budget-conscious alternative, stay in an inexpensive efficiency unit at* **Prince of Wales Motel**, *513 S. Scenic Hwy., 863/676-1249, and just make dinner or breakfast reservations at the Chalet.*

*If antique shopping in a hilly Old-Florida town appeals, drive along sparkling Lake Dora to picturesque* **Mount Dora**. *For a British-style lunch or afternoon tea, try the pretty* **Windsor Rose Tea Room** *on Fourth Avenue, or have a casual dinner at the* **Palm Tree Grille** *on North Donnelly Street. Stay downtown at the landmark* **Lakeside Inn**, *800/556-5016 or 352/383-4101, where Calvin Coolidge and his wife vacationed for a month after he completed his presidency. A rocking chair on the large, covered porch is a fine place for afternoon tea, and you can dine in the romantic formal dining room,* **The Beauclaire**, *or a couple of blocks away at the gourmet* **Gables Restaurant**. *At sunset you can stroll over to a boardwalk along Lake Dora where you can listen to whippoorwhills calling across the water and watch the herons fish for their supper.*

*On weekends, serious collectors visit the enormous* **Renninger's Twin Markets**, *800/522-3555 or 352/383-8393, a few miles away, where hundreds of dealers offer antiques and collectibles (there's a farmer's market and a flea market, too).*

*Central Florida is also baseball country at certain times of the year: Winter visitors flock here during major league baseball's spring training. Look for the* **Cleveland Indians** *in Winter Haven, the* **Detroit Tigers** *in Lakeland, and the* **Kansas City Royals** *in Haines City.*

**SPLURGE: THE HYATT REGENCY GRAND CYPRESS**

If you can afford it, the Hyatt Regency Grand Cypress, 1 Grand Cypress Blvd., Orlando, 800/233-1234 or 407/239-1234, offers one of the most memorable accommodations experiences in the region. Orchids bedeck the tall palms that rise from the resort grounds and giant philodendrons cascade from above. Many units overlook 20-acre Lake Windsong, a lovely setting for watching local wildlife as the early morning mist lifts. The highly regarded golf club boasts 45 championship holes and a pitch-and-putt course; the Equestrian Center offers Western and English riding and instruction. Other amenities include a fitness center, jogging trails, beach and marina with sailboat and canoe rentals, rental bikes, a pool area with an 80-foot water slide, tennis, shuffleboard and racquetball courts, and a daycare facility.

800/584-0014 or 407/324-9238, www.higginshouse.com, offers the charm of an 1894 Victorian inn, and your hosts will treat you like family if you encourage it; ask about special local events when you call.

In Kissimmee, **Best Western Kissimmee**, 2261 E. U.S. 192, 800/944-0062 or 407/846-2221, and **Days Inn–Hwy. 192**, 4104 W. U.S. 192, 800/647-0010 or 407/846-4714, offer inexpensive lodging. If you'll be staying a few nights, you can spread out in a reasonably priced furnished apartment at **Condo Lodge**, 3187 W. Vine St., 800/866-2660 or 407/931-2383. The low-priced **Sun Motel**, 5020 W. U.S. 192, 800/541-2674 or 407/396-2673, offers limited shuttle service to attractions. In the Historic Kissimmee area, the British owners serve American or English breakfast at the attractive **Unicorn Inn,** 8 S. Orlando Ave., 800/865-7212 or 407/846-1200.

## CAMPING

In Sanford, the **Twelve Oaks RV Resort**, 6300 SR 46 W., 800/633-9529 or 407/323-0880, has 27 acres of shaded, level sites with large patios and some pull-throughs, a pool, and fishing nearby. **Katie's Wekiva River Landing**, 190 Katie's Cove, Sanford, 407/628-1482, www.ktland.com, has limited camping for tents, plus furnished log cabins on the river's edge so you can rest after a canoe or kayak trip.

In Altamonte Springs, **Orlando Green Acres RV Resort**, 9701 Forest City Rd. (SR 434), 407/295-3461, has 450 sites to accommodate tents or RVs, with grassy, level sites; some pull-throughs; cable TV; and recreational facilities including a swimming pool, kiddie pool, and playground.

## NIGHTLIFE

For more than 40 years the **Orlando Opera Company**, 800/336-7372 or 407/426-1717, has been presenting professional, world-class grand opera from November through March. The **Southern Ballet Theatre**, 407/426-1728, performs September through May, and the **Bob Carr Performing Arts Center**, 407/849-2020, hosts the Pace Theatrical Broadway Series of concerts, performers, and Broadway hits. Orlando's professional Equity theater company, the **Mark Two Dinner Theater**, 407/843-6275, produces a number of live Broadway shows every season.

Let the good times roll at **Church Street Station**, 129 W. Church St., 407/422-2434 (cheapest city parking is under I-4). This is Orlando's premier dining and entertainment complex, and it's still a winner for visitors. Admission to much of the complex is free; street performers such as mimes, jugglers, and magicians entertain in the public areas. A single cover charge ($17.95 adults, $11.95 children) lets you into all the clubs. Wear your cowboy boots to the **Cheyenne Saloon**, which offers a Grand Ol' Opry–style house band and line-dance lessons. (Don't miss the photos of legendary Old West characters and the antique gun collection.) The **Orchid Garden**'s band plays '50s–'90s favorites; Saturday evenings are Big Band ballroom dance night. Be sure to at least step inside to see this ornate, multilevel Victorian palace, originally created as a hotel lobby, with its original, highly polished brick dance floor. Antique brass chandeliers, etched mirrors, and leaded glass adorn the Bourbon Street–style **Rosie O'Grady's**, which has its own Red Hot Mama, singing bartenders, cancan girls dancing on the bartop, and an outstanding Dixieland band. Church Street holds frequent street parties and special events, which are good fun and popular with locals. Oh, and if you think what Orlando needs is a good nickel beer, come to **Phineas Phogg's** on Wednesdays between 6:30 and 7:30 and get high amid authentic balloon paraphernalia.

International Drive is never quiet, but it really howls when evening comes. **Blazing Pianos**, 407/363-5104, at the Mercado, is a three-piano rock 'n' roll sing-along party hall. The Clarion Plaza Hotel's **Backstage at the Clarion**, 407/996-1719, has dancing nightly to live bands and a DJ. For a friendly pint, drop in for an imported brew at the **Lucky Leprechaun** Irish pub, 407/352-7031, or play some darts and watch live English soccer on a giant-screen TV at the **Cricketers Arms** English pub.

There's live comedy nightly and family-suitable shows at **Sak Comedy Lab**, 380 W. Amelia St., 407/648-0001. If you prefer a sophisticated evening of martinis and tapas, try the **Sapphire Supper Club**, 54 N. Orange Ave., 407/246-1599, with an eclectic mix of live jazz and blues, plus occasional Southern rock or folk music.

## SHOPPING

Factory outlet centers are big business in the Orlando area. The good thing is that, because they're so abundant and huge, they're rarely too crowded to be enjoyed. Start with the **Belz Factory Outlet World**, 5401 W. Oakridge Rd., 407/352-9611, the mother of all outlet centers, with more than 170 stores; and across the street, the **Belz Designer Outlet Center**, with another 60 designer clothing and accessory shops. Just south is the **Off 5th–Saks Fifth Avenue Outlet**.

**Lake Buena Vista Factory Stores,** 15591 SR 535, in Kissimmee, 407/238-9301, has plenty of outlets and a playground. (The VF Factory Outlet here sells name-brand fashions at half off the lowest ticket price.)

More than 200 stores, including Saks Fifth Avenue, are at Orlando's **Florida Mall**, 407/851-6255. Near downtown, **Orlando Fashion Square Mall**, 407/896-1131, has another 165 stores, with covered parking—a real boon in summer months.

The **Pointe Orlando Mall,** 9101 International Dr., 407/363-7900, is a huge retail venue, with Versace, Chico's, Zales, Banana Republic, and a movie complex. You can't miss it—look for the 40-foot-high teddy bear out in front of F.A.O. Schwartz and the enormous, three-story Wonderworks white colonial-style mansion, tottering precariously on its roof, a science/entertainment center that supposedly was lifted from its foundation hundreds of miles away and blown here by a tornado.

Posh, trendy-casual, and not very well known as a tourist stop, **Park Avenue** in Winter Park is a charming shopping area with more than 100 clothing and specialty shops, art galleries, jewelry stores, and restaurants. Watch for the Wine & Cheese Cellar, for a worldly selection of wines, meats, cheeses, and fancy imported groceries.

In Sanford on Friday through Sunday, rain or shine, you'll find more than 1,000 dealers and zillions of bargains at **Flea World**, 4311 U.S. 17-92, 407/330-1792.

# 6
# THE UPPER GOLD COAST AND THE PALM BEACHES

The lifestyles are as varied as the origins of the names of the towns along Florida's Gold Coast, a label attached a century ago because of the gold found in wrecked ships not far out into the Atlantic Ocean. There may be more gold in tourist dollars than in salvage today, because as railroad magnate Henry Flagler pushed his Florida East Coast Railroad tracks southward, tourists came to modest towns like Melbourne, named after the 1879 postmaster's hometown of Melbourne, Australia. Then more visitors came to Vero Beach and lovely little Stuart, and Jupiter, and finally to tropical paradises like Singer Island and Palm Beach, where Flagler himself and others like him decided to settle.

Wealth followed the railroad south. Melbourne is a working town, even if lately it has benefited from the proximity of the Kennedy Space Center and developed a high-tech industrial core. Anchoring the southern edge, Palm Beach is a mixture of sedentary inherited wealth and entrepreneurial nouveau riche. Melbourne began as a village of African American freedmen in the 1860s, while Singer Island, next to Palm Beach, was once the private playground of Paris Singer, son of the sewing machine magnate.

For many settlements here, riches come from the soil. Some of this territory is Indian River country, famed for its citrus products as well as its beaches and rocky inlets. Fort Pierce, built as a United States Army post during the Seminole wars of 1838, is still a center of beef ranching and vegetable

# GOLD COAST

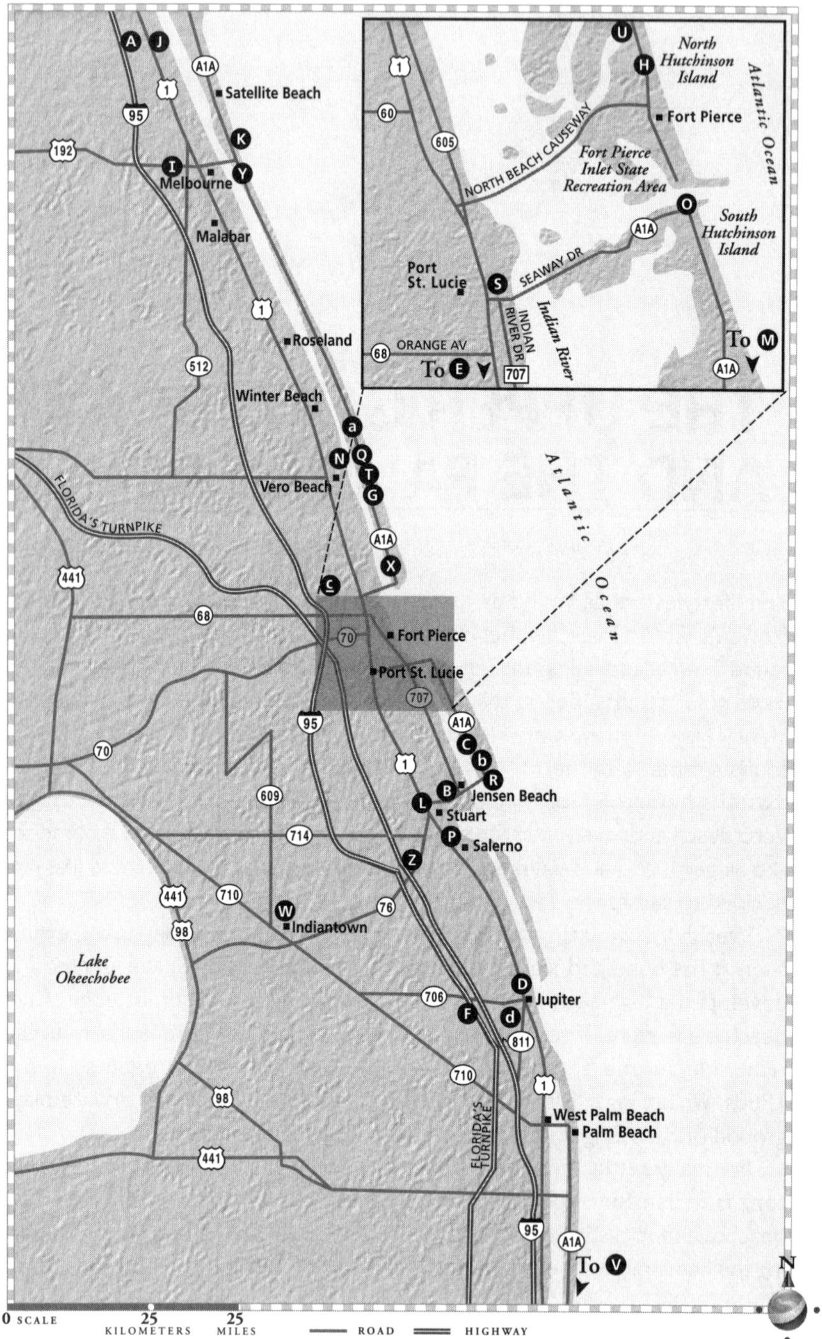

Satellite Beach
Melbourne
Malabar
Roseland
Winter Beach
Vero Beach
FLORIDA'S TURNPIKE
Fort Pierce
Port St. Lucie
Jensen Beach
Stuart
Salerno
Indiantown
Lake Okeechobee
Jupiter
West Palm Beach
Palm Beach
Atlantic Ocean
To V
North Hutchinson Island
Fort Pierce
NORTH BEACH CAUSEWAY
Fort Pierce Inlet State Recreation Area
South Hutchinson Island
Port St. Lucie
SEAWAY DR
INDIAN RIVER DR
Indian River
ORANGE AV
To E
To M
0 SCALE
25 KILOMETERS
25 MILES
ROAD
HIGHWAY
N

farming. And Stuart serves as the eastern terminus of the Okeechobee Waterway, which runs basically east–west from the Gulf of Mexico to the Atlantic Ocean and effectively makes a very large island out of the bottom third of Florida. Visitors will be hard-pressed to find another area of Florida with such varied character.

## A PERFECT DAY IN THE PALM BEACHES

Where there is much to see and do along this lengthy coast, you might choose to explore the Palm Beaches for a day. Rise early enough to watch the tangerine sun rise out of the Atlantic to the east of Ocean Boulevard in Palm Beach. Take careful note of the opulent series of palatial homes along the west side of the boulevard. These are the mansions of the Kennedys, the Trumps, and other unimaginably wealthy denizens of this exclusive island. (By the way,

---

### SIGHTS

- A Brevard Zoo
- B Coastal Science Center
- C Elliott Museum
- D Florida History Center and Museum
- C FPL's Energy Encounter
- C Gilberts Bar House of Refuge Museum
- E Heathcote Botanical Gardens
- F Jonathan Dickinson State Park
- G McLarty Treasure Museum
- H UDT–Seal (Frogman) Museum

### FOOD

- I Banana Bay Waterfront Restaurant
- J Captain Katanna's Dockside Restaurant & Bar

### FOOD *(continued)*

- K The Dove Restaurant
- L Flagler Grill
- M Kristi's on the Ocean
- N The Lobster Shanty
- O Mangrove Mattie's
- P Mario's Italian Restaurant
- Q Ocean Grill
- P Riverwalk Cafe
- R Scalawags Restaurant
- S Toucans & Top of the Dock Restaurant

### LODGING

- T Aquarius Oceanfront Resort
- L HarborFront Inn Bed & Breakfast
- L The Homeplace Bed & Breakfast Inn
- R Indian River Plantation Marriott Resort

### LODGING *(continued)*

- U Mellon Patch Inn
- V Palm Beach Shores Resort
- Q Reef Ocean Resort
- T Riviera Inn
- W Seminole Country Inn
- X Villa Nina Inn
- Y Windermere Inn by the Sea

### CAMPING

- Z Huckleberry Finn RV Resort
- a Long Point County Recreation Park
- b Nettles Island
- c Road Runner Travel Resort
- a Sebastian Inlet State Recreation Area
- d West Jupiter Camping Resort

*Note: Items with the same letter are located in the same area.*

**THE ALL-EMBRACING WORLD OF DISNEY**

Travelers are sometimes surprised to find that Disney isn't confined to Lake Buena Vista. Walt Disney World tries to transfer the magic from Central Florida to the beach at **Disney Vero Beach Resort**, 9250 Island Grove Terrace, Vero Beach, 800/359-8000 or 561/234-2000, www.disney.com/DisneyVacationClub/VeroBeach. Members of the Disney Vacation Club (Disney's spin on the time-share world), have special privileges but, space permitting, nonmembers also can stay here. Choose a garden-view room or a three-bedroom beach cottage, then take the kids to a Disney Character Breakfast with Goofy and friends. The resort offers an optional visit to a real Florida cattle ranch, the Adam's Ranch, followed by a Cracker-style barbecue. In June and July a guided Turtle Patrol walk takes visitors beachside to watch sea turtles digging their nests in the sand.

obey all the speed limit signs here.) Two must-see museums are near. Stop at the Henry Morrison Flagler Museum first, then spend a few minutes at the lovely Bethesda-by-the-Sea Episcopal Church before exploring Worth Avenue, Florida's most famous shopping street. It's only a few blocks long, but both sides of the street are lined with elegant shops. If you can tear yourself away, cross the bridge to the Norton Museum of Art in West Palm Beach. After dinner, cap this day by attending a performance at the magnificent Kravis Center for the Performing Arts in West Palm.

## SIGHTSEEING HIGHLIGHTS

### ★★★★ ELLIOTT MUSEUM

**825 N.E. Ocean Blvd. (A1A), Hutchinson Island, 561/225-1961**

This unexpected gem of a museum, filled with a variety of Americana and collectibles, dates from only 1961, when it was founded by Harmon Elliott as a monument to his inventor father. Eight of Sterling Elliott's inventions, as well as 222 of the items he patented, are on display. In the Americana wing, early twentieth-century shops, a hand-carved miniature circus, and an ice cream parlor are re-created, while the Main Gallery has bicycles, a wonderful collection of music boxes, and a collection of memorabilia in its Baseball Hall of Fame. The star of the museum's automobile collection (there are 24 cars in all) is a rare 1926 Bugatti Grand Prix racing car.

***Details:*** *Located 4½ miles northeast of U.S. 1 on A1A. Open Oct–Aug, Mon–Sat 10–4, Sun 11–4. Admission: $6 adults, $2 children. (1–2 hours)*

## ★★★★ THE HENRY MORRISON FLAGLER MUSEUM

**One Whitehall Way, Cocoanut Row, Palm Beach, 561/655-2833, www.flagler.org**

When Florida railroad tycoon Henry Flagler opened his gleaming white $2.5-million Whitehall estate in 1902, admirers called it the "Taj Mahal of North America." After its second life as a posh hotel, the mansion was restored as a museum in 1960. Inside are many of its original Gilded Age furnishings (which cost Henry an additional $1.5 million). The mansion also has a Louis XIV music room and a Louis XV ballroom. Outside, Flagler's private railroad car is open for inspection.

***Details:*** *Open Tue–Sat 10–5, Sun noon–5. Admission: $7 adults, $3 children. (1½–3 hours)*

## ★★★★ HIBEL MUSEUM OF ART

**150 Royal Poinciana Plaza, Palm Beach, 561/833-6870**

This lovely museum holds 10 galleries devoted to the lithographs, paintings, drawings, and porcelain work of Edna Hibel. The elderly artist, who lives on Singer Island just north of here, is well served by a devoted museum staff who may not let you leave until you know every detail of her work and her artistic life.

***Details***: *Open Tue-Sat 9–5, Sun 1–5. Free. (1–1½ hours)*

## ★★★★ JONATHAN DICKINSON STATE PARK

**16450 S.E. Federal Hwy., Hobe Sound, 561/546-2771**

In this state park, hikers can traverse a nine-mile segment of the Florida Trail, while canoeists can paddle on the Loxahatchee River. There are bike and horse trails, too, in these 12,000 acres of sandy scrub where bald eagles and sandhill cranes pay you no heed. But the chief reason to visit is to board the *Loxahatchee Queen II* for a relaxing, educational, and memorable two-hour excursion along the river through some of Florida's prettiest country.

***Details:*** *Park open daily 8–dusk. Admission: $3.25 per car, otherwise $1 per person. River cruise at 9 and 11 a.m., and 1 and 3 p.m.; $10 adults, $5 children. (2–4 hours)*

## ★★★★ LION COUNTRY SAFARI

**Southern Blvd. W. (SR 80/98/441), West Palm Beach, 561/793-1084, www.lioncountrysafari.com**

The nation's first "cageless zoo," a 500-acre park where rhinoceroses, gnus, lions, elephants—in all, about 1,300 animals—run free, is still going strong. Keep your doors locked and the car windows closed as you drive through the park's five sections: Lake Nakaru, the Great Plains, the Gorongosa Preserve, the Serengeti Plain, and the Wankie. They're all separated by landscape barriers. Pull into the right lane at any time and take photos. The animals are accustomed to cars, but they're still wild, and sometimes they show their authority by lying down in front of your vehicle or coming up to your window. You can drive through as many times as you wish on one ticket, but don't miss visiting the baby animal nursery, the petting zoo, and Safari World amusement park, a compact, nicely arranged walkabout section with small animals and birds in cages for more close-up viewing.

*Details: Open daily 9:30–5:30 (last ticket sold at 4:30 p.m.). Admission: $14.95 adults, $9.95 children and seniors. Convertibles not allowed, but rental cars available at $6 per hour. (3–4 hours)*

## ★★★★ NORTON MUSEUM OF ART

**1451 S. Olive Ave., West Palm Beach, 561/832-5194**

Without a doubt, this is one of the country's premier art museums. Its grand collection of more than 4,500 works focuses on French Impressionism and Post-Impressionist painting and American painting after 1900. The Norton has an extensive array of Chinese art as well. In its 19 galleries you can ponder the works of Renoir, Gauguin, Degas, Matisse, and Braque, then Edward Hopper, Andy Warhol, and Georgia O'Keeffe, before moving on to examine the Chinese bronzes, jades, and monumental Buddhist sculpture.

***Details:*** *Open Tue–Sat 10–5, Sun 1–5. Guided tours Dec–Mar daily at 2 p.m. Admission: $5 adults, $2 children. Free Wednesdays. (1–3 hours)*

## ★★★★ SOCIETY OF THE FOUR ARTS

**2 Four Arts Plaza, Palm Beach, 561/655-7226**

### EXPLORING WRECKS AND REEFS

Diving is a big part of life on Florida's coast, but it is particularly intriguing off Boynton Beach Inlet, just north of Delray Beach, where you can visit two shipwrecks, the 167-foot coastal freighter *Budweiser* and the 70-foot treasure hunter *Swordfish*. Lying in about 80 feet of water, the *Budweiser* is easy to explore, and the mature coral growth around it hosts an amazing array of sea life. Lying just west of the *Budweiser* is the *Swordfish*, a more recent wreck (1992) that's still in the process of attracting coral, tropicals, and game fish. Divers warn to watch out for a resident scorpion fish. A reef system stretches down the Atlantic coastline, but some formations in this region, like Boynton Falls, Grouper Hole, and Gulfstream Ledge, stand out for their large overhangs and deep cuts—and for the large fish that live in them. Information and supplies are available from **Splashdown Divers**, 561/736-0712, or **TNT Dive Charters**, 561/762-7668, both in Boynton Beach.

This small cultural complex, in buildings that are architectural landmarks, includes a library, an art museum, the Philip Hulitar Sculpture Garden, and a botanical garden, as well as an auditorium where writers—John Updike, for example—and other noted speakers stand and deliver. Art exhibits in the galleries change each month. If you're going to be in the area for a few days, ask about the film series, recitals, and concerts that go on regularly.

***Details:*** *Galleries open Dec–Apr, Mon–Sat 10–5, Sun 2–5. Library and gardens open Nov–Apr Mon–Fri 10–5, Sat 9–1; rest of the year Mon–Fri 10–5. Donations. (30 minutes–1 hour)*

## ★★★★ UDT-SEAL (FROGMAN) MUSEUM

**3300 N. A1A, Fort Pierce, 561/595-5845**

And now for something completely different. You've heard of Underwater Demolition Teams (UDTs), Sea, Air, Land Teams (SEALS), Naval Combat Demolition Units, Scouts, and Raiders? Well, this collection shows off the weapons, equipment and suits used by these daring Navy men, and a 25-minute videotape details just how arduous the training program really is. Outside, the museum has a landing craft and an Apollo space capsule.

**Details**: *Open Mon–Sat 10–4, Sun noon–4. Admission $3.25 adults, $1.50 children. (1–2 hours)*

### ★★★ ATLANTIC COASTAL CRUISES

**900 E. Blue Heron Blvd., Phil Foster Park, Singer Island, 800/390-7464 or 561/848-7827, www.fun-cruises.com**

Unless you have your own boat, the cruises on the 600-passenger yacht *Atlantic Star* or the 300-passenger paddlewheeler *The Star of Palm Beach* offer the best way to get an up-close view of the mansions that front the Intracoastal Waterway. For 1 1/2 hours, well-informed narrators tell you stories of the rich and famous who have lived here. The Kennedy mansion has been sold, but you'll sail past Peanut Island, the site of the bomb shelter from which JFK would have run the country if nuclear weapons had started to fly. Current well-known residents of the barrier islands include golfers Jack Nicklaus and Greg Norman.

**Details**: *Sightseeing cruises daily, 12:30 and 3 p.m., $11.95 adults, $8.95 children. Lunch cruise, $20.95 adults, $15.95 children. Dinner cruises 7 p.m., $32.95 adults, $21.95 children. Sunday Brunch cruise 12:15 p.m., $23.95 adults, $19.95 children.*

### ★★★ BETHESDA-BY-THE-SEA EPISCOPAL CHURCH

**141 S. County Rd., Palm Beach, 561/655-4554**

This is an Episcopal church, not an attraction, but don't leave Palm Beach without a brief look at the wonderful lines of its fifteenth-century modified Gothic design and the lovely, formal Cluett Memorial Gardens in back. Built in 1926 to replace an original 1889 structure, the church has impressive stained glass and acoustics that serve its choral works series very well indeed.

**Details:** *Church and gardens open daily 8–5. Free. (30 minutes)*

### ★★★ COASTAL SCIENCE CENTER

**890 N.E. Ocean Blvd., Stuart, 561/225-0505**

This small place across the street from the Elliott Museum looks like somebody's modest home, but your children won't want to get back into the car soon, and maybe you'll stay longer than planned yourself as you examine the tropical fish in four 300-gallon aquariums, touch the horseshoe crabs and starfish in the shallow tank, and realize you still have to gaze at the Frances Langford wall of mounted fish and play the computer game that tests whether you know what kind of fish you're staring at. All this, and nature walks. Neat place.

**Details:** *Open Mon–Sat 10–5. Admission: $3.50 adults, $2 children. (1–2 hours)*

## ★★★ FLORIDA HISTORY CENTER AND MUSEUM

**805 N. U.S. 1, Jupiter, 561/747-6639**

The collection of photos and memorabilia in this museum may tell you more than you'll want to know about Florida's history, the coastline, the Florida East Coast Railroad, and other glories of the past. You can also tour the wonderfully intact 1896 Dubois Pioneer Home and the 1860 Jupiter Inlet Lighthouse Museum. The nearby lighthouse is worth the tour. It still throws a beam 18 miles out to sea to warn ships off the Florida coast. Climb up 105 feet for a wonderful perspective of the Atlantic.

**Details**: *Open Tue–Fri 10–5, Sat–Sun 1–5. Dubois Home tours Wed, Sun 1–4. Admission: $4 adults, $2 children, $3 seniors. Lighthouse open Sun–Wed 10–4. Admission: $5 (under 48 inches tall not permitted). (1–2 hours)*

## ★★★ GILBERTS BAR HOUSE OF REFUGE MUSEUM

**Off A1A, Hutchinson Island, 561/225-1875**

This is a basic lifesaving station dating from 1875, when sea travel up and down the Atlantic coastline seems to have been particularly dangerous. The museum details the nautical and marine history of the area, while saltwater tanks show off lobsters, sharks, and other local sea life.

**Details:** *On A1A east through the Indian River Plantation Resort. Open Oct–Aug, Mon–Sat 10–4, Sun 11–4. Admission: $4 adults, $2 children. (30 minutes–1 hour)*

## ★★★ MCLARTY TREASURE MUSEUM

**13180 N. A1A, Vero Beach, 561/589-2147**

This little museum is devoted chiefly to the wreck of the Spanish Plate Fleet in 1715, and a diorama illustrates its history and the shipwreck survivors' camp. Artifacts are also on display, and an audiovisual presentation shows how the continuing salvage operations are revealing the secrets of the treasure fleet.

**Details**: *Located five miles north of CR 510 on A1A at the south end of Sebastian Inlet State Recreation Area. Open daily 10–4:30. Admission: $1, small children free. (1 hour)*

# PALM BEACH AREA

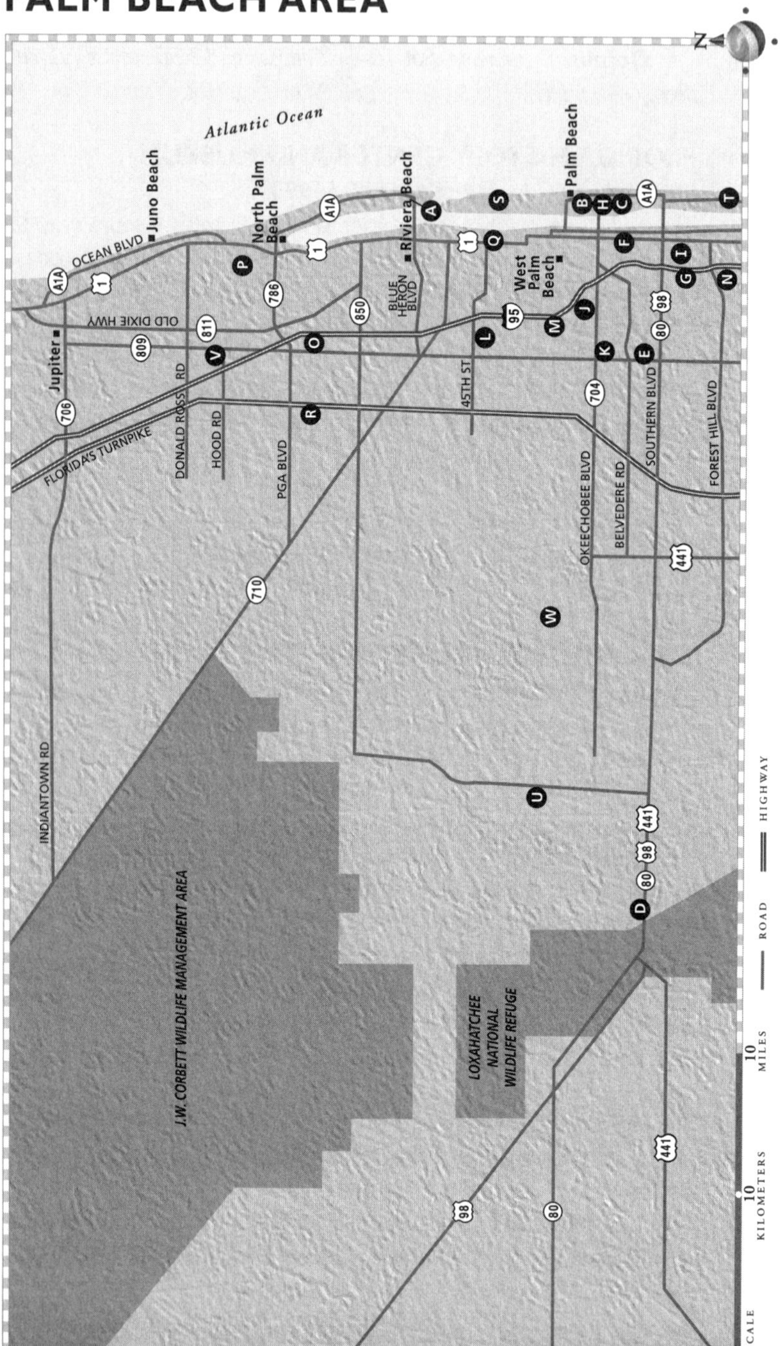

### ★★★ MOUNTS BOTANICAL GARDEN

**531 N. Military Tr., West Palm Beach, 561/233-1749**

It's amazing what you can do with just 15 acres if you plan well. This garden has a small rain forest, an herb garden, rose gardens, hibiscus gardens, and walkways through tropical and subtropical flora. Sometimes guided tours are available; otherwise, you're free to walk through at your own pace.

***Details:*** *Open Mon–Sat 8:30–5, Sun 1–5. Free. (1 hour)*

### ★★★ PALM BEACH ZOO AT DREHER PARK

**1301 Summit Blvd., West Palm Beach, 561/533-0887**

A Florida panther, giant tortoises, Bengal tigers, and more than 400 other animals from 100 different species fill this relatively small 25-acre zoo. It has the only outdoor exhibit of Goeldi monkeys in the United States. Red kangaroos and wallabies hop around in the popular Australian Outback exhibit.

***Details:*** *Open daily 9–5. Last tickets sold at 4:15. Admission: $6 adults, $4 children, $5 seniors. (2–3 hours)*

---

## SIGHTS

- Ⓐ Atlantic Coastal Cruises
- Ⓑ Bethesda-by-the-Sea Episcopal Church
- Ⓒ Henry Morrison Flagler Museum
- Ⓒ Hibel Museum of Art
- Ⓓ Lion Country Safari
- Ⓔ Mounts Botanical Garden
- Ⓕ Norton Museum of Art
- Ⓖ Palm Beach Zoo at Dreher Park
- Ⓗ Society of the Four Arts
- Ⓘ South Florida Science Museum

## FOOD

- Ⓒ 264 The Grill
- Ⓚ Aleyda's
- Ⓒ Café L'Europe
- Ⓛ Café Protégé
- Ⓑ Chuck & Harold's
- Ⓜ No Anchovies! Neighborhood Pastaria
- Ⓝ Rain Dancer Steak House
- Ⓑ Ta-Bóo
- Ⓞ Ta-Kil-Ya Café

## LODGING

- Ⓑ The Breakers
- Ⓟ Chesterfield Hotel Deluxe
- Ⓗ Clarion Hotel of the Palm Beaches
- Ⓠ Hibiscus House Bed & Breakfast

## LODGING *(continued)*

- Ⓑ Palm Beach Historic Inn Bed & Breakfast
- Ⓖ Parkview Motor Lodge
- Ⓡ PGA National Resort & Spa
- Ⓢ Riviera Beach Motel
- Ⓣ Sea Lord Hotel
- Ⓠ Tropical Gardens Bed & Breakfast

## CAMPING

- Ⓤ Lion Country Safari KOA-West Palm Beach
- Ⓥ Palm Beach Gardens RV Park
- Ⓦ Sunspot Gardens Nudist Retreat

*Note: Items with the same letter are located in the same area.*

## ★★★ SOUTH FLORIDA SCIENCE MUSEUM

**4801 Dreher Trail N., West Palm Beach, 561/832-1988**

If you have children traveling with you, come here and let them get their hands on just about everything they see. Permanent and changing exhibits explore visual phenomena, and there's a small aquarium with sea life from South Florida and the Caribbean. The museum also contains the Aldrin Planetarium and Gibson Observatory, which has one of the largest telescopes in the state. The Native Plant Center highlights Florida flora along an outdoor nature trail.

***Details**: Open daily 10–5, Fri until 10. Call for planetarium and laser light show times. Admission: $5 adults, $3 students, $4.50 seniors; planetarium shows, $1.75; laser light shows, $2. (1–2 hours)*

## ★★ BREVARD ZOO

**8225 N. Wickham Rd., Melbourne, 407/254-3002**

The focus of this small zoo is Latin America, and 60 species are represented by about 200 animals. Visitors can get great views of the wildlife from shaded boardwalks. You may never see giant anteaters, jaguars, sloths, and alligators closer than this. An Australia section features red kangaroos, wallabies, emus, and kookaburras.

***Details:** Open daily 10–5. Admission: $5 adults, $3 children, $4 seniors. (2–3 hours)*

## ★★ FPL'S ENERGY ENCOUNTER

**6501 S. A1A, Hutchinson Island, 561/468-4111**

Drive through Gate B at Florida Power and Light Company's St. Lucie nuclear power plant to encounter intriguing displays on the history of energy production and a see-through nuclear reactor model. Take the Turtle Beach Nature Trail for a self-guided walk through three habitats of a typical coastal barrier island—beach, mangrove, and tropical hammock.

***Details**: Open Mon–Fri and Sun 10–4. Free. (1–2 hours)*

## ★★ HEATHCOTE BOTANICAL GARDENS

**210 Savannah Rd., Fort Pierce, 561/464-4672**

Several gardens flourish in this small acreage, including a Japanese garden, herb garden, and several species of palms and orchids.

***Details:** Located 1½ blocks east of U.S. 1. Open Nov–Apr, Tue–Sat 9–5, Sun 1–5; rest of year, Tue–Sat 9–5. Admission: $2.50 adults, children free. (1 hour)*

LION COUNTRY SAFARI

Rose M. Wilson

## FITNESS AND RECREATION

Head to **Sebastian Inlet State Recreation Area**, 561/984-4852, for the premier saltwater fishing site on Florida's east coast. There are two Atlantic jetties, a beach area, and the nearby Indian River (Intracoastal Waterway) to keep snook, redfish, bluefish, and Spanish mackerel on your line. Of course, you can also do all the other beach activities. There's much to explore at **Hobe Sound National Wildlife Refuge**, U.S. 1, Hobe Sound, 561/546-6141, which has three miles of beach, sand dunes, and a mangrove swamp on Jupiter Island, plus a sand pine scrub forest on the mainland. Snorkelers and divers favor the offshore reefs to the east and north of the refuge. A barrier island with a mixture of coastal and tropical hammock and mangroves, considered to be one of the finest examples of subtropical coastal habitat in the state, is **John D. MacArthur Beach State Park**, 10900 SR 703 (A1A), North Palm Beach, 561/624-6950. Go fishing, collect shells, snorkel, picnic, or just take a walk across the 1,600-foot boardwalk that spans Lake Worth Cove and explore two miles of beach in this unspoiled patch of Florida.

Drop in at **Canoe Outfitters of Florida**, SR 706, Jupiter, 407/746-7053, if you want to explore the scenic Loxahatchee River, where you may see bald eagles, ospreys, barred owls, bobcats, otters, and alligators.

Baseball fans are in a kind of spring training heaven in this part of Florida.

The **Montreal Expos** and **St. Louis Cardinals** share Roger Dean Stadium in Jupiter; the **New York Mets** train at Thomas J. White Stadium in Port St. Lucie; the **Los Angeles Dodgers** play at Holman Stadium at Dodgertown, Vero Beach; and the **Florida Marlins** get ready for the season at Space Coast Stadium in Melbourne.

If baseball doesn't appeal to you, maybe the dogs at the **Palm Beach Kennel Club** will. If you want to see horses run but not race, settle in at the **Palm Beach Polo & Country Club** in Wellington. Matches are held Sundays at 3 p.m., generally from late December to late April.

Golf is to die for here, from the tough courses at the **PGA National Resort & Spa** in Palm Beach Gardens to individual semi-private gems like **Emerald Dunes** in West Palm Beach.

## FOOD

Just north of Melbourne, in Satellite Beach, settle in at **The Dove Restaurant**, 1790 A1A, 407/777-5817, for excellent, moderately priced pasta and shrimp entrees. In Melbourne, don't worry about its ramshackle appearance, just head to the oceanfront **Captain Katanna's Dockside Restaurant & Bar**, 4263 N. Harbor City Blvd., 407/253-1369. Its comprehensive menu is sure to have something to please everyone, after you decide whether to sit outside overlooking the pier or inside behind a wall of glass. On the Indian River, try the **Banana Bay Waterfront Restaurant**, 2425 Pineapple Ave., 407/242-2401, known for its creative and trendy Florida menu.

There's no need to leave the waterfront to eat in Vero Beach. **The Lobster Shanty**, 1 Royal Palm Blvd., 561/562-1941, serves chicken and beef as well as seafood in casual dining areas overlooking the Indian River, while the **Ocean Grill**, 1050 Sexton Plaza, 561/231-5409, offers a rustic setting overlooking the Atlantic.

In Fort Pierce, wander over to **Mangrove Mattie's**, 1640 Seaway Dr., 561/466-1044, for its seafood, served to you as you overlook the Intracoastal Waterway. Another good find here is **Kristi's on the Ocean**, 2400 S. Ocean Dr. (in the Ocean Village residential complex), 561/465-4200, where you might want to make reservations for dinner or Sunday brunch. Yet another stop in Fort Pierce could be **Toucans & Top of the Dock Restaurant**, 201 Fisherman's Wharf, 561/465-1334, which carries a varied menu and offers good Intracoastal water views in air-conditioned comfort or outside.

In downtown Stuart, stop at **The Flagler Grill**, 47 S.W. Flagler Ave.,

561/221-9517, whose health-conscious menu is dressed up with innovative American cuisine. If you like bustling bistros and want to stay downtown, try the **Riverwalk Cafe**, 1201 S.W. St. Lucie Ave., 561/221-1511, which revels in its international tastes and flavors. On the way to Hutchinson Island, **Mario's Italian Restaurant**, 1924 S. Federal Hwy. (U.S. 1), 561/283-6660, may provide a lasting memory. It's a simple place, but portions are generous and the owner, who doubles as the chef, learned his craft well. If you're looking to splurge a bit, go to the Indian River Plantation Marriott Resort and **Scalawags Restaurant**, 555 N.E. Ocean Blvd., 561/225-6818, for its excellent seafood presented *nouvelle Americain* style.

Unless you're Donald Trump, you're likely to run out of money before you run out of especially wonderful restaurants in the Palm Beaches. One to try is **Café L'Europe**, 331 S. County Rd., Palm Beach, 561/655-4020, winner of so many awards that it takes a separate menu page to recount them. Several others are worth your attention, however. Try the **Café Protégé**, 2400 Metrocentre Blvd., West Palm Beach, 561/687-2433, where you'll be a test subject for students of the Florida Culinary Institute. There's an observation kitchen, and the students in this upscale but casual place serve continental cuisine. **Chuck & Harold's**, 207 Royal Poinciana Way, Palm Beach, is a popular spot for its fresh fish and homemade pasta dishes. If you've been strolling the posh shops on Worth Avenue, stop in **Ta-Bóo**, 221 Worth Ave., 561/835-3500, a Palm Beach tradition for more than 50 years, known for prime rib, veal, fish, main course salads, and gourmet pizza, all served with piano music. Just north of Worth Avenue, stop in at **264 The Grill**, 264 S. County Rd., 561/833-6444, a small, well-to-do-neighborhood, American-menu kind of spot located in the historic Mizner building. Devotees of Tex-Mex are not forgotten, even on the edge of the Atlantic Ocean. **Aleyda's**, 1890 Okeechobee Blvd., West Palm Beach, 561/688-9033 (and at 1890 S. Military Tr., West Palm Beach, 561/642-2500), is consistently chosen the best Mexican restaurant in the county. Eat here and you'll learn why. You'll also be pleased to know that, as this is very chic Palm Beach, the kitchen uses only low-fat, low-cholesterol oils. In an unlikely setting in a Comfort Inn, you'll have a tough time not being pleased at **No Anchovies! Neighborhood Pastaria**, 1901 Palm Beach Lakes Blvd., West Palm Beach, 561/689-6100. Critics and locals love this simple and amazingly inexpensive Italian place, with its specialty pastas and meals cooked in a wood-burning oven. Not far down the street, if steak is your choice, go to the nearby **Rain Dancer Steak House**, 2300 Palm Beach Lakes Blvd., West Palm Beach, 561/684-2810, a casual place known for its desserts as well as thick-cut filet mignon.

Travelers with families might like the **Ta-Kil-Ya Café** at the PGA National

Resort & Spa, Palm Beach Gardens, 561/627-2000. For not much more than $20 on weekdays between 5 and 8 p.m., this café serves a family of four dinner (two entrees, refills of soda, salsa, chips, rice, and beans) and hands out 20 game tokens for the restaurant's video arcade.

## LODGING

Lodgings in this region are generally so good that you might as well choose the one whose design you like best. In Vero Beach, the inns and resorts along Ocean Drive all offer the Atlantic Ocean, soft-sand beaches, and generally more moderate rates than similar lodgings farther south. Try the **Aquarius Oceanfront Resort**, 1526 S. Ocean Dr., Vero Beach, 561/231-5218, a family-oriented place that offers two locations, notably moderate rates, and ties to all the recreation possibilities. More adult-oriented is the **Riviera Inn**, 1605 S. Ocean Dr., Vero Beach, 561/234-4112, a new Mediterranean-style hotel with a restaurant, Chez Yannick, 561/234-4115, that is already drawing rave reviews. A little more secluded yet directly on the Atlantic is the **Reef Ocean Resort**, 3450 Ocean Dr., Vero Beach, 800/662-7333 or 561/231-1000, which is really a time-share that rents accommodations at fairly reasonable rates.

In Indialantic, near Melbourne Beach, a private beach is available at **Windermere Inn by the Sea**, 815 S. Miramar Ave., 800/224-6853 or 407/728-9334, www.windermereinn.com, an Italianate home with eight antiques-furnished rooms.

In Stuart, stop for the night at **The Homeplace Bed & Breakfast Inn**, 501 Akron Ave., 561/220-9148, www.homeplacebb.com. Rates are on the high end of moderate for its four 1913-era bedrooms, but the gracious, romantic ambience may make you forget that.

At Fort Pierce on North Hutchinson Island, try the **Mellon Patch Inn**, 3601 N. A1A, 800/656-7824 or 561/461-5231, www.sunet.net/mlnptch, if you can stay at least two days. This is pricier territory than Vero Beach, but this highly rated inn, built in 1994, puts you in the middle of every sort of activity in an especially relaxing setting. Hutchinson Island's **Indian River Plantation Marriott Resort**, 555 N.E. Ocean Blvd., Stuart, 800/775-5936 or 561/225-3700, is a sprawling resort complex built around a first-class executive golf course. From most of its facilities, you're quite literally only a few steps from the Atlantic. If you're looking for a private Indian River beach, try the **Villa Nina Inn**, 3851 N. A1A, North Hutchinson Island, 561/467-8673, www.gate.net/~villanin, a regular on lists of recommended bed-and-breakfast inns, both for its location and its amenities. Right on the St. Lucie River, five minutes from the restored historic shopping district of Stuart, is **HarborFront Inn Bed & Breakfast**, 310 Atlanta Ave., Stuart, 561/288-7289, www.harborfrontinn.com, a place that conjures up Old Florida ambience, aided by the fact that the house was built in 1908 and is a good example of early 1900s architecture. You can study that from your hammock.

West of Stuart, **Seminole Country Inn**, 15885 S.W. Warfield Blvd., Indiantown, 561/597-3777, www.bbonline.com/fl/seminole, is not merely a 25-room restored 1920s-era citrus and cattle country inn. Its ceiling of pecky cypress (a decorative wood often used in Florida interiors), hardwood floors, and grand double French doors whisk you back to the reduced but nevertheless charming grandeur of the post–Civil War South.

Don't be surprised by high prices in the Palm Beaches, because this is one of the wealthiest areas in the country. Even in the off-season the bill for a night at **The Chesterfield Hotel Deluxe**, 3632 Cocoanut Row, Palm Beach, 800/243-7871 or 561/659-5800, with its famous Leopard Lounge and luxurious ambience, is likely to be $150 for a room for two. And you can't mention Palm Beach without suggesting **The Breakers**, 1 S. County Rd., Palm Beach, 561/655-6611, the ultimate in luxury in a splendid early-1900s Italianate pile set in the kind of landscape you'd expect to have been hand-trimmed by artists with scissors. It has everything, and you pay handsomely for it. But this is an attraction as well as a hotel, so if you don't stay here, stop in for breakfast or lunch in one of its five restaurants and take a tour.

An alternative is to stay at the **Palm Beach Historic Inn Bed & Breakfast**, 365 S. County Rd., Palm Beach, 561/832-4009, a 1921 building in the heart of the island, offering an easy walk to Worth Avenue or The Breakers. And for Palm Beach, its rates are moderate. Even more reasonable is the **Sea Lord Hotel**, 2315 S. Ocean Blvd., Palm Beach, 800/638-6217 or 561/582-1461, which has 40 guest rooms and a coffee shop but lacks the atmosphere of the previously mentioned properties.

The choices are legion back across the Intracoastal Waterway in West Palm Beach. Try the **Parkview Motor Lodge**, 4710 S. Dixie Hwy., 561/833-4644, which has perfectly good rooms and an attractively landscaped setting. The **Hibiscus House Bed & Breakfast**, 501 30th St., 561/863-5633, www.hibiscushouse.com, was the mayor's mansion in 1922 and its eight rooms still have an air of tropical elegance. The **Tropical Gardens Bed & Breakfast**, 419 32nd St., 800/736-4064 or 561/848-4064, is another good choice.

Just north of Palm Beach, try the **Riviera Beach Motel**, 3124 Broadway, Riviera Beach, 561/844-1857, a well-kept older motel with very moderate rates. **The Clarion Hotel of the Palm Beaches**, 11360 U.S. 1, North Palm Beach, 888/696-9692 or 561/624-7186, is two miles from the beach,

## BOCA RATON AND DELRAY BEACH

*Try if you can to find time for at least a brief foray south of the Palm Beaches, into the region that famed architect Addison Mizner sought to construct as the "world's most architecturally beautiful playground." For a splendid few months after February 1926, the glitterati of the era strutted like kings and queens through Mizner's $1.25-million Cloister Inn (today's Boca Raton Resort & Club). Then the Florida land boom died abruptly, and the Cloister Inn locked its doors before the year was out. The eccentric, six-foot-two-inch, 300-pound Mizner, who made a habit of shuffling around in silk pajamas with a macaw on one shoulder, a monkey on the other, and two larger apes trailing behind, left a wonderfully indelible mark of elegance on Boca Raton's architecture. Its appealing facades, white beaches, and immaculate parks are not to be missed.*

*On the way south, stop in Delray Beach to visit* ***The Morikami Museum and Japanese Gardens****, 4000 Morikami Park Rd., 561/495-0233, a 200-acre landscaped park with fascinating museums. Morikami is a tribute to early-1900s Japanese farmers who established Boca Raton's Yamato Colony. Try the home-style Japanese food at the museum's Cornell Café.*

*If there's a nature lover in your party, stop at* ***Arthur R. Marshall Loxahatchee National Wildlife Refuge*** *at U.S. Hwy. 441 and SR 7, Delray Beach, 561/734-8303, where boardwalk trails lead through a cypress swamp filled with herons, egrets, limpkins, pileated woodpeckers, great-horned owls, wood storks, and even endangered Everglade kites.*

*In Boca Raton, head straight for the* ***Boca Raton Resort & Club****, 501 E. Camino Real, 800/327-0101 or 561/395-3000, even if you're not staying in one of its 963 guest rooms. Have breakfast or lunch, then wander through the inspired landscaping and architectural*

but visitors like its style and Spanish Mediterranean look, which allows the management to describe it as a "boutique hotel."

If it's splurge time north of Palm Beach, whether or not you love golf, you'd regret not staying at the **PGA National Resort & Spa**, 400 Avenue of the *features that still make this stone palace a stopover for the rich and famous. Elsewhere in town, you'll find the small but impressive* ***Boca Raton Museum of Art****, 801 W. Palmetto Park Rd., 561/392-2500, which has an absorbing collection of works by Degas, Matisse, Picasso, Prendergast, Demuth, and Warhol. And while you're in the neighborhood, don't miss a stroll north through the Old Floresta Historic District to gain a sense of the old town.* ***The International Museum of Cartoon Art****, 201 Plaza Real, 561/391-2200, is a must for anyone fascinated by the art. If you're still on the lookout for more of natural Florida, stop in at the small, unspoiled patch of land occupied by the* ***Gumbo Limbo Nature Center****, 1801 N. Ocean Blvd. (A1A), 561/338-1473.*

*You won't have a problem finding restaurants here, as they are legion and rated from good to absolutely fabulous. In Delray Beach, food critics would like to make it mandatory to eat at* ***Boston's On The Beach****, 40 S. Ocean Blvd., 561/278-3364, with its impressive choices of fresh seafood and New England-style meals. Eat upstairs at* ***Boston's Upper Deck*** *for a more romantic evening. If you don't hate Pete Rose, when you're in Boca Raton, try his* ***Pete Rose Ballpark Cafe****, 8144 W. Glades Rd., 561/488-7383, a 12,000-square-foot restaurant filled with sports memorabilia. Rose broadcasts his live radio show from here on weekend nights, and you can meet him afterwards for an autograph. Just don't mention Cooperstown.* ***Maxaluna's Tuscan Grill****, 21150 Military Trail, in Shops at Boca Center, will nick your credit card, but it's another special place with an unusually creative menu.*

*If you want to stay the night at a place other than the resort, try* ***The Inn at Boca Teeca****, 5800 N.W. Second Ave., Boca Raton, 800/344-6995 or 561/994-0400, a lodge at the Boca Teeca Country Club.*

Champions, 561/627-2000, located next to the PGA headquarters. It's a golf mecca, of course, but the European-style spa and its four pools of world waters, including one from the Dead Sea, plus its schools of tennis and croquet instruction are powerful incentives.

On the beach in Palm Beach Shores, check in at **Palm Beach Shores Resort**, 181 Ocean Ave., 800/328-2289 or 561/863-4000, which has 255 suites, including amenities for children.

## CAMPING

You won't have any trouble finding both beach and inland camping facilities all through this mid-state stretch of Florida's Atlantic Coast, but campers planning to travel south should be aware that between West Palm Beach and Miami there are far fewer choices, so plan accordingly.

In the Melbourne area, pull into **Long Point County Recreation Park**, 700 Long Point Rd., 407/952-4532, a 60-acre, 112-site campground with 84 full hookups. Or, not far away, try **Sebastian Inlet State Recreation Area**, 9700 S. A1A, Melbourne Beach, 561/984-4852, a 587-acre park with 51 sites with electricity and water, a lovely area where the main activities are swimming, surfing, and fishing. As you move south, you'll probably find an available site at the **Road Runner Travel Resort**, 5500 St. Lucie Blvd., Fort Pierce, 800/833-7108 or 561/464-0969, which has 300 full-hookup pull-through and tent sites, cabins to rent, and both open and shaded grassy sites.

Northeast of Stuart, stop at **Nettles Island**, 9801 S. Ocean Dr., Jensen Beach, 561/229-1300, which has 100 RV grassy sites with cement pads on 140 acres bordering the Indian River (Intracoastal Waterway). You're a long way from the Mississippi River in Stuart, but you can still go to the **Huckleberry Finn RV Resort**, 7601 S.W. Lost River Rd., 561/220-0909, which offers pull-through sites, paved pads, tent sites, and full hookups, plus an array of recreational amenities.

Farther south, the **West Jupiter Camping Resort**, 17801 N. 130th Ave., Jupiter, 888/6746-6073 or 561/746-6073, has 85 full-hookup sites in a quiet setting near both city amenities and the beach, and it offers a full choice of recreation from fishing to shuffleboard and canoe rentals. In the Palm Beach area, the **Palm Beach Gardens RV Park,** 4063 Hood Rd., 561/622-8212, has 106 level, pull-through, full-hookup sites near the PGA National Resort & Spa, in case you've brought your golf clubs. On the other hand, it's sometimes special to stay near well-known attractions, so you could head to the **Lion Country Safari KOA-West Palm Beach**, 2000 Lion Country Rd., Loxahatchee, 800/562-9115 or 561/793-9797, which is right next to the wild animal park. Its pleasantly shaded 211 sites are well protected from the wild beasts, however, with tent sites and full-hookup pull-through RV sites.

If you want to treat your entire body to Florida's subtropical sun—and remember that it doesn't take long for pale skin to turn red in this relentless sunlight—head for the **Sunsport Gardens Nudist Retreat**, 14125 North Rd., Loxahatchee, 800/551-7217 or 561/793-0423, which has grassy, shaded sites, full hookups, tent sites, and recreation ranging from the hot tub to hiking trails. Don't pull in here unless you're prepared to enjoy the nudist lifestyle.

## NIGHTLIFE

Who can think of nightlife in Palm Beach without recalling William Kennedy Smith and his uncle, Sen. Ted Kennedy, having a drink or two at a chic nightspot? **Françoise's Place**, 336 Royal Poinciana Way, in the Royal Poinciana Plaza, 561/832-4800, (formerly the Kennedy hangout Au Bar), is a central meeting place for the elite and the elite wannabes, where well-dressed men get acquainted with stylishly and provocatively dressed women, and they all drink too much and stumble off into the night. If your inquiring mind wants to know what goes on among the upper-crust residents of this posh little island, this is without a doubt one of the best people-watching spots in Florida. (The food here is excellent, too.) If this doesn't appeal to you, there are dozens of other nightspots in both Palm Beach and West Palm Beach.

Major cultural events occur at the glorious **Kravis Center for the Performing Arts**, 701 Okeechobee Blvd., West Palm Beach, 800/572-8471 or 561/833-8300, which has a 2,200-seat concert hall, a black box theater, a restaurant, and an outdoor amphitheater featuring major touring acts plus regular concerts by the Florida Philharmonic Orchestra. **The Barn Theatre**, 2400 S.W. Ocean Blvd., Palm Beach, 561/287-4884, regularly puts on well-performed musicals. The **Royal Poinciana Playhouse,** 70A Royal Poinciana Plaza, Palm Beach, 561/659-3310, is a 900-seat showplace for traveling Broadway shows. And if you're in West Palm Beach, try out the various establishments along Clematis Street, including locally famous places such as **Roxy's**, 518 Clematis St., 561/833-1003, or the **Bimini Bay Café**, 104 Clematis St., 561/833-9554, with live music to entertain while you watch night traffic on the Intracoastal.

## SHOPPING

There's perfectly good shopping anywhere in this section of Florida, but you won't find anything like the four glitzy blocks of **Worth Avenue**, Palm Beach, anywhere else. It may be the most exclusive third-of-a-mile of shops in the country, and it fits in perfectly with the Mediterranean mansions along Ocean Boulevard. Shop at Cartier, Chanel, Gucci, Armani, Georgio, Gallery Versailles, Frances Brewster, and countless others, but don't look at the price tags unless your heart is in good shape. And don't just stick to the sidewalk. Wander into the little landscaped courtyards, like **Esplanade Palm Beach**, 150 Worth Ave., 561/659-6090, a Mediterranean-style shopping court with tropical gardens and splashing fountains. At **Greater Royal Poinciana Way**, 139 N. County Rd., Palm Beach, 561/655-1207, you'll find a central area of Palm Beach studded with boutiques, booteries, music shops, book shops, restaurants, and cafés.

Not-so-famous **Clematis Street** in West Palm Beach offers noticeably less opulence but still considerable charm, with 50 storefronts housing a variety of art galleries, jewelry, home decor, and clothing shops. If you haven't seen enough, try **The Gardens Mall**, 3101 PGA Blvd., Palm Beach Gardens, 561/775-7750, which has 180 shops and restaurants, including Bloomingdale's, Burdines, Macy's, Sears, Saks Fifth Avenue, and a large number of uncommon specialty stores. **Oakbrook Square**, on U.S. 1, North Palm Beach, 561/626-3880, is another upscale center with Spanish-style architecture featuring tropical flowers and fountains.

Hard as it is to believe, there is actually a **Palm Beach Outlet Center**, 5700 Okeechobee Blvd., West Palm Beach, 561/684-5700, an enclosed mall. And in Fort Pierce you'll find the **Manufacturer's Outlet Center** at I-95 and Florida's Turnpike, a small complex of 35 factory stores, including Bass, Gitano, and London Fog.

# 7 GREATER FORT LAUDERDALE

For most of its existence overshadowed by star-studded, more sophisticated Miami and Miami Beach, Fort Lauderdale was long known as an unremarkable town. For several decades it wallowed in infamy as a Spring Break mecca, its citizens apparently content to allow undisciplined college students to overrun its beaches and streets, drunkenly smashing up the place. But by the 1980s Fort Lauderdale residents had had enough of the annual mayhem and decided to reinvent their city. Every such movement should be as successful as this one.

The Fort Lauderdale you're about to visit is an attractive city of islands joined by a web of canals, rivers, bays, and waterways, a city of museums and cultural facilities second to none in Florida. Attend orchestral concerts or Broadway shows at the glittering Broward Center for the Performing Arts, and you may choose to arrive by water taxi. An array of first-rate restaurants offers the best of American and world cuisines. Nightlife didn't disappear with the college students, but beer swilling and beachside wet T-shirt contests have been replaced by wine-tastings and jazz clubs.

Flanked by pleasant (if crowded) oceanside communities like Pompano Beach to the north and Hollywood to the south, Fort Lauderdale has emerged as a viable contestant for a traveler's attention. The March Spring Break destructiveness has been replaced by the PGA's Honda Golf Classic and the Fort Lauderdale Festival of the Arts. Some who come here are amazed that it has become such a cultural center, while local residents have developed a new kind of civic pride. At one time it might have seemed laughable to want to visit Fort Lauderdale, or to take a horse-and-carriage ride along Las Olas Boulevard. Now, it seems an entirely appropriate thing to do.

## A PERFECT DAY IN FORT LAUDERDALE

Go ahead, get up early and watch the sun rise over the Atlantic Ocean from anywhere along this stretch of beach, then head to Port Everglades to see which impressive cruise ships and freighters are in dock this morning. Eat a satisfyingly cheap breakfast at Joe Bel Air's Diner before heading to town to stroll the undulating Riverwalk path and visit the Museum of Art (if you have kids, choose the Museum of Discovery and Science instead). Then hop aboard the *Jungle Queen* riverboat for the 2 p.m. cruise to explore the New River and the Intracoastal Waterway while you get a peek at Millionaire's Row and the incredible fleet of mega-yachts. You'll remember this day even more if, whenever you get a chance, you take a water taxi. Make sure you take one in the early evening when you head for Las Olas Boulevard to dine and to enjoy a horse-and-carriage ride along the wonderfully restored, lamplit street.

## SIGHTSEEING HIGHLIGHTS

### ★★★★ ANNE KOLB NATURE CENTER AND MARINA

**West Lake Park, 751 Sheridan St., Hollywood, 954/926-2410**

This 1,500-acre coastal mangrove forest wetland located in the heart of densely populated Southeast Florida is a natural habitat for ibises, herons, and most other Florida birds. Climb the 65-foot observation tower to get a perspective on the park, then stroll the boardwalks or rent a canoe, kayak, or rowboat to see the mangrove islands up close. A narrated, 40-minute boat tour leaves the nature center hourly, and visitors not inclined to go off on their own can get a true picture of the area's natural life from the knowledgeable tour guides.

***Details***: *Open daily 7:30–5:30. Admission: $3 adults, $1.50 children. Boat tours of West Lake: $8 adults, $4 children. (2–4 hours)*

### ★★★★ FLAMINGO GARDENS AND ARBORETUM

**3750 Flamingo Rd., Davie, 954/473-2955**

In a state that's filled with well-designed, highly publicized tourist at-

## FORT LAUDERDALE

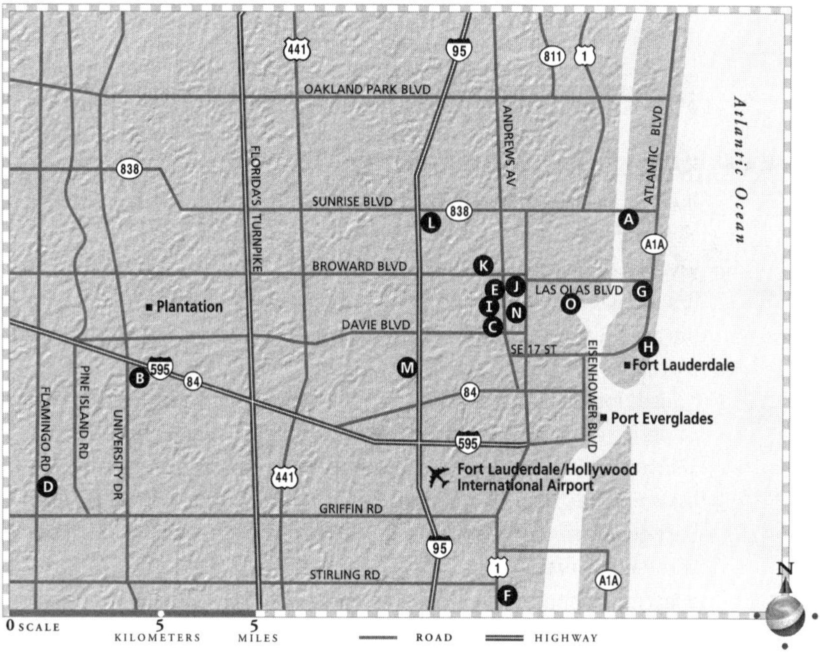


## SIGHTS

- **A** Bonnet House
- **B** Buehler Planetarium
- **C** *Carrie B.* Sightseeing Cruise
- **D** Flamingo Gardens and Arboretum
- **E** Fort Lauderdale Historical Museum
- **F** The Graves Museum of Archaeology and Natural History
- **G** International Swimming Hall Of Fame
- **H** *Jungle Queen* Riverboat
- **I** Las Olas Horse and Carriage Tours
- **J** Museum of Art
- **K** Museum of Discovery and Science/ Blockbuster 3-D IMAX Theater
- **L** Old Dillard Art & Cultural Museum
- **M** Riverwalk, A Linear Park
- **N** Stranahan House
- **O** Water Taxis

---

tractions, some smaller parks tend to get overlooked. This is one of them, an unheralded gem originally set aside to educate the public rather than to satisfy a theme-park company's bottom line. It's enchanting to visit these subtropical forests, wetlands, half-acre free-flight aviary, crocodile lagoon, and the historic house of the founding Wray family. Start with the narrated tram ride through the aromatic citrus groves, bromeliads, orchids, hammocks, and wetlands, then wander at will. Don't miss the birds-of-prey exhibit, in addition to the wandering flamingos and other wildlife.

***Details**: Open daily June–Sept 9:30–5:30. Admission: $8 adults, $4.50 children, $6.40 seniors. Tram ride, $2. (2–4 hours)*

### ★★★★ *JUNGLE QUEEN* RIVERBOAT

**801 Seabreeze Blvd., Bahia Mar Yachting Center, A1A, Fort Lauderdale Beach, 954/462-5596, www.junglequeen.com**

It's actually quite satisfying to explore the New River and the Intracoastal Waterway while listening to a cruise guide dish out information about the occupants of Millionaire's Row, the luxury houses located between the Intracoastal and the Atlantic. It's the sort of stuff you would normally find in the *National Enquirer*. The cruise also takes you around the downtown area of the city that is reasserting its "Venice of America" claim. Dinner cruises specialize in barbecued ribs or steamed shrimp, and there's a creditable variety show to entertain you. There are actually two all-steel *Jungle Queens*, a larger 550-passenger vessel and a smaller 180-passenger version.

***Details**: Sightseeing cruises depart at 10 a.m. and 2 p.m., $11.50 adults, $7.50 children; four-hour dinner cruise departs at 7 p.m., $24.50 adults, $13 children. Special cruises to Miami's Bayside Marketplace, $14.95 adults, $10 children.*

### ★★★★ MUSEUM OF ART

**One E. Las Olas Blvd., 954/525-5500**

One of Florida's most impressive collections of twentieth-century European and American art is housed in this eclectic building that anchors the western end of Las Olas Boulevard. Pablo Picasso, Andy Warhol, Henri Matisse, Alexander Calder, Salvador Dalí, Henry Moore, and Frank Stella are all well represented, but the highlight may be the works of William Glackens, a lesser-known American Impressionist whose *Artist's Daughter in Chinese Costume* or *Outside the Guttenburg Race Track* may make you wonder why he's not numbered among the top Impressionist artists. An African art collection of religious and ceremonial masks, plus the colorful and wild CoBrA collection (works from the radical post-WWII CoBrA movement of Copenhagen, Brussels, and Amsterdam artists), will lure you to every nook, even if your legs and feet have developed museum fatigue.

***Details**: Open Tue 10–9, Wed–Sat 10–5, Sun noon–5. Admission: $6 adults, $3 children, $5 seniors. (2–4 hours)*

### ★★★★ MUSEUM OF DISCOVERY AND SCIENCE/ BLOCKBUSTER 3-D IMAX THEATER

**401 SW Second St., 954/467-6637**

One of the best, most successful hands-on science museums anywhere, the Museum of Discovery and Science could easily occupy you and your children for an entire day, especially if you take in an IMAX film. Featured are seven interactive exhibit areas, including "Florida Ecoscapes," where appropriate animal and natural sounds surround you as you wander through hammocks, swamps, and eight other areas that represent the state's 10 different ecosystems. The staff is likely to appear with baby alligators and sea turtles, because endangered species are raised at the museum. Don't miss Gizmo City, a "how things work" museum within the museum featuring dozens of gadgets and contraptions. Outside, check out the 52-foot-high Great Gravity Clock, said to be Florida's largest kinetic energy sculpture.

***Details:** Open Mon-Sat 10–5, Sun noon–6. Admission: $6 adults, $5 children and seniors. IMAX theater admission: $9 adults, $7 children, $8 seniors. Combination ticket: $12.50 adults, $10.50 children. (2–4 hours)*

### ★★★★ RIVERWALK, A LINEAR PARK

**From S.W. Seventh Avenue to S.W. Second Avenue, 954/468-1541**

This is a stroll, not a themed attraction, but you'll remember the curving, beautifully landscaped, engraved brick walkway along the banks of the New River as it gently winds it way through the city's historic district, which is filled with small cafés and intimate boutiques. If you want to be part of the walkway forever (well, at least for a very long time), the city will be happy to sell you an engraved paving brick.

***Details:** Free.*

### ★★★★ STRANAHAN HOUSE

**S.E. Sixth Ave. at Las Olas Blvd., on the New River, 954/524-4736**

Built as a trading post for Ohio immigrant Frank Stranahan to conduct business with the Seminole Indians, this 1901 building has also been a private home and restaurant. Built of tough Dade County pine, the house is a prime example of Florida frontier design, with wide porches, tall windows, and tropical gardens. Original Stranahan furnishings include the family's hand-painted china. Stranahan built a Fort Lauderdale empire only to see it crumble in the stock-market confusion of the 1920s, and he didn't have to go far when he committed suicide by jumping into the New River.

***Details**: Located on the New River, behind the Hyde Park supermarket. Open Wed–Sat 10–4, Sun 1–4. Admission: $5 adults, $2 children. (30 minutes–1 hour)*

## ★★★★ WATER TAXIS

**Along the New River and Intracoastal Waterway, 954/467-6677**

Traveling by water taxi along the New River and Intracoastal Waterway is an attraction in itself to many visitors, simply because there are so few places where it can be done. In a city with 300 miles of rivers and canals, Fort Lauderdale's flotilla of floating taxis with green-and-yellow awnings is surprisingly efficient—the boats fairly zip from place to place—and inexpensive if you buy an all-day pass. It's very pleasant to leave your car and float to your destination. Perhaps it's not quite as colorful as that gondolier scene on the other side of the Atlantic, but take a ride and you'll see why Fort Lauderdale boosters are not embarrassed to have adopted the "Venice of America" slogan.

***Details**: The taxis travel everywhere between 10 a.m. and 1:30 a.m. Fare: one-way, $7; round-trip, $12; unlimited all-day pass, $15. Taxis pick up at marinas, motels, restaurants, theaters. Phone for schedules and precise pick-up/drop-off information.*

## ★★★ BONNET HOUSE

**900 N. Birch Rd., 954/563-5393**

Think Great Gatsby South as you tour this 35-acre estate, built in 1926 between the ocean and a small lake as the winter home of not-so-starving artists Frederic and Evelyn Bartlett. Enter their world of private luxury and take in orchid-draped gardens, an art gallery featuring the Bartletts' work, and even their hand-painted ceilings.

***Details**: Open for guided tours Wed–Fri at 10 a.m. and 2 p.m., Sat–Sun at noon and 3 p.m. Admission: $9 adults, $7 children, $8 seniors. (2 hours)*

### ★★★ BUTTERFLY WORLD

**3600 W. Sample Rd., Coconut Creek, 954/977-4400**

Butterfly World's breeding laboratory, insectarium, and English rose garden are all very interesting, but the most delightful experience here is walking through the two-story aviaries, where butterflies flit about and are likely to land on you. Rangers explain the life cycle of these creatures and point out which plants are the most likely to attract butterflies.

**Details**: *Located in Tradewinds Park just west of Florida's Turnpike. Open Mon–Sat 9–5, Sun 1–5; last admission at 4. Admission: $10.95 adults, $6 children. Park entrance fee on weekends and holidays, $1. (1–1 ½ hours)*

### ★★★ *CARRIE B.* SIGHTSEEING CRUISE

**S.E. Fifth Ave. and W. Las Olas Blvd., 954/768-9920**

A sightseeing cruise aboard this replica nineteenth-century riverboat takes you down the New River and through the Intracoastal Waterway, past the yachts, cruise ships, and U.S. Navy ships at Port Everglades. It is a satisfying, shorter version of the *Jungle Queen* trip (see above), and also gives you a close-up view of Millionaire's Row.

**Details**: *Daily cruises at 11 a.m. and 1 and 3 p.m. Fares: $9.95 adults, $5 children. (1 ½ hours)*

### ★★★ FORT LAUDERDALE HISTORICAL MUSEUM

**219 S.W. Second Ave., 954/463-4431**

This moderate-sized museum features artifacts from the Seminole Wars and displays an extensive photographic history of the city. The collection is spread through historic buildings that have been collected at the site. Ask at the museum desk about historical walking, river, and city tours, available for separate fees.

**Details**: *Open Tue–Fri, 10–4. Admission: $2 adults, $1 children. (30 minutes–1 hour)*

### ★★★ THE GRAVES MUSEUM OF ARCHAEOLOGY AND NATURAL HISTORY

**481 S. Federal Hwy., Dania Beach, 954/925-7770**

If local archaeologist Wilburn "Sonny" Cockrell unearthed an artifact, it ended up here. That's why this museum is so eclectic: On display are pottery, carved stone and horn, and what is said to be

# GREATER FORT LAUDERDALE

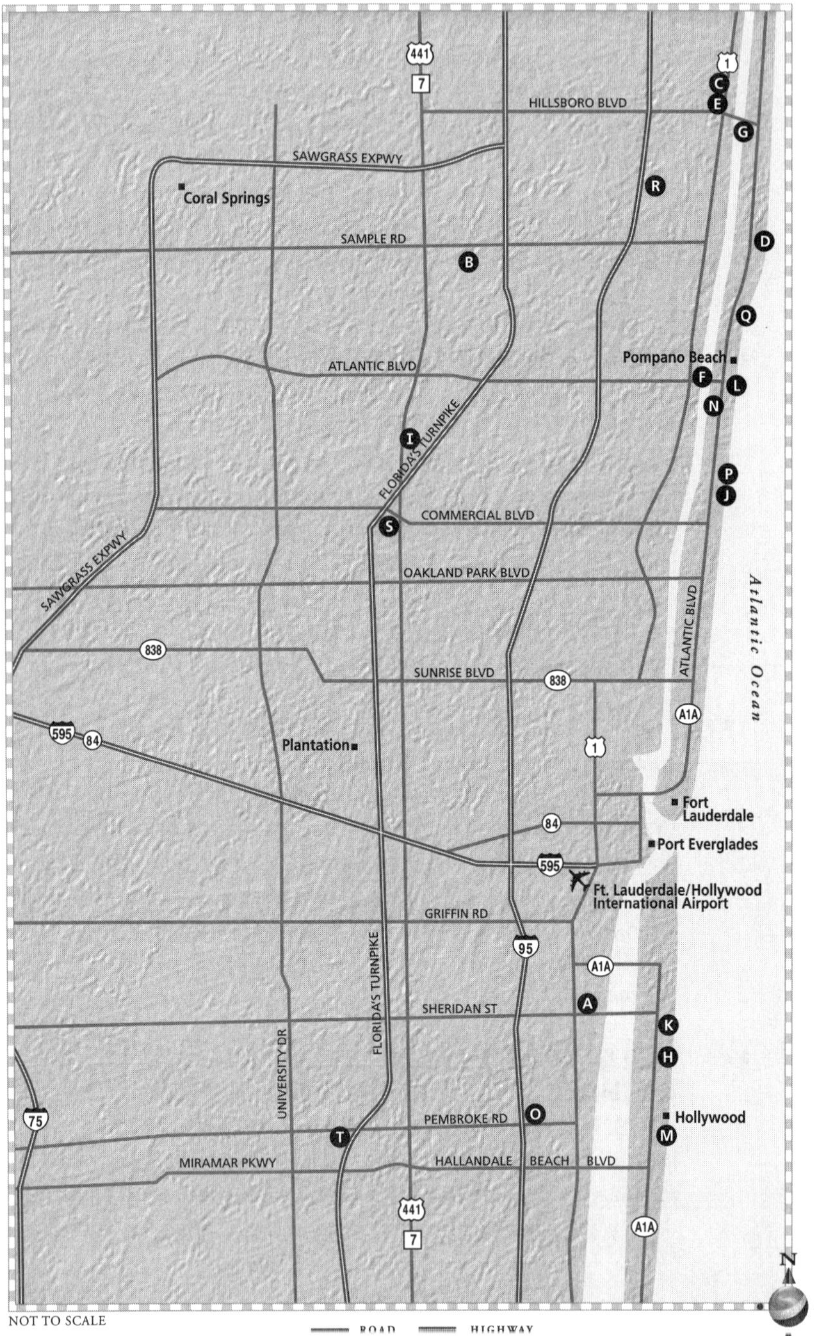


NOT TO SCALE

ROAD HIGHWAY

the world's most complete 100-million-year-old triceratops skull. Dioramas depict the Tequesta Indians, the area's original settlers, while separate rooms are devoted to intriguing specimens of Egyptian art, African tribal art, Columbian art, the bones of various reptiles and primates, and—something to really marvel at—a double-terminated quartz crystal that weighs more than 3 tons.

***Details***: *Open Tue–Sat 10–4, Sun 1–5. Admission: $6 adults, $4 children. (2–3 hours)*

## ★★★ INTERNATIONAL SWIMMING HALL OF FAME

**501 Seabreeze Blvd., 954/468-1580**

Esther Williams, Johnny Weissmuller ("Tarzan"), and Greg Louganis may be among the most famous names honored in this vast monument to swimmers, aquatic art, and aquatic life since the fifteenth century. It's full of medals, uniforms, photographs, and computerized information modules that show great swimmers in action. The facility is also host to a variety of national and international swimming competitions, during which the museum and art gallery are closed. Two first-class 50-by-25-meter pools out back are open to the public.

***Details***: *Open daily 8–4, also Mon–Fri 6–8 p.m. Admission: $3 adults, $2 students, seniors. (1–2 hours)*

---

### SIGHTS

- A Anne Kolb Nature Center and Marina
- B Butterfly World

### FOOD

- C Brooks
- D Cap's Place
- E Carafiello's
- F Darrel and Oliver's Cafe Maxx
- G Pal's Charley's Crab

### FOOD *(continued)*

- H Sugar Reef Tropical Bar & Grill
- I Yips

### LODGING

- J Blue Seas Courtyard
- K Bougainvillea on the Beach
- L Ebb Tide Hotel
- J A Little Inn by the Sea
- M Manta Ray Inn
- N Ronny Dee Resort Motel

### LODGING *(continued)*

- O Shell Motel
- P Tropic Seas Resort
- Q Villamar Inn

### CAMPING

- R Breezy Hill Travel Trailer Park
- S Candlelight Park
- R Highland Woods Travel Trailer Park
- T Trinity Towers RV Park

*Note: Items with the same letter are located in the same place.*

**WHERE'S THE BEACH?**

*You might think that Florida towns with "beach" in their names have extensive beaches. It would be logical, but you would be wrong. Dania Beach, for instance, was just plain Dania until November 1998, when voters changed its name to try to attract more tourists. The town, located about 5 miles south of Fort Lauderdale, has just 900 yards of Atlantic coastal beach. By the way, Dania Beach is the third name for the town that started out as Modello. In 1904 it was changed to Dania for its first settlers—Danish farmers.*

## ★★★ LAS OLAS HORSE AND CARRIAGE TOURS

**S.E. Eighth Ave. at E. Las Olas Blvd., 954/763-7393**

Ride in a carriage because you can, and because single-horsepower is a thoroughly enchanting way to see the revived Fort Lauderdale, lit romantically, if dimly, by lamplight.

***Details**: Rides available Thu–Sat, 8 p.m.–12:30 a.m. Fares: \$8–\$90 depending on length of ride chosen. (20 minutes–1 1/2 hours)*

## ★★ BUEHLER PLANETARIUM

**2501 S.W. Davie Rd., Davie, 954/475-6680**

Time- and space-travel are the main themes of the planetarium shows on the Broward Community College campus. Its small Zeiss star machine projects constellations visible only from the North or South Poles. Fascinating laser light shows are set to the music of various pop groups.

***Details**: Main shows Fri–Sat 7 p.m. Family shows Sat–Sun 1:30, 3. Call for laser light show schedule. Admission: features \$5; family shows, \$4. (1 hour)*

## ★★ OLD DILLARD ART AND CULTURAL MUSEUM

**1009 N.W. Fourth St., 954/765-6952**

This collection of African art, jewelry, and tribal masks is housed in a school building that's listed in the National Register of Historic Places.

***Details**: Open Tue–Sat noon–4, Wed noon–8. Free. (30 minutes–1 hour)*

## FITNESS AND RECREATION

It's fascinating how, even in heavily populated areas of Florida, large greenbelts survive and even flourish. So it is with the 180-acre **Hugh Taylor Birch State Recreation Area**, on E. Sunrise Blvd., Fort Lauderdale, 954/468-2791, which lies between the Atlantic and the Intracoastal Waterway. Hike the interior trails through its four distinct biological communities, or use the 1.7-mile exercise course that traces its outer boundaries. A tunnel under A1A leads to the beach. Another excellent outdoor stop in this region is the **John U. Lloyd Beach State Recreation Area**, 6503 N. Ocean Dr., Dania Beach, 954/967-1297. It too has nature and hiking trails, canoe rentals, and fishing and picnicking possibilities, and it's a particularly pleasant coastal gem, with dunes, a coastal hammock, and mangroves to explore.

Golfers can find good courses from **Crystal Lake Country Club** in Pompano Beach to the **Raintree Golf Resort** in Pembroke Pines, and you can fish from the piers up and down the coast, in the rivers, or go to sea on half- or all-day deep-sea fishing boats that sail from the **Bahia Mar Marina**, **Marina del Americana**, or **Pier 66 Marina** in Fort Lauderdale; from **Sands Harbor Marina** or **Hillsboro Inlet Marina** in Pompano Beach; or from **Diplomat** or **Goombay** marinas in Hollywood. If you want to join the fishes, you can outfit yourself for scuba diving at shops such as **Ocean Promotion Scuba & Snorkel Adventures,** Pompano Beach, 954/561-4499; **Lauderdale Diver,** 800/654-2073 or 954/467-2822, or **Atlantic Marine**, 954/583-4000, in Fort Lauderdale; or **Frog International,** 954/963-0757, or **Giant Stride Divers**, 954/987-9030, in Hollywood.

Like to bet on the ponies or the dogs? Head for the **Pompano Harness Track**, Florida's only harness track, in Pompano Beach, 954/972-2000. For thoroughbred racing, it's **Gulfstream Park** in Hallandale, 954/454-7000. Greyhounds chase mechanical rabbits at **Hollywood Greyhound Track**, also in Hallandale, 954/454-9400.

## FOOD

You'll find more good dining in this small section of Florida than you could sample if you stayed two months, but for a fairly expensive dining highlight, stop at **Darrel and Oliver's Cafe Maxx**, 2601 E. Atlantic Blvd., Pompano Beach, 954/782-0606. Its eclectic menu draws crowds every night of the week. Diners line up for a seat here at *Zagat Guide*'s top-rated Florida restaurant, one of 22 top-rated regional restaurants nationwide. The menu is always changing, but the servers know it well. Follow their recommendations as you navigate through grilled or sautéed seafood entrees, many of the dishes unlike

# FORT LAUDERDALE

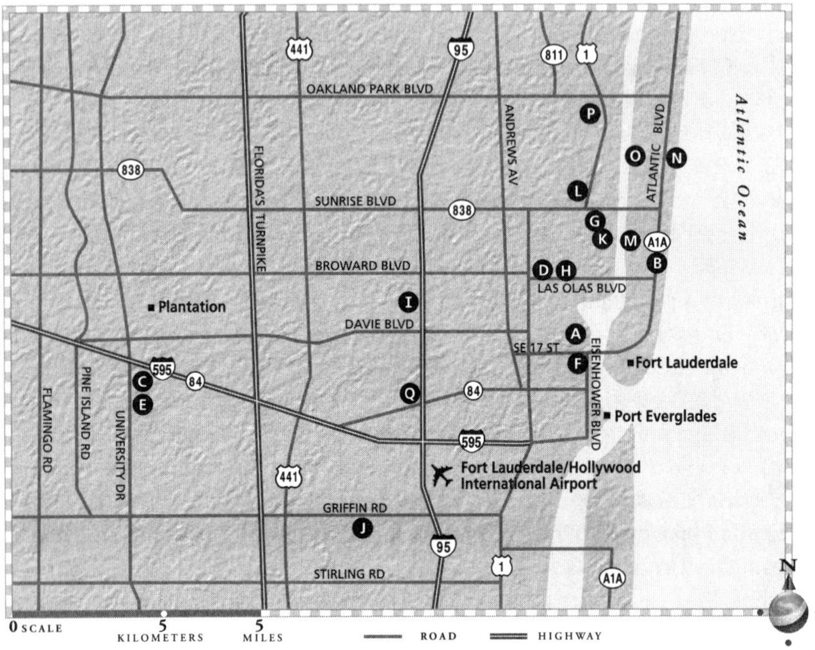


## FOOD

- A 15th Street Fisheries
- B Casablanca Cafe
- C Davie Ale House
- D Galleria G'vanni
- E Geronimo's Grill
- D Indigo
- F Joe Bel Air's Diner
- G La Tavernetta–Bistro by the Water
- H Mango's
- I Shirttail Charlie's Crab
- J Vincent's on the Water
- D Zan Z Bar

## LODGING

- K Aqua Mar Resort and Marina
- L By-Eddy Apartments & Motel
- M La Casa Del Mar Bed & Breakfast
- N Pelican Beach Resort
- K Sandpiper Island Resort & Marina
- O The Trevers at the Beach

## CAMPING

- P Buglewood RV Resort
- Q Yacht Haven Park & Marina

*Note: Items with the same letter are located in the same area.*

anything you'll find elsewhere, such as the Szechuan barbecue salmon or andouille-braised collard greens. This restaurant's wine list is locally famous, and its desserts are to dream for, so splurge on the dessert sampler.

There's another must-stop here. You don't go to **Cap's Place**, Cap's Dock, 2765 N.E. 28 Court, Lighthouse Point, 954/941-0418, merely for its excellent grouper chowder and hearts of palm salad. This rustic, shanty-like island restaurant—an old wooden motorcraft takes you from the dock to the restaurant—fairly shouts its history. It was a rum-runners' haven during Prohibition days. The table and chairs where Winston Churchill and President Franklin Delano Roosevelt dined during furtive World War II visits by Churchill are still here, in the side room where the two leaders plotted an Allied victory. President John F. Kennedy liked Cap's food and felt its history. Of course, knowing all that might tend to diminish the significance of any television celebrity you find dining here today.

Now, back to just good dining. Wear semiformal attire when you try **Brooks**, 500 S. Federal Hwy., Deerfield Beach, 954/427-9302, for its fairly pricey menu that offers wonderful Florida seafood specialties and dessert soufflés. During the winter season, it may offer only a prix fixe menu. Not far away is the more modestly priced **Carafiello's**, 949 S. Federal Hwy., Deerfield Beach, 954/421-7337, which also offers a continental menu but in a more casual setting. **Pal's Charley's Crab**, 1755 S.E. Third Court, in Cove Plaza, Deerfield Beach, 954/427-4000, not only offers superb seafood, but its position on the Intracoastal Waterway gives you great views of general boat traffic as well as a ringside seat to the comings and goings of those who take their mega-yachts to dinner. If it's been a while since you've stopped for Chinese, pull in at **Yips**, 1327 SR 7, North Lauderdale, 954/978-9477, a nondescript place favored locally because of its first-rate food, such as crab in black-bean sauce.

If the dining choices north of Fort Lauderdale present too many excellent options, then when you get to the city, just throw a dart at a restaurant list. Of course, it's not quite that easy, but a very long list of excellent restaurants confronts you here, and what follows is merely a small sampling of mostly moderately priced eateries, starting in the heart of the city on Las Olas Boulevard. **Indigo**, in the landmark Riverside Hotel, 620 E. Las Olas Blvd., 954/467-0671, is a sidewalk café in the city's oldest continuously occupied hotel, and it features three meals a day of "Colonial Southeast" Asian cuisines with a South Florida twist. **Galleria G'vanni**, 625 E. Las Olas Blvd., 954/524-5246, features elegantly eclectic displays of artwork to complement its nouvelle American and Italian dishes. At **Zan Z Bar**, 602 E. Las Olas Blvd., 954/767-3377, you'll find another cozy coffeehouse and sidewalk café, this one featuring contemporary South African dishes and African decor. Try the ostrich or the pepper-seared filet of salmon. For simpler American fare, sit down outside or indoors at **Mangos**, 904 E. Las Olas Blvd., 954-523-5001, a place with nightly musical entertainment.

Eating by the water is always pleasant, and Fort Lauderdale has an abundance of great waterside dining. The world could eat at **Casablanca Cafe**, 3049 Alhambra St., 954/764-3500, and not know it wasn't at home, because the menu at this chic, historic beachside house shows influences from Argentina to Spain, from Morocco to New Orleans. Nautical themes are overwhelming at the rustic **15th Street Fisheries**, 1900 S.E. 15th St., 954/763-2777, but the kitchen provides exceptionally good seafood dishes, served while you look out over the Intracoastal Waterway. **La Tavernetta–Bistro By The Water**, 926 N.E. 20th Ave., 954/463-2566, is worth getting off the water taxi for its health-conscious Italian menu, served as you watch boat traffic on the Middle River. On the south bank of the New River, **Shirttail Charlie's Restaurant**, 400 S.W. Third Ave., 954/463-3474, serves good, moderately priced American menu items on a popular deck right on the water. If you're scoping out the cruise ships in Port Everglades and want to eat cheaply, stop in at the oddly named **Joe Bel Air's Diner**, 1717 Eisenhower Blvd., 954/527-5637, for good diner food, 24 hours a day.

In Dania Beach stop in at **Vincent's On The Water**, 3445 Griffin Rd., 954/961-5030, for its seafood and well-prepared dishes served in a homey kind of atmosphere. The **Sugar Reef Tropical Bar & Grill**, 600 N. Surf Rd., Hollywood, 954/922-1119, maintains a good reputation for moderately priced seafood and poultry, with European-style desserts. In Davie, try the **Davie Ale House**, 2080 University Dr., 954/236-0062, a busy, inexpensive burger, chicken, and pasta place with excellent microbrewed beers. If you want a little more variety, try **Geronimo's Grill**, 3528 S. University Dr., 954/474-9992, which offers a creative, California-chic menu.

## LODGING

This is one of Florida's most visited areas, so you'll find chain lodgings everywhere from Pompano Beach to Hollywood, most of them clean, well tended, and not very far from the beaches. If you want to get away from the chains for a night or two, try some of the following moderately priced hotels and resorts. All are close to good restaurants, shopping, and cultural amenities, and most have heated pools for those who find even the Florida section of the Atlantic too cold.

In Pompano Beach, the **Ronny Dee Resort Motel**, 717 S. Ocean Blvd., 954/943-3020, is a good bet, a nicely landscaped, family-friendly place just a short hop from the beach. You'll probably be mixing with European holiday-makers at the slightly pricier **Villamar Inn**, 740 N. Ocean Blvd., 800/946-3556 or 954/941-3530, www.villamar.com, an 18-unit European inn just a grass strip away from the beach sand. The **Ebb Tide Hotel**, 300 Briny Ave., 954/941-7200, www.ebbtidehotel.com, is a particularly handsome place, with 200 feet of private Atlantic beach.

Lauderdale-by-the-Sea is an enclave of good hotels, including **A Little Inn By The Sea**, 4546 El Mar Dr., 800/492-0311 or 954/772-2450, www.travelbase.com/destinations/ftlaud/alittleinn, a beachside, tropical bed-and-breakfast kind of place built around a courtyard. In fact, El Mar Drive is lined with good lodgings, including the slightly less expensive **Blue Seas Courtyard**, 4525 El Mar Dr., 954/772-3336; and the **Tropic Seas Resort**, 4616 El Mar Dr., 800/952-9581 or 954/772-2555, a small lodging, quiet except for the lapping of the waves just across the sand.

In Fort Lauderdale itself, you'll find considerable comfort at internationally popular **Aqua Mar Resort and Marina**, 90 Isle of Venice, 954/763-5501, www.aqua/mar.com. It's only a few steps from fashionable Las Olas Boulevard, yet on a waterway and also near the beach. Next door is the **Sandpiper Island Resort & Marina**, 800/543-2006 or 954/527-0026, www.ssl-online.com/sandpiper, equally good and equally well-placed for everything in town. **The Trevers at the Beach**, 552 N. Birch Rd., 800/533-4744 or 954/564-9601, is a slightly less expensive, small, family-run resort. Yet another good choice is the **By-Eddy Apartments & Motel**, 1021 N.E. 13th Ave., 954/764-7555, a find if you want to sleep away from the beach.

The appeal of **La Casa Del Mar Bed & Breakfast**, 3003 Granada St., 800/739-0009 or 954/467-2037, www.lacasadelmar.com, is its moderate rates that put you into nicely decorated Monet, Stolen Kiss, Southwest, or Vizcaya theme rooms. And 400 feet of private beach awaits you at the **Pelican Beach Resort**, 2000 N. Atlantic Blvd., 800/525-6232 or 954/568-9431, another family kind of place convenient to restaurants, shopping, and attractions.

Many of Hollywood's best lodgings are along Surf Road, including **Bougainvillea on the Beach**, 2813 N. Surf Rd., 954/925-1368, a particularly pleasant, small place with a tropical garden near the Hollywood Broadwalk. The **Manta Ray Inn**, 1715 S. Surf Rd., 800/255-0595 or 954/921-9666, www.mantarayinn.com, has large rooms on its beachfront property. If the sound of the waves keeps you awake at night, try the **Shell**

**Motel**, 1201 S. Federal Hwy., 800/547-0044 or 954/923-8085, a nicely landscaped lodging close to but not on the beach.

## CAMPING

In Pompano Beach, pull into the 594-site **Breezy Hill Travel Trailer Park**, 800 N.E. 48th St., 954/942-8688, which has 115 full-hookup, open RV sites just two miles from the Atlantic Ocean. Nearby, **Highland Woods Travel Trailer Park**, 900 N.E. 48th St., 954/942-6254, offers 148 sites, 40 with complete hookups, for self-contained vehicles only, and offers a heated swimming pool, whirlpool, and recreation room.

Several choices are available in Fort Lauderdale, which you may find convenient enough to use as a base while visiting Miami and Miami Beach (it's just 25 miles away). Drive into **Candlelight Park**, 5731 S. SR 7, 954/791-5023, a huge place with 800 sites, 500 of them grassy with cement pads and full hookups. For pleasant waterside camping, try the **Yacht Haven Park & Marina**, 2323 SR 84, 800/581-2322 or 954/583-2322, which has 250 full-hookup sites, many of them fronting a river, canal, or marina. **Buglewood RV Resort**, 2121 N.W. 29th Court, 800/487-7395 or 954/485-1150, is six miles inland and doesn't allow tents, but many of its 232 sites are shaded. Between Fort Lauderdale and Miami you'll find **Trinity Towers RV Park**, 3300 Pembroke Rd., Pembroke Park, 954/962-7400, with 203 sites on a lakeside parcel. Electrical and water hookups are offered at 53 sites, which have paved pads. There are no tenting facilities.

## NIGHTLIFE

Fort Lauderdale didn't throw away partying with the Spring-Breakers, it just ratcheted the definition of nightlife up several rungs. The **Broward Center for the Performing Arts**, 201 S.W. Fifth Ave., 800/764-0700 or 954/462-0222, which glitters at night along the banks of the New River, is one of Florida's largest and most important arts halls. It's the home of the Florida Philharmonic Orchestra and the Florida Grand Opera company, and also hosts top-notch Broadway musicals, the Miami City Ballet, and a full schedule of concerts by visiting orchestras and singers. Touring Broadway shows also hit the **Parker Playhouse**, 707 N.E. Eighth St., Fort Lauderdale, 954/763-2444; and leading popular music stars and groups perform at the **Sunrise Musical Theater**, 5555 N.W. 95th Ave., Sunrise, 954/741-8600, which has a huge, 4,000-seat auditorium.

The nightclub scene thrives on an adult crowd. There's live blues at **Cheers** and the **Downtowner Saloon** (where on Wednesdays at 10:30 p.m. you move out back to the New River to moon the *Jungle Queen* cruise—a tradition honoring the city's Spring Break past), and there are popular music and dance clubs along Federal Highway. A fairly strong gay and lesbian element is evident in Fort Lauderdale, so keep in mind that perhaps 20 to 30 of the city's nightspots cater largely to that audience.

## SHOPPING

Every day, even during the off-season, 40 to 50 busloads of tourists pull up to the 270 shops at 2.35-million-square-foot **Sawgrass Mills**, 12801 W. Sunrise Blvd., Sunrise, 954/846-2350, the world's largest outlet mall. While shopping here is a special and often crowded experience, be alert to the fact that this is a tourist haven and an entertainment center (with giant video screens, and a Steven Spielberg Gameworks with racing, sports, and fighting simulators), too. In fact, its "outlet" status is questionable. Tourists make up nearly half the shoppers, and about 60 percent come from Latin America.

If you'd like less company while you shop, head to **The Shops of Las Olas**, Las Olas Blvd., Fort Lauderdale, 954/480-4942, a region of upscale boutiques and trendy art galleries. It doesn't yet rank up there with Worth Avenue in Palm Beach, but it's trying. **The Galleria**, 2414 E. Sunrise Blvd. (between A1A and U.S. 1), Fort Lauderdale, 954/564-1015, is an established high-end shopping center, with Neiman Marcus, Saks Fifth Avenue, Lord & Taylor, Dillard's, Burdines, and 120 other shops and restaurants from which to choose. And in downtown Dania Beach, more than 100 dealers in antiques, fine art, and collectibles have formed a kind of antiques row called **Dania Beach Historic Antique Shopping District**, 800/903-2642.

Flea-market shoppers should head for the **Festival Indoor Flea Market Mall**, 2900 Sample Rd., Pompano Beach, 954/979-4555, where there are about 600 vendors.

# 8
# MIAMI BEACH

Miami and Miami Beach may sound pretty much like the same place if you've not visited here before, but they are in fact totally unalike. Miami, the mainland city, is a hodgepodge of diverse and sometimes fractious communities, a gritty kind of place. Miami Beach, a 7.5-square-mile island between the Bay of Biscayne and the Atlantic Ocean, is and always has been for tourists and beautiful people. South Beach in particular (the bottom third of this long, narrow strip of sand) is a gorgeous illusion, where all the prices are high, all the hotels and condos are elegantly furnished, and all the restaurants casually serve gourmet food 24 hours a day.

That's not as much of an exaggeration as it might seem, because this city has been through a kind of cultural, entertainment, and commercial renaissance during the past decade. It was called the "American Riviera" during the 1920s. The luster disappeared for a few decades, but it's back. Miami Beach claims its nightlife sizzles, and it does. Its restaurants say they let you taste the culture, and they do. You'll know what this means as you amble down revitalized Lincoln Road Mall, an open-air shopping mecca whose $16 million facelift put even more polish on its haute couture boutiques, art galleries, and sidewalk cafés. Speaking of food, there are about 250 restaurants on this slim island. Their menus will expand your culinary imagination.

The decadence of it all, along with its New World architecture, draws thousands of visitors every year. The Art Deco district of South Beach—actually,

# MIAMI BEACH

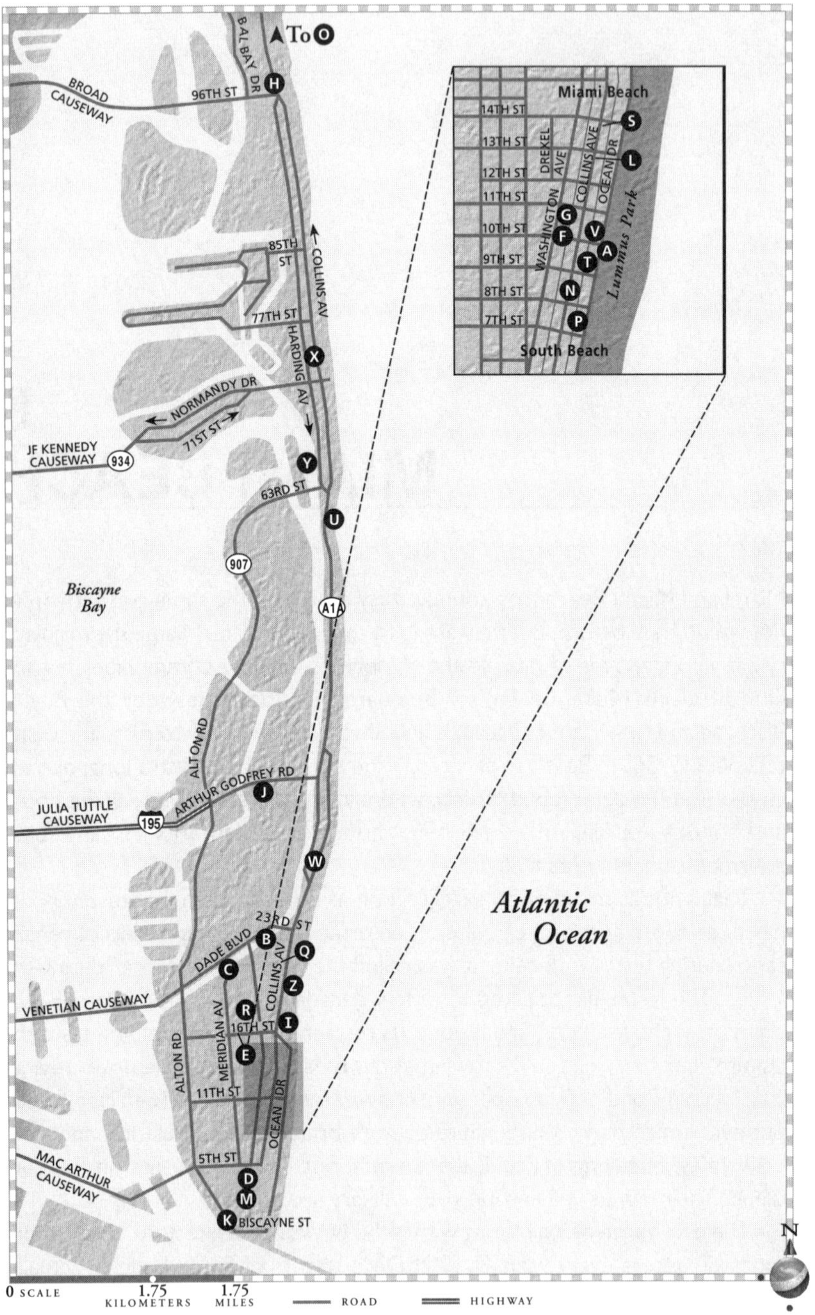

To O
BAL BAY DR
BROAD CAUSEWAY
96TH ST
85TH ST
COLLINS AV
77TH ST
HARDING AV
NORMANDY DR
71ST ST
JF KENNEDY CAUSEWAY
934
63RD ST
907
Biscayne Bay
A1A
ALTON RD
ARTHUR GODFREY RD
JULIA TUTTLE CAUSEWAY
195
23RD ST
DADE BLVD
VENETIAN CAUSEWAY
MERIDIAN AV
16TH ST
11TH ST
OCEAN DR
5TH ST
MAC ARTHUR CAUSEWAY
BISCAYNE ST
Atlantic Ocean
Miami Beach
14TH ST
13TH ST
12TH ST
11TH ST
10TH ST
9TH ST
8TH ST
7TH ST
DREXEL AVE
WASHINGTON
COLLINS AVE
OCEAN DR
Lummus Park
South Beach
0 SCALE
1.75 KILOMETERS
1.75 MILES
ROAD
HIGHWAY
N

Miami Beach's contribution to the style is more properly termed "Tropical Art Deco"—is a must-see for anyone interested in the marriage of art and functionality in city design, while North Beach is just right for those wanting a whiff of '50s motifs.

Miami Beach, a small place jammed with some of the finest shopping, restaurants, and nightclubs anywhere, is as much an attitude as a place. You might not want to live your entire life like this, but let it take you over for a day or two, and silently thank the preservationists who prevailed about 20 years ago, when there was a concerted move afoot to demolish all those aging Art Deco structures and replace them with high-rise casino hotels.

## A PERFECT DAY IN MIAMI BEACH

If you have just one day, make it a SoBe (South Beach) day. Take a tour of a historic Art Deco hotel, spend just enough time on the beach and in the aqua ocean to get a South Beach tan (swimsuit models claim these tans are the best), and get a close-up look at those strange-looking lifeguard towers designed by famous artists for the city's Beach Patrol. Take a walk on the beachfront boardwalk. Wander among Lincoln Road's art galleries and glitzy shops. If you're young or young at heart and in good shape, rent some inline skates—everyone else seems to have them. If your feet tire, take the Electrowave, a

### SIGHTS

- Ⓐ Art Deco Welcome Center
- Ⓑ Bass Museum of Art
- Ⓒ The Holocaust Memorial
- Ⓓ Sanford L. Ziff Jewish Museum of Florida
- Ⓔ South Florida Art Center
- Ⓕ The Wolfsonian Foundation Gallery

### FOOD

- Ⓖ 11th Street Diner
- Ⓗ Bal Harbour Bistro
- Ⓘ Blue Door
- Ⓙ Crystal Cafe
- Ⓚ Joe's Stone Crab Restaurant
- Ⓛ Les Deux Fontaines
- Ⓜ Memo Restaurant
- Ⓝ Mezzaluna
- Ⓝ The News Cafe
- Ⓔ Norma's on the Beach
- Ⓞ Tivoli
- Ⓟ Wet Willie's
- Ⓠ Wolfie's
- Ⓡ Yuca Restaurant

### LODGING

- Ⓢ Bayliss Guest House
- Ⓣ Breakwater Hotel
- Ⓤ Castillo del Mar Resort
- Ⓥ The Clevelander Hotel
- Ⓘ Delano Hotel
- Ⓝ Hotel Leon
- Ⓦ Indian Creek Hotel
- Ⓧ Ocean Surf Hotel
- Ⓨ Pelican Creek Hotel
- Ⓩ Shelborne Beach Resort–South Beach

*Note: Items with the same letter are located in the same area.*

free electric shuttle-bus system that runs up and down Washington Avenue. Have lunch at an Ocean Drive café; stop, if you must, outside No. 1114 Ocean Drive, at the palatial Casa Casaurina (House of the Pine), to see what memorial has been left today on the steps where fashion designer Gianni Versace died; then stroll over to The Promenade south of 16th Street to observe a fashion shoot, linger over dinner at one of the chic restaurants or cafés, and watch for celebrity patrons. For even more entertainment, attend a performance at the Jackie Gleason Theater of the Performing Arts or dance the night away at one of this town's hot clubs.

## SIGHTSEEING HIGHLIGHTS

### ★★★★ ART DECO WELCOME CENTER
**1001 Ocean Dr., 305/672-2014**

Perhaps it's not what is normally thought of as an attraction, but the architectural style that is considered one of the first successful breaks with traditional revival forms is everywhere in Miami Beach. A 27-block area of pastel greens, blues, yellows, and pinks (every colorful square foot of it on the National Register of Historic Places) makes up the heart of the city's architectural appeal. Ziggurat rooflines, geometric detailing, glass-block construction, and "eyebrow" cornices combine with the pastels to make this remarkable variety of Art Deco styles a visual delight. Other architectural styles are prominently represented here, too, including Post-War Deco, Post-War Modern, Eclectic, and Garden.

***Details:*** *The Miami Design Preservation League will suggest individual walking tours; it offers structured tours on Sat mornings. Two men lead well-known cultural walking safaris of the area. Milton Heller's half-day group walks cost $5, 305/931-1782. Miami history professor Dr. Paul George leads particularly engaging tours of other parts of Miami as well as the Art Deco district, 305/237-3723, with varying costs.*

### ★★★★ BASS MUSEUM OF ART
**2121 Park Ave., 305/673-7530**

In 1963 John and Johanna Bass placed their collection of about 500 paintings by European masters from the fourteenth to nineteenth centuries in this massive coral rock Art Deco building with a Mayan motif. Since then the Bass has developed South Florida's largest collection (more than 2,000 works, only a small portion on view at any one time) of European painting, sculpture, and textiles, including ecclesiastical vestments and two enormous tapestries. There are also impressive collections of period furniture, Oriental art, and modern American painting, architecture, and design. Don't miss *The Holy Family* by Rubens and works by Toulouse-Lautrec and Albrecht Dürer. The museum itself is on the National Register of Historic Places.

***Details:*** *Open Tue–Sat 10–5, Sun 1–5. Admission: $7 adults, $5 students. (1–2 hours)*

## ★★★★ THE WOLFSONIAN FOUNDATION GALLERY

**1001 Washington Ave., 305/531-1001**

In the heart of the Art Deco district, this relatively new institution in a renovated Mediterranean-style 1920s warehouse, recently acquired by Florida International University, displays furniture, ceramics, books, posters, architectural design models, and other objects that portray the history, art, and architecture of the late nineteenth and early twentieth centuries. Particularly impressive is its collection of Depression-era prints and mural work by WPA artists and European artifacts of political propaganda. What you see is drawn from more than 70,000 items of the Michael Wolfson, Jr., collection of decorative arts.

***Details:*** *Open Tue–Sat 11–6, Sun 12–5. Admission: $5 adults, $3.50 children. (1–2 hours)*

## ★★★ THE HOLOCAUST MEMORIAL

**1933-45 Meridian Ave., 305/538-1663**

A 42-foot-high bronze arm being climbed by figures apparently scrambling to escape is the central feature of this memorial to the six million Jews who died in Nazi Germany during World War II. Victims' names are etched into a black granite wall and there is a meditation garden as well as the Dome of Contemplation, where an eternal flame burns.

***Details:*** *At the channel at the north end of Meridian Ave. Open daily 9–9. Free. (30 minutes–1 hour)*

## ★★★ SANFORD L. ZIFF JEWISH MUSEUM OF FLORIDA

**301 Washington Ave., 305/672-5044**

Through a permanent collection of artifacts called "Mosaic: Jewish Life in Florida," the museum chronicles the more than 230-year history of immigration, rituals, community building, acculturation, and identity-building among the state's Jewish population. It is all nicely displayed in a restored 1936 Art Deco synagogue.

***Details:*** *Open Tue–Sun 10–5. Admission: $5 adults, $4 students and children. (30 minutes–1 hour)*

### ★★ SOUTH FLORIDA ART CENTER

**924 Lincoln Rd., 305/674-8278**

Work by up to 60 visual artists being supported by the Center is often on display in changing exhibits. Supported artists are in all stages of career development, so quality varies widely.

***Details:*** *Open studios, exhibits, and art classes are at multiple addresses on Lincoln Road and Lenox Avenue. Free.*

## FITNESS AND RECREATION

You can't visit Miami Beach without soaking up some sun at the edge of the Atlantic Ocean, so head for the beach anywhere from the island's southernmost point to 83rd Street—but be aware that from 5th to 21st Streets, you're in the topless-sunbathing district. Try **Lummus Park** (6th Street to 14th Place east of Ocean Drive), with its palm trees and thatched-roof *chickees;* or **North Shore** (76th to 87th streets along Collins Avenue), which has a vita course and wooden boardwalks. Farther north still is **Haulover Beach**, 10800 Collins Ave., 305/947-3525, with picnic facilities and a nude beach area.

It won't be tough to dive into these waters—they're seldom colder than January's average 71 degrees, and in July about 86 degrees. Strong onshore winds can whip up rip currents that can carry even the strongest swimmer out to sea, so the **Beach Patrol**, 305/673-7714, guards 21 locations.

Golfers can head to two 18-hole courses: **Bayshore Municipal Golf Course**, 2301 Alton Rd., 305/532-3350, which also happens to have two tennis courts, or, farther north, **Normandy Shores Golf Course**, 2401 Biarritz Dr., 305/868-6502.

If you're concerned that your major physical activity in Miami Beach has been lifting cool glasses or food from the plate, rent some inline skates—try **Fritz's Skate Shop**, 726 Lincoln Rd., 305/532-1954—and join the locals zipping up and down the city's streets or The Promenade.

## FOOD

Eat at ordinary places elsewhere. In Miami Beach, especially in South Beach, you can hardly turn around without spotting a restaurant you'd really like to try. Some say the **11th Street Diner,** 1065 Washington Ave., 305/534-6373, has the best hamburger in town. It certainly has reasonable prices, and its hip

### HERE'S A TIP

*Explore South Beach on foot, if you possibly can. Parking is tough to find and expensive when you do. Use valet parking at restaurants that offer it—it's cheaper than paying a fine. The rule here is: Don't stretch the parking rules. Parking enforcement officers smile a lot and are very friendly to tourists, but they have a well-deserved reputation for spotting even tiny infractions and they offer no pity for rule violators.*

crowd may be one of the reasons this 24-hour indoor/outdoor eatery makes just about every food critic's top-ten list. Celebrity-spotting is a sport at **Mezzaluna,** 834 Ocean Dr., 305/674-1330, which serves everything Northern Italian, from brick-oven pizza to exotic pastas, on the oceanfront.

The **Crystal Cafe**, 726 41st St. (Arthur Godfrey Rd.), 305/673-8266, is another casually elegant place that's always boasting of another culinary award for its new continental cuisine. **Les Deux Fontaines**, 1230-38 Ocean Dr., 305/672-7878, a French seafood restaurant in the Ocean Front Hotel, has live jazz and Dixieland music to entertain if the ocean view isn't enough. **Memo Restaurant**, 100 Collins Ave., 305/532-9822, serves American cuisine from a health-conscious menu. Be prepared for wok-charred salmon or curried lentil stew.

If you want to read *Le Monde*, the *Singapore Business Times*, or *Folha de Sao Paulo*, why not have a bite to eat while you're browsing? Stop in at **The News Cafe**, 800 Ocean Drive, 305/538-6397, www.newscafe.com, at any hour to read these or 42 other domestic and world newspapers, plus an impressive selection of magazines. This casual sidewalk café is South Beach to the core, the perfect people-watching spot as models and producers drop by for the healthy menu items. Fashion designer Versace bought his last cup of coffee here.

In North Beach, try the **Bal Harbour Bistro**, 9700 Collins Ave., Bal Harbour, 305/861-4544, in The Bal Harbour Shops, for its elegant sandwiches; or make some wild choices from the eclectic menu at **Tivoli**, 3439 N.E. 163rd St. (Sunny Isles Blvd.), 305/945-7080: rack of lamb, roast duck, or swordfish.

Maybe it would be easiest just to try the most famous places in South Beach not already mentioned, like the original 24-hour gourmet deli, **Wolfie's**, Collins Ave. at 21st St., 305/538-6626; or **Wet Willie's**, 760 Ocean Dr.,

305/532-5650, the cash-only place that serves food but really specializes in attitude improvement through its lengthy list of alcoholic beverages, such as the aptly named "Call-a-Cab." Don't forget **Joe's Stone Crab Restaurant**, 227 Biscayne St., 305/673-0365, where the same family has been serving for more than 80 years, or the **Yuca Restaurant**, 501 Lincoln Rd., 305/532-9822, with its Cuban specialties. **Norma's on the Beach**, 646 Lincoln Rd., 305/532-2809, fancies itself a "New World Caribbean" kind of place, and you're not likely to disagree after you've had the rum-glazed ribs, the Rasta chicken, or prawns in red-pepper sauce. But if nouvelle American is more to your taste, make reservations at the Delano Hotel's **Blue Door**, 1685 Collins Ave., 305/674-6400, for roast duck in sour-cherry sauce, potato-wrapped trout, or young chicken filled with lemon rind, garlic, and onion.

## LODGING

Travelers on a strict budget often choose inexpensive accommodation at the usual chain motels on the mainland in Miami or Fort Lauderdale, then nip over one of the causeways to visit Miami Beach. Some chains have Miami Beach properties that offer reasonable rates, so you don't have to stay at the **Delano Hotel,** 1685 Collins Ave., 800/555-5001 or 305/672-2000, an intimate Art Deco property where the former operator of New York's Studio 54 discotheque, Ian Schrager, charges up to $2,000 a night for a room.

Instead, try the **Breakwater Hotel**, 940 Ocean Dr., 800/454-1220 or 305/532-1220, another historic property with moderate rates; or that Art Deco masterpiece, the **Ocean Surf Hotel**, 7436 Ocean Terr., 800/555-0411 or 305/866-1648, www.oceansurf.com. Others worth trying include the **Castillo del Mar Resort,** 5445 Collins Ave., 888/352-3224 or 305/865-1500, which has fairly moderate rates along so-called "Millionaires' Row," and **The Clevelander Hotel,** 1020 Ocean Dr., 305/531-3485. **Shelborne Beach Resort–South Beach**, 1801 Collins Ave., 800/327-8757 or 305/531-1271, is in a great location; some suites cost two weeks' pay, but the resort also offers moderately priced rooms. **The Hotel Leon**, 841 Collins Ave., 305/673-3767, www.hotelleon.com, also with reasonable rates, is a pleasantly renovated 1929 property a block from the Atlantic Ocean.

The **Bayliss Guest House**, 1340 Collins Ave., 888/305-4683 or 305/531-3755, is one of three small hotels with room rates from inexpensive to total luxury. Away from the beach, try the **Indian Creek Hotel**, 2727 Indian Creek Dr., 305/531-2727, a moderately priced 1936 Art Deco hotel, or the nearby **Pelican Creek Hotel**, 6580 Indian Creek Dr., 800/588-7918 or 305/868-3371.

## NIGHTLIFE

When the sun goes down, the lights come up. Put on something chic and head for the **Lincoln Theatre**, 555 Lincoln Rd., 305/673-3331, to take in a concert by the **New World Symphony**, the orchestra founded in 1986 by Michael Tilson Thomas. Tickets are available by phone from the theater, in person at the orchestra's box office at 555 Lincoln Rd., or remotely by fax, 305/673-2302, or E-mail, tickets@nws.org. **The Miami City Ballet**, 905 Lincoln Rd., 305/532-4880, one of the country's top ballet troupes, performs at the **Jackie Gleason Theater of the Performing Arts,** 1700 Washington Ave., 305/673-7300. The 2,700-seat theater is also home to the Miami Beach Broadway Series and hosts touring orchestras, singers, and other performers. There's usually something worthwhile at the **Colony Theater**, 1040 Lincoln Rd., 305/674-1040, a renovated Art Deco movie house built by Paramount Pictures in the 1930s. The 465-seat theater hosts five film festivals each year.

High-energy nightclubs worth checking out include **Amnesia**, 136 Collins Ave., 305/531-5535; the **Shadow Lounge**, 1532 Washington Ave., 305/531-9411; and **Club 737**, 737 Washington Ave., 305/534-4469. The wannabe-famous are drawn to **Liquid**, 1439 Washington Ave., 305/532-9154; and the **Groove Jet**, 323 23rd St., 305/532-2002. For a truly glitzy show, go to the **Club Tropigala** at the Fontainebleau Hilton Resort & Towers, 4441 Collins Ave., 305/672-7469, for both dining and an award-winning floor show with 30 performers and special guests.

## SHOPPING

The only questions are where to start and when to stop. Miami Beach is as much a shopper's as a sun-worshipper's paradise. The goods tend to be chic and the prices high, but there's nothing like strolling among the 175 stores at pedestrian-only **Lincoln Road Mall** at 16th Street. Stop in to admire the fashions at **The 24 Collection,** 744 Lincoln Rd., 305/673-2455; pick up some hard-to-find Canary Islands cigars at **Condal & Penamil House**, 741 Lincoln Rd., 305/604-9690; or treat yourself to new luggage at **Chatani Luggage Gallery**, 320 Lincoln Rd., 305/532-1289. There's even a **Farmer's Market** at Lincoln Road and Meridian Avenue, 305/673-4166.

The shops stretch from south to north along Collins Avenue, but the true shopper's destination is toward the north end, at **Bal Harbour Shops**, 9700 Collins Ave., Bal Harbour, 305/866-1816, a world apart, where from one doorway to the next you'll find Neiman Marcus, Saks Fifth Avenue, Lord & Taylor, Gucci, Bvlgari, Tiffany & Co., Chanel, St. John, and just about every other famous name in haute couture among its 90 specialty stores.

# 9
# GREATER MIAMI

The metropolis of Miami is often called the Magic City, probably because of its continual self-transformation. In fact, change seems to have been the only constant in the region's hundred-year history. The area arose from the vision of wealthy pioneers such as Julia Tuttle and Henry Flagler, who arrived here in the late 1800s, when the palm-tree paradise was no more than a rugged outpost ravaged by hurricanes and mosquitoes. Tuttle, the "Mother of Miami," envisioned a thriving city along the wild mangrove-lined river and implored Flagler, the railroad tycoon, to extend his track from West Palm Beach to Dade County, which was cut off from the rest of the country by water. He resisted for years, but her persistence won out. Reluctantly laying the final 66 miles of track to Miami in 1896, Flagler predicted huffily, "The town will never be more than a fishing village for my hotel guests."

Oh? The growth of Greater Miami has been phenomenal, its skyline ever-evolving, its diverse peoples ever-melding, merging newcomers into the fold. Some 45 percent of the population is foreign-born—predominantly Cubans, followed by Canadians, Haitians, Germans, and Jamaicans. It's a mosaic of big-city sophistication, commerce, and culture, with quaint Caribbean and hot Latin influences. Shimmering skyscrapers tower over locals dressed on the cutting edge of urban chic. Coconut Grove, long a bohemian hangout, offers an eclectic, art-colony ambience ranging from funky earring and accessory shops to home furnishings, haute couture, and fine cuisine.

# GREATER MIAMI

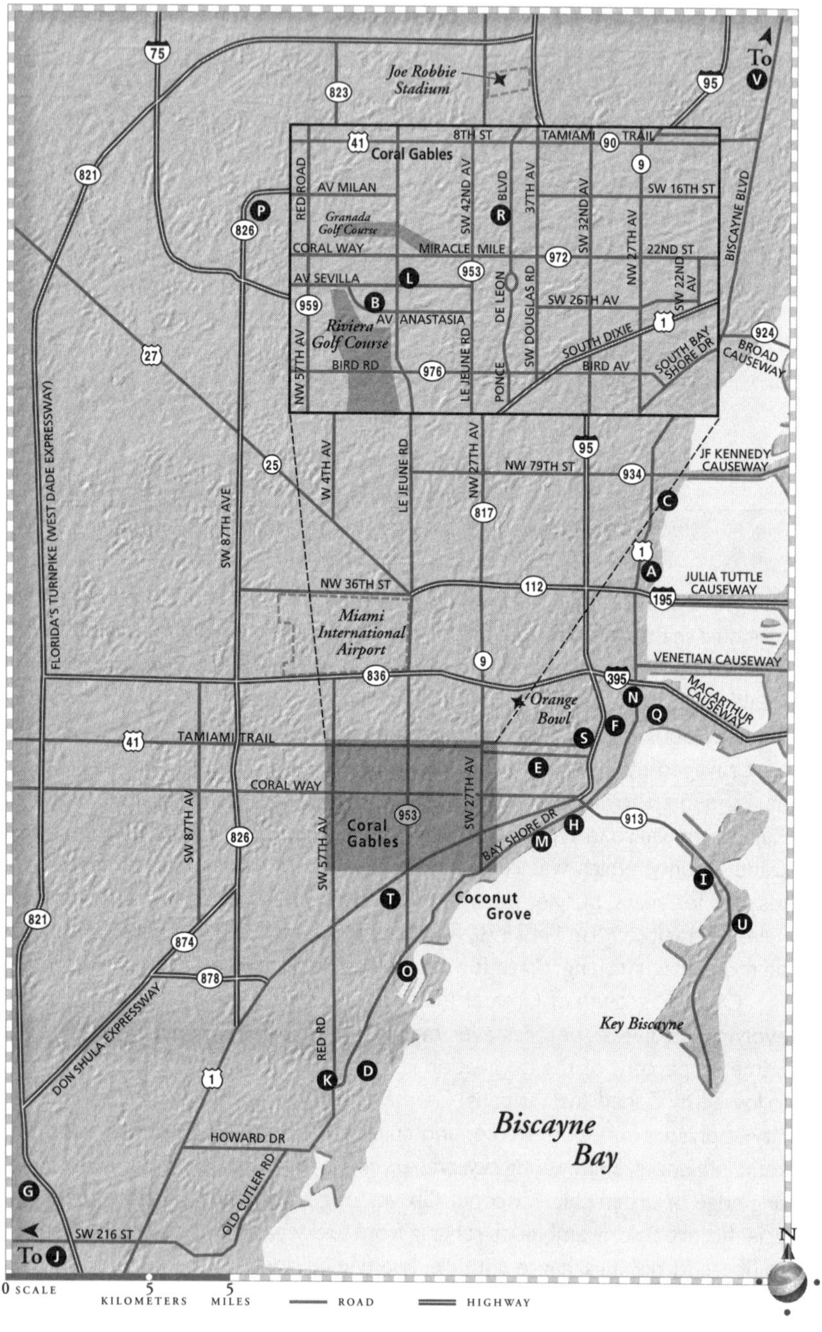

Divers come to explore North America's only living coral reef, which stretches south along the Florida Keys; nature lovers walk or ride airboats through thousands of acres of unspoiled wilderness in Everglades National Park, just a few miles west of the city; and the Port of Miami is the cruise capital of the world, with more than 3 million passengers a year sailing on huge liners, departing for the Bahamas, the Caribbean, Europe, Asia, and other exotic lands.

But don't worry. If you prefer to keep your feet planted securely on terra firma, you'll have no problem finding enough sights, shopping, and activities to make your stay seem all too short.

## A PERFECT DAY IN GREATER MIAMI

Make this a day of romance—leave the car windows down and let the wind blow through your hair. Stop at an outdoor café for a breakfast of guava pastries and strong Cuban coffee. Visit the shops in Coconut Grove, and take a rollicking rickshaw ride, or tour downtown Miami by horse and carriage. Visit the Coral Castle, Vizcaya Museum, and Fairchild Tropical Garden. If being out in the midday sun has you a little sweaty, stop for a kiss in the shade of a fragrant ylang-ylang tree. You can rent a bicycle-built-for-two and pedal around town, inhaling sea spray and jasmine. As nighttime falls, make your way over to the Bayside Marketplace and take a romantic gondola ride while you watch a laser light show at Bayfront Park, or charter a boat for a moonlight sail. Feel

### SIGHTS

- A American Police Hall of Fame and Museum
- B Biltmore Hotel
- C Caribbean Marketplace
- D Fairchild Tropical Garden
- E Little Havana, Miami
- F Metro-Dade Cultural Center
- G Metrozoo
- H Miami Museum of Science and Space Transit Planetarium

### SIGHTS *(continued)*

- I Miami Seaquarium
- J Monkey Jungle
- K Parrot Jungle and Gardens
- L Venetian Pool
- M Vizcaya Museum and Gardens

### LODGING

- N Best Western Marina Park Hotel
- B Biltmore Hotel
- O Coconut Grove Bed & Breakfast

### LODGING *(continued)*

- P Don Shula's Hotel & Golf Club
- Q Everglades Hotel
- R Hotel Place St. Michel
- S Miami River Inn
- T Riviera Court
- U Silver Sands Beach Resort
- U Sonesta Beach Resort Hotel
- V Turnberry Isle Resort & Club

*Note: Items with the same letter are located in the same place.*

like dancing? Dress, dress, dress, and choose a club with pulsing lights and a sensuous salsa beat, or enjoy a little cheek-to-cheek at a smoky jazz café.

## SIGHTSEEING HIGHLIGHTS

### ★★★★ BILTMORE HOTEL

**1200 Anastasia Ave., Coral Gables, 800/727-1926 or 305/445-1926**

If you can't muster the lucre to spend an evening, it's worth a visit just to stroll the grounds of this Old World European–style hotel, from which gangster Al Capone once conducted his questionable affairs. It's been designated as a National Historic Landmark, and its 315-foot tower looms over the city. Historic tours are complimentary. The classical statuary between the columns surrounding a huge pool recalls a grand version of the Roman Baths, and you can relax with a cool drink at the poolside café. If you enjoy a good cigar, stop by the cigar shop in the lower lobby for one of the area's best. Al would have.

***Details:*** *Open daily. Tours Sun, 1:30, 2:30, and 3:30 p.m. Free.*

### ★★★★ METROZOO

**12400 S.W. 152nd St. (Coral Reef Dr.), Miami, 305/251-0401**

Some of the world's most beautiful and endangered animals roam freely in settings similar to their natural habitats in this premier cageless zoo. Take the air-conditioned monorail for a cool overview of the zoo's 290 acres of free-roaming primates, antelopes, elephants, koalas, blood pythons, and large cats. Pathways and animal displays are creatively landscaped and a picnic area is available for lunch, whether you buy it here or bring your own. Don't miss the Asian River Life exhibit, where you can walk among waterfalls amid a tropical mist and the exotic sounds of wild Asian animals, such as otters, leopards, water monitors, and Muntjac deer. Also top-notch is Wings of Asia, a free-flight aviary and rain forest that's home to hundreds of vibrantly colored birds. Elephant rides, a pair of primitive-looking Komodo dragons, and a petting area with a ferret and pot-bellied pig are highlights for youngsters.

***Details:*** *U.S. 1 to S.W. 152nd St., then west three miles. Open daily 9:30–5:30. Admission: $8 adults, $4 children. (half-day minimum)*

**786 OR 305**

Greater Miami has an "overlay" telephone area code system, in which two area codes, 786 and 305, may apply to phones across the street from or next door to each other, or even to a phone and fax within the same office.

## ★★★★ VIZCAYA MUSEUM AND GARDENS

**3251 S. Miami Ave., Coconut Grove, 305/250-9133**

International Harvester farming-equipment magnate James Deering hired a tenth of Miami's 1914 population as labor, it is said, and put more than $15 million into this palatial estate at the edge of Biscayne Bay. Serene, formal botanical gardens with decorative statuary, fountains, reflecting pools, and a maze of canals ring the vast 10-acre Italian Renaissance–style villa. Romantics will find the gardens delightful for an afternoon stroll. One Roman altar is thought to be from the first century A.D. The mansion's 34 elaborately appointed rooms and halls are adorned with frescoed ceilings and priceless European antiques, art, and tapestries. A huge, carved-stone gondola serves as a breakwater in the bay behind the house.

***Details:*** *Open daily 9:30–4:30 (gardens until 5:30). Admission: $10 adults, $5 children. (2 hours)*

## ★★★ FAIRCHILD TROPICAL GARDEN

**10901 Old Cutler Rd., Miami, 305/667-1651**

The fragrance of the ylang-ylang tree, the primary ingredient in Chanel No. 5, perfumes the air at this 83-acre expanse of exotic plants, flowers, rain forest, streams, and waterfalls. The guided tram tour is just the thing to get you oriented, or open the pamphlet provided and set off at your own pace to explore the lush, well-signed trails lined with flowers, unusual trees, and extraordinary beauty. This is one of the largest tropical parks in the country, known worldwide among botanists for its variety and preservation of endangered species of palms. The gardens, lakes, and grottos are magnificent. Look for the Moos Memorial Sunken Garden, a private oasis surrounded by towering palms, ferns, and flowers, created in a natural sinkhole.

**Details:** *Open daily 9:30–4:30. Admission: $8 adults, children free. (1 1/2–2 hours)*

### ★★★ METRO-DADE CULTURAL CENTER

**101 W. Flagler St. at First Ave., Miami, 305/375-1700**

A Mediterranean-style plaza and cascading fountains lend Old World ambience to this handsome complex, each entity of which is worth a visit. The **Miami Fine Arts Museum**, 305/375-3000, is itself a visual masterpiece, featuring major touring exhibitions of contemporary art and works of international artists. Lectures and concerts at the four-story **Miami-Dade Public Library**, 305/375-2665, are open to the public, and the facility houses nearly four million books, including a stellar collection of Florida-related titles. The **Historical Museum of Southern Florida,** 305/375-1492, illuminates the area's history over the last 10,000 years, including the days of Indian camps through the boom years of the '20s, and Miami's golden years as the nation's playground. Be sure to see the extensive photo library, with thousands of photos that bring Florida's evolution to life.

**Details:** *Library open Mon–Sat 9–6 (Thu 9–9), free. Art museum open Tue–Fri 10–5 (Thu 10–9), Sat–Sun noon–5; $5 adults, children free, $2.50 students/seniors, Thu evening free to all. Historical museum open Mon–Sat 9–5 (Thu 9–9), Sun noon–5; $4 adults, $2 children, $3 seniors, by donation Mon. Combo tickets available at Cultural Center. (1 hour minimum)*

### ★★★ MIAMI SEAQUARIUM

**4400 Rickenbacker Cswy., Miami, 305/361-5705, www.miamiseaquarium.com**

This 35-acre attraction, bordered by water on three sides, has been entertaining Miami visitors for more than 40 years. Its biggest stars include 20-foot-long Lolita, a 3 1/2-ton killer whale, plus TV superstar Flipper. (You can even see the original set used in Flipper's TV series.) The Top Deck Dolphin Show features high-flying Atlantic bottlenose dolphins, and Salty the Sea Lion and her slippery friends put on a hilarious show. The Seaquarium also has an excellent manatee exhibit that highlights the efforts of its Marine Mammal Rescue Team.

**Details:** *Open daily 9:30–6. Admission: $19.95 adults, $14.95 children, $16.95 seniors. (3–5 hours)*

## ★★ AMERICAN POLICE HALL OF FAME AND MUSEUM

**3801 Biscayne Blvd. (U.S. 1), Miami 305/573-0070**

Test your sleuthing skills and try to catch the bad guy in a mock crime scene at this museum, which highlights the history of crime fighting. You'll see jail-cell replicas, gruesome execution equipment, and more than 10,000 items pertaining to past and present modes of law enforcement. Included are a gas chamber, an electric chair you can actually sit in, an authentic guillotine, gangster memorabilia, and weapons confiscated from real-life villains. The primary exhibit is a memorial to the thousands of U.S. police officers who've been killed in the line of duty.

***Details:*** *Open daily 10–5:30. Admission: $6 adults, $4 seniors, $3 children, $1 police officers. (1 hour)*

## ★★ LITTLE HAVANA, MIAMI

**SW Eighth Street between S.W. 12th and S.W. 22nd Avenues, Miami**

Music stores with flashing neon signs blast passersby with a salsa beat; old men in guayabera shirts play chess or dominoes on benches; young men ogle women sauntering past in short, tight skirts; and everybody now is smoking cigars! The older architecture of Little Havana reflects its early Spanish influence. Wander onto the side streets and perhaps nobody will speak English. Stop at one of the bakeries for a tasty guava-filled pastry and *café con leche*, but beware the high-octane *café Cubano* (espresso), which is intensely different from its Italian counterpart. (Some say it's an acquired taste; others liken it to motor oil!)

From the first Saturday of March through the following Sunday, Carnaval Miami, an enormous street party, draws about a million revelers to the streets of Miami, mostly to Little Havana, for music, dancing, street performers, costume parties, fireworks, and tons of Cuban food.

## ★★ MIAMI MUSEUM OF SCIENCE AND SPACE TRANSIT PLANETARIUM

**3280 S. Miami Ave., Miami, 305/854-4247 (museum), 305/854-4242 (planetarium)**

National touring and permanent exhibits at the **Miami Museum of Science** offer hands-on activities for all ages. The museum also features presentations about Florida fauna and flora, a natural history gallery, and a wildlife center. Computer types can play virtual-reality basketball in CyberCity, while other exhibits feature insects, lizards, frogs, and snakes. The **Space Transit Planetarium** offers multimedia laser and star shows daily, an observatory on Saturday evenings, and telescopic viewing; free space lectures are given Fridays and Saturdays (call for times).

**Details:** *Open daily 10–6. Museum admission: $6 adults, $4 children and seniors. Planetarium admission: $5 adults, $2.50 children; with laser show, $6 adults, $3 children. Combo tickets available. (2 hours museum, 1 1/2 hours planetarium)*

## ★★ PARROT JUNGLE AND GARDENS

**11000 S.W. 57th Ave. at S.W. 112th St., S. Miami, 305/666-7834, www.parrotjungle.com**

One of Miami's oldest and best-known attractions, this institution opened just before Christmas in 1936, on the site of a former nudist colony. Back then, visitors paid 25 cents to see Franz Scherr's tropical parrot paradise. Today, parrots, macaws, cockatoos, flamingos, and other exotic birds ride bikes, roller-skate, shoot hoops, pose coyly, and fly freely about in this subtropical jungle of flowering trees, shrubs, orchids, and bromeliads. Bring film and a camera—if you want, you can hold a friendly scarlet macaw on your arm (they're heavier than they look). Wander along the winding paths and you'll find a baby-bird area, wildlife and reptile shows, baby apes, gators, and a petting zoo and playground.

**Details:** *Open daily 9:30–6. Admission: $12.95 adults, $8.95 children, $11.95 seniors. (half-day)*

## ★★ VENETIAN POOL

**2701 DeSoto Blvd., Coral Gables, 305/460-5356**

What was once an abandoned, unsightly coral rock quarry is now a historic landmark and gorgeous, spring-fed public swimming lagoon that's surrounded by caves, waterfalls, stone bridges, tropical flowers, and palm trees. The Venetian-style architecture of the adjacent buildings makes this an attraction worth seeing, even if you don't intend to take a dip.

**Details:** *Open Tue–Fri 11–5:30, Sat–Sun 10–4:30. Admission: $5 adults, $2–$4 children (under 3 not allowed in pool). (1–2 hours)*

## ★ CARIBBEAN MARKETPLACE

**Little Haiti, 5927 N.E. Second Ave., Miami, 305/751-2251**

You'll think you've stepped into the Iron Market in Haiti's Port-au-

Prince when you enter this quaint and colorful open-air marketplace. Vendors with lilting accents call you "hon" and "ma'am," as they tend their stalls selling Caribbean art, clothing, exotic fruits, spices, and Creole delicacies. Caribbean and Creole musicians perform on weekends between the brightly painted bungalows.

***Details:*** *Open Tue–Thu 10:30–7, Fri–Sat 10:30–9, Sun 10:30–5. Free.*

### ★ MONKEY JUNGLE

**14805 S.W. 216th St., S. Miami, 305/235-1611**

It's the visitors who are caged here. They're enclosed in an observation tunnel, while bands of free-roaming chimpanzees, gorillas, orangutans, and baboons swing freely through a natural habitat that resembles a lush Amazonian rain forest. Call ahead for feeding times if you want to enjoy the most entertaining visit: The monkeys dive into a pool for crabs and fruit treats.

***Details:*** *Located three miles west of U.S. 1. Open daily 9:30–5. Admission: $11.50 adults, $6 children, $9.50 seniors. (2–3 hours)*

## FITNESS AND RECREATION

Natural and man-made sporting opportunities in the Greater Miami area make it a magnet for sports enthusiasts. Professional sports teams include baseball's **Florida Marlins**, 305/626-7400; the NBA's **Miami Heat**, 305/530-4400; the NFL's **Miami Dolphins**, 305/623-6100; and the NHL's **Florida Panthers**, who play just north of Dade County in Sunrise, 954/835-7000.

Fishing is excellent from the piers and bridges, and all kinds of boats are available for hire, with or without captains. The calm waters around Key Biscayne or the Miami River make the area popular with windsurfers and sailors. Diving and snorkeling trips may be arranged to **Biscayne National Underwater Park**, and glass-bottom boat trips leave daily from the Convoy Point Visitor Center on S.W. 328th St., 305/230-1100.

Pari-mutuel wagering is exceptionally popular throughout South Florida. Dog-racing tracks include **Flagler Greyhound Track** and **Biscayne Kennel Club**, both in Miami, and **Hollywood Greyhound Track** in Hollywood. Horse-racing fans have several choices of where to place their bets, including **Calder Broward Race Course**, 305/625-1311; **Hialeah Park**, 305/885-8000, with its lush tropical landscaping, formal gardens, and striking French Mediterranean–style clubhouse; or **Gulfstream Park Race Track** in

# GREATER MIAMI

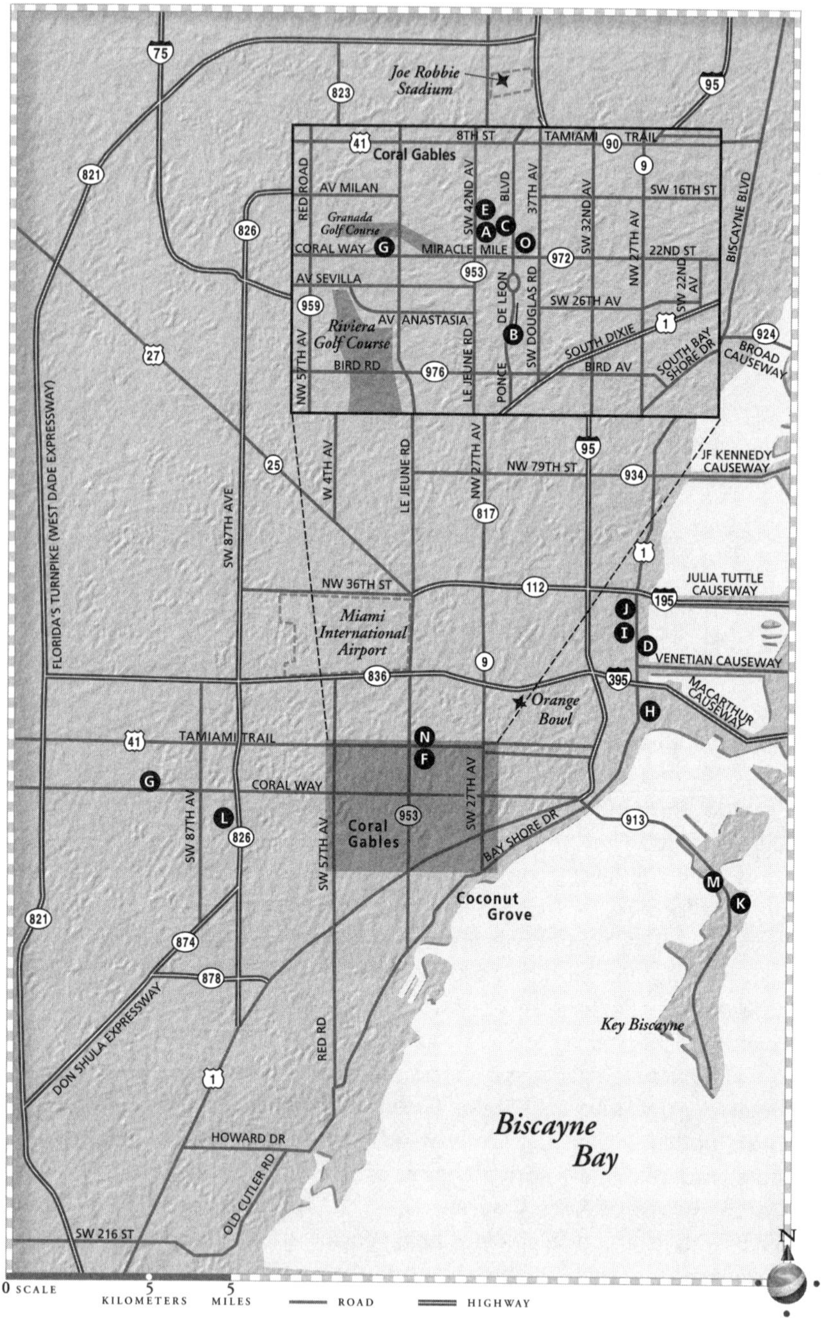

Hallandale, 954/454-7000. The **Miami Jai Alai Fronton**, 305/633-6400, offers high-speed Basque-style sporting action year-round.

Subtropical surroundings and cooling sea breezes make Greater Miami one of the country's most beautiful year-round golf destinations. Outstanding courses abound, including the world-class Blue Monster at the **Doral Golf Resort and Spa**, 305/592-2000, home of the Doral-Ryder Open.

## FOOD

The assortment of restaurants in the Greater Miami area is staggering, from New World cuisine to European standards; small, ethnic cafés and trendy, modern bistros to superstar-owned restaurants; and everything in between.

In Coral Gables, if you love meat and plenty of it, you'll rave about **Christy's**, 3101 Ponce de Leon Blvd. (Malaga Ave.), 305/446-1400, a terrific steak house that's also noted for great lamb and Caesar salads. **Darbar**, 276 Alhambra Cir., 305/448-9691 serves top-notch Indian food including curries, tandoori chicken, and fragrant basmati rice at moderate prices. For the best in Italian cuisine, at prices to match, treat yourself to dinner at **Giacosa**, 394 Giralda Ave., 305/445-5858, or the **Caffe Abbracci**, 318 Aragon Ave., 305/441-0700, where the service and food are always top-flight. Svelte women in native Thai dress serve creative, upscale cuisine at the **Thai Orchid**, 317 Miracle Mile, 305/443-6364, where Asian art and exotic flowers set the stage for a saucy, sensual dining experience. For nouvelle Cuban dishes, visit **Yuca**, 177 Giralda Ave., 305/444-4448, where a torchy chanteuse performs in the evenings.

In Miami, Chinese food doesn't get any better than at the **Tropical Chinese Restaurant**, 7991 S.W. 40th St., 305/262-7576, where service and

---

### FOOD

- A Caffe Abbracci
- B Christy's
- C Darbar
- D Fish Market
- E Giacosa
- F Hy-Vong
- G Latin American Cafeteria
- H Le Pavillon
- I S & S Restaurant
- J Smitty's
- K Sundays on the Bay
- A Thai Orchard
- L Tropical Chinese Restaurant
- M Two Dragons
- N Versailles Restaurant
- O Yuca

*Note: Items with the same letter are located in the same area.*

the dim sum are outstanding. One of the most popular chains among the city's Latinos, the mom 'n' pop **Latin American Cafeteria** has several locations serving good, cheap Cuban fare, including 2940 Coral Way, 305/448-6809, and 9796 Coral Way, 305/226-2393. In Little Havana, the **Versailles Restaurant,** 3555 S.W. Eighth St. at 36th Ave., 305/445-7614, serves great Cuban sandwiches in a kitschy, mirrored dining room.

Fans of Vietnamese foods may have to wait out on the street to get a table at the unassuming and pleasantly inexpensive **Hy-Vong**, 3458 S.W. Eighth St., Miami, 305/446-3674. It's no wonder. Those in the know come here often for delicious authentic dishes such as squid salad or spicy pork in coconut milk. For lunch only, American "blue-collar" foods are dished up in hearty portions at the inexpensive **Smitty's**, 3195 N.E. Second Ave., Miami, 305/573-3162. Downtown, don't bypass the hole-in-the-wall, diner-style **S & S Restaurant**, 1757 N.E. Second Ave., 305/373-4291, which offers home cooking, such as open-face turkey sandwiches, to a busy lunchtime crowd who wait for stools at the counter. For fine dining, two hotel restaurants are excellent: Try the **Fish Market** in the Crowne Plaza Hotel, 1601 Biscayne Blvd., 305/374-0000, for creative seafood and desserts in a setting of mirrors and marble, or the Intercontinental Hotel's highly regarded **Le Pavillon**, 100 Chopin Plaza, 305/577-1000, whose French continental menu makes prominent use of local ingredients.

Just past the Seaquarium, on the right at the northern end of Key Biscayne, **Sundays on the Bay**, 5420 Crandon Blvd., 305/361-6777, can be noisy but has a bountiful Sunday brunch and a sunset view. For romantic Mandarin and Szechuan dining, try **Two Dragons** at the Sonesta Beach Resort, 350 Ocean Dr. (Crandon Blvd.), Key Biscayne, 305/361-2021, with its black-lacquer furnishings and wicker seating; prices tend to be high, but food and service are outstanding.

## LODGING

Staying in the more upscale cities of southeast Florida can set you back a pretty penny for lodging, but the high-priced hoteliers here know how to put on the dog.

For the ultimate in exclusivity north of Miami in Aventura, the **Turnberry Isle Resort & Club**, 19999 W. Country Club Dr., 305/932-6200, is the place to stay in an elegant, residential setting. Amenities include two championship golf courses; 20 tennis courts; racquetball courts; and enough saunas, steam baths, and whirlpools to drown a grouper; and the resort's landscaping is drop-dead gorgeous. In Miami Lakes, athletes and sports fans opt for **Don**

**Shula's Hotel & Golf Club**, 15255 Bull Run Rd., 305/821-1150, which has a variety of higher-priced accommodations. The facility offers professional health programs, lighted tennis courts, racquetball, a championship golf course, and another 18-hole par-3 that's lighted for night play. The consistently top-rated Shula's Steakhouse on the premises is decorated with Miami Dolphins memorabilia.

In downtown Miami, adjacent to the Bayside Marketplace Village shopping area and opposite the Port of Miami, the 17-story 1926 **Everglades Hotel**, 244 Biscayne Blvd., 800/327-5700 or 305/379-5461, is moderately priced and offers a large rooftop pool and bar with sweeping views overlooking Biscayne Bay. Just north, the **Best Western Marina Park Hotel**, 340 Biscayne Blvd., 800/526-5655 or 305/371-4400, also convenient to the port, has a comfortable, European ambience. Right on the river downtown, your bed and breakfast are reasonable in several historic buildings with early-1900s antiques-furnished rooms or apartments at the **Miami River Inn**, 118 S.W. South River Dr., 305/325-0045.

Lavish Mediterranean architecture and landscaped parkways are the rule in the lovely planned community of Coral Gables. The Old World ambience of the **Hotel Place St. Michel**, 162 Alcazar Ave., 305/444-1666, gives it the warm, welcoming feeling of a European pension. Rooms are furnished with antiques and fresh flowers, the restaurant is top-notch, and breakfast of fresh croissants is served in your room or the downstairs sitting room. Coral Gables' 1925 landmark, the crescent-shaped **Biltmore Hotel**, 1200 Anastasia Ave, 800/228-3000 or 305/445-1926, attracts the beautiful people from around the world. If money's no object (and we mean it), you might reserve the posh Everglades tower suite that once sheltered Al Capone from his enemies, with its 360-degree view of the area. Perhaps you'll swim in the huge hotel pool, the former aquatic stage of Esther Williams, or simply sit with a book and admire the hand-painted ceilings in one of the lavishly appointed public rooms. For a well maintained family-style motel, try the **Riviera Court**, 5100 Riviera Dr. at U.S. 1, 800/368-8602 or 305/665-3528, which is reasonably priced for the area and overlooks a scenic waterway.

In Coconut Grove, the 1900-vintage **Coconut Grove Bed & Breakfast**, 4286 Douglas Rd., 800/339-9430 or 305/665-2274, offers spacious, bright second-floor suites, gourmet breakfasts, and a guest membership to an exclusive island resort.

On Key Biscayne, the pyramid-shaped **Sonesta Beach Resort Hotel**, 350 Ocean Dr., 800/766-3782 or 305/361-2021, is a deluxe, 292-room complex whose amenities include several good restaurants, a palm tree–studded oceanfront pool, water-sports activities and rentals, and a fitness

## HOMESTEAD

*Homestead, about 30 miles southwest of Miami, sits on the edge of the Everglades and offers a few sights of its own.*

*The word "farm" usually calls to mind a totally different type of facility, but* **Everglades Alligator Farm** *(40351 S.W. 192nd Ave., Homestead, 305/247-2628) is a real, working alligator farm, with alligators from eggs to adults and every stage in between. Alligator shows, snake shows, and alligator feedings are held several times a day; it's amazing to watch how the local Indians used to capture some of the larger gators. Pay the extra fee for the half-hour airboat ride through the surrounding canals and into the Everglades. The farm's wild setting at the edge of the 'glades is ideal for seeing a variety of native Florida wildlife.*

*The* **Coral Castle** *(28655 S. Dixie Hwy./U.S. 1, Homestead, 305/248-6344) is an architectural wonder. A heartsick Latvian immigrant, working alone for 28 years, using only homemade pulleys and tools salvaged from junkyards, built this mammoth monument in tribute to the lovely 16-year-old bride who deserted him on their wedding night. Some say he knew the secret of the construction of the pyramids, because the mansion and its massive stone furnishings are all hand-hewn from limestone rock.*

*If you've always wanted to skydive, you can try it with a licensed instructor after only a one-hour class at* **Skydive Miami,** *Homestead General Aviation Airport, 305/759-3483. The* **Metro-Dade Homestead Motorsports Complex** *hosts a a variety of NASCAR and motorcycle competitions, including the* **Marlboro Grand Prix of Miami**.

*For lunch or dinner, try* **White Lion Cafe & Antiques**, *146 N.W. Seventh St., 305/248-1076. The menu includes meat loaf, grilled skirt steak, rumaki, and snapper, made with all-fresh ingredients like purple onions, artichoke hearts, spinach, and garlic, and served with pasta or real mashed potatoes. (Restaurant profits are donated to Alzheimer's research.)*

*If you'd like to stay the night, you'll find no frills but bright, clean rooms and inexpensive rates at the* **Everglades Motel**, *605 S. Krome Ave., 305/247-4117, or try the* **Coral Roc Motel**, *1100 N. Krome Ave., 305/247-4010, a small place with contemporary efficiencies or kitchenettes, is just over the border in Florida City.*

center; for more private accommodations, three-bedroom villas are also available. Oceanfront cottages and efficiency apartments with patios are offered at the **Silver Sands Beach Resort,** 301 Ocean Dr., 305/361-5441. Mini-suites are large rooms with pantry areas, refrigerators, and microwaves, but they're convenient and reasonable for this part of town.

## NIGHTLIFE

By night, downtown Miami is a dynamic neon rainbow of activity. To find out what's going on when you're there, pick up a free copy of *New Times*, a local arts-and-entertainment publication that's invaluable for restaurant, gallery, theater, and nightclub information.

Clubs are plentiful and ever-changing. World music or old-fashioned blues bands, Afro-Cuban drummers, sassy salsa ensembles, and flamenco dancers clattering across polished parquet floors wow audiences at lively clubs around town. You can listen to dance bands at **Tobacco Road**, 305/374-1198, a former speakeasy that held the city's first liquor license, and look for the secret closet where gaming tables and illegal hooch were stashed. **Bayside Marketplace,** 305/577-3344, which often has outdoor entertainment, also has several clubs, including Dick Clark's American Bandstand Grill.

There's usually a performance of one kind or another at the **James L. Knight International Center** or the lovely **Gusman Center for the Performing Arts**, 305/374-2444, an ornate 1920s Mediterranean palazzo built for Paramount Studios. The Gusman holds various film festivals as well as performances by the culturally diverse **New World Symphony** and widely acclaimed **Florida Philharmonic Orchestra**. One of the area's oldest cultural institutions, **Florida Grand Opera**, 305/854-1643, offers presentations of some of the most revered works in the operatic repertoire.

Performance art is plentiful in Greater Miami. In Coconut Grove, the **Coconut Grove Playhouse**, 305/442-4000, when not showing its own performances, hosts popular Broadway road shows and other events on its two stages. **Florida Shakespeare Theatre** has occasional performances at the Biltmore Hotel in Coral Gables, performing classic and contemporary drama in addition to Shakespeare's works.

Lovers of dance will find plenty of evidence of the area's diversity. Performances include modern dance, ballet, flamenco, Haitian dance, salsa, African themes, and every combination imaginable. Top companies include Miami City Ballet, Florida Dance Association, Inner City Children's Dance Company, Momentum Dance Company, and Ballet Flamenco La Rosa.

## SHOPPING

Shopping in the Greater Miami area runs the gamut from Haitian sidewalk stands to Bloomingdale's and Saks Fifth Avenue. The bargains won't be gone if you arrive after 5 a.m. at the humongous (more than 1,000 vendors on weekends) **Opa-locka/Hialeah Flea Market**, 12705 N.W. 42nd Ave., but you can start shopping that early if you want to, seven days a week. In downtown Miami, the lively and fashionable **Bayside Marketplace** at 401 Biscayne Boulevard offers more than 150 shops, restaurants, dining spots, artisans, and galleries; the spectacular waterfront setting is a great place for the street performers and open-air concerts that are held here. Nearby, the **Downtown Miami Shopping District** is the place for bargain hunters in search of electronics, trendy casual clothing, and jewelry. North of downtown in the **Miami International Arts and Design District,** you can shop for furniture, accessories, antiques, and interior-decorating items.

In Coral Gables, the **Miracle Mile** on S.W. 22nd Street between Douglas Road (S.W. 37th Avenue) and S.W. 42nd Avenue lives up to its name, comprising several blocks of elegant boutiques, specialty shops, antiques and curio stores, and international art galleries.

Coconut Grove offers two areas across the street from each other that are great for people watching or power shopping and salon hopping: the **Streets of Mayfair**, an elegant, atrium-style structure of exclusive specialty shops; and the **CocoWalk** retail and entertainment complex, a European-style open-air mall of unusual shops and outdoor bistros.

For mall shopping, the **Dadeland Mall** on Kendall Drive, between U.S. 1 and the Palmetto Expressway, is tops, housing 165 top retailers, including huge Burdines, The Limited, and Express stores, plus Lord & Taylor, Saks Fifth Avenue, a Disney Store, The Gap, and Ann Taylor. A few miles south, **The Falls** at U.S. 1 and S.W. 136th Street has a Macy's, Bloomingdale's, Coach, Pottery Barn, and 100 more stores in a beautiful complex amid tropical landscaping, lakes, and waterfalls.

For outlet shopping in Florida City, a Mediterranean-style marketplace is also the setting for the **Florida Keys Factory Shops** at 250 E. Palm Drive (S.W. 344th St.), where the Florida Turnpike meets U.S. 1. In addition to brand-name stores like Nike, Bass, Bugle Boy, Nine West, London Fog, Mikasa, and another 60, the single-story open-air complex has a small children's playground and an enclosed food court.

# 10 THE KEYS AND KEY WEST

When Henry Morrison Flagler's Florida East Coast Railway provided land access from Miami to Key West in 1912, the Keys were changed forever. In 1938 the railroad was replaced by the exotic Overseas Highway, whose 42 bridges comprise 15 percent of the 126-mile drive—if you've a fear of bridges, best to let someone else do the driving.

Mile markers along the way (indicated in this chapter as MM) tell you how far you are from the southernmost tip of the continental United States. The first and largest key, 30-mile-long Key Largo, is known as the "Sport Diving Capital of the World." Half a dozen inhabited islands comprise the Islamorada area, a sportfishing paradise with the Keys' largest charter fishing fleet. You'll pass through Conch Key, reminiscent of a tiny New England seaport; Crawl Key, named for the huge sea turtles; and Vaca Key, for the manatees, or "sea cows," found here in abundance by Spanish explorers. Less densely populated, the "Lower Keys" are home to some 300 miniature deer found nowhere else in the world.

While there's no place for memorable sunsets like Cayo Hueso, or "the island of bones," as the Spaniards originally called Key West, this eclectic, romantic community just 90 miles from Havana has much more to recommend it. Notables in its history—Ernest Hemingway, Tennessee Williams, Calvin Klein, President Harry Truman, Thomas Edison, and many others—left their mark on its quaint streets and in its historic gingerbread mansions.

# KEY WEST

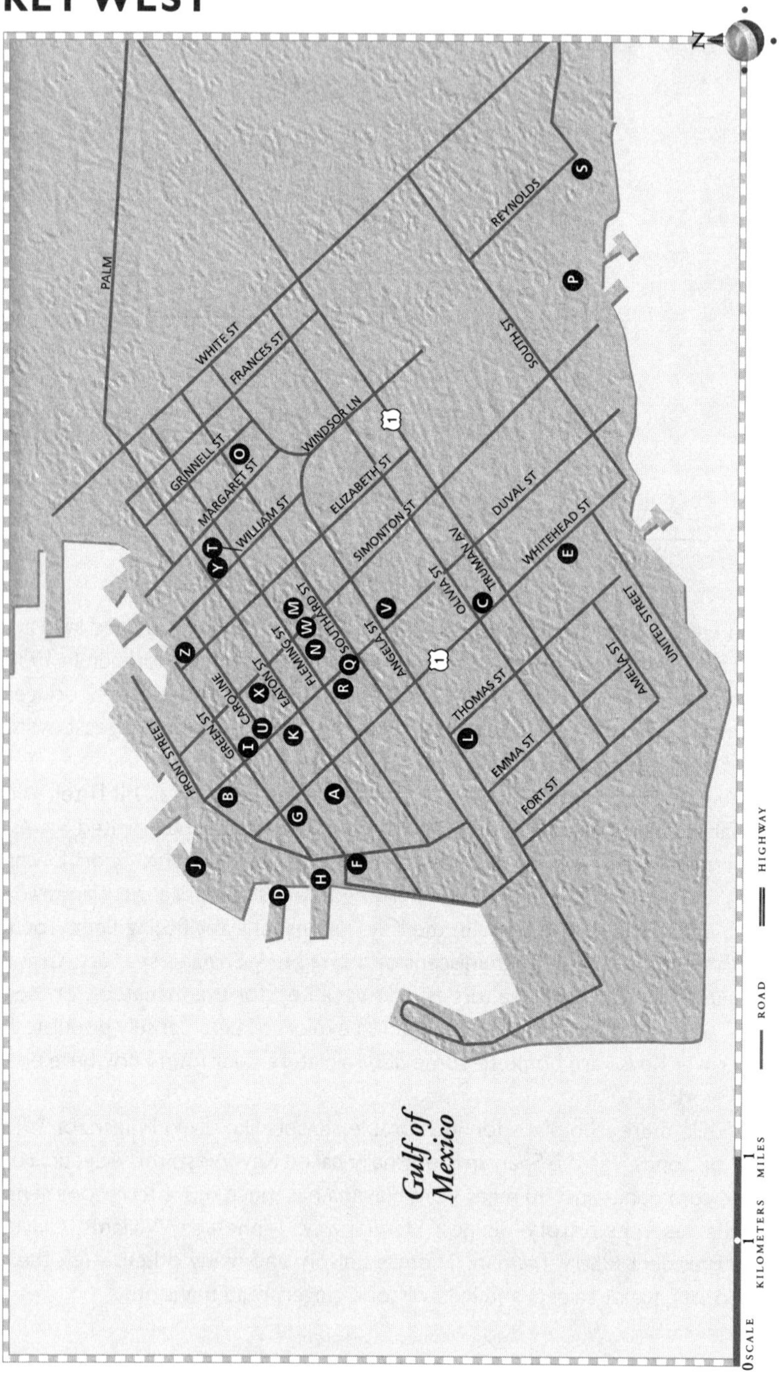
PALM
WHITE ST
FRANCES ST
GRINNELL ST
MARGARET ST
WILLIAM ST
WINDSOR LN
ELIZABETH ST
SIMONTON ST
SOUTHARD ST
FLEMING ST
EATON ST
CAROLINE
GREEN ST
FRONT STREET
ANGELA ST
OLIVIA ST
TRUMAN AV
DUVAL ST
WHITEHEAD ST
SOUTH ST
REYNOLDS
THOMAS ST
EMMA ST
FORT ST
AMELIA ST
UNITED STREET
Gulf of Mexico
HIGHWAY
ROAD
SCALE
KILOMETERS
MILES
N

High season here is during the drier months of December through April, but a summer or fall visit has its own merit. Sipping rumrunners or salty margaritas on a porch swing can be even better after a day spent amid fewer tourists, on less-crowded streets and restaurants, amid more laid-back attitudes—and at off-season rates.

## A PERFECT DAY IN THE FLORIDA KEYS

Rise with the sun at your guest house on Marathon or Islamorada and begin the scenic drive south. At MM37, stop and get some sand between your toes on the beach at Bahia Honda State Recreation Area. If you dive, stop at Looe Key National Marine Sanctuary, an underwater site renowned for its variety of coral and fish. Take a break for lunch at an open-air café with an ocean view. Then continue to Key West and rent a bike or just set off on foot to explore the island. When shadows grow long, make your way to the dock to watch a magical sunset as the sky changes from powder blue to fire and orange, violet, and indigo. Bring a few singles to tip the street performers if you enjoy their gigs. And leave your watch in your luggage. You won't need it here.

## SIGHTSEEING HIGHLIGHTS

### ★★★★ HEMINGWAY HOUSE

**907 Whitehead St., Key West, 305/294-1575**

The periwinkle-tiled swimming pool dug into the coral limestone

---

**SIGHTS**

- A Audubon House
- B Conch Tour Train
- C Hemingway House
- D Key West Aquarium
- E Key West Lighthouse
- F Little White House
- G Mel Fisher Maritime Heritage Society Museum
- H Old Town Trolley
- I Sloppy Joe's Bar
- J Sunset Celebration
- K Wrecker's Museum

**FOOD**

- L Blue Heaven
- M Cafe Marquesa
- N Fausto's Food Palace
- O Five Brothers Grocery and Sandwich Shop
- P Louie's Backyard
- Q Mangoes Restaurant
- R Margaritaville Cafe

**LODGING**

- S Casa Marina Marriott
- T Curry House Mansion
- U Curry Mansion
- V Gardens Hotel
- W Heron House
- X Simonton Court
- Y Whispers Bed & Breakfast Inn

**CAMPING**

- Z Jabour's Trailer Court

foundation here cost more than the entire house to build, but you can tour Papa Hemingway's large, airy Key West home, where he lived almost until his death in 1961, and see the desk where he wrote many of his novels, including *A Farewell to Arms* and *For Whom the Bell Tolls*. We don't know how the docents can keep track of such things, but they say the dozens of six-toed cats you'll see wandering freely about the place are all descended from the writer's own feline companions. Watch as you tour the house for a casually placed ceramic cat on an armoire—it was a gift to the writer from Picasso.

***Details:*** *Open daily 9–5. Admission: $6.50 adults, $4 children. (30–45 minutes)*

## ★★★★ MEL FISHER MARITIME HERITAGE SOCIETY MUSEUM

**200 Greene St., Key West, 305/294-2633**

Here are all the precious-metal artifacts and gold bars, jewelry, and coins you ever thought you'd see in a Spanish treasure-ship. Fisher's underwater salvage expeditions in the early 1980s yielded awesome treasures from the sunken Spanish galleons *Atocha* and *Santa Margarita*. This collection is dazzling.

***Details:*** *Open daily 9:30–5. Admission: $6 adults, $2 children. (1–2 hours)*

## ★★★★ SUNSET CELEBRATION

**Mallory Square Pier, Key West**

The whole town turns out for this nightly hippie-style happening, when musicians, magicians, mimes, and other street performers vie for attention an hour or so before sunset. Bra-less vendors in flowery dresses sell handmade candles and silver jewelry. Seers and tarot readers divine the future. A clown's costume advertises his services: "Jokes, 50¢; Better Jokes, $1.00." A bicycling juggler hoists a shopping cart onto his chin, while a guy down at the end is playing *Danny Boy* on his nose. Come at least once to watch the glorious glowing ball of the sun hover above the horizon before the last glint of hot red-and-gold light is sucked into the hungry Gulf of

*Key West is home to a large gay population. Your best source for current information on gay-friendly businesses and lodging around the city is the Key West Business Guild, 424 Fleming St., 305/294-4603.*

Mexico. Some of the mesmerized crowd break into applause; some drift away. Still others just stare reverently, as if maybe, if they wait long enough or wish hard enough, there will be an encore. There will be—tomorrow.

## ★★★ CONCH TOUR TRAIN/OLD TOWN TROLLEY

**Conch Tour Train, 1 Key Lime Sq., Key West, 305/294-5161; Old Town Trolley, 1910 N. Roosevelt Blvd., 305/296-6688**

Owned by the same parent company, these tour vehicles run every 20 to 30 minutes. The tours will help familiarize you with the layout of the island, passing more than 100 of Key West's sites on a route once traveled by horse-drawn trolleys. Tours feature a running narration of island lore, legend, local color, and easy commentary provided by personable driver/guides. The Conch Train, an open tram, offers a continuous 90-minute tour, while the enclosed Trolley lets you get on and off all day long.

***Details:*** *Tours daily 9–6 (varies seasonally). Admission: $14–$15 adults, $6 children. (1 1/2 hours)*

## ★★★ FORT JEFFERSON NATIONAL PARK

**Dry Tortugas**

Well off the beaten track in the Dry Tortugas, just 70 miles southwest of Key West, this largest of the nineteenth-century American coastal forts is accessible by a low-altitude seaplane in just about half an hour. Your pilot directs your attention to the sights below, circling for photo opportunities: A huge turtle or barracuda, the lighthouse at Loggerhead Key, or the wreckage of the *Atocha*, the legendary Spanish galleon whose treasure Mel Fisher recovered in 1985. Brown noddies, pelicans, and frigate birds cruise above the clear, shallow Gulf of Mexico, searching for fish and squid. As the seaplane approaches the Tortugas, a spectacular hexagonal structure comes into view, afloat on the glistening azure surface: The ghostly remains of Fort Jefferson cover virtually the entire 16 acres of sun-baked Garden Key.

The plane beaches at the fort's entrance and cuts the engines. But for a gust of wind or the raucous calls of gulls and terns perched on the pilings, the stillness enshrouds you. A 70-foot moat surrounds the half-mile perimeter of the red-brick monolith that slumbers in the bright tropical sunshine. Its eight-foot-thick walls stand 50 feet high. Still in amazingly good condition, the remains of two huge buildings, foundations of the officers' quarters and soldiers' barracks, can

FORT JEFFERSON NATIONAL PARK

David J. Wilson

be explored in a self-guided tour. You can easily find the dark, stark brick cell occupied by Dr. Samuel Mudd from 1865 to 1869 after he was imprisoned by the federal government for treating the broken leg of Abraham Lincoln's assassin, John Wilkes Booth.

Diving and snorkeling are spectacular, and various charter boats and flying services can take you out to swim, snorkel, and explore the old fort. It's a visually splendid day trip. Limited camping permits are available through the Everglades National Park office, 305/242-7700.

***Details:*** *Open Mon–Fri 8–6 (varies seasonally). Transportation: The Yankee Freedom, 800/634-0939; Key West Air Service, 888/359-3678 or 786/292-5201; Seaplanes of Key West, 800/950-2359; Key West Seaplane Service, 305/294-6978. (4 hours minimum)*

## ★★★ SLOPPY JOE'S BAR

### 201 Duval St., Key West, 305/294-5717

If you have only one beer while you're in Key West, have it here. You might also shoot a game of pool in the cantina behind the louvered doors where Ernest Hemingway did his drinking—that's Papa at the typewriter in the painting behind the bar. (Beware the signature Hemingway Hammer potion, made with 151-proof rum.) The old watering hole looks to have endured little, if any, renovation over the years, and has all the color an old Key West bar should, with its uneven floors, seedy tattooed sots, and old beer smells.

***Details:*** *Hours vary. Free.*

### ★★ AUDUBON HOUSE

**205 Whitehead St., Key West, 305/294-2116**

Red and magenta bougainvilleas, birds-of-paradise, hibiscus, and jasmine thrive in the lovely tropical gardens here. Ships' carpenters built this meticulously crafted three-story structure in the early 1800s for Capt. John Geiger. Though the renowned artist/ornithologist never lived here, John James Audubon was a visitor of the Geiger family, and his lithographs are on display throughout the home.

***Details:*** *Open daily 9:30–5. Admission: $7.50 adults, $2 children. (1 hour)*

### ★★ KEY WEST AQUARIUM

**1 Whitehead St., Key West, 305/296-2051**

Though this small, low-tech aquarium is more than a half-century old, it does provide a close-up look at a wide variety of underwater life commonly found in the Keys, including giant grouper, moray eels, barracuda, and tarpon. Touch tanks allow you to feel and hold some of the marine life you'll likely see offshore, including small sharks; friendly docents offer encouragement for the timid. Ask for times of daily shark and turtle feedings.

***Details:*** *On Mallory Square. Open daily 10–6. Admission: $6.50 adults, $3.50 children. (1–1 ½ hours)*

### ★★ LITTLE WHITE HOUSE

**111 Front St., Key West, 305/294-9911**

The Harry S. Truman Annex, adjacent to the U.S. submarine base at the edge of the sea where the Gulf of Mexico meets the Atlantic Ocean, was President Harry S. Truman's home away from Washington. The Little White House here was his private residence while visiting Key West. Inside you can see the home as it was furnished when he lived here, including his favorite poker table. On the tour you'll get a good feel for the man, as a docent describes the president's fondness for card playing. If it's not volunteered, ask for the story about Truman's daughter Margaret's musical debut.

# The Overseas Highway to Key West

Stretching southwest from Key Largo, the scenic, 113-mile Overseas Highway is the only land route to Key West. The drive takes about 2 1/2 hours total, but there are plenty of interesting things to see along the way.

For outstanding snorkeling and scuba diving, stop at **Key Largo,** home of **John Pennekamp Coral Reef State Park** (see "Fitness and Recreation," page TK) and **Key Largo Undersea Park** (MM 103.2; tel. 305/451-2353). A ride on the ***Key Largo Princess* glass-bottom boat** (305/451-4655) lets you stay dry and still see the dazzling undersea life. The original, charcoal-powered ***African Queen*** steamboat (skippered by Humphrey Bogart in the film of the same name) is often docked at the Holiday Inn Key Largo Marina; call 305/451-2121 for more information.

**Islamorada** (pronounced EYE-lah-more-AH-dah) is renowned for sport fishing and has a number of great shops and art galleries.

For a pleasant half-day side trip, stop at MM 78 on Indian Key Fill for an excursion either to the 10-acre island **Indian Key State Historic Site**, once a prosperous settlement owing its wealth to the salvage business, or to **Lignumvitae Key State Botanical Site**, where rangers lead walks through virgin tropical forest.

In **Marathon** hike the nature trails at the **Museum of Natural History (305/743-9100)** or take a tram to historic **Pigeon Key**. The original 1950s *Flipper* movie was shot at **Dolphin Research Center** on Grassy Key (MM 59, 305/289-1121), where visitors who make reservations 30 days in advance can swim with the dolphins.

**The Lower Keys** are perhaps the most ecologically attuned of the Keys and natural activities here abound. A great beach and dive shop beckons at **Bahia Honda State Park** (MM 37, 305/872-2353), while birdwatchers can observe rare endangered species at the **Great White Heron National Wildlife Refuge**. Early morning or late afternoon hours are best for spotting the two-foot-high white-tailed Key deer that live in the **National Key Deer Refuge**, which is headquartered, ironically, in Big Pine Shopping Plaza at MM 30.5. Call 305/872-2239 for information on the deer and great white heron refuges.

***Details:*** *Open daily 9–5. Admission: $7.50 adults, $3.75 children. (1 hour)*

### ★★ WRECKERS' MUSEUM

**322 Duval St., Key West, 305/294-9502**

Also called the Oldest House, this is the former residence of a sea captain, a dashing "wrecker" who risked his life to sail the treacherous reefs in search of treasure and adventure. Owing to its bottom-heavy, shiplike design, the building has survived dozens of storms. Friendly guides lead you into another era as you look at the ship models, an 1824 insurance policy, and little girls' playthings belonging to some of the home's inhabitants since 1829.

***Details:*** *Open daily 10–4. Admission: $4 adults, 50¢ children. (30–45 minutes)*

### ★ KEY WEST LIGHTHOUSE

**938 Whitehead St., Key West, 305/294-0012**

The oddest thing about this 1848 lighthouse is that it's several blocks from the water. It is on the island's high point, though, and you can tour the lighthouse-keeper's house, which now holds a museum of lighthouse and Key West memorabilia. Climb the 88 steps to the top, stand inside the lens, and get a great view of Key West.

***Details:*** *Open daily 9–5. Admission: $5 adults, $1 children. (1 hour)*

## FITNESS AND RECREATION

Diving, snorkeling, and fishing and sailing excursions and charters are available throughout the Keys. Key Largo has long enjoyed a reputation as the Sport Diving Capital of the World, due in no small part to the world-famous **John Pennekamp Coral Reef State Park**, MM 102.5, 305/451-1202, a fragile underwater wonderland that also offers phenomenal sailing. The Keys' premier dive site is world-famous for its 178-nautical-mile underwater garden of living coral reefs, sea grass beds, and mangrove swamps. The natural habitat is home to more than 300 species of fish and dozens of varieties of coral. Nondivers can enjoy its breathtaking beauty via a glass-bottom boat tour or by renting a boat, canoe, kayak, or sailboat. Call for details on sailing, snorkeling, boat tours, or open-water and night diving. The dive shop offers instruction, equipment, and watercraft rentals. The visitors center and family recreation area offers bumper boats, seacycles, and rafts.

# FLORIDA KEYS

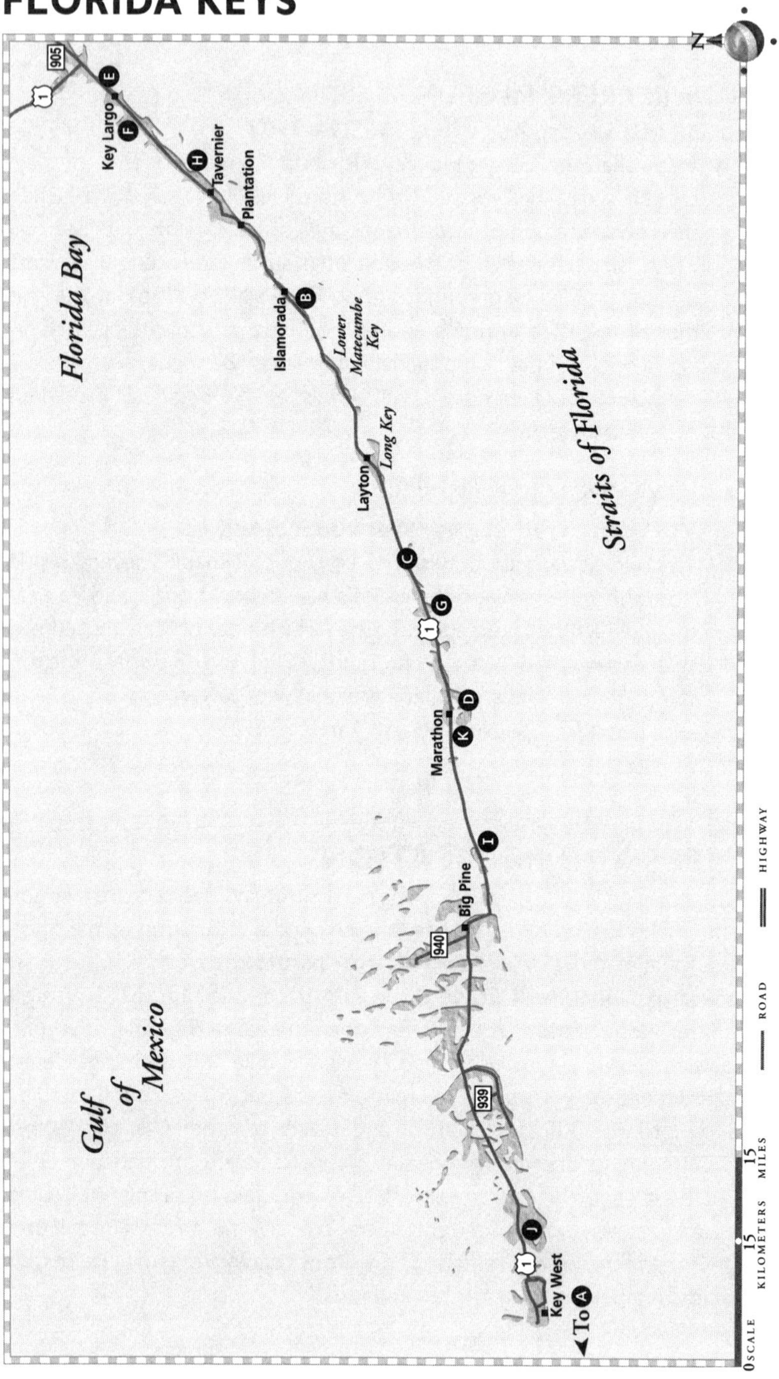

The Islamorada area is particularly renowned among fishermen for prize tarpon, bonefish, snook, permit, redfish, trout, and grouper. Boat rentals and charters are readily available.

In Key West, a number of dive companies are located around Mallory Square and along Duval Street, including **Dive Masters of the Keys**, 305/292-9110, and **Key West Pro Dive**, 305/296-3823. Bicycling is a great way to get some exercise while exploring the side streets and seeing the whole island. Several shops and some of the guest houses offer rentals. Guided bike tours are available through **Lloyd's Original Nature Bike Tours**, 305/294-1882.

## FOOD

Just about every restaurant in the Keys has a liquor license, but some are more bar-like than others. Most are fine for family dining. In Islamorada, the **Green Turtle Inn,** MM81.5, 305/664-9031, is legendary for its fresh seafood, turtle soup, and Key lime pie at moderate prices in a casual, roadhouse-type '40s-style atmosphere. More laid-back is the **Hog Heaven Sports Bar**, MM85.3 Oceanside, 305/664-9669, which features man-sized steaks and sandwiches, several big-screen TVs, and a bar that stays open until 4 a.m. For a romantic spot to dine and watch the sunset, ask for a window at **Lorelei Restaurant and Cabana Bar** at the Yacht Basin, 305/664-4657, or the two-level **Marker 88** at MM88 on Plantation Key, 305/852-9315, both are well-patronized by locals because of their outstanding food.

In Key West's Bahama Village, try the huge, fruit-filled Caribbean-style pancakes in the small indoor dining room at **Blue Heaven**, 729 Thomas St., 305/296-8666, or eat outdoors—if you don't mind the resident chickens and

---

### SIGHTS

- Ⓐ Fort Jefferson National Park

### FOOD

- Ⓑ Green Turtle Inn
- Ⓑ Hog Heaven Sports Bar
- Ⓑ Lorelei Restaurant and Cabana Bar
- Ⓑ Marker 88

### LODGING

- Ⓑ Cheeca Lodge
- Ⓑ Hampton Inn & Suites
- Ⓒ Hawk's Cay Resort and Marina
- Ⓓ Hopp-Inn Guest House
- Ⓔ Jules' Undersea Lodge
- Ⓕ Kona Kai Resort
- Ⓑ Pelican Cove Resort

### LODGING *(continued)*

- Ⓖ Rainbow Bend Fishing Resort
- Ⓗ Tavernier Hotel

### CAMPING

- Ⓘ Bahia Honda State Park
- Ⓙ Boyd's Campground
- Ⓚ Knights Key Park

*Note: Items with the same letter are located in the same place.*

dogs that may come looking for a handout. **Mangoes Restaurant,** 700 Duval St., 305/292-4606, is an open-air favorite of the conchs (locals), with a shady corner patio where you can sit and watch the goings-on in Old Town. For an intimate atmosphere and fine dining, visit the **Cafe Marquesa**, serving creative continental dishes in the Marquesa Hotel, 600 Fleming St., 305/292-1244, an old, high-ceilinged conch mansion. **Louie's Backyard**, 700 Waddell Ave., 305/294-1061, is renowned for attractive presentations of Cuban, Caribbean, and "Floribbean" specialties; unfortunately, despite the high prices, service can be a tad plodding. If so, just sit back and enjoy the gorgeous view of the Atlantic or dine under the huge banyan trees in the backyard.

On a more casual note, you'll find the Key West ambience is everything you'd hoped for at Jimmy Buffett's **Margaritaville Cafe**, 500 Duval St., 305/292-1435, where a cheeseburger in Paradise won't set you back too much and you can sing along with the songs you know by heart. Even less expensive for sandwiches or takeout, try **Five Brothers Grocery and Sandwich Shop**, 930 Southard St., 305/296-5205, a fine neighborhood market that makes great fresh Cuban sandwiches, Cuban espresso, *café con leche*, and sugar cookies. If you see **Fausto's Food Palace**, 522 Fleming St., 305/296-5663, stop in for a crusty loaf of Cuban bread and some of the locally made sausage for lunch, and pick up some Cuban spices and Key lime juice for souvenirs.

## LODGING

On Key Largo, divers love the idea of staying at **Jules' Undersea Lodge**, 51 Shoreland Dr. (MM103.2), 305/451-2353, which has only two rooms, submerged some 30 feet on the floor of a lagoon; diving gear is provided. Continuing south, the **Kona Kai Resort**, MM97.8 Bayside, 800/365-7829, a restored 1940s retreat, is a quiet, intimate place to unwind, with a sandy beach, Jacuzzi, bayfront heated pool, and romantic view of the sunset. The historic, English-owned **Tavernier Hotel**, 91865 U.S. 1 (MM91.8), 800/515-4131, a cluster of nicely renovated old pink buildings in the heart of the historic district, has a great bakery on the premises.

In Islamorada, the **Hampton Inn & Suites**, 80001 Overseas Hwy. (MM80), 800/426-7866 or 305/664-0073, has kitchens, plenty of water sports, and an on-site dive shop. The **Cheeca Lodge**, 81801 Overseas Hwy. (MM82), 305/664-4651 or 800/327-2888, has a huge, palm-lined beach, a nine-hole par-three golf course, a 525-foot fishing pier, and a kids' club. Personal attention is the rule at **Pelican Cove Resort**, 84457 Old

Overseas Hwy. (MM84.5), 800/445-4690 or 305/664-4435, with water sports, fishing, a heated pool, and whirlpool.

At Marathon on Duck Key, **Hawk's Cay Resort and Marina**, MM61, 800/432-2242 or 305/743-7000, is a luxurious yet casual West Indies–style resort on a private island, with a complete dive shop, glass-bottom boat, freshwater pool, and lagoon. On the ocean side at MM58 on Grassy Key, **Rainbow Bend Fishing Resort**, 800/929-1505 or 305/289-1505, is a natural for barefoot family vacationing. If you prefer a B&B, try the **Hopp-Inn Guest House**, 5 Man-O-War Dr., 305/743-4118, a waterfront bungalow with both canal and ocean views.

Kinky, quirky Key West is a mixed bag, as lodgings go. Those with special affinities, alternate lifestyles, pets, children, or aversions to any of the above, can generally be accommodated; contact the Key West Visitors' Bureau at 800/352-5397 for a current lodging directory by visitor "type." The grand old 1920s **Casa Marina Marriott**, 1500 Reynolds St., 800/626-0777 or 305/296-3535, Henry Flagler's ultimate luxury resort hotel, is still impressive, with a 1,000-foot private beachfront, tennis courts, gracious verandahs, wicker furnishings, and aristocratic dining ambience. Another stylish and romantic choice is the **Gardens Hotel**, 526 Angela St., 800/526-2664, a gracious, walled estate that takes up nearly a whole block in the historic district. Accommodations in the 1870s main house are outfitted with imported English furnishings and original art; the carriage house and cottage have porches overlooking tropical botanical gardens full of colorful frangipani, fringed hibiscus, palms, and banyan trees.

If you're traveling without children, stay in a converted 1880 cigar factory at **Simonton Court**, 320 Simonton St., 305/294-6386, offering charming cottages with porches and private decks. Or you might try the **Heron House**, 512 Simonton St., 888/265-2395 or 305/294-9227, a small luxury inn with private sundecks, balconies, and gardens; watercolor art; and fresh orchids. The romantic Victorian-style **Curry Mansion**, 511 Caroline St., 800/253-3466 or 305/294-5349, www.currymansion.com, is now a guest house, furnished with hand-sewn quilts, antiques, and decorative arts. There's a daily cocktail party and breakfast served for guests. (Don't confuse this with the **Curry House Mansion**, 806 Fleming St., 800/633-7439 or 305/294-6777, a late-1800s Victorian-style manse that caters exclusively to gay men.) In the heart of Old Town, **Whispers Bed & Breakfast Inn**, 409 William St., 800/856-7444 or 305/294-5969, is a 150-year-old antiques-filled guest house on a quiet, shady street, which offers access to a private beach, pool, and health club, and features a hot tub and sundeck on the premises.

## CAMPING

In Marathon, **Knights Key Park**, U.S. 1 at MM47, 305/743-4343, has extensive grounds with large open and shaded waterfront or dock sites for tents or RVs; there's a boat ramp, rec room, shuffleboard, horseshoes, laundry, restaurant, and lounge on the premises. Just south, at MM37, **Bahia Honda State Park** on U.S. 1, 305/872-2353, has sites for tents or RVs, plus cabins, marinas, picnic grounds, watercraft rentals, and one of the most beautiful stretches of beach in the Keys.

You'll have to call well in advance if you want a beachfront site at **Boyd's Campground**, 6401 Maloney Ave., on Stock Island in Key West, 305/294-1465 or 305/293-9301. Amenities include oceanfront and shaded sites for tents or RVs, full hookups including cable TV, a heated pool, laundry facilities, fishing, and a boat ramp and dock. Downtown, there's a waterfront campground at **Jabour's Trailer Court**, 223 Elizabeth St., 305/294-5723, which has sites for tents, vans, motor homes, and trailers; amenities include restrooms with hot showers, full hookups, a guest house, and bike rentals, plus trailer, cottage, and mobile-home rentals.

## NIGHTLIFE

Water taxis depart from Holiday Inn Key Largo Resort and Marina at MM100, Key Largo, 800/843-5397, every two hours Sunday through Thursday from 5 to 11 p.m. (last return to shore 2 a.m.), and Friday and Saturday from 5 p.m. to 12:30 a.m. (last return 3 a.m.), shuttling passengers to the **SunCruz Casino Cruises** for full casino-gaming action.

In Key West, the **Red Barn Theater**, 319 Duval St., 305/296-9911, has performances during winter and spring months. On the Mallory Docks, the **Waterfront Playhouse**, 305/294-0431 or 305/294-5015, offers theater and opera performances in season.

Key West has always been a drinking town. Duval Street in the late 1800s had several saloons named Bucket of Blood. These days there's still a lot of heavy drinking in a number of the restaurant/bars, but you won't need a guidebook to recognize them. Of course, you'll have stopped in to Sloppy Joe's during the day, but for a real taste (and smell) of old Key West nighttime color, pull up a bar stool at **Che Che's**, 1000 Truman Ave., 305/294-4721. For a lively Cole Porter–style sing-along with a more upscale but equally convivial group, check out the piano bar at one of Key West's first hotels, the **Pier House**, 1 Duval St., 305/296-4600.

# 11 NAPLES AND THE EVERGLADES

No one has been more eloquent than the late Marjory Stoneman Douglas in describing the vast, saltwater flatness of the Everglades. "There are no other Everglades in the world," she wrote, "their vast glittering openness, wider than the . . . visible round of the horizon, the racing free saltness. . . ."

As you leave the Keys or Florida's East Coast and head west, you are skirting this wondrous watery land, which remains as it does largely because of the attention Douglas focused on the area in the late 1940s, half a century ago. More than 1.5 million acres of natural habitat, sawgrass prairies, mangrove swamps, and subtropical jungle form the southern boundaries of Florida, where land and water become indistinguishable from one another, and the birds and reptiles and mammals thrive on the confusion here at the southernmost point on the U.S. mainland. A caveat for visitors: You *must* carry insect repellent.

But Southwest Florida is not entirely alligators and swamps. The small, pretty city of Naples fancies itself the Palm Beach of the Gulf coast, with its upscale shopping, art galleries, and long list of truly wonderful restaurants and resorts. However, it is the city's 10 miles of usually uncrowded public beaches that lure visitors. Much of the development is recent, as a photographic history of Marco Island shows. While old Captain Bill Collier enjoyed his Marco Hotel at the end of the nineteenth century, Marco Island remained largely empty until the late 1960s.

# MARCO ISLAND/EVERGLADES CITY

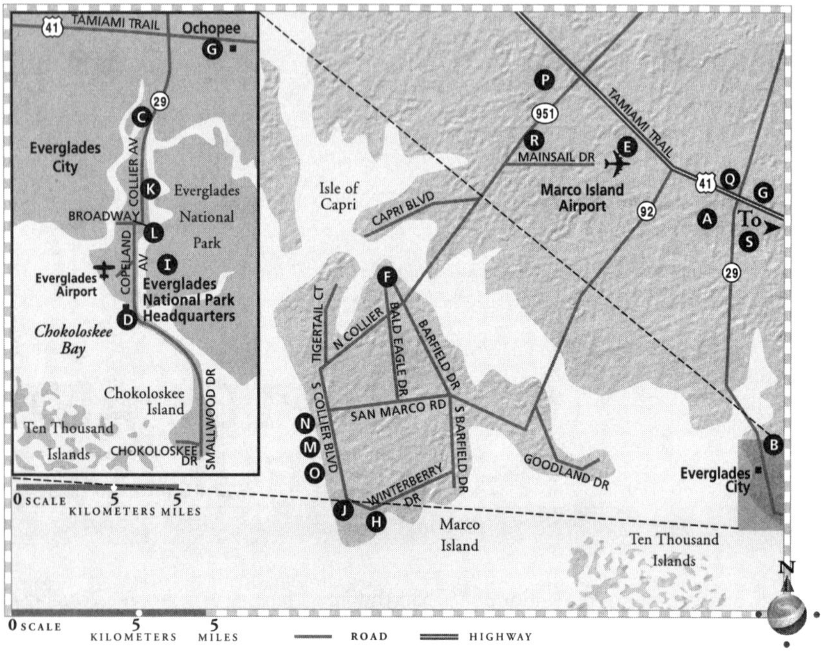


## SIGHTS

- **A** Collier-Seminole State Park and Boat Tours
- **B** E.J. Hamilton Observation Tower
- **C** Eden of the Everglades
- **D** Everglades National Park
- **D** Everglades National Park Boat Tours
- **E** Island Nature Cruises
- **F** Ten Thousand Islands Airboat Tours
- **G** Wooten's

## FOOD

- **H** Konrad's Steak & Seafood Grill
- **I** The Oyster House Restaurant
- **J** Sandcastles
- **F** Vito's Waterfront

## LODGING

- **K** The Ivey House
- **L** On the Banks of the Everglades
- **M** Marco Island Hilton Beach Resort
- **N** Marco Island Marriott Resort and Golf Club
- **O** Radisson Suite Beach Resort

## CAMPING

- **P** Naples/Marco Island KOA
- **Q** Port of the Islands Waterfront RV Resort
- **R** Silver Lakes RV Resort
- **S** Southern Comfort RV Resort

*Note: Items with the same letter are located in the same area.*

Sanibel and Captiva Islands off Fort Myers are becoming overcrowded, but that's because they have some of the best shelling beaches in the world and one of the nation's best birding preserves.

## A PERFECT DAY IN SOUTHWEST FLORIDA

If you've not been to the Everglades before, spend your day immersing yourself in the wonders of this unusual land and the life it supports. While there are many other attractions worth a visit in this area, none are equal to the Everglades. Visit E. J. Hamilton Observation Tower in Everglades City, then take a boat tour given by park rangers from the Everglades City–area ranger station. Walk some of the hammock trails from various visitor centers, then stop at Wooten's at least for the swamp-buggy ride. If you want a varied Everglades experience but want to leave the planning to someone else, take the all-day Everglades excursion that leaves from various Naples or Marco Island hotels. Should the Everglades not be your cup of tea, head for Sanibel and Captiva Islands for their wonderful shops, the sugar-consistency beaches, clear, warm Gulf of Mexico waters, and nature and golfing possibilities. End with dinner at the Bubble Room on Captiva Island.

## SIGHTSEEING HIGHLIGHTS

### ★★★★ CARIBBEAN GARDENS/JUNGLE LARRY'S ZOOLOGICAL PARK

**1590 Goodlette Rd. N., Naples, 941/262-5409, www.caribbeangardens.com**

This 52-acre bit of lush paradise is one of a dwindling number of Old Florida gardens that evolved into pleasant tourist attractions, having begun as the personal gardens or collections of the people who lived on the premises. The gardens don't try to be all things to all visitors, and they make a point of not trying to compete with the Central Florida theme parks. Larry Tetzlaff and wife, Jane ("Safari Jane," that is), planted bamboo, calabash, lychee nut, and banyan trees, plus hundreds of blooming plants (more than 3,000 species in all) and created a tropical canopy under which they stashed their collection of endangered animals. Soon they had an attraction people were willing to pay to see. You can take the 20-minute boat trip to a primate-inhabited island, watch alligator feedings, and take a self-guided walking tour through a tropical setting filled with birds and animals that

**LOST FOREVER IN THE EVERGLADES**

*If you're traveling along U.S. 41, the Tamiami Trail (Tampa to Miami), stop for a moment about 15 miles west of Miami at the rows of 110 coral stone columns that memorialize the 110 victims of the crash of ValuJet Flight 592 on Mothers' Day weekend in 1996. Many bodies were never recovered from the deep Everglades mud.*

include a tiger, elephants, lions, lemurs, an albino python, and an anteater. Birds and cats put on animal shows in Safari Canyon, and a maze of video screens presents footage of wild animals similar to those you are viewing.

***Details:*** *Open daily 9:30–5:30. Admission: $13.95 adults, $8.95 children. (4–6 hours)*

## ★★★★ CORKSCREW SWAMP SANCTUARY

**375 Sanctuary Rd., Naples, 941/657-3771**

This 11,000-acre wilderness and wildlife sanctuary, a National Audubon Society preserve, is a natural wonder. A two-mile boardwalk leads you among the towering trees of the world's largest old-growth bald-cypress forest. Alligators abound, and among the bird population is a large colony of American wood storks. The sanctuary is a popular spot for local as well as visiting nature lovers, birders, and photographers.

***Details:*** *Located off CR 846, 16 miles east of I-75, Exit 17. Open daily Dec–Apr 7–5, May–Nov 8–5. Admission: $6.50 adults, $3 children. (1–3 hours)*

## ★★★★ EDEN OF THE EVERGLADES

**Everglades City, 800/543-3367 or 941/695-2800**

This is much more than an elevated boardwalk that takes you through a mangrove forest. A 45-minute pontoon boat ride tours the grassy waterways of Ten Thousand Islands, the uncounted mangrove islands that lie south of Naples. You'll get a first-class Everglades experience without ever getting your feet in the muck. At additional cost, various airboat rides are also available.

***Details:*** *Located south of the junction of U.S. 41 and SR 29. Open daily 9–5. Admission: $13.95 adults, $8 children. (2–3 hours)*

## ★★★★ EVERGLADES EXCURSIONS

**800/592-0848 or 941/262-1914**

If you have a full day and want to immerse yourself in the Everglades, so to speak, without getting lost or trying to find sometimes-elusive trails and boardwalks, this is the tour to take. You'll be picked up at your hotel, and in the course of a day take a narrated cruise through sawgrass prairie and mangroves, visit Everglades City, and strap into an airboat for a ride through sections of the Ten Thousand Islands. The strangely beautiful Fakahatchee Strand State Preserve, with its impressive stands of royal palms and bald cypress, its 2,000-foot-long boardwalk, and the largest concentration of epiphytic orchids in the United States, is on your itinerary, and you'll visit a replica Seminole Indian village.

You'll be more prepared for the Fakahatchee visit if you've read *The Orchid Thief* by Susan Orlean, whose account of the theft of rare orchids from the preserve by a white man and three Seminole Indians evokes Frontier Florida, as well as the weirdness of the Fakahatchee itself.

***Details:*** *Departs daily 8 a.m., from various hotels in Naples and Marco Island. Reservations required. Fares: $79 adults, $64 children. (8 hours)*

## ★★★★ EVERGLADES NATIONAL PARK

**Superintendent: 40001 SR 9336, Homestead, 305/242-7700**

Everglades National Park was established to prevent the loss of this unique ecosystem, where flora and fauna struggle to survive in a savagely beautiful environment that is, ironically, as fragile as a butterfly wing. "Everglades" is a newer name for the old word *Pahayokee*, which means "grassy waters." The "river of grass" that is the Everglades is a slow-moving freshwater river 50 miles wide and a few inches deep, fed by Lake Okeechobee. Much of it is a maze of mangrove waterways and sawgrass marsh, relieved by an occasional hammock or salt prairie. Except for pinelands and the highest hammocks, the entire Everglades region is likely to be a swamp during the summer rainy season.

The main park entrance to Everglades National Park is on SR 9336, 10 miles southwest of Homestead and 35 miles south of

### THE EVERGLADES IN BLACK AND WHITE

*If you have the opportunity, stop in at the* ***Big Cypress Gallery****, 52388 Tamiami Tr., Ochopee, 941/695-2428. Open from 9 to 5:30 daily, it is the home gallery of Florida's extraordinary Everglades photographer Clyde Butcher, and it houses the originals of the amazing photos he has taken by wading into the swamps of the Everglades and waiting for just the right moment, when lighting conditions come into perfect alignment with his intended subject. Clouds float by, wildlife appears . . .* click.

Miami, near the East Coast, while Everglades City provides entry from the Gulf Coast. From December through April, you can expect a pleasant, mild climate; during summer both temperature and humidity indexes are likely to be in the 90s. Expect afternoon thunderstorms in summer, and wear loose-fitting, long-sleeved shirts and pants because this is mosquito territory. Carry inspect repellent, and bring sunscreen—the combination of insects and sun can be unbearable. You can find out the mosquito level by calling 305/242-7700 between 8:30 a.m. and 4 p.m.

When you're in the park, walk the nature trails, rent a canoe, or take a boat or tram tour; these are the only practical ways you will see wildlife, including alligators and more than 350 species of both tropical and temperate bird life. Only two bird species stay here all year, the Cape Sable sparrow and the great white heron. More than 600 species of fish, snakes, and sea turtles call the park home.

From the main entrance, a winding road takes you 38 miles to the **Flamingo Visitor Center** (941/695-3101). Here, at the tip of the state on Florida Bay, is one of the largest mangrove forests in the world. You can bicycle or take canoe trips, the tram tour, or one of the sightseeing cruises that leave from the marina daily during the winter season. **Royal Palm Visitor Center**, inside the park, south of SR 9336, is a place to begin naturalist-led walks and talks in winter. The **Gulf Coast Visitor Center** in Everglades City has natural-history exhibits and is the departure point for park ranger–led boat tours. Here you really are among the Ten Thousand Islands, a beautiful, tranquil, tide-swept maze of oyster bars, mud shallows, and mini-islands. Local flora is much the same as that in Cuba and the West Indies.

***Details:*** *Park admission at the main entrance is $10 per car, $5 for a pedestrian or cyclist. Prices are slightly lower at the Shark Valley or Chekika entrances. Backcountry camping is allowed within the park.*

## ★★★★ EDISON-FORD WINTER ESTATES

**2350 McGregor Blvd., Fort Myers, 941/334-3614**

The country's industrial elite discovered Florida's winter warmth toward the end of the nineteenth century, and two of the biggest names of the era, inventor Thomas A. Edison and industrialist Henry Ford, wintered side by side in their two Florida homes, Seminole Lodge and Mangoes, respectively. Edison's trips here were "working vacations," and in the laboratory next to the visitors center and Florida's largest banyan tree, he perfected the phonograph, the incandescent light bulb, and the storage battery, among other inventions. Ford didn't work as much as he enjoyed life as the world's first billionaire and puttered in his wonderful garden.

***Details:*** *Open Mon–Sat 9–4, Sun noon–4. Admission to museum and both homes by guided tour only: $10 adults, $5 children. (2–3 hours)*

## ★★★ BAILEY-MATTHEWS SHELL MUSEUM

**3075 Sanibel-Captiva Rd., Sanibel Island, 941/395-2233**

Sanibel Island has one of the country's best shelling beaches, so it's an appropriate place for a fascinating museum of shells from around the world. About 275 kinds are found in Sanibel's shallow waters, and another 500 in the Gulf of Mexico. If you want to learn to tell a whelk from a turkey wing or a fighting conch from a lettered olive, this is the place. The museum offers information on habitats and includes exhibits depicting the seashell's role in medicine, religion, and art in various cultures.

***Details:*** *Open Tue–Sun 10–4. Admission: $5 adults, $3 children. (1 hour)*

## ★★★ THE CONSERVANCY-NAPLES NATURE CENTER

**450 Merrihue Dr., Naples, 941/262-0304**

This wildlife rehabilitation center features snakes, a loggerhead sea turtle, a touch tank, an outdoor aviary, and an aquarium exhibit tank. The center is surrounded by a network of nature trails, and canoes and kayaks are available for rent. Don't miss the 45-minute narrated

# FORT MYERS AREA

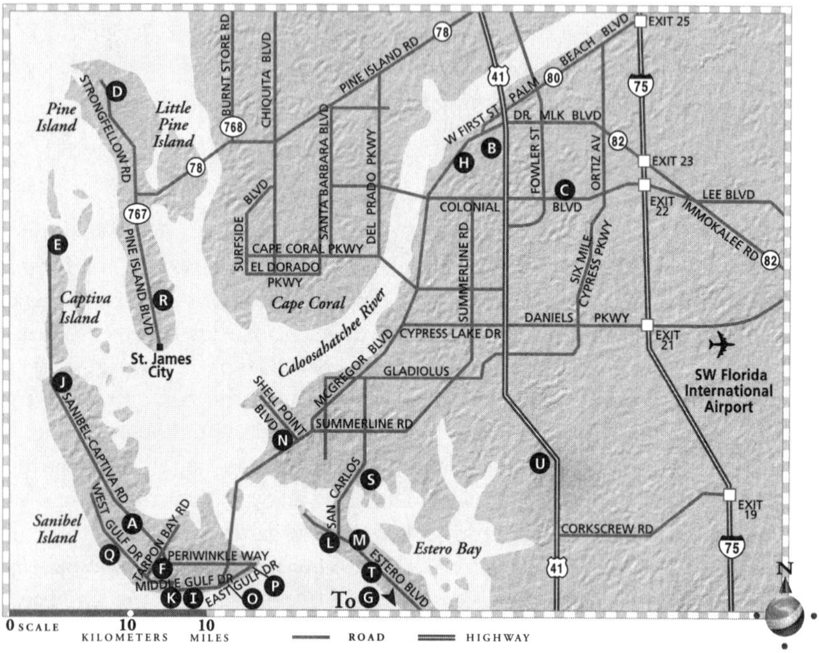


## SIGHTS

- **A** Bailey-Matthews Shell Museum
- **B** Edison-Ford Winter Estates
- **C** Seminole Gulf Railway
- **D** *Tropic Star* Cruise Boat

## FOOD

- **E** The Bubble Room
- **E** Chadwick's
- **E** Charley Brown's Restaurant
- **F** Greenhouse Grill
- **G** Rooftop Restaurant
- **H** Smitty's on McGregor
- **I** Windows on the Water

## LODGING

- **J** Blind Pass Condominium
- **K** Casa Ybel Resort
- **L** Lighthouse Island Resort
- **M** Outrigger Beach Resort
- **N** Sanibel Harbour Resort and Spa
- **O** Sanibel Inn
- **P** Seaside Inn
- **P** Song of the Sea
- **D** South Seas Plantation
- **I** Sundial Beach Resort
- **Q** West Wind Inn Beach Resort

## CAMPING

- **R** Fort Myers/Pine Island KOA
- **S** Gulf Air Travel Park
- **T** Red Coconut RV Resort
- **U** Woodsmoke Camping Resort

*Note: Items with the same letter are located in the same place.*

boat tour (included with admission) that takes you into nearby mangrove forests and lagoons for a look at creatures in the wild.

***Details:*** *Open Apr–June and Oct–Dec Mon–Sat 9–4:30, Sun 1–4:30. Rest of year Mon–Fri 9–4:30. Grounds free. Admission to complex: $5 adults, $2 children. (1–2 hours)*

## ★★★ E. J. HAMILTON OBSERVATION TOWER

**Everglades City**

Visit the tower for one of the best panoramic views of the Everglades and the Ten Thousand Islands you're likely to get. Flat may never seem uninteresting again. The wooden tower is 80 feet high, with 180 steps, and there is also a short boardwalk that takes you through the mangrove swamp to a waterway where you are likely to see marine birds.

***Details:*** *Follow signs south on SR 29. Open 24 hours. Admission: $1. (30 minutes)*

## ★★★ EVERGLADES NATIONAL PARK BOAT TOURS

**Everglades City, 800/445-7724 or 941/695-2591**

This is the official tour, and chances are you'll be spellbound for 1½ to 1¾ hours as park rangers steer you through the world's largest mangrove forest. There's a good possibility you'll see manatees and dolphins, and you're virtually certain to spy bald eagles, ospreys, roseate spoonbills, and the whole pantheon of Florida bird life. Boats—canvas-shaded, twin-hulled flatboats—depart every half-hour beginning at 9 a.m. on a first-come, first-served basis.

***Details:*** *Boats depart from Park Ranger station a half-mile south of Everglades City at 30-minute intervals daily 8:30–5. Fare: $13 adults, $6.50 children. (2 hours minimum)*

## ★★★ ISLAND NATURE CRUISES

**25000 Tamiami Tr. E. (U.S. 41), Port of the Islands, 800/237-4173**

Float through the Everglades to the mouth of the Gulf of Mexico on this informative, 14-mile cruise through the Everglades and Ten Thousand Islands.

***Details:*** *Departs daily at 10. Fare: $15 adults, $7.50 children, $13.50 seniors. (2–3 hours)*

### ★★★ NAPLES TROLLEY TOURS

**179 Southbay Dr., Naples, 941/262-7300**

Hop onto a rubber-tired trolley for a pleasant, 1¾-hour ride around Naples, stopping at or cruising slowly past nearly 100 points of interest. It's a good way to check out the shopping areas, historic sites, and posh residential sections of town before setting off on your own, and unless you read Naples history, you're not likely to hear some of the humorous stories about Ponce de León and the pirate Gasparilla anywhere else. Your ticket, valid for one day, allows you to get off and reboard anywhere you want.

***Details:*** *Operates daily 8:30–5:30, departing from various points along its route. Fare (includes all-day boarding pass): $12 adults, $5 children. (2 hours)*

### ★★★ TROPIC STAR CRUISE BOAT

**Four Winds Marina, Pine Island, 941/283-0015**

This full-day narrated cruise through the protected waters around Pine Island Sound, Cabbage Key, and the Rookery (where frigate birds soar in never-ending ellipses) takes visitors to the Cayo Costa State Park, which is accessible only by boat. The park has miles of beaches, oak palm hammocks, pine forests, mangrove swamps, and an unending variety of bird life. Shelling is good, particularly in the winter months, and you can pack a picnic and use the state park's facilities.

***Details:*** *Departs daily 9:30, returns at 4. Fare: $25 adults, $15 children. Tram: 50 cents. Reservations required. (full day)*

### ★★★ WOOTEN'S

**U.S. 41 (Tamiami Tr.), Ochopee, 800/282-2781 or 941/695-2781, www.wootens.com**

Wooten's is a kind of early Everglades theme park, locked firmly in the pleasant backwater atmosphere that must have prevailed in the 1950s, when it opened. Panthers, bobcats, a Siberian tiger, really big alligators, and snakes live in an animal sanctuary amid all the natural wildlife of the Everglades. Alligator-wrestling goes on all day. If you don't do it elsewhere, take the half-hour swamp-buggy tour through the wetlands and swamps. Airboat tours, also about 30 minutes long, put you in the thick of things, skimming on top of the water and grasses for close-up views of sleepy alligators and Everglades vegetation.

**Details:** *Open daily 8:30–5:30. Admission to animal sanctuary: $6 adults and children over 6. Swamp buggy and airboat tours leave every half hour and cost $12.50 for adults and children over 6. (1 1/2 -2 hours)*

### ★★ COLLIER-SEMINOLE STATE PARK AND BOAT TOURS

**20200 E. Tamiami Tr., Naples, 800/842-8898 or 941/642-8898**

Think of the Everglades and you'll have a sense of the vegetation and wildlife of this tropical park, with its hardwood hammock and Florida royal palms. Wildlife includes brown pelicans, wood storks, bald eagles, red-cockaded woodpeckers, Florida black bears, panthers, and mangrove fox squirrels. A walk on the 6.5-mile nature trail gives you ample time to experience the natural surroundings, and a pontoon boat tour provides an hour's worth of first-rate narration about the area's pioneers as well as the natural life.

**Details:** *Pontoon boat tours depart daily 9–4. Fare: $8.50 adults, $5.50 children. (1–2 hours)*

### ★★ EVERGLADES WONDER GARDENS

**27180 S. Tamiami Tr., Bonita Springs, 941/992-2591**

The Wonder Gardens opened in 1936 as a refuge for injured animals but has since become home to exotic birds, panthers, alligators, flamingos, bears, and otters—even an endangered Everglades crocodile (the ones with the pointy snouts). Grounds include botanical gardens, trees from around the world, and a natural history museum.

**Details:** *Open daily 9–5. Admission: $9 adults, $5 children. (30 minutes–2 hours)*

### ★★ MARCO ISLAND TROLLEY TOURS

**Marco Island, 941/394-1600**

Marco Island isn't very big, so a 90-minute tour takes you just about everywhere, including to sites once occupied by the Calusa Indians. You'll also see what's left of the grand hotels built by entrepreneurs who saw the area's tourist potential back in the late 1890s. You may be surprised to learn, however, that the island was basically empty as late as the mid-1960s.

**Details:** *Departs at intervals daily 10–3:15, boarding at hotels on Marco Island. Fare (includes all-day boarding pass): $10 adults, $4 children. (1 1/2 hours)*

### ★★ SEMINOLE GULF RAILWAY

**4110 Centerpointe Dr., Fort Myers, 941/275-8487**

Florida has few train rides to offer, and this is a chance for visitors to ride the same rails that Thomas Edison did. Visitors sit in vintage passenger cars behind a diesel engine as an informative narration provides history and an overview of the area from Fort Myers north to the Caloosahatchee Trestle and south to Bonita Springs.

***Details:*** *Trains depart from Colonial Station in Fort Myers and the Old Bonita Springs Station. Fares: $7–$11 adults, $4–$6 children, depending on route. Dinner and murder-mystery trips depart from Fort Myers only. Call for changeable hours and schedules.*

### ★★ THE TEDDY BEAR MUSEUM OF NAPLES

**2511 Pine Ridge Rd., Naples, 941/596-2722**

To every facet of human invention there is, somewhere, a dedicated museum, and who *doesn't* like the cuddly bears named for the 26th president? This "dream home for teddy bears" (as the museum calls itself) is home to more than 3,500 bears, from miniature (less than an inch) to larger-than-life-size, from antiques to new limited-edition collectibles.

***Details:*** *Dec–Apr, open Mon, Wed–Sat 10–5, Sun 1–5. Rest of year Wed–Sat 10–5, Sun 1–5. Admission: $6 adults, $2 children, $4 seniors. (30 minutes–1 hour)*

### ★★ TEN THOUSAND ISLANDS AIRBOAT TOURS

**Factory Bay Marina, 1079 Bald Eagle Dr., Marco Island, 941/642-6717**

If you've not been on an airboat yet, you might want to board this ride through the Ten Thousand Islands, where you may see manatees and dolphins and are guaranteed to see pelicans, hawks, and the whole range of Florida waterbirds, while the guide provides an excellent history of the Ten Thousand Islands.

***Details:*** *Departs daily 10 a.m. and 2 p.m. Fare: $25 adults, $12.50 children. Reservations required. (1½–2 hours)*

### ★ NAPLES DEPOT CIVIC AND CULTURAL CENTER

**1051 Fifth Ave. S. (at U.S. 41), Naples, 941/262-1776**

Little is left of the railroad network that once connected parts of South Florida, so it's worth having a look at this renovated 1927 train station, which has become a civic and cultural center. Inside, a

# NAPLES

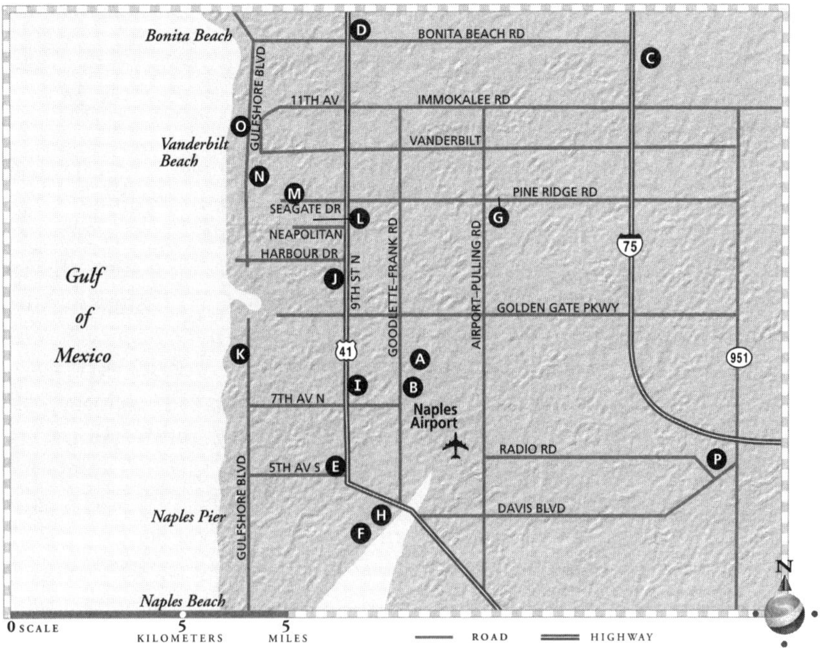


## SIGHTS

- **A** Caribbean Gardens/ Jungle Larry's Zoological Park
- **B** The Conservancy–Naples Nature Center
- **C** Corkscrew Swamp Sanctuary Everglades Excursions
- **D** Everglades Wonder Gardens
- **E** Naples Depot Civic and Cultural Center
- **F** Naples Trolley Tours
- **G** The Teddy Bear Museum of Naples

## FOOD

- **H** Merriman's at Tin City
- **I** Pippin's
- **H** Riverwalk Fish & Ale House

## LODGING

- **J** Inn of Naples
- **K** Naples Beach Hotel and Golf Club
- **L** Park Shore Resort
- **M** The Registry Resort, Naples

## LODGING *(continued)*

- **N** The Ritz-Carlton, Naples
- **O** Vanderbilt Inn on the Gulf

## CAMPING

- **P** Endless Summer RV Estates

*Note: Items with the same letter are located in the same place.*

collection of railroad memorabilia is displayed, while outside you can visit an old caboose.

***Details:*** *Open Mon–Fri 10–4. Free. (30 minutes)*

## FITNESS AND RECREATION

Still have some energy after exploring all the parks and trails in the Everglades and the southwestern coastal parks? Then head to **Delnor-Wiggins Pass State Recreation Area**, 11100 Gulf Shore Dr. N., Naples, 941/597-6196 to explore this narrow barrier island, lush with sea oats, sea grapes, cabbage palms, mangroves, and swimming and fishing in the Gulf. **Briggs Nature Center** in the Rookery Bay National Estaurine Research Reserve, located north of Marco Island, is a good place to study the area's ecosystems (all five of them) plus explore mangrove islands with their rare birds and rich marine life.

The famous **J. N. "Ding" Darling National Wildlife Refuge** on Sanibel Island, one of the nation's finest birding areas, can be explored by canoe or bicycle. And everywhere there is water, and wherever you find that, you'll also find canoes and kayaks for rent and bait fish for sale.

If you've got time to hit the links, you'll find more than 100 golf courses in the Naples/Fort Myers area, from the treacherous, watery **Dunes** course on Sanibel Island to pleasingly palm-studded courses attached to a variety of Naples resorts.

## FOOD

It's a popular opinion that the Naples area has more good restaurants per 1,000 population than any other area of Florida. There is no objective measure, of course, but from café casual to bow-tie elegant, there is an unusually large number from which to choose.

Near tiny Everglades City, try **The Oyster House Restaurant**, 905 Copeland Ave. (three miles south of town on SR 29, the Chokoloskee Island causeway), 941/695-2073, which features not only local seafood and stone-crab claws (in season) but also alligator and frog legs.

There really isn't a bad choice on Marco Island, but the somewhat pricey, semiformal **Sandcastles**, 560 S. Collier Blvd., 941/394-5000, in the Marco Island Hilton Beach Resort, will provide a first-class taste of the upscale nature of the island. **Konrad's Steak & Seafood Grill,** 599 S. Collier Blvd., 941/642-3332, where required attire is merely "dressy casual," is less expensive and offers outdoor patio seating and gourmet entrees. **Vito's Waterfront**, 1079 Bald Eagle Dr., 941/394-7722, right on the water,

**GO, SWAMP BUGGIES, GO**

*If you'd like to be able to boast that you did something on your vacation that your friends probably didn't, visit Naples in March, May, or October and head to Florida Sports Park, at the junction of Rattlesnake Hammock Rd. and CR 951, Naples, 800/897-2701 or 941/774-2701, for the swamp-buggy races. In the 1930s and '40s these peculiar vehicles with the huge balloon tires were invented by hunters as they tried to find more effective ways to penetrate the Everglades. Hunters would get together to test and waterproof their vehicles, and, well, one day one of 'em challenged another, and off they went. The first official race was in November 1949, when about 50 competitors dashed through the mud. Naples immediately claimed the world's most bizarre motor sport as its own. Time and celebrity changed the nature of the races. Buggies built for racing were impractical for actual hunting expeditions, and it seemed more fun to splash around in the "Mile O'Mud" oval track than to hunt, anyway. Stay until the end of the meet to witness another Naples tradition—throwing the usually pretty Swamp Buggy Queen, white gown and all, into the watery track for her mudbath.*

regularly wins national attention for its creative Italian and seafood dishes, all moderately priced.

In Naples you can hardly turn around without seeing another attractive restaurant, but even casual dining here, as on Marco Island, may be slightly more expensive than in most areas of Florida. Expect a $15 entree elsewhere to run $20 or $22 in Naples. So take your credit cards and head for the waterfront and **Merriman's at Tin City**, 1200 Fifth Ave. S., 941/261-1881, a restaurant often honored for its imaginative seafood and beef entrees. Nearby is the slightly less expensive **Riverwalk Fish & Ale House**, 1200 Fifth Ave. S., 941/263-2734, also in the Tin City shopping complex. A moderately priced local favorite is **Pippin's**, 1390 Ninth St. N., 941/262-2880, which has a salad bar and a family-dining menu.

North of Naples, in Bonita Springs, take the elevator up to the **Rooftop Restaurant**, 25999 Hickory Blvd. (four miles west of U.S. 41 on SR 865 in Casa Bonita Plaza). No prizes for its unimaginative name, but the health-conscious Florida regional cuisine is appealing, and there is a wonderful view of the water.

**Charley Brown's Restaurant**, 6225 Estero Blvd., 941/463-6660, at Fort Myers Beach on Estero Island, features seafood and beef, a casual atmosphere, and dining on a porch that overlooks the island's back bay, home to Florida's exotic waterbirds. **Smitty's on McGregor**, 3583 McGregor Blvd., Fort Myers, 941/489-2226, located a half-mile west of the U.S. 41 Caloosahatchee River Bridge, specializes in aged prime rib but offers a full menu.

Even if you don't like seafood, you won't go hungry on Sanibel and Captiva Islands. But why not sample some of Florida's best harvest from the sea? It will be difficult to avoid excess at **Chadwick's**, at South Seas Plantation at the northern end of the public road on Captiva Island, 941/472-5111. It features extravagant luncheon and dinner buffets and an exquisite Sunday brunch. **The Bubble Room**, 15001 Captiva Rd., 941/472-5558, doesn't take reservations, but the experience of dining at its glass-topped, display-box tables is worth the wait. Save a lot of room for dessert, because the portions of its famous cakes would make a meal for most people. On Sanibel Island, try the **Greenhouse Grill**, 2407 Periwinkle Way S., 941/472-6882, a modern diner offering a sophisticated "Floribbean" menu. The airy **Windows on the Water** restaurant at the Sundial Beach Resort, 1451 Middle Gulf Dr., 941/472-4151, has a complete menu, but features Florida seafood with special seasonings.

## LODGING

It's not at all difficult to find accommodations in the immediate Naples area, but you need to ratchet your definition of "moderate" back up to its Palm Beach mode. The low-priced chains exist but seem scarce, and you might prefer to stay in one of the numerous local resorts that have flourished over the years. Given the local definition, some of them are moderately priced.

On Marco Island, accommodations are at the high end of the price scale, period. The **Hilton**, **Marriott**, and **Radisson** chains have their beachfront resorts lined up on South Collier Avenue: Try the **Marco Island Hilton Beach Resort**, 800/221-2424 or 941/394-5000, the **Marco Island Marriott Resort and Golf Club**, 800/438-4373 or 941/394-2511, or the **Radisson Suite Beach Resort**, 800/992-0651 or 941/394-4100. So choose your style or the name you find easiest to spell. They're similar peas from a choice pod.

In Naples, **Park Shore Resort**, 600 Neapolitan Way, 800/548-2077 or 941/263-2222, www.sunstream.com, in the heart of this small city, is beautifully landscaped, which you can appreciate from your patio. The more elegant **Inn of Naples**, 4055 Tamiami Tr. N., 800/237-8858 or 941/649-5500, operated by the same small resort chain, is slightly more expensive, a Mediterranean-styled villa with rather luxurious rooms. The **Vanderbilt Inn on the Gulf**, 1100 N. Gulf Shore Dr., 800/643-8654 or 941/597-3151, www.vanderbiltinn.com, is a stylish resort with either luxury or standard accommodations along its 300 feet of white-sand beach. Nearby, the **Naples Beach Hotel and Golf Club**, 851 N. Gulf Shore Blvd., 800/237-7600 or 941/261-2222, www.naplesbeachhotel.com, a family-oriented, medium-sized resort, not only is on the beach but also has its own highly rated golf course. If you have unlimited means or want to splurge, opt for one of two wonderfully luxurious, magically landscaped resorts where the dining is both varied and superb. **The Registry Resort, Naples**, 475 Seagate Dr., 800/489-8686 or 941/597-9151, www.registryhotels.com, prides itself on its mangrove sanctuary, the hotel trolley that takes you through it to the beach, and the "cool tropical" colors of its plush furnishings. **The Ritz-Carlton, Naples**, 280 Vanderbilt Beach Rd., 941/598-3300, www.ritzcarlton.com, likes to boast that it exudes Old World elegance in its 13 stories. It does. And it may be the most luxurious resort on Florida's Gulf Coast.

The prices have dropped considerably by the time you get to the pleasant but much less tony Fort Myers Beach area. Stay at the moderately priced **Lighthouse Island Resort,** 1051 Fifth St., 800/778-7748 or 941/463-9392, and you're across the street from the beach and a fishing pier. Slightly less expensive is the **Outrigger Beach Resort**, 6200 Estero Blvd., 888/429-3131 or 941/463-31313, right on the beach, and with its tiki bar and palm trees it looks as though it might have been dropped here from a Caribbean island.

Staying on the islands of Sanibel or Captiva can be one of the loveliest experiences you'll have in Florida, but there are no budget motels and you can expect to pay island prices. Before you cross the causeway, you might investigate the **Sanibel Harbour Resort and Spa**, 17260 Harbour Pointe Dr., Sanibel Harbour, 800/767-7777 or 941/466-4000, www.sanibel-resort.com, a modern resort that faces the islands. On the islands themselves, in the past few years there has been considerable consolidation of lodging ownership in the hands of South Seas Resorts, 800/952-6574, www.southseas.com, which runs, among others, the gracious **South Seas Plantation,** 5400 Southseas Plantation Rd., 941/572-5111, at the northern end of Captiva Island; and the more modern resortlike **Sundial Beach Resort,** 1451 Middle Gulf Dr., 941/472-4151 on Sanibel Island. South Seas' other properties on Sanibel include the charming, intimate, European-style (and often filled with European guests) **Song of the Sea**, 863 E. Gulf Dr., 941/472-2220; the palm-surrounded **Seaside Inn**, 541 E. Gulf Dr., 941/472-1400; and the **Sanibel Inn**, 937 E. Gulf Dr., 941/472-3181, all of them right on the Gulf of Mexico. Other excellent choices include (but are not limited to) **Blind Pass Condominium**, 5117 Sea Bell Rd., 800/852-2038 or 941/472-6981, which rents large units right at Blind Pass, the narrow saltwater channel that separates Sanibel and Captiva Islands; the 23-acre, family-oriented **CasaYbel Resort**, 2255 W. Gulf Dr., 941/472-0939; and the **West Wind Inn Beach Resort**, 3345 W. Gulf Dr., 800/824-0476 or 941/472-1541, www.westwindinn.com.

Few lodgings are very close to the Everglades. In Everglades City, consider sleeping at the bank: **On the Banks of the Everglades**, 201 W. Broadway, 888/431-1977 or 941/695-3151, www.banksoftheeverglades.com, is a moderately priced Old Florida–style bed-and-breakfast in the 1923 Bank of the Everglades building. It was the home of Collier County's original and only bank until 1962, and you might think it still is. Breakfast is served in the walk-in vault, and rooms have names like Checking Department, Foreclosures Department, and Stocks & Bonds. A remodeled 1928 boardinghouse, **The Ivey House**, 107 Camellia St., 941/695-3299, www.iveyhouse.com (closed June through October), which also charges moderate rates and is another good place to stay, has a useful library of Everglades-related books. The owners offer watercraft rentals and shuttles for canoeists, half- or full-day and overnight guided eco-tours, and complimentary bicycle use.

## CAMPING

Campgrounds abound in the Fort Myers area, but there are fewer choices in the southernmost reaches of Florida's Gulf Coast. **Port of the Islands Waterfront RV Resort**, 12425 Union Rd., Naples, 800/319-4447 or 941/642-5343, www.portoftheislands.com, has 99 level grass sites on a freshwater river, conveniently near the heart of the Ten Thousand Islands. The **Naples/Marco Island KOA**, 1700 Barefoot Williams Rd., Naples, 800/562-7734 or 941/774-5455, is a lush place with palms shading its 66 mostly pull-through sites, and canoes and cabins for rent. It has access to the Gulf and is just a few minutes from Marco Island. **Endless Summer RV Estates**, 2 Tina Lane off Radio Road, Naples, 941/643-1511, has 75 long, grassy, full-hookup sites, including tent plots, about five miles from the beaches, while **Silver Lakes RV Resort**, 1001 Silver Lakes Blvd., Naples, 800/843-2836 or 941/775-2575, offers large lots, full hookups, and a nine-hole golf course on its 110-acre site.

More camping choices emerge as you drive north. In Fort Myers Beach, pull in right next to the Gulf of Mexico to the **Red Coconut RV Resort**, 3001 Estero Blvd., 888/262-6226, ext. 204, or 941/463-7200, ext. 200, for the sort of family camping that lends itself to picture postcards. The 170-site facility offers pull-throughs, paved pads, tent sites, full hookups, cabins, and the usual recreation activities. **Gulf Air Travel Park**, 17279 San Carlos Blvd. S.W., 941/466-8100, two miles from the beaches, has 40 full-hookup sites with a heated pool. **Woodsmoke Camping Resort**, 19551 U.S. 41 S., 800/231-5053 or 941/267-3456, has 80 full-hookup pull-through sites between Fort Myers and Estero Island.

If the isolation of Gilligan's Island appealed to you, drive west of North Fort Myers to Pine Island, then south to St. James City, to the **Fort Myers/Pine Island KOA**, 5120 Stringfellow Rd., 800/562-8505 or 941/283-2415, where you can walk the beaches alone, pick up shells, or take a free bus or boat trip (seasons vary) back to town. The facility has full hookups and tent sites, and rents cabins and bicycles for exploring the pine-covered barrier island.

If you're visiting the Everglades, you might try the **Southern Comfort RV Resort**, 345 E. Palm Dr., Florida City, 305/248-6909, located immediately south of the Florida's Turnpike southern terminus. It offers 270 grassy or gravel, open or shaded, full-hookup sites, convenient to the Royal Palm Visitor Center at the eastern edge of the Everglades. As noted above, backcountry camping is permitted within Everglades National Park.

## SHOPPING

Skip the regular malls with Burdines and Sears and the usual suspects. Instead, head for **Tin City Waterfront Shops & Restaurants** at the corner of U.S. 41 and SR 851 (Goodlette-Frank Road) in Naples, designed to capture the flavor of pioneer-era Naples. Built on the site of a 1920s clam-shelling and oyster-processing plant, it does a good job of aping the rustic maritime spirit inside and out, even though it is now home to some good restaurants, boutiques, and a variety of antiques and gift shops. At **Village on Venetian Bay**, 4200 Gulf Shore Blvd. N., Naples, you'll find nifty boutiques, restaurants and galleries done in Mediterranean style. Determined shoppers will love the **Waterside Shops** at U.S. 41 and Seagate Drive because it has a fine collection of shops like Banana Republic, Jacobsons, and Saks Fifth Avenue. **The Third Street South** shopping area, in Old Naples' historic district, is home to more than 100 shops, galleries, restaurants, and cafés.

Some might say that the main drag on Sanibel Island is one long shopping center, but that's not literally true. There are innumerable fine, small shops of every description along Periwinkle Way, but don't miss browsing at **Periwinkle Place**, at 2075 Periwinkle Way, which is filled with one-of-a-kind eateries, clothing boutiques, and gift shops, all cleverly built around what looks like the corner of a palm-tree park.

# 12 SARASOTA TO BRADENTON

As you cross the impressive Caloosahatchee River north of Fort Myers, you are entering a relatively unspoiled area of bays, islands, fishing villages, and broad, slow-moving rivers. Florida black vultures may be circling high overhead, but so are so white-headed ospreys. Pelicans fly in formation along the bridge railings, or wait patiently near fishermen, hoping for a handout.

You'll see this part of Florida more closely if you stay on U.S. 41, the Tamiami (Tampa-to-Miami) Trail, which crosses the Peace River, then arcs toward Italianate Venice, the aptly named picturesque little city of canals that is also the shark's-tooth capital of the world.

The jewel of this area is Sarasota. For its size an unparalleled cultural center, the city not only is blessed geographically with a fabulous location on the Gulf of Mexico, but also is a mecca for artists in every discipline, a tradition fostered by John Ringling when he established the area as a winter home for his Ringling Bros. & Barnum and Bailey Circus in 1927. He didn't merely build a palace, he also built an art museum. Performing-arts centers and playhouses are sold out regularly, evidence that the city has been settled by a population that is educated, wealthy, and intensely interested in music and theater. City boosters have taken to calling the area Florida's "Cultural Coast," and no one has objected.

A few miles north, along the banks of the Manatee River, Bradenton lives in Sarasota's shadow. It's much more of a working-class town, but Bradenton is an excellent staging point for visits to the barrier islands in the Gulf.

# SARASOTA/BRADENTON

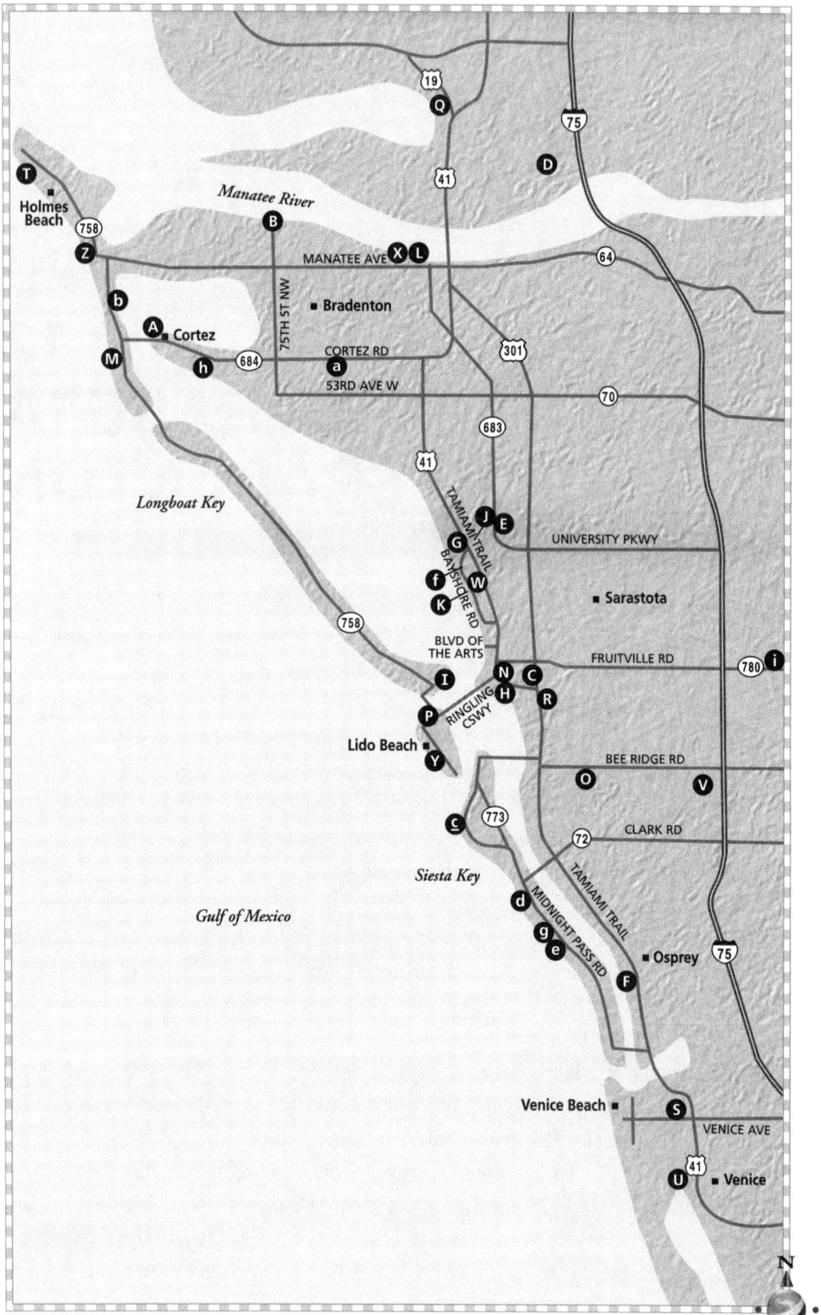


NOT TO SCALE

ROAD HIGHWAY

## A PERFECT DAY IN SARASOTA

Start with an early morning walk along the beach on Longboat Key, then head for the Ringling complex, taking the next two or three hours to explore the mansion, the magnificent art museum, and the truly fabulous circus museum. Take care not to walk into the trunks of the huge banyan tree or the outdoor statuary as you stroll the grounds. Then take the quick drive north on I-75 to Ellenton and the Gamble Plantation, one of the very few Florida antebellum homes still standing. View it from underneath the magnificent live oaks that sway with Spanish moss. If outlet shopping is your pleasure, you're sure to enjoy an afternoon at the Prime Outlets mall in Ellenton at U.S. 301 and I-75. Drive west to the Gulf of Mexico at Holmes Beach, then head north up to lovely Anna Maria Island, or south on the narrow strips of barrier islands that will take you to the Mote Marine Aquarium, with its *Mote Explorer* nature cruise. Shop or window-shop around St. Armands Circle, dine alfresco at Cafe L'Europe, then from the beach on Longboat Key, watch the sinking of the huge tangerine sun into the Gulf.

---

### SIGHTS

- A *Cortez Lady* Egmont Key Excursion
- B DeSoto National Memorial
- C F.S.U. Center for the Performing Arts
- D Gamble Plantation State Historic Site
- E Gulf Coast Wonder and Imagination Zone (G.WIZ)
- F Historic Spanish Point
- G John and Mable Ringling Museum of Art
- H Marie Selby Botanical Gardens
- I Mote Marine Aquarium
- J Museum of Cars & Music of Yesterday
- I Pelican Man's Bird Sanctuary

### SIGHTS *(continued)*

- K Sarasota Jungle Gardens
- L South Florida Museum, Bishop Planetarium, and Parker Manatee Aquarium

### FOOD

- M Beach House Restaurant
- N The Bijou Cafe
- O Cafe Campestre Mexican Restaurant
- P Cafe L'Europe
- N First Watch Restaurant
- Q Lee's Crab Trap I
- R Michael's on East
- S Patches Restaurant
- T Sandbar Restaurant
- U Sharky's on the Pier
- V Sugar & Spice

### LODGING

- W Best Western Royal Palms
- X Betts House
- Y Coquina on the Beach Resort
- N The Cypress
- Z Harrington House
- a Park Inn Club and Breakfast Hotel
- b Sunset Beach Motel
- c Tropical Breeze Inn
- d Tropical Shores Beach Resort
- e Turtle Beach Resort
- f Wellesley Inn

### CAMPING

- g Gulf Beach Campground on the Beach
- h Sarasota Bay Travel Trailer Park
- i Sun-N-Fun Resort

*Note: Items with the same letter are located in the same place.*

## SIGHTSEEING HIGHLIGHTS

### ★★★★ GAMBLE PLANTATION STATE HISTORIC SITE

**3708 Patten Ave., Ellenton, 941/723-4536**

Here, under spreading live oak trees dripping with Spanish moss, is a rare chance to feel what life was like in pre–Civil War Florida. Built by Major Robert Gamble in 1844, this was once the most successful sugar plantation in Florida. (It once comprised 3,000-acres, and it produced 230,000 tons of sugar and 10,000 gallons of molasses at its peak.) The plantation house, one of the very few antebellum mansions left in the state, contains period furnishings and is constructed of tabby (crushed oyster shell, other broken shells, oyster shell lime, sand and sugar as a binder) and wood. Its windows are aligned, Florida fashion, to allow pass-through breezes.The United Daughters of the Confederacy saved the mansion from destruction in 1925 and donated it to the state.

***Details:*** *On U.S. 301 a mile west of I-75. Grounds are free. Admission to house by tour only (9:30 and 10:30 a.m., and 1, 2, 3, and 4 p.m.): $3 adults, $1.50 children. (1–1 1/2 hours)*

### ★★★★ JOHN AND MABLE RINGLING MUSEUM OF ART

**5401 Bay Shore Rd., Sarasota, 941/351-1660**

The Ringlings may have made their money by providing Big Top entertainment, but at home they lived like royalty rather than circus barkers, and their estate is perhaps the supreme attraction of this area. The art museum houses what is said to be the world's largest collection of Baroque, Italian, and Flemish Renaissance paintings, as well as seventeenth-century tapestries. A few steps away is the Ringling home, **Ca 'd'Zan** (House of John), a 30-room palazzo built right on Sarasota Bay in 1926 at a cost of $1.5 million. The terracotta mansion, built to resemble a Venetian palace, is an architectural showcase dripping with opulence. Also on the 66-acre estate grounds is the **Circus Museum**, a fascinating place for anyone interested in the history of the circus, and in the Ringling Bros. & Barnum and Bailey Circus in particular.

***Details:*** *Open daily 10–5:30. Grounds free. Admission to museums and home: $9 adults, children free, $8 seniors. (3–4 hours)*

### ★★★★ MARIE SELBY BOTANICAL GARDENS

**811 S. Palm Ave., Sarasota, 941/366-5731, www.selby.org**

Perhaps the finest botanical gardens in the state, if not in the entire Southeast, this 8.5 acres of Sarasota bayfront shows off a living collection of more than 6,000 orchids and 20,000 other colorful plants in both open-air and greenhouse displays. There are 20 garden areas on the grounds of the historic Selby estate, including a butterfly garden, a bamboo pavilion, a banyan grove, a palm grove, a bromeliad display, and gardens of succulents and cycads. An impressive display of the botanical art of five centuries may highlight zeniths of artistic achievement—but the real-life flora is more satisfying.

***Details:*** *Located just south of U.S. 41 junction with S. Palm Avenue. Open 10–5 daily. Admission: $7 adults, $3 children. (1–2 hours)*

## ★★★★ MOTE MARINE AQUARIUM

**1600 Ken Thompson Pkwy., City Island, Sarasota, 800/691-6683 or 941/388-4200**

More than 200 varieties of fish and sea invertebrates reside in this not-to-be-missed aquarium, which is, in fact, a real scientific research laboratory. Among the highlights: a 30-foot touch-tank, where visitors can touch starfish, sea urchins, hermit crabs, horseshoe crabs, lightning whelks, sand dollars and sometimes stingrays, and an impressive 135,000-gallon shark tank. Other tanks hold manatees, eels, rays, and sea turtles. Visitors will learn how fish are bred and grown for farming, and how snook, fish that are all born male, can turn into females as they grow, a biological wonder that allows the species to survive. The aquarium's boat, the *Mote Explorer*, takes visitors on tours of nearby mangrove islands where herons, ibises, ospreys, eagles, and pelicans reside.

***Details:*** *Located between St. Armands Key and Longboat Key. Open daily 10–5. Admission: $8 adults, $6 children. Boat tours extra. (1–2 hours)*

## ★★★★ MYAKKA RIVER STATE PARK

**13207 SR 72, Sarasota, 941/365-0100**

Florida's largest park (and one of the country's outstanding wildlife sanctuaries) comprises 29,000 acres of wetlands, dense woodlands, and prairies. Deer, alligators, and more than 200 bird species live here, along with hundreds of species of subtropical plants, flowers, and trees. Stop in at the natural history museum for some background information before you set out on the walking trails. An airboat trip on Upper Myakka Lake provides a good narrated tour—get your boarding pass when you arrive at the park. Tram tours cover some of the park's land portions.

**Details:** *From I-75, take Exit 37 and drive nine miles east on SR 72. Park open daily 8–sunset. Tram tours daily at 1 and 2:30 Dec–May. Airboat tours daily at 10, 11:30, 1, and 2:30 Dec–May. Tour fares: $7 adults, $3 children. (1–3 hours)*

### ★★★ *CORTEZ LADY* EGMONT KEY EXCURSION

**4330 127th St.W., Bradenton, 941/761-9777**

If a nifty trip to a little-known island seems like an attractive idea to you, then board the 65-foot *Cortez Lady* for a 45-minute trip to historic Egmont Key National Wildlife Refuge in the mouth of Tampa Bay. Foot-long gopher tortoises are everywhere, and a good beach fronts the Gulf side of the island. Be careful when exploring the crumbling Spanish–American War fort. The lighthouse is closed, but pilots who guide ships in and out of Tampa Bay live on the south side of the island. The trip will give you about 2½ hours to explore, take a swim, or feed the tortoises. Watch where you step!

**Details:** *Departs from Cortez Fleet wharf, northeast side of Cortez Bridge, at 1 p.m. Tue, Thu, and Sun (more frequently in high tourist season). Fare: $20 adults, $10 children, $15 seniors. (4 hours)*

### ★★★ DESOTO NATIONAL MEMORIAL

**75th St. N.W., Bradenton, 941/792-0458**

This engaging little park, largely mangrove swamp, commemorates the first noteworthy European exploration of the territory that became the southeastern United States. The visitor center details the expedition of ambitious Spanish soldier Hernando de Soto, who landed near here in May 1539 and embarked on a 4,000-mile journey of exploration and conquest that ended three years later when he died of a fever and was buried in the Mississippi River mudflats. At Camp Ucita, a model of the village DeSoto and his men captured and used as base camp after their arrival, costumed guides explain what life was like here in the sixteenth century. Walk down the boardwalk to the Manatee River for a look at the unusual gumbo-limbo trees native to this area.

**Details:** *Located five miles west of Bradenton on SR 64, then 2.5 miles north on 75th Street S.W. Camp Ucita is open from mid-December through mid-April, daily 9–5. Free. (1 hour)*

### ★★★ SARASOTA JUNGLE GARDENS

**3701 Bayshore Rd., Sarasota, 941/355-5305**

These 10 acres of winding trails, luxuriant gardens, and exotic waterfowl are a showplace for Florida's snakes, turtles, alligators, and birds. The setting will make you forget how close you are to major highways. In fact, you're in one of those Old Florida attractions that grew not as a lure for tourists but because local residents created a tropical garden for their home and later realized people would pay money to see it. Don't miss the reptile and bird shows; also featured are a small shell museum, a petting zoo, and a Gardens of Christ section, which features dioramas depicting the life of Jesus.

***Details:*** *Located a quarter-mile west of U.S. 41 via Myrtle Street. Open daily 9–5. Admission: $9 adults, $5 children, seniors $7.50. (2 hours)*

### ★★★ SOUTH FLORIDA MUSEUM, BISHOP PLANETARIUM, AND PARKER MANATEE AQUARIUM

**201 10th St. W., Bradenton, 941/746-4131**

This Bradenton complex offers attractions for every taste. The **South Florida Museum** highlights southwest Florida history from Native American times to the present. An interesting medical wing displays early surgical instruments and replica 1900-vintage doctor's and pharmacist's offices. The innovative **Bishop Planetarium** hosts a wide variety of projected, laser, and special-effect shows, and opens its rooftop observatory Friday and Saturday evenings, weather permitting, for stargazing. And if you've never seen a manatee, visit the **Parker Manatee Aquarium**, where you can watch Snooty through underwater windows in his 60,000-gallon tank.

***Details:*** *Open Mon–Sat 10–5, Sun noon–5. Admission for combination museum and one planetarium show: $6 adults, $3.50 children. (1½–2½ hours)*

### ★★ FLORIDA STATE UNIVERSITY CENTER FOR THE PERFORMING ARTS

**5555 N. Tamiami Tr., Sarasota, 941/351-8000**

Yes, this is the university's theater for training for film and stage, but it's also home to the first-class professional Asolo theatre company and the Sarasota Ballet. If you can't take in a performance, come for a tour—the interior of this arts complex is a reconstructecd 1903 opera house and well worth a visit.

***Details:*** *Free tours offered Wed–Sat 10–noon, but schedule may vary, so call ahead. (1 hour)*

## ★★ GULF COAST WONDER AND IMAGINATION ZONE (G.WIZ)

**1001 Boulevard of the Arts, Sarasota, 941/957-4969**

The G.WIZ center features more than 60 hands-on exhibits. Visitors can play laser harps, dig for fossils, or touch live animals, including rat snakes, black pine snakes, pythons, gopher tortoises, and other creatures indigenous to Southwest Florida. There's an echo chamber and a "frozen shadow" exhibit. You can picnic on the grounds.

***Details:*** *Open Tue–Sat 10–5, Sun 1–5. Admission: $3 adults, $1.50 children (1 hour)*

## ★★ HISTORIC SPANISH POINT

**337 N. Tamiami Tr. (U.S. 41), Osprey, 941/966-5214**

Take the nature trail in this 30-acre archeological site at the edge of Little Sarasota Bay and you'll get a rare view of the remains of a prehistoric community and a burial mound. The park also contains a restored pioneer homestead, a formal garden established by one of Sarasota County's great landowners early in the twentieth century, and a citrus-packing house.

***Details:*** *Open Mon–Sat 9–5, Sun noon–5. Admission: $5 adults, $3 children and seniors. (1 1/2–2 hours)*

## ★★ MUSEUM OF CARS & MUSIC OF YESTERDAY

**5500 N. Tamiami Tr., Sarasota, 941/355-6228**

Well, why not? Cars and music boxes both age and become antiques. And people like to see what their ancestors thought was new and wonderful. So admire the old Pierce Arrows and Rolls Royces, then hit the Great Music Hall, which has more than 1,000 music boxes that play tunes from the Gay Nineties (the *other* Gay Nineties) and the Roaring Twenties, then pry loose some coins and play some penny-arcade games your grandfather might have known.

***Details:*** *Open daily 9–6. Admission: $9 adults, $5 children. (1 1/2–2 hours)*

## ★★ PELICAN MAN'S BIRD SANCTUARY

**1708 Ken Thompson Pkwy., Sarasota, 941/388-4444**

# GREATER SARASOTA

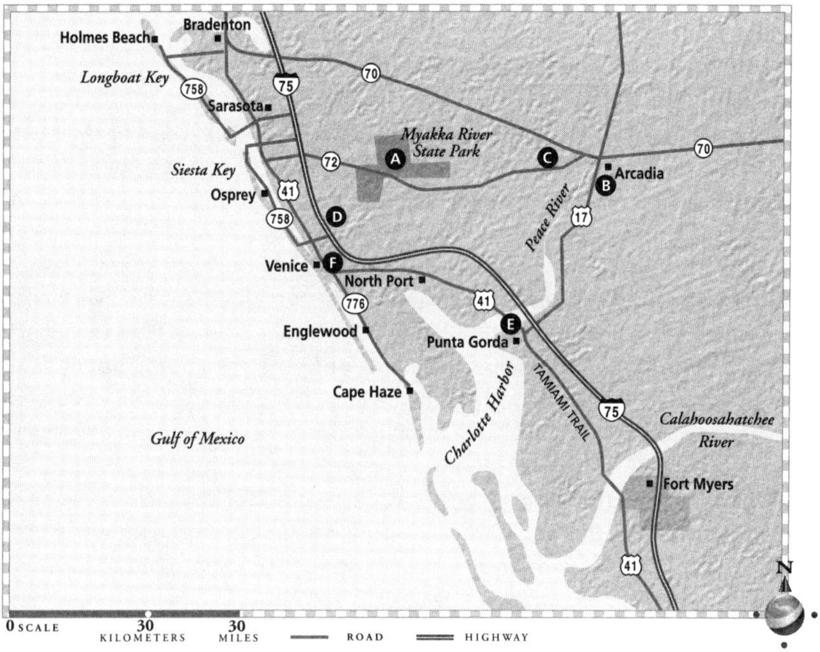


## SIGHTS

- A Myakka River State Park

## LODGING

- B Arcadia's Magnolia Manor

## CAMPING

- C Arcadia Peace River Campground
- A Myakka River State Park
- D Oscar Scherer State Recreation Area
- E Punta Gorda/Charlotte Harbor KOA
- F Venice Campground

*Note: Items with the same letter are located in the same area.*

---

Licensed wildlife rehabilitator Dale Shields has created an open-air home for as many as 39 different species of Florida birds that are not fit to be returned to the wild, even after they've recovered from their injuries. Boardwalks allow close-up views of pelicans, owls, herons, hawks, and egrets.

***Details:*** *Located between Longboat Key and St. Armands Key, east* *of the Mote Marine Aquarium, north of St. Armands Circle. Open daily 10–5. Free. (30 minutes)*

## FITNESS AND RECREATION

The nation's best golf-course designers seem to delight in creating their best work in this section of Florida, weaving fairways and greens around watery hazards and Florida wasteland in ways you may find dismaying as well as enjoyable. If you play, don't leave without a round at Arnold Palmer's tough **Legacy Golf Club** at Lakewood Ranch, Ron Garl's picturesque **University Park Country Club** in Bradenton, Ted McAnlis's very challenging **Pelican Pointe Golf Club** in Venice, Gene Bates's superb **Riverwood Golf Club** near Cape Haze, or Bob Tway's new **Bobcat Trail Golf Club** in North Port. All of this seems fitting, as Sarasota is the site of the state's first golf course, built by an immigrant Scot late in the nineteenth century.

Of course, not everyone enjoys chasing a little ball around a lot of acreage, so if you'd prefer something a little more rigorous, spend a day paddling a canoe anywhere on the Peace River or the impressively broad and slow—under 2 mph, usually—Manatee River. You can fish for striped bass or bream. **Ray's Canoe Hideaway**, 1247 Hagle Park Rd., Bradenton, 941/747-3909, rents canoes by the half-day or for overnight trips, and offers detailed information on what to see and do along the river. This entire area is a canoeist's paradise, with inlets, canals, and natural waterways everywhere.

If you want your water frozen, head to the **Venice Ice Pavilion**, one of 27 skating rinks in Florida (and more are on the way). The new **J. P. Igloo & Inline Sports Complex** in Ellenton has two ice rinks and one inline skating rink, a restaurant, and an arcade.

More passive recreation is available, too. On Sundays from December through April, head to the **Sarasota Polo Club** for traditional tailgating before watching the ponies and their riders compete; they play for the 14-goal Ringling Cup final on the first Sunday in April. During those same months you can watch the greyhounds run at the **Sarasota Kennel Club**.

## FOOD

If there weren't so many things to see and do, you could simply eat your way from Venice to Bradenton, enjoying something different every meal. In Venice, busy **Sharky's On The Pier**, on the beach at the Venice Fishing Pier, 1600 S. Harbor Dr., 941/488-1456, offers seafood broiled, blackened, grilled,

**CELEBRATE THE STONE CRAB**

*If you visit Florida between the middle of October and the middle of May, you're here in stone-crab season, and you may find special stone-crab festivals to attend, like the Stone Crab, Seafood, and Wine Festival held at the end of October every year at the upscale Colony Beach and Tennis Resort on Longboat Key, 1620 Gulf of Mexico Dr., 941/383-5558. Well-known chefs from around the country participate in this four-day, three-night splurge, so tickets are often sold out weeks in advance. There's no need to do anything other than remove the succulent meat and dip it in mustard sauce. By the way, stone-crab eating has lots of things going for it. These crabs are a renewable resource: Only the large claw is removed, and the crab is returned to the water to grow another. And three ounces of cooked stone-crab claw meat contains no fat, just 60 calories, 15 grams of protein, 45 milligrams of cholesterol, 300 milligrams of sodium, and 4 grams of calcium!*

or fried, served under a covered porch or indoors. **Patches Restaurant**, 501 E. Venice Ave., 941/484-6713, offers inexpensive family dining.

If in Sarasota you crave Mexican, try the popular, consistently top-rated **Cafe Campestre Mexican Restaurant**, 3164 Bee Ridge Rd., 941/923-5356. For breakfast or lunch, try the crepes, omelets, or sandwiches of the moderately priced flagship eatery of the small Sarasota-based chain, **First Watch Restaurant**, 1395 Main St., 941/954-1395. For inexpensive, simple fare, sit down at **Sugar & Spice**, 1850 S. Tamiami Tr., 941/953-3340, which offers a children's menu and Amish-style cooking. It's easy to find superb food at moderately expensive, special places in Sarasota. Local favorites include the contemporary bistro, **Michael's On East**, 1212 East Ave. S., 941/366-0007; the continental **Cafe L'Europe**, 431 St. Armands Cir., 941/388-4415, where you can eat outside facing St. Armands Circle; and **The Bijou Cafe**, 1287 First St., 941/366-8111, known for its innovations in Florida seafood.

In Bradenton's environs, watch the sun set over the Gulf of Mexico while enjoying steaks and fresh seafood from the moderately priced **Sandbar Restaurant**, 100 Spring Ave., Anna Maria Island, 941/778-0444, or the

**Beach House Restaurant**, 200 Gulf Dr., North Bradenton Beach, 941/795-1115. A favored local seafood house in rustic, Florida "Cracker" style is **Lee's Crab Trap I**, 5611 U.S. 19, Palmetto, 941/722-6255, just south of the Sunshine Skyway Bridge over Tampa Bay.

## LODGING

If you've been canoeing on the Peace River near Arcadia, there's no reason to drive anywhere else for the night. Stop at **Arcadia's Magnolia Manor**, 500 W. Oak St., Arcadia, 888/494-5748 or 941/494-4299, a nicely restored century-old home with just two rooms and moderate rates.

In downtown Sarasota, **The Cypress**, 621 Gulfstream Ave. S., 941/955-4683, will accommodate you among the European and American antiques and paintings that fill this 1940 structure. Rates are characteristically Sarasota-high for its four rooms with private baths.

Even the ubiquitous chain motels seem to have added a few dollars to their rates because of their Sarasota addresses, but during the off-season, reasonable rates prevail at places like the **Wellesley Inn**, 1803 N. Tamiami Tr., 800/444-8888 or 941/366-5128, and the **Best Western Royal Palms**, 1701 N. Tamiami Tr., 800/528-1234 or 941/365-1342. In season, rates rise substantially. You might try the **Coquina on the Beach Resort**, 1008 Ben Franklin Dr., 800/833-2141 or 941/388-2141, which sits directly on the Gulf of Mexico on Lido Beach. On Siesta Key, the **Tropical Breeze Inn**, 140 Columbus Blvd., 800/300-2492 or 941/349-1125, has a dozen "Old Florida" apartments in a tropical garden, and four beachfront apartments. **Tropical Shores Beach Resort**, 6717 Sara Sea Cir., 800/235-3493 or 941/349-3330, also has a seaside location with private beach access. For even more luxury, try the **Turtle Beach Resort**, 9049 Midnight Pass Rd., 941/349-4554, www.sarasota-online.com/turtle, a Key West–style waterfront inn a short walk to Turtle Beach. There's a hot tub on each secluded patio.

In Bradenton, spend a night at **Betts House**, 1523 First Ave. W., 941/747-3607, a very moderately priced 1913 "Four-Square" house with 1,000 square feet of porches and leaded windows in its two bedrooms. The location is convenient for exploring the city's historic riverfront as well as its downtown attractions. Everywhere in town, you'll find the usual chains at reasonable prices. There is also good value at the **Park Inn Club and Breakfast Hotel**, 4450 47th St. W., Bradenton, 800/437-7275 or 941/795-4633. On Bradenton Beach, try the **Sunset Beach Motel**, 2201 Gulf Dr. N., 941/778-7900, which has some efficiencies and offers beach proximity at moderate rates.

**CALL OF THE ISLANDS**

*If you can, find an extra day or two (and some extra cash) to stay on a relatively unknown Gulf island off Cape Haze in Charlotte County. Cars aren't allowed on Palm Island, where the* ***Palm Island Resort****, 7092 Placida Rd., Cape Haze, 800/824-5412 or 941/697-4800, awaits. You can walk, rent a golf cart, or take resort-provided trams to explore the far reaches of the island. Accommodations are spacious, moderately luxurious, and close to an endless white-sand beach.* ***Collier Inn****, on the 100-acre private island of Useppa, is another option. You'll feel time recede as you take the boat from Boca Grande or Bokeelia to the recently restored inn (mailing address: P.O. Box 640, Bokeelia, FL 33922, 941/283-5255). Walk, kayak, bicycle (though the island's not very big), fish, visit the little museum that documents the lifestyle of the Calusa Indians, or simply enjoy the gourmet meals and the nineteenth-century island elegance that surrounds you.*

Few bed-and-breakfast inns can match the combined casual elegance and location of **Harrington House**, 5626 Gulf Dr., Holmes Beach, 941/778-5444, www.harringtonhouse.com. The meals are terrific and the island location is literally 20 feet from the beach. Rates are moderately high, but you're not likely to regret spending a few extra dollars.

## CAMPING

Ample choices await campers in Florida's Sarasota region. South of the city, south of the Peace River, **Punta Gorda/Charlotte Harbor KOA**, 6800 Golf Course Blvd., Punta Gorda, 800/562-4786 or 941/637-1188, has a tent village and air-conditioned "Kamping Kabins," as well as wide pull-through sites. Northeast of the KOA, the **Arcadia Peace River Campground**, 2996 N.W. U.S. 70, Arcadia, 800/559-4011 or 941/494-9693, has 182 pull-through sites, full hookups, and an emphasis on outdoor recreation, with bicycle and hiking trails and canoe rentals for use along the picturesque Peace River.

**Venice Campground**, 4085 E. Venice Ave., Venice, 941/488-0850, is on the Myakka River just east of downtown, offering a good chance of finding isolation on nearby Gulf of Mexico beaches. There are 96 pull-through sites, full hookups, and cabin, boat, and canoe rentals. The **Myakka River State Park**, about nine miles east of Sarasota on SR 72, 941/361-6511, http://myakka.sarasota.fl.us/, is in a 28,875-acre park developed by the Civilian Conservation Corps in the 1930s to entice visitors to explore its large wildlife population, including alligators, deer, red-shouldered hawks, roseate spoonbills, and an unending cavalcade of other Florida birds. It offers 76 sites, 48 with electric and water hookups.

In Sarasota itself, **Gulf Beach Campground on the Beach**, 8862 Midnight Pass Rd., 941/349-3839, is on an island, directly on the Gulf of Mexico, with miles of beach and full hookups and tent sites. **Sun-N-Fun Resort**, 7125 Fruitville Rd., Sarasota, 800/843-2421 or 941/371-2505, is an RV city if there ever was one. It has 1,600 full-hookup, pull-through sites; paved pads; and complete recreation facilities, including lighted tennis courts and bicycle rentals.

In Osprey, just south of Sarasota, the **Oscar Scherer State Recreation Area** offers 104 sites with water and electric hookups. This park is another nature-lover's special with its extensive scrubby flatwoods, home to the Florida scrub jay, gopher tortoises, gopher frogs, and indigo snakes. Recreation includes canoeing, swimming, fishing, and hiking.

North of the city, **Sarasota Bay Travel Trailer Park**, 10777 44th Ave. W., Bradenton, 800/247-8361 or 941/794-1200, offers 50 full-hookup grass sites, plus some transient RV sites in a standing mobile-home subdivision right on Sarasota Bay. It accepts adults only—and no pets—from October through April.

## SHOPPING

You may find yourself reciting that bumper sticker, "So many shops, so little time," when you consider the alternatives in the Sarasota–Bradenton area of Florida. Sarasota boasts a Gulf Coast shopping mecca at **St. Armands Circle** on Lido Key, where fine dining is mixed with galleries and exclusive jewelry shops and boutiques. **South Gate Mall** has more than 150 shops, including Saks Fifth Avenue, Dillard's, and Burdines, while **Sarasota Square Mall** is anchored by Sears and JCPenney.

Salmon-colored, Mediterranean-style **Prime Outlets** at Ellenton (formerly Gulf Coast Shops) is hands-down the best and largest outlet mall on Florida's West Coast, with 135 stores. Famous names here include Royal Doulton, Elisabeth, Le Creuset Co., and Coach. Shop here and compare yourself to the averages Prime Retail has tabulated: time spent shopping, 2 hours,

22 minutes; stores visited, 15.4; dollars spent, 114; percentage who visit the food court, 48; percentage of repeat shoppers, 66.

## NIGHTLIFE

In a state full of dinner theaters, the professional troupe at the **Golden Apple Dinner Theatre**, 25 N. Pineapple Ave., Sarasota, 941/366-5454, wins consistently good reviews for its ambitious productions of Broadway shows from *Showboat* to *Camelot*. But your choices of evening entertainment are unending in the heart of what claims to be Florida's "Cultural Coast." There is excellent professional theater at the **Asolo Theatre**, 555 N. Tamiami Tr., 941/351-8000. One of the state's premier ballet companies, the **Sarasota Ballet of Florida**, performs at the same venue, while the **Florida West Coast Symphony** plays in centers in Venice, Sarasota, and Bradenton. The crowning jewel among the area's performing-arts centers is the shocking purple **Van Wezel Performing Arts Hall**, 777 N. Tamiami Tr., Sarasota, 800/826-9303, on Sarasota's bayfront, which presents top-rated traveling artists and shows. If you're an opera buff, don't miss a performance by **The Sarasota Opera**, 61 N. Pineapple Ave., 941/366-8450, considered the "Jewel on the Gulf" by *Opera News*.

Community theater is strong here, too. The **Venice Little Theatre**, 140 W. Tampa Ave., Venice, 941/488-1115, is one of the country's most successful community theaters; and **The Players of Sarasota**, 838 N. Tamiami Tr., Sarasota, 941/365-2494, has consistently been called the most professional of nonprofessional groups.

# 13
# TAMPA BAY

Variety is the watchword in the "tri-city" Tampa Bay area, which encompasses the cities surrounding Tampa, St. Petersburg, and Clearwater. Remnants of the Old South still find a home here in the natural habitats of Tampa's wild Hillsborough River. Vestiges of Indian mounds molder, and springs with legendary healing powers burble. Children build sand castles, teens play volleyball, men flex, and women hunt for shells on gently sloping beaches. Roller coasters thunder and roar. Latinos in Ybor City hand-roll cigars by day, and watch from their wrought-iron balconies as the old neighborhood turns to a hedonistic party city when night falls. Farmers inspect their strawberries.

Pinellas is Florida's most densely populated county, and that's before the population swells with the winter snowbird arrivals. While the West Coast, and St. Petersburg in particular, was once discounted as "heaven's waiting room," the area has been revitalized with younger residents in recent years. The rejuvenation has demanded more active pastimes, more cultural venues, more recreational choices, in fact, all the best features of a thriving metropolis, within easy access of deserted islands, beaches, and other natural recreation areas.

## A PERFECT DAY IN TAMPA BAY

The simplest way to ensure a grand time for all ages is to visit Busch Gardens in Tampa, the state's best theme park. The road less traveled might be a ferry

# TAMPA AREA

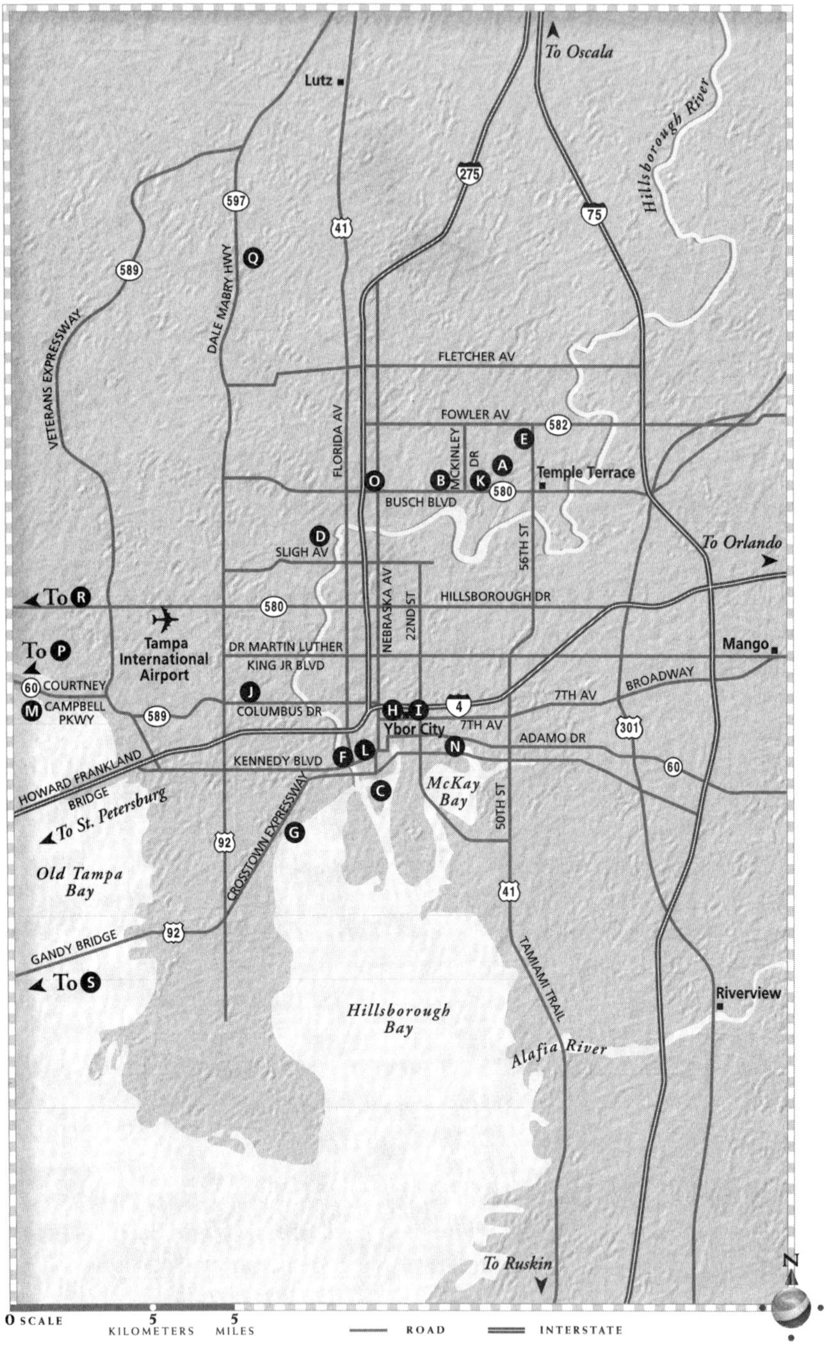
To Oscala
Lutz
Hillsborough River
275
597
75
41
589
DALE MABRY HWY
VETERANS EXPRESSWAY
FLETCHER AV
FOWLER AV
582
FLORIDA AV
MCKINLEY DR
Temple Terrace
580
BUSCH BLVD
56TH ST
SLIGH AV
To Orlando
To R
NEBRASKA AV
22ND ST
HILLSBOROUGH DR
To P
Tampa International Airport
DR MARTIN LUTHER KING JR BLVD
Mango
60 COURTNEY CAMPBELL PKWY
BROADWAY
7TH AV
4
COLUMBUS DR
Ybor City
301
ADAMO DR
KENNEDY BLVD
HOWARD FRANKLAND BRIDGE
McKay Bay
50TH ST
To St. Petersburg
92
CROSSTOWN EXPRESSWAY
Old Tampa Bay
GANDY BRIDGE
To S
TAMIAMI TRAIL
Riverview
Hillsborough Bay
Alafia River
To Ruskin
N
0 SCALE
5 KILOMETERS
5 MILES
ROAD
INTERSTATE

from Honeymoon Island in Dunedin to tranquil, uncrowded Caladesi Island, even if all you do is walk around a bit on the wide, white sandy beach, check out some wildlife, and then catch the first boat back. It's a short drive from here to Tarpon Springs to explore this quaint Greek seaside Mediterranean village and have lunch at Pappas or the Oxford House Tea Room. If your primary interest is beachside activity, head for busy Clearwater Beach, quiet Sand Key, multipurpose Fort DeSoto—or artsy St. Pete Beach, where you can shop, sunbathe, and find yourself on the Hurricane Restaurant rooftop at sunset, scanning the horizon for waterspouts or dolphins. If you're a foreign film or alternative/classic movie buff, end your day at the Beach Theatre in St. Pete Beach or at the exotic Tampa Theatre.

## ORIENTATION

On the south side of the peninsula, the four-mile-long, 192-foot-high Sunshine Skyway Bridge offers a stunning vista over Tampa Bay, connecting Sarasota and Manatee counties with Tampa or St. Petersburg and the West Coast via I-275.

In Tampa, I-4 and I-275 crisscross through downtown, with I-275 heading north to I-75 or southwest to St. Petersburg, and I-4 leading east to Lakeland and Orlando.

Three east-to-west bridges—the Gandy, the Howard Frankland (I-275), and the Courtney Campbell Causeway (SR 60)—link Tampa with Pinellas County, which encompasses the cities basically from St. Petersburg north to

### SIGHTS

- A Adventure Island Water Park
- B Busch Gardens
- C Florida Aquarium
- D Lowry Park Zoo
- E Museum of Science and Industry
- F Tampa Museum of Art
- F Tampa Theatre

### FOOD

- F Armani's
- G Bern's Steak House

### FOOD *(continued)*

- H Cafe Creole
- I Columbia
- J La Teresita
- K Mel's Hot Dogs
- L Mise En Place
- M Oystercatchers
- K Rumpelmayer's

### LODGING

- N Baymont Inn
- O Best Western Resort
- P Days Inn Rocky Point Island

### LODGING *(continued)*

- P DoubleTree Guest Suites
- M Hyatt Regency Westshore
- Q Saddlebrook Resort

### CAMPING

- R Bay Bayou Traveler RV Park
- S Tampa East Green Acres Campground

*Note: Items with the same letter are located in the same place or area.*

Tarpon Springs. North of the bridges, land access is through Oldsmar via SR 580 or SR 586, which connect with Tampa's Hillsborough Avenue.

Within Pinellas County, it's easy to go from one city to another without noticing any distinction. Streets can change names, though: Take Duhme Boulevard north from the 150th Avenue Causeway at Madeira Beach, and you'll find yourself on New Ridge Road, 113th Street, Ridge Road, Clearwater-Largo Road, Fort Harrison Avenue, Edgewater Drive, Bayshore Boulevard, Alternate 19, 10th Street, and Pinellas Avenue before you get to Tarpon Springs, so check your map again if you can't find what you're looking for. This is definitely the more touristy side of the Tampa Bay area. Traffic here is noticeably more congested from November through April, and roads along the beaches can slow to a crawl January through March.

## SIGHTSEEING HIGHLIGHTS

### ★★★★ BUSCH GARDENS

**3000 E. Busch Blvd., Tampa, 800/372-1797 or 813/987-5082, www.buschgardens.com**

This extensive, multifaceted attraction is pure gold. Its 300 acres are packed full of African-themed shows, shops, exhibits, wild animals, and thrill rides. It has five of the best roller coasters in the Southeast, including its newest wind-whipping, wooden, dueling double coaster, the **Gwazi**. Named after a fabled lion with a tiger's head, the two coasters speed past each other six times at a combined speed of 100 mph; the looping, swirling, 2-minute 20-second ride rises 90 feet on 6,800 feet of track. If you ride the 20-passenger **Tanganyika Tidal Wave**, you're sure to get wet, but in the midday heat you may welcome it, and you'll find yourself dry before you know it. You'll be just inches from huge, powerful gorilla and chimpanzee families who can't see you from the other side of the glass at the **Myombe Preserve**. A lushly landscaped pathway through colorful **Orchid Canyon** winds between high cliffs, a spider-monkey island habitat, and more than 250 exotic tropical orchids. The **Moroccan Palace** features spectacular sets and costumes, and the **Hollywood On Ice** skating show. Don't miss the truly unique **King Tut's Tomb** exhibit, a realistic replica of the 1920s excavation site and the treasures found there.

***Details:*** *Open daily; hours vary seasonally. Admission: $46 adults, $37 children, plus $4–$6 parking. (full day)*

### ★★★★ FORT DESOTO PARK

**Pinellas Bayway Exit off I-275, St. Petersburg, 727/866-2484; campground 727/582-2267**

Fort DeSoto Park encompasses 900 tranquil acres, including seven miles of glistening beaches on five keys, at the south end of St. Petersburg. The park offers good fishing, swimming, and bathing facilities; its very shallow water makes it great for families with small children. Kids also might enjoy the old fort, built during the Spanish-American War, which is set up for a self-guided tour. Rent a kayak, canoe, or bike and explore the park, or follow the winding nature trail through the Arrowhead area across from North Beach. Be sure to wear sturdy shoes or sneakers to keep from getting stuck by the prickly sand spurs that grow here.

***Details:*** *Open daily dawn–dusk, except piers and boat ramp, which never close. Free. Pets are welcome.*

### ★★★★ SALVADOR DALÍ MUSEUM

**1000 Third St. S., St. Petersburg, 727/823-3767, www.Daliweb.com**

The only difference between a madman and this eccentric surrealist master, according to Dalí himself, is that "I am not mad." This always-striking, sometimes-disturbing museum houses the world's largest collection of works by Salvador Dalí, including *Galacid, The Dream,* and others, as well as traveling exhibits of other surrealists. Take the docent-led tour for a better understanding of some of the recurring themes employed by the unforgettable artist.

***Details:*** *Open Mon–Sat 9:30–5:30, also Thu 5:30–8, Sun noon–5:30. Admission: $8 adults, $4 children, $7 seniors. (1 1/2–2 hours)*

### ★★★ ADVENTURE ISLAND WATER PARK

**10001 McKinley Dr. at Busch Blvd., Tampa, 800/423-8368 or 813/987-5600, www.adventureisland.com**

If your gang likes waterparks, this one tops the heap. Adventure Island offers extreme activity and plenty of super-sopping rides for good summer fun on the hottest Florida days. Young folks can't get enough of the seven-story Tampa Typhoon, the park's tallest water slide, or the side-by-side tube-slides in Key West Rapids. The less adventurous will enjoy the Rambling Bayou, a slower-paced, lazy-river float ride. Pools are heated in cooler weather, and smaller rides are available for small children. The park offers lifeguards, lockers, changing facilities, and electronic games. Be sure to bring waterproof sunscreen and reapply it every couple of hours.

***Details:*** *Open daily mid-Feb–early Sept, weekends only Sept–Oct; hours vary seasonally. Admission: $24.92 adults, $22.95 children. Parking $3. (half-day minimum)*

## ★★★ CALADESI ISLAND STATE PARK

**Dunedin, 727/734-1501**

This is the Florida you came to see. After a 15-minute ferry ride from Honeymoon Island to Caladesi, you'll find yourself on a gently sloping, baby-powder-soft white beach. The three-mile stretch of sand is relatively uncrowded, and the park has nicely kept bathhouses with showers, picnic shelters, and tables (though these are a bit of a walk from the beach). See the island's interior on a three-mile nature trail or explore the mangroves at the water's edge—they're full of herons, egrets, and wood storks.

***Details:*** *Take Curlew Road west to Honeymoon Island. Admission: $4 carload to enter Honeymoon Island State Recreation Area. Ferry from Honeymoon: $6 adults, $3.50 children.*

## ★★★ FLORIDA INTERNATIONAL MUSEUM

**100 Second St. N., St. Petersburg, 800/777-9882 or 727/821-1448**

Blockbuster international traveling exhibits at this relatively new museum have included "Treasures of the Russian Czars" and "Empires of Mystery: The Incas, the Andes and Lost Civilizations." Galleries are designed anew, walls moved, and special areas erected for each show, and the presentations get better every time. The world's largest collection of John F. Kennedy memorabilia is also in permanent residence here. Items include Kennedy's christening ring, doodles drawn on White House paper during the 1962 Cuban missile crisis, and flags flown from the presidential limo in Dallas on November 22, 1963.

***Details:*** *During exhibitions open daily 9–8 (last tours at 6). Admission: $13.95 adults, $5.95 children, $12.95 seniors. (1½–2 hours)*

## ★★★ GREAT EXPLORATIONS

**The Pier, 800 Second Ave. NE, St. Petersburg, 727/821-8992**

Engaging interactive exhibits involve you in the arts and sciences at this innovative hands-on museum, and you needn't be a kid to love it.

Take off your shoes and crawl through the 90-foot, pitch-black Touch Tunnel linear maze, examine a 25-foot model of a diamondback rattlesnake, investigate the principles of physical science in Explore Galore, solve brain-teasing 3-D logic puzzles in the Think Tank, make music and magic in the Phenomenal Arts area, and test your reflexes, fitness, and flexibility in the Body Shop. The museum store is full of fun things, too—try the freeze-dried ice cream, for starters.

***Details:*** *Open Mon–Sat 10–5, Sun noon–5. Admission: $6 adults, $5 children, $5.50 seniors. (1–2 hours)*

## ★★★ HERITAGE VILLAGE

**11909 125th St. N., Largo, 727/582-2123**

If you want to know what life was like for Florida's early settlers, this 21-acre complex provides a fascinating window into a bygone era. Twenty-three pioneer buildings have been relocated to this site, where a museum displays artifacts, early photos, and archeological finds. The focus is on preserving the history of Pinellas County and showing how people lived. The oldest structure, the 1852 McMullen-Coachman Log House, exemplifies the Cracker-style architecture used before air-conditioning, in which buildings were separated by a breezeway or "dog trot," allowing breezes to flow through even in midsummer. The 1896 Plant-Sumner House, built by the Henry Plant Co. to house the men working on the Belleview Biltmore Hotel, has a seven-foot bathtub, similar to those installed in the historic hotel. Occasional weddings are still performed at the 1905 Safety Harbor First Methodist Church, which holds the original pulpit and altar rail. A Garden for the Blind, housed in a gazebo, holds nontoxic plants and herbs to be touched and smelled, identified by braille markers.

***Details:*** *Open Tue–Sat 10–4, Sun 1–4. Free; donations welcome. (1–2 hours)*

## ★★★ MUSEUM OF FINE ARTS

**255 Beach Dr. N.E., St. Petersburg, 727/896-2667**

It's not too large, but it's one of the best fine-art museums in the Southeast, with a collection of more than 4,000 works. Significant French and American artists represented include Cézanne, Gauguin, Renoir, Rodin, George Inness, and Georgia O'Keeffe. Photography, Native American, pre-Columbian, African, and Asian collections are displayed in 20 galleries, including a beautiful Steuben glass exhibit.

# SOUTHERN PINELLAS COUNTY

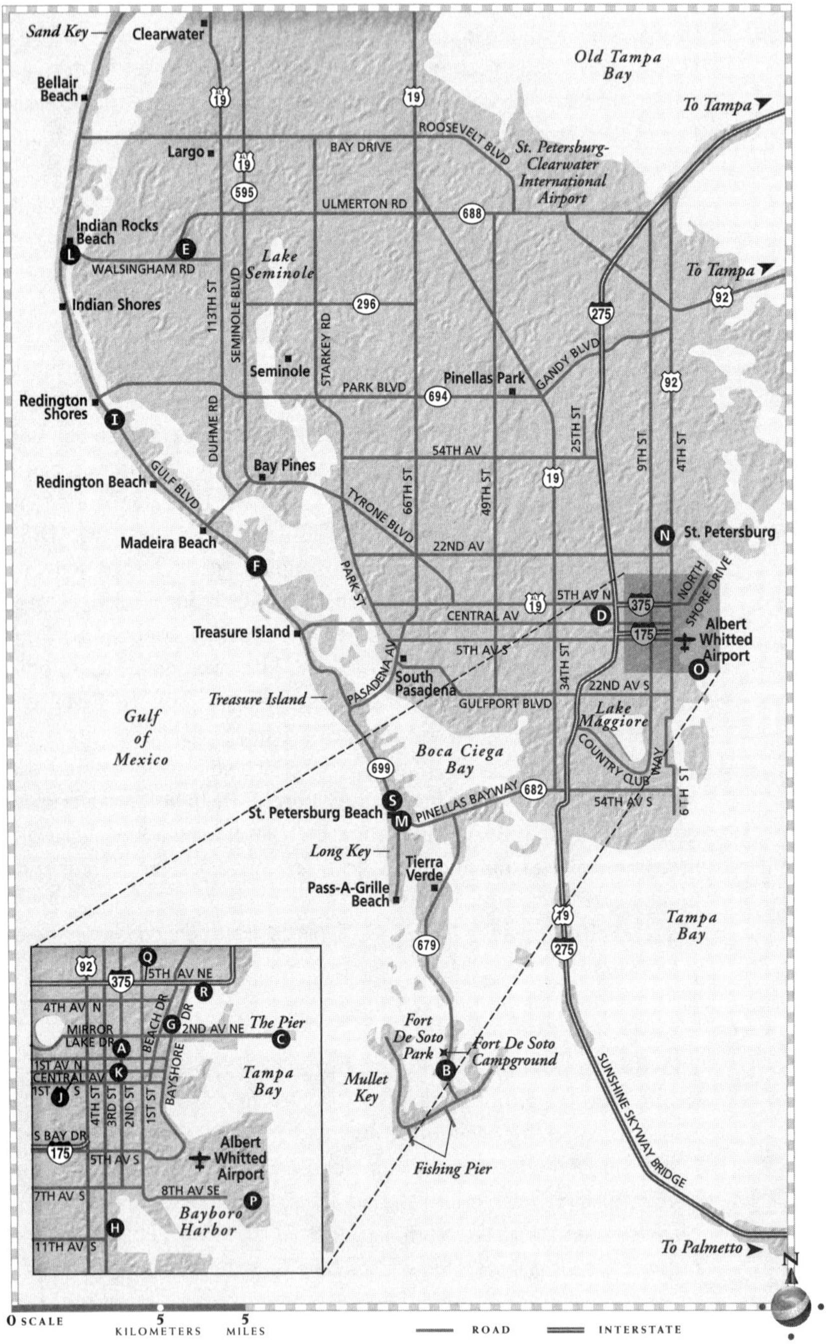

***Details:*** *Open Tue–Sat 10–5, Sun 1–5. $6 adults, $2 students, $5 seniors; free to all on Sun.*

### ★★★ TAMPA THEATRE

**711 N. Franklin St., Tampa, 813/274-8981, tampatheatre@juno.com**

If you have a chance to catch a classic, independent, or foreign film or a musical performance at this restored 1926 movie palace, you'll long remember the visit. Find a water fountain, and the basin is likely to be strewn with fragrant rose petals. While the sound system isn't state-of-the-art, the elaborately decorated Rococo-style theater will give you plenty to look at while you listen or sing along during a mini Mighty Wurlitzer organ concert before the show. The illusion is that you're looking up into the sky on a starry summer night from within the courtyard of a Spanish palazzo, while cherubim, seraphim, and other statuary adorn the intricately carved pillars and walls around you.

***Details:*** *Downtown Tampa. Call for schedule of events.*

### ★★★ TARPON SPRINGS

**727/937-6109**

For years, sponging was the leading industry of this Greek-American community. It's still a prime source of income, and many shops sell

---

#### SIGHTS

- Ⓐ Florida International Museum
- Ⓑ Fort DeSoto Park
- Ⓒ Great Explorations
- Ⓓ Haslam's
- Ⓔ Heritage Village
- Ⓕ John's Pass Village and Boardwalk
- Ⓖ Museum of Fine Arts
- Ⓖ The Pier
- Ⓗ Salvador Dalí Museum
- Ⓘ Suncoast Seabird Sanctuary
- Ⓙ Tampa Bay Holocaust Museum

#### FOOD

- Ⓚ Garden Restaurant
- Ⓚ Guppy's
- Ⓛ Hurricane Restaurant
- Ⓜ Ringside Cafe
- Ⓝ Smokey's Texas Bar-B-Que

#### LODGING

- Ⓞ Bayboro House
- Ⓛ Don Cesar Beach Resort and Spa
- Ⓛ Dolphin Beach Resort
- Ⓟ Mansion House

#### LODGING *(continued)*

- Ⓚ Pelican West
- Ⓠ Renaissance Vinoy
- Ⓡ Shifting Sands Cottages

#### CAMPING

- Ⓑ Fort DeSoto Park Campground
- Ⓢ St. Petersburg-Madeira Beach Resort KOA

*Note: Items with the same letter are located in the same place.*

the sea's bounty of natural sponges, from the tiny cosmetic-size to huge ones for washing the SUV. Gift and clothing shop prices are reasonable, and delectable Greek pastries and coffee make this a great afternoon's stop. For a delectable lunch, try some spanakopita (spinach and feta-cheese pie) or a gyro sandwich made of thinly sliced, roasted lamb or pork, served with a spicy cucumber and yogurt sauce and wrapped in a rolled-up pita bread. Shops are open late on weekend evenings, and the bakeries and cafés offer patio or sidewalk tables for people watching over a casual dessert or postprandial of ouzo or Metaxa.

Along the **Sponge Docks** where the fishermen tie up their boats on Dodecanese Boulevard, visit the open-air **Spongeorama Exhibit Center,** 727/943-9509, a free attraction that shows a 30-minute film and houses a museum with sponging artifacts dating to the early 1900s. You can try the ancient art of brass rubbing at the **Medieval Brass Rubbing Center**, 727/934-6760; or visit the **Coral Sea Aquarium**, 727/938-5378, which has a simulated coral reef, tidal-pool touch tank, and separate tanks for Pacific Ocean marine life and South Pacific predators.

Built in 1943, the **St. Nicholas Greek Orthodox Cathedral** downtown at the corner of U.S. Alt. 19 and Orange St., 727/937-3540, is a replica of St. Sophia's in Constantinople, and weeping icons have been reported here. The church is the center of many Greek festivals, including the huge annual Epiphany celebration on January 6. The **Unitarian Universalist Church** at 230 Grand Blvd., 727/937-4682, is worth a visit to see the religious paintings by American artist George Inness, Jr., celebrated for his innovative use of light and luminous shades of green.

***Details:*** *From Tampa, take Keystone Road west; from Clearwater, go north on U.S. 19 about 10 miles then turn left on Anclote Road (Keystone goes off here on your right).*

## ★★ FLORIDA AQUARIUM

**701 Channelside Dr., Tampa, 813/273-4000**

The Florida Aquarium, housed in a glass-domed building on Tampa's waterfront, is home to more than 5,300 animals. Call ahead for times if you want to chat one-on-one with a marine biologist who answers you from underwater in the shark tank. Look for the tank of white moon jellyfish, whose ethereal, white gossamer threads wave rhythmically before you. This is a rapidly improving aquarium. Don't miss the Frights of the Forest exhibit, which features live animals that thrive in wet forest habitats, and other special exhibits. You'll see vampire bats, electric eels, tarantulas, and poison dart frogs, and you'll get a close-up look at assorted skulls and skeletons, a bee stinger, a human louse, and a bedbug's mouth.

***Details:*** *Open daily 9:30–5. Admission: $11.95 adults, $6.95 children, $10.95 seniors. Parking: $3. (2–4 hours)*

## ★★ JOHN'S PASS VILLAGE AND BOARDWALK

**Gulf Blvd., Madeira Beach, 727/367-4529**

Perched at the edge of a Gulf of Mexico inlet, this lively area has more than 100 unique shops, restaurants, and art galleries, plus boat and watercraft rentals and charters. The annual Seafood Festival, held the last full weekend of October, features continuous outdoor entertainment, arts and crafts, and plenty of fresh fish, shrimp, and other seafood.

***Details:*** *Located just south of 150th Avenue. Generally open daily 10–9. Free. (30 minutes minimum)*

## ★★ LOWRY PARK ZOO

**North Blvd. at Sligh Ave., Tampa, 813/935-8552**

Answer the call of the wild at this unpretentious but satisfying zoo. It's home to the state's largest collection of native Floridian wildlife, including alligators, panthers, bears, and manatees, plus primates, exotic Asian tigers, a free-flight aviary, and kids' petting zoo. Look for a fascinating golden lion tamarin and the woolly monkey in Primate World, and an extremely rare Indian rhino in the Asian Domain. An extensive manatee exhibit gives you a fabulous underwater look at these lumbering sea cows.

***Details:*** *Open daily 9:30–5 (varies seasonally). Admission: $8.50 adults, $4.95 children, $7.50 seniors. (2–3 hours)*

## ★★ MUSEUM OF SCIENCE AND INDUSTRY (MOSI)

**4801 E. Fowler Ave., Tampa, 813/987-6300**

The MOSIMAX theater's 10,500-square-foot screen is the best thing about this large science-and-technology museum, and films here are really impressive. Step inside the Gulf Coast Hurricane exhibit for an idea of just how powerful a 74-mph wind is. Some good flight and space, physics, and engineering exhibits may outweigh your disappointment if some of the hands-on activities or buttons don't work.

***Details:*** *Open daily 9–6 or so (closing hours vary). Admission: $11 adults, $7 children, $9 seniors. IMAX admission also available separately. (3 hours)*

### ★★ THE PIER

**East end of Second Ave. N.E., St. Petersburg, 727/821-6164**

One of the most recognizable landmarks in this part of Florida is this inverted five-story pyramid in downtown St. Petersburg. It features two cylindrical fish tanks rising from the first floor to the second-floor aquarium, the third-floor Great Explorations hands-on museum, a food court, and entertaining shops and restaurants. The Pier extends some 2,400 feet out into Tampa Bay, and the windows from the Columbia Restaurant offer a spectacular view. A 300-foot guided missile–carrying Russian submarine, docked on the north side of the pier and formerly used to hunt U.S. aircraft, is open for touring.

***Details:*** *Open daily; shops 10–9, restaurants close later. Parking $3 at foot of pier with free shuttle service; valet parking free for restaurant patrons. Free. (1 hour minimum)*

### ★★ PHILIPPE PARK

**2355 Philippe Pkwy., Safety Harbor, 727/461-0011**

French Count Odet Philippe, head surgeon of Napoleon Bonaparte's navy, landed at the site of the Espiritu Santo Springs about a mile south of here in 1823. The doctor called the springs God's own medicine, "stirred by His hand and deposited on this shore to heal man's suffering." Philippe stayed and planted the first grapefruit, limes, and oranges in this part of Florida. The citrus trees or their progeny still flourish here at the edge of Old Tampa Bay, and Philippe's grave mound is marked. The park offers recreation areas, covered shelters, grills, softball fields, boat slips, and a tiny spit of sandy beach. It's a lovely place for practicing tai chi at sunrise, midday rollerblading or napping, or just taking a walk at dusk, listening to the cicadas humming and watching the sky and water turn shades of salmon and gold.

***Details:*** *On SR 590 about a mile north of downtown Safety Harbor. Open daily sunrise–dusk. Free.*

### ★★ SAND KEY PARK

**SR 699 (Gulf Blvd.), south of Clearwater Beach, 727/595-7677**

Just a short drive south of Clearwater Beach brings you to a quiet, palm tree–studded beach at Sand Key. If you like your beaches huge, broad, and serene, this one's for you. Bring everything you'll want with you, as there's no concession stand.

**Details:** *Open daily sunrise–dusk. Free. Parking: 20 minutes for 25 cents.*

## ★★ TAMPA BAY HOLOCAUST MUSEUM

**55 Fifth St. S., St. Petersburg, 727/820-0100, tampabayholocaust.org**

The fourth-largest holocaust museum in the country is downtown St. Petersburg's newest. Vibrant exhibits illuminate the era of Nazi tyranny when 11 million Jews, Gypsies, Jehovah's Witnesses, physically disabled people, homosexuals, and political dissidents were murdered or condemned to death in ghettos and concentration camps between 1933 and 1945. Exhibits tell the stories of Anne Frank, Maximilian Kolbe, and Oskar Schindler, among others. A particularly powerful display in the central atrium confronts visitors with the power and massiveness of Auschwitz Boxcar #113-0695-5, resting on railroad tracks from Treblinka, formerly used by the Nazis to transport victims to the killing centers.

**Details:** *Open Mon–Fri 10–5, Sat–Sun noon–5. Admission: $6 adults, $2 children, $5 seniors. (1 hour)*

## ★★ TAMPA MUSEUM OF ART

**600 N. Ashley Dr., Tampa, 813/274-8130**

The attractive, modern building in downtown Tampa with all the public space and reflecting pools out front is the home of an impressive permanent collection that includes Greek, Roman, and South American antiquities and contemporary American art. It also hosts unusual, first-rate traveling exhibits in a variety of media.

**Details:** *Open Mon–Sat 10–5, also Wed 5–9, Sun 1–5. Admission: $5 adults, $3 children, $4 seniors, except Wed 5–9 and Sat 10–noon, free to all. (2 hours)*

## ★ HASLAM'S

**2025 Central Ave., St. Petersburg, 727/822-8616**

It's an especially worthy rainy-day attraction, but book-lovers will need no excuse to pay a visit to Florida's largest independent bookseller, which stocks over 300,000 new, used, and rare books.

# NORTHERN PINELLAS COUNTY

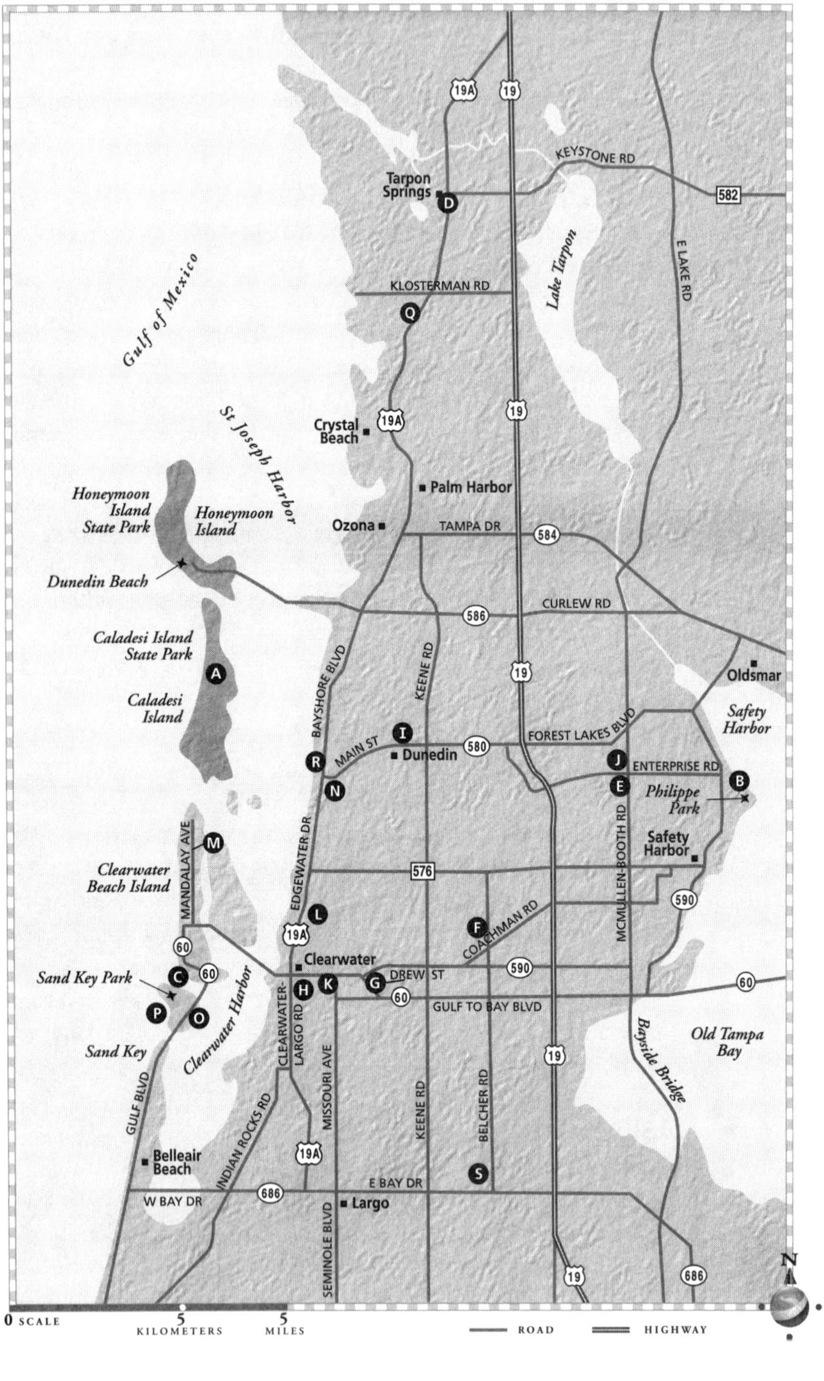

It's easily spotted by its extensive frontage along St. Petersburg's main drag.

***Details:*** *Open Mon–Sat 10–6:30, Sun 12:30–5:30. Free. (30 minutes)*

★ **SUNCOAST SEABIRD SANCTUARY**
**18328 Gulf Blvd., Indian Shores, 727/391-6211**

This beachfront avian hospital is home to hundreds of injured wild birds, most of which are released when sufficiently healed. The staff rescues and rehabilitates nearly 5,000 birds a year, from songbirds to pelicans and birds of prey. Generally, you're on your own to tour the modest one-acre facility; guided tours are held Wednesday and Sunday at 2.

***Details:*** *Open daily 9–dusk. Free, donations welcome. (30 minutes)*

## FITNESS AND RECREATION

It should come as no surprise that golf is big around Tampa Bay, and an abundance of good courses are open to the public. Sure, it's hot in summer, but that's when you can join the locals to play in the least-crowded conditions. In winter the game's popularity with the area's huge snowbird population makes advance tee times a must.

You can wager on greyhounds racing on the country's oldest continually operated track at **Derby Lane** in St. Petersburg. **Tampa Bay Downs** in

---

**SIGHTS**

- A Caladesi Island State Park
- B Phillippe Park
- C Sand Key Park
- D Tarpon Springs

**FOOD**

- E Alley Cat's
- F Azara's
- G Caramba's
- H Carmelita's

**FOOD** *(continued)*

- I Casa Tina
- D Dino's
- J G. Bellini's
- K Johnny's Italian Restaurant
- L Made in Italy
- J Marco Polo
- D Pappa's

**LODGING**

- M Clearwater Beach Hotel

**LODGING** *(continued)*

- N J.O. Douglas House
- O Radisson Suite Resort
- P Sheraton Sand Key Resort
- Q Westin Innisbrook Resort

**CAMPING**

- R Dunedin Beach Campground
- S Travel Towne RV Resort

*Note: Items with the same letter are located in the same place.*

Oldsmar has live thoroughbred racing from December through May, and year-round simulcasts from other racing and jai alai venues. If polo is your game, call the **Tampa Polo Club**, 813/754-2234.

Windsurfing, parasailing, and boating opportunities are plentiful. You can canoe downstream on the Hillsborough River through a 16,000-acre wilderness park in the heart of Tampa by calling **Canoe Escape**, 813/986-2067. For fishing, **Pier 60**, at the end of SR 60 on Clearwater Beach, 727/462-6466, is open 24 hours, as are St. Petersburg's **Sunshine Skyway Fishing Piers**, which offer bait, tackle, restrooms, and nighttime security. For fishing license information, call 813/272-6040.

Tampa's **Seminole Indian Casino**, 800/282-7016 or 813/621-1302, a full-fledged casino on an Indian reservation, offers 24-hour gaming, including high-stakes bingo, stud poker, and Texas Hold-em. Gamblers in Pinellas can try their luck on the twice-daily ***SunCruz*** casino cruise from Tarpon Springs, 800/464-3423 or 727/843-3423, which features blackjack, roulette, dice, table games, slots, bingo, and live entertainment.

Professional sports are well represented throughout the area, including the **Tampa Bay Mutiny** soccer team, NHL's **Tampa Bay Lightning**, NFL's **Tampa Bay Buccaneers**, and baseball's **Tampa Bay Devil Rays**. Spring training is held beginning the first week in March by the **New York Yankees** in Tampa, the **Philadelphia Phillies** in Clearwater, the **Toronto Blue Jays** in Dunedin, and the **Tampa Bay Devil Rays** in St. Petersburg.

## FOOD

In Tampa, lovers of German food will enjoy the family-owned **Rumpelmayer's**, 4812 E. Busch Blvd., 813/989-9563, near Busch Gardens. Lederhosen-clad musicians play while you dine on brats, sauerbraten, and apple strudel, or choose from more than 80 German beers at moderate prices. For a faster bite, locals of all financial means revere the Vienna beef tube-sausage at **Mel's Hot Dogs**, 4136 E. Busch Blvd., 813/985-8000.

Tampa's Ybor City district once had more than 120 cigar factories, employing mostly Cuban, Spanish, and Italian immigrants, and their descendants still are prominent throughout the city, ensuring the continued popularity of the **Columbia**, 2117 E. 7th Ave., 813/248-4961, Tampa's darling for fine Spanish cuisine. Call for show times of the flamenco dancers who perform nightly. For Cajun and Creole specialties, try **Cafe Creole**, 1330 Ninth Ave. E., 813/247-6283. The bar here is popular, too, with live jazz on weekends. Just a couple of blocks off Dale Mabry, there's a fine Spanish dining room at **La Teresita**, 3248 W. Columbus Dr., 813/879-4909, but huge portions are served faster next door if you want to belly up to the old, casual, counter-seating area.

A longtime favorite, **Mise En Place**, 442 W. Kennedy Blvd., 813/254-5373, is a smart, brasserie-style American bistro across from the University of Tampa. **Bern's Steak House**, 1208 S. Howard Ave., 813/251-2421, is a Tampa institution for fine aged beef, Bern Laxer's own home-grown organic vegetables, a 200-page wine list, and a truly unique dessert room. If funds are limited, have dinner elsewhere and make just a dessert-room reservation here.

Just before the SR 60 causeway to Pinellas County, **Armani's**, 813/281-9165, and **Oystercatchers**, 813/281-9116, both at the Hyatt Regency, 6200 Courtney Campbell Causeway, are favorites. Oystercatchers has a waterfront patio that's great for casual drinks and often has an island or reggae-type ensemble playing after 5 p.m. or on weekends. The restaurant is highly regarded for its fresh seafood from around the world and spectacular upscale Sunday brunch. Armani's, perched atop the hotel, offers Tampa's best in service, cuisine, presentation, and romantic ambience, with a gorgeous sunset view overlooking Tampa Bay and the causeway to Clearwater.

You'll have to vie with locals for a table at the artsy **Garden Restaurant** at Jannus Landing, 217 Central Ave., St. Petersburg, 727/896-3800. It's a popular café with a varied Mediterranean menu. Jazz bands play in the outdoor patio area, where umbrellas protect tables from the sparrows that flit about in the trees overhead. The **Ringside Cafe**, 2742 Fourth St. N., 727/894-8465, offers good casual dining amid lots of boxing paraphernalia, due to its proximity to an old boxing venue next door, and there's live blues on Friday and Saturday nights. Big, meaty ribs, slow-smoked over hickory; friendly service; and excellent value are the draw at **Smokey's Texas Bar-B-Que**, 8180 49th St. N., Pinellas Park, 727/546-3600, which features Texas-style appetizers, chicken, seafood, and burgers.

On the beaches, you may have to elbow your way through a crowd for the locally famous grouper sandwich and a tall, cool drink inside or out on the rooftop deck overlooking Pass-a-Grille Beach at the huge, three-story **Hurricane Restaurant**, Ninth Ave. and Gulf Way, St. Pete Beach, 727/360-9558. Casual dress is the rule, indoors or on the patio, for innovatively prepared fresh seafood, sandwiches, and salads at **Guppy's**, 1701 N. Gulf Blvd., Indian Rocks Beach, 727/593-2032.

In Clearwater's Countryside area, **Marco Polo**, 2516 McMullen-Booth Rd. at Enterprise Road in Northwood Oaks Plaza, 727/791-7979, offers excellent value with a moderately priced menu of gourmet continental cuisine. **G. Bellini's**, 727/724-5716, in the same complex, is fashionable with the after-work crowd, offering wood-oven baked pizzas and regional Italian dishes.

Just across the street in Oakbrook Plaza, **Alley Cat's**, 727/797-5555, is a good, casual place for seafood dishes, generous sandwiches and salads, and informal evening entertainment.

Italian restaurants figure prominently in Clearwater. For its setting in a small strip center, **Azara's** at Belcher Road just north of N.E. Coachman Road, 727/441-1644, is surprisingly charming inside. **Johnny's Italian Restaurant**, just east of U.S. 19 in the Mission Hills Plaza at 2907 SR 590, 727/797-2940, is also excellent. It's casual, and offers excellent value at pleasingly affordable prices. Just north of Countryside Mall, housed in an old steakhouse on the west side of the highway, try **Made in Italy**, 27964 U.S. Hwy. 19 N., for savory chicken, fresh veal, or the delicious bowtie pasta with prosciutto in asiago sauce.

Mexican lovers can't go wrong at any of these three cantinas. The best is **Caramba's,** 1842 Drew St., Clearwater, 727/336-7469, for terrific seafoods or chicken and a marvelous mole sauce. **Carmelita's,** at either 5211 Park St. N., St. Petersburg, 727/545-2956, or 5100 Easy Bay Dr., Clearwater, 727/524-8226, has good Mexican and Tex-Mex at bargain prices, with mariachi singers in the evenings. For fresh, healthy dishes, try the wild mushroom quesadillas at **Casa Tina,** 369 Main St., Dunedin, 727/734-9226; they open early on weekends for huevos rancheros or other brunch-type dishes.

In the Greek village of downtown **Tarpon Springs**, the huge landmark restaurant is **Pappas**, 10 W. Dodecanese Blvd., 727/937-5101—its trademark Greek salad is a visual masterpiece. For more casual dining, **Dino's Taverna**, 604 Athens St., 727/938-9082, has good, authentic Greek cuisine and ambience.

## LODGING

North of Tampa off I-75, Wesley Chapel has a terrific, condo-style complex that's great for active families. The **Saddlebrook Resort**, 5700 Saddlebrook Way, 813/973-1111, has 36 holes of golf, the Arnold Palmer Golf Academy, and a tennis academy and 45 tennis courts, plus fishing-equipment and bicycle rentals. Lodging is in a walking village on beautifully landscaped grounds that surround a meandering, lagoon-type swimming pool.

If you're planning to visit Busch Gardens, you can easily stay close by. All the chains are here as well as along the major roads near the airport. Near Busch, the **Baymont Inn**, 9202 30th St. N., 813/930-6900 won't cost an arm and a leg, and has a pool and free continental breakfast. Also reasonable, the full-service **Best Western Resort** at 820 E. Busch Blvd., 800/288-4011 or

813/933-4011, offers indoor and outdoor pools, lighted tennis courts, exercise facilities, and a sauna.

Near the airport, if you're here on business or planning to spend much time in your hotel, you won't regret staying at the **Hyatt Regency Westshore** high-rise, 6200 Courtney Campbell Cswy., 800/233-1234 or 813/874-1234, built on a scenic nature preserve that hosts lots of readily visible wildlife at the edge of Tampa Bay. The complex has a health club with tennis and racquetball, plus two of Tampa's best restaurants. Just a mile or so west, the **Days Inn Rocky Point Island**, 7627 Courtney Campbell Cswy., 800/237-2555 or 813/281-0000, and the more expensive **DoubleTree Guest Suites**, 3050 Rocky Point Dr. W., 813/888-8800, are set on a protected inlet and canal with a small beach area offering water sports, Jet Ski rentals, and beach volleyball courts.

Downtown St. Petersburg has a number of historic guest houses. Across from the waterfront, the **Bayboro House**, 1719 Beach Dr. S.E., 727/823-4955, is a luxurious family-owned and -operated B&B, with a swing on the verandah from which you can watch the seabirds and boats passing by. In the heart of the entertainment district, the historic, owner-occupied 1904 **Mansion House**, 105 Fifth Ave. N.E., 800/274-7520, www.mansionbandb.com, offers nicely restored common areas, and it's within an easy walk of the waterfront, art galleries, museums, and shops. For luxurious waterfront lodging within walking distance of many area attractions, reserve at the Mediterranean Revival–style **Renaissance Vinoy**, 501 Fifth Ave. N.E., 800/678-8946 or 727/894-1000.

If you drive over the Pinellas Bayway from St. Petersburg to St. Pete Beach, the huge pink castle you'll see is the **Don CeSar Beach Resort and Spa**, 3400 Gulf Blvd., 800/637-7200 or 727/360-1881. This historic resort has a full-service spa, water sports, parasailing, and a lavish Sunday brunch. It's a fine place to spend a night to say you did, but while the setting and public areas are spectacular, guest rooms can be small and antique furnishings just old. The **Dolphin Beach Resort**, 4900 Gulf Blvd., 800/237-8916 or 727/360-7011, is more reasonable and still has an impressive beach frontage, heated pool, and water-sports facilities.

**Shifting Sands Cottages**, 10232 Gulf Blvd., Treasure Island, 800/458-8728 or 727/360-7777, offer inexpensive beachfront cottages with kitchens, outdoor grills, and shuffleboard. Also on Indian Rocks Beach, low-priced, neatly furnished beachfront apartments are available at **Pelican West**, 108 21st Ave., 727/595-9741.

On Sand Key, all the units at the **Radisson Suite Resort**, 1201 Gulf Blvd., 800/333-3333 or 727/596-1100, have private balconies so you can

**SAY SPA—AHH!**

*The **Safety Harbor Resort and Spa**, 105 N. Bayshore, 727/726-1161, a National Historic Landmark, has a long history. Built over five natural mineral springs believed by Hernando de Soto to be the legendary "Fountain of Youth" somehow missed by Ponce de León, its waters have been bottled and sold as far back as 1855 as cures for maladies from skin diseases and indigestion to diabetes and high blood pressure. A sanitorium was developed, porcelain bathtubs and a large pool were installed, and in 1944 the facility opened as a health spa, offering body treatments and overnight accommodations on a picturesque setting at the edge of Old Tampa Bay. Long patronized by celebrities, athletes, and visiting dignitaries, the resort offers an extensive fitness center, skin-care institute, and tennis academy. The sunny decor reflects its historic Spanish heritage; hand-colored vintage photos grace the walls. The crystal-clear spring waters are used throughout the resort for drinking, bathing, and a lengthy roster of European-style spa services. The main dining room's domed ceiling recalls the original Espiritu Santo Springs pavilion. The Café here has a superb Sunday brunch that's open to the public.*

watch the sun set over the Gulf. The complex includes a fitness center, sauna and spa services, and a huge, free-form pool for cooling off after you step in from the beach. Slightly less expensive just north is the **Sheraton Sand Key Resort**, 1160 Gulf Blvd., 727/595-1611, which offers a variety of beachfront activities and water sports.

If you long for the ambience of a grand old Southern-style hotel, stay at the **Clearwater Beach Hotel**, 500 Mandalay Ave., Clearwater Beach, 800/292-2295 or 727/441-2425, which has an excellent restaurant and beautiful vistas of the water.

Close to everything in Dunedin, yet off the beaten track, the **J. O. Douglas House,** 209 Scotland St., 727/735-9006, an 1878 Victorian B&B across from the marina, is listed in the National Register of Historic Places. Hardwood floors are polished to a gleam and the large, screened front porch is a peaceful refuge with comfortable swings. Just a couple of minutes' walk away are quaint shops and restaurants downtown, and the house overlooks the Pinellas Trail, a 32-mile paved recreation trail. Bike and inline-skate rentals are available.

Spacious condos are offered at **Westin Innisbrook Resort**, 36750 U.S. 19 N., Palm Harbor, 727/942-2000, a renowned golf resort set on 1,000 manicured and wooded acres that, from within, you'd never know are so close to a major highway. There's excellent golf on five championship courses, including the venomous Copperhead, plus tennis, racquetball, fishing, and a superb on-site steak house.

## CAMPING

East of Tampa in Dover, about 15 minutes from Busch Gardens, is a large, private park with 262 grassy and shaded sites. Tent sites and full RV hookups are available with all the amenities at **Tampa East Green Acres Campground**, 12720 U.S. 92, 800/454-7336 or 813/659-0002. **Bay Bayou Traveler RV Park**, 12622 W. Memorial Hwy., Tampa, 813/855-1000, has full hookups for 200 RVs. The facility offers a winter recreation program and low long-term rates, and it accepts pets.

In south St. Petersburg you'll have to call well in advance for a site at **Fort DeSoto Park Campground**, SR 679, 727/582-2267, but the natural setting and scenery are splendid. It offers tent and RV sites with electric and water hookups, a boat ramp, bike and nature trails, and clean, well-lit facilities. Heading north, just a half-mile off U.S. Alt. 19 on Long Bayou, on the Pinellas Trail recreation area, the **St. Petersburg–Madeira Beach Resort KOA**, 5400 95th St. N., 727/392-2233, offers sites for tents and RVs with some pull-throughs. On-site are a boat ramp, heated pool and whirlpools, shuffleboard, bocce ball court, horseshoes, and canoe and bike rentals.

About a mile north of SR 580 in Clearwater, **Travel Towne RV Resort,** 29850 U.S. 19 N., 727/784-2500, has 18 acres of paved sites with full hookups, a heated pool, rec room, playground, and shuffleboard. Closer to Dunedin Beach and Honeymoon Island State Park, **Dunedin Beach Campground**, 2920 U.S. Alt. 19, Dunedin, 800/345-7504 or 727/784/3719, welcomes tenters and RVs to 17 acres of grassy, shaded sites with full hookups beside a lagoon adjacent to the Pinellas Trail.

## NIGHTLIFE

Whatever your interests, pick up a copy of the free *Weekly Planet* newspaper for current listings of nighttime entertainment in this vibrant and varied area.

One of Tampa's best-kept secrets, **Skipper's Smokehouse**, 910 Skipper Road, 813/971-0666, has an outdoor stage and sand dance floor under the stars, booking national and local blues, folk, and alternative acts. This place is lots of fun. Cover charges and drinks are cheap, as are meals like beans and rice, smoked seafood, and alligator black-bean chili. It's in a residential neighborhood, so the music stops at 11 p.m.—and you can bring the kids.

For envelope-pushing nightlife, young adults head for Tampa's Ybor City, a hotspot for clubs and weekend late-night revelry. If you're looking for a relatively less frenetic experience, go early (and leave early), but visit the **Blues Ship** for good live blues, or **Frankie's Patio**, which has live entertainment in a two-story indoor/outdoor setting, and great food, from snacks and appetizers to home-style meat loaf. National comedy acts are regularly booked at **Side Splitters Comedy Club** on North Dale Mabry Highway in Tampa.

In St. Petersburg there's usually a lively crowd at **Cha Cha Coconuts** at The Pier, listening to oldies and top-40s music. Entertainment varies widely at the **Coliseum**, 535 Fourth Ave. N., 727/892-5202, a historic ballroom and local institution where you can find a '50s sock-hop one night, an orchestra performance the next, and Big Band tea-dances in the afternoons.

Major performing-arts halls host a wide variety of entertainment, including Broadway shows, music, dance, comedy, opera, cabaret, experimental theater, and children's shows. Call for schedules at Tampa's **Tampa Bay Performing Arts Center**, 800/955-1045 or 813/229-7827; St. Petersburg's **Bayfront Center**, 727/892-5767; or Clearwater's **Ruth Eckerd Hall**, 727/791-7400. Lovers of theater arts can call St. Petersburg's professional company, **American Stage**, 727/822-8814, or see good community productions at **St. Petersburg Little Theater**, 727/866-1973.

For a schedule of its performances, call the **Florida Orchestra** at 813/286-2403.

## SHOPPING

For upper-crust shopping in fashionable European ambience, check out Tampa's **Old Hyde Park Village**, 813/251-3500, which offers trendy sidewalk cafés and coffee bars, sophisticated shops like Mondi, Williams-Sonoma, and Jacobson's, and a movie theater. More casual pockets full of unique, antique-artsy shops and pleasant walking areas are located downtown in **Palm Harbor**, **Dunedin**, and **Plant City**, among others. There's also a unique assortment of craft and specialty shops, galleries, and antiques emporiums in **Ybor Square**, a historic cigar factory in Tampa's Ybor City.

For mall shopping, the largest and best include **Brandon Town Center** in Brandon; **Countryside Mall** in Clearwater; **Tyrone Mall** in St. Petersburg; and **University Mall**, **West Shore Plaza**, and the huge **Citrus Park Town Center**, all in Tampa.

Flea-market aficionados and bargain hunters can check out large venues at **Big Top Flea Market** in Tampa, 813/986-4004; **Wagon Wheel Flea Market** in Pinellas Park, 727/544-5319; or **Oldsmar Flea Market**, 813/855-5306.

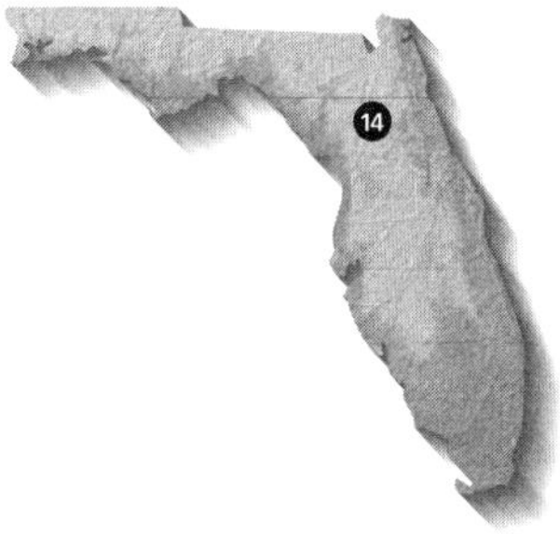


# 14
# GAINESVILLE AND HILL COUNTRY

North of Tampa Bay, Florida's long string of Gulf of Mexico beaches that tourist officials have labeled the "Suncoast" gradually gives way to a largely beachless mix of flat country and rolling hills that make this one of the more geographically interesting parts of the state. Most of this area has been labeled the "Nature Coast," and it turns out to be an apt designation. A good deal of this section of the state is as rural as it gets, a region of small villages here and there interspersed with larger ones. Gainesville, with 85,000 people, is by far the region's largest city.

This is still Florida, of course, so it has its share of attractions. But instead of the rather plastic tourist havens so common in some other parts of the state, the attractions here carry moderate prices and most of them revolve around natural phenomena. Brooksville has been dismissed as a "redneck" town, but in fact it is an Old Florida village careful to preserve the best of its legacy.

Visitors are sometimes surprised by the proliferation of horse farms around Ocala, but it is one of the country's prime producers of racing horses and the home of Native Dancer. Drive through the scenic, rolling hill country to the south and west of town and you'll find yourself looking for bluegrass. Gainesville is a college hub, but its active cultural life and renovated old downtown blocks draw more than just the relatives of University of Florida students. And far from just about everything, including its unimaginably glorious past, is Cedar Key, sitting three miles from the coastline on its close-knit set of

# GAINESVILLE

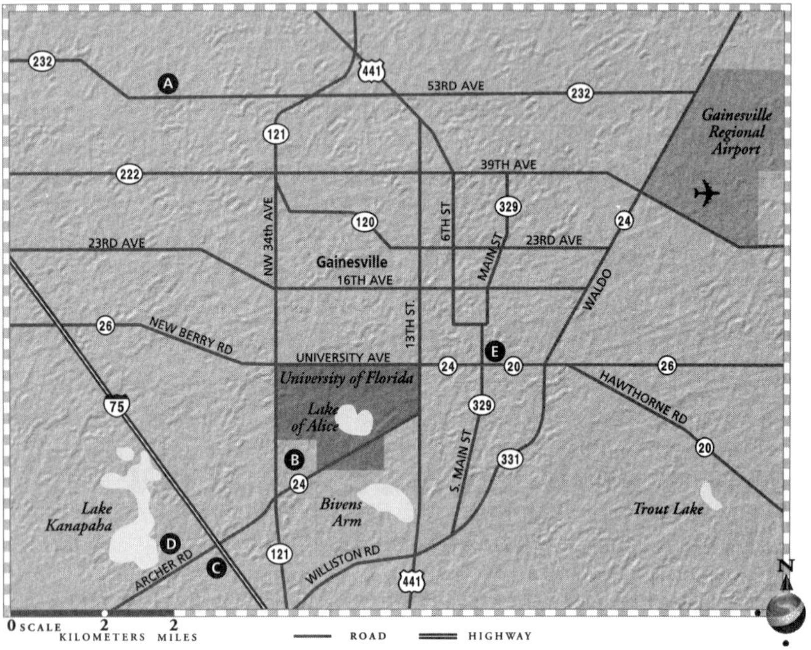


## SIGHTS

- **A** Devil's Millhopper State Geological Site
- **B** Florida Museum of Natural History
- **C** Fred Bear Museum
- **D** Kanapaha Botanical Gardens
- **B** Samuel P. Harn Museum of Art

## FOOD

- **E** Amelia's
- **E** Emiliano's Bakery and Cafe
- **E** Steve's Cafe Americain

## LODGING

- **E** Magnolia Plantation
- **E** Sweetwater Branch Inn

*Note: Items with the same letter are located in the same area.*

little islands, a living lesson in how the best-laid plans can go awry when you live at the edge of the sea in the path of unpredictable hurricanes.

## A PERFECT DAY IN GAINESVILLE AND FLORIDA HILL COUNTRY

This is a largely rural patch of Florida, easily explored. Brooksville is a modern enough town, but start with a stroll or even a slow drive down its 1900-vintage South Brooksville Avenue, an elegant, live oak–canopied street that is listed on the National Register of Historic Places. While you're in town, even if it's not Christmas, visit Rogers' Christmas House and Village. Drive west to Weeki Wachee and take in an underwater mermaid show—it's such a classic attraction that missing it would be like visiting Paris and forgetting to glance at the Eiffel Tower. Drive northeast toward Ocala, with a stop at Don Garlits Museum of Drag Racing, then take SR 475 north into Ocala, following the hills through some of Florida's finest horse country. North of Ocala off U.S. 441, browse for antiques at wonderful little Micanopy, then head for the Fred Bear Museum in Gainesville. To cap off this involved but quite doable day, order something Caribbean from a patio table at Emiliano's Bakery and Cafe in downtown Gainesville.

## SIGHTSEEING HIGHLIGHTS

### ★★★★ THE APPLETON MUSEUM OF ART

**4333 N.E. Silver Springs Blvd., Ocala, 352/236-7100**

This architecturally magnificent museum would not be at all out of place in Chicago or Philadelphia, with its wonderful collections of European paintings and sculpture and immensely impressive displays of Asian and West African art. Yet here it sits, half-hidden, in north-central Florida. A docent will be happy to tell you the story of the Appleton family and how the collections ended up here. It's safe to say that if you are an art lover, you'll regard the eclectic displays and the museum itself a genuine, totally unexpected "find."

***Details:*** *Located on the north side of Silver Springs Boulevard just east of Ocala. Open Tue–Sat 10–4:30, Sun 1–5. Admission: $3 adults, $2 children. (1–2 hours)*

### ★★★★ DON GARLITS MUSEUM OF DRAG RACING

**13700 S.W. 16th Ave., Ocala, 352/245-8661**

Growing up in Tampa, Don Garlits tinkered with cars in his back yard. He grew up to become the "Big Daddy" of drag racing, and in four decades of racing won 17 world championship titles and set numerous racing milestones. His museum, established in 1977, is a must-stop for anyone even remotely interested in antique and/or racing cars. He has 175 of them on display, including his *Swamp Rat* series of race cars that set world records, the 1956 Chrysler that Mamie gave President Dwight D. Eisenhower, and a 1904 Orient Buckboard.

***Details:*** *From I-75 take Exit 67 east to CR 475A, then go south to the museum. Open daily 9–5. Admission: $7.50 adults, $3 children (under 13 must be accompanied by an adult), $6 seniors. Antique car museum admission: $5. Combination ticket, $10. (1–2 hours)*

## ★★★★ FLORIDA'S SILVER SPRINGS

**5656 E. Silver Springs Blvd., Ocala, 800/234-7458 or 352/236-2121**

This natural park is centered around the source springs for the Silver River. Among them is the world's largest artesian limestone spring, named (appropriately enough) Mammoth. Glass-bottomed boats allow you to peer through the crystal-clear spring waters to the caves—and the fish, tortoises, and vegetation—below. During the past few years, to compete with the larger theme parks in Orlando, Silver Springs has added a bear enclave, a Florida panther exhibit, a jeep safari ride, and an alligator lagoon.

***Details:*** *On the south side of SR 40 just east of Ocala. Open daily 9–5:30. Admission: $29.95 adults, $20.95 children, plus tax and $3 parking charge. (4–8 hours)*

## ★★★★ THE FRED BEAR MUSEUM

**4600 S.W. 41st Blvd. (Fred Bear Drive), Gainesville, 352/376-2411**

Fred Bear was a great bow hunter, founder of Bear Archery—now the world's largest manufacturer of bows—and creator of this unexpectedly fascinating museum of, frankly, the animals that he killed and the weapons he used to do them in. Wander among huge grizzlies, an elephant, a tiger, and rooms with artifacts that illustrate the history of the bow and arrow. Glass walls allow you to observe the bow-making process in the manufacturing plant below.

***Details:*** *Located just south of SR 24 (Archer Road), west of I-75.*

*From I-75 take Exit 75 west (Archer Road) and turn south to the museum. Open daily 10–6. Admission: $5 adults, $3 children, $12 family ticket. (1–2 hours)*

## ★★★★ TED WILLIAMS MUSEUM AND HITTERS HALL OF FAME

**2455 N. Citrus Hills Blvd., at The Villages of Citrus Hills, Hernando, 352/527-6566**

Some famous sports figures have called this wonderful baseball museum the "Cooperstown of the South," and while that may be a bit fanciful, the former Boston Red Sox slugger, undeniably one of the greatest players of all time, has created a gem of a museum built in the shape of a baseball diamond. Eight galleries have photos, artwork, and bats, gloves, and balls from Williams' career. Get a feel for life in the Bigs in two life-size dugouts, and watch a video that features Williams narrating his choices of the 25 greatest hitters ever.

***Details:*** *On CR 486 about three miles west of U.S. 41. Open Tue–Sun 10–4. Admission: $3 adults, $1 children. (1–2 hours)*

## ★★★★ WEEKI WACHEE SPRINGS/BUCCANEER BAY

**U.S. 19 at SR 50, Weeki Wachee, 800/678-9335 or 352/596-2062**

Real mermaids? Maybe not, but the women dressed as mermaids in the Weeki Wachee Springs underwater shows move so smoothly that the fantasy isn't spoiled. The mermaids perform daily while audiences watch through the glass-walled side of a spring-fed pool. Other attractions include the compelling Birds-of-Prey and Exotic Birds shows. Buccaneer Bay, right next door, offers more family fun, with flume rides, float rides on the Weeki Wachee River, and a sandy beach.

***Details:*** *From I-75 take Exit 61 and drive west on SR 50. Open daily 9:30–5:30. Admission: $16.95 adults, $12.95 children. Combination ticket with Buccaneer Bay, $1 more. (3 hours minimum)*

## ★★★ DEVIL'S MILLHOPPER STATE GEOLOGICAL SITE

**4732 Millhopper Rd., Gainesville, 352/955-2008**

Florida's landscape is prone to caving in, creating good visuals for television cameras as houses fall apart or cars plunge up to their radiators in sinkholes that open without warning. Here is one of the best places in the state to discover how sinkholes form. Learn how

# HILL COUNTRY

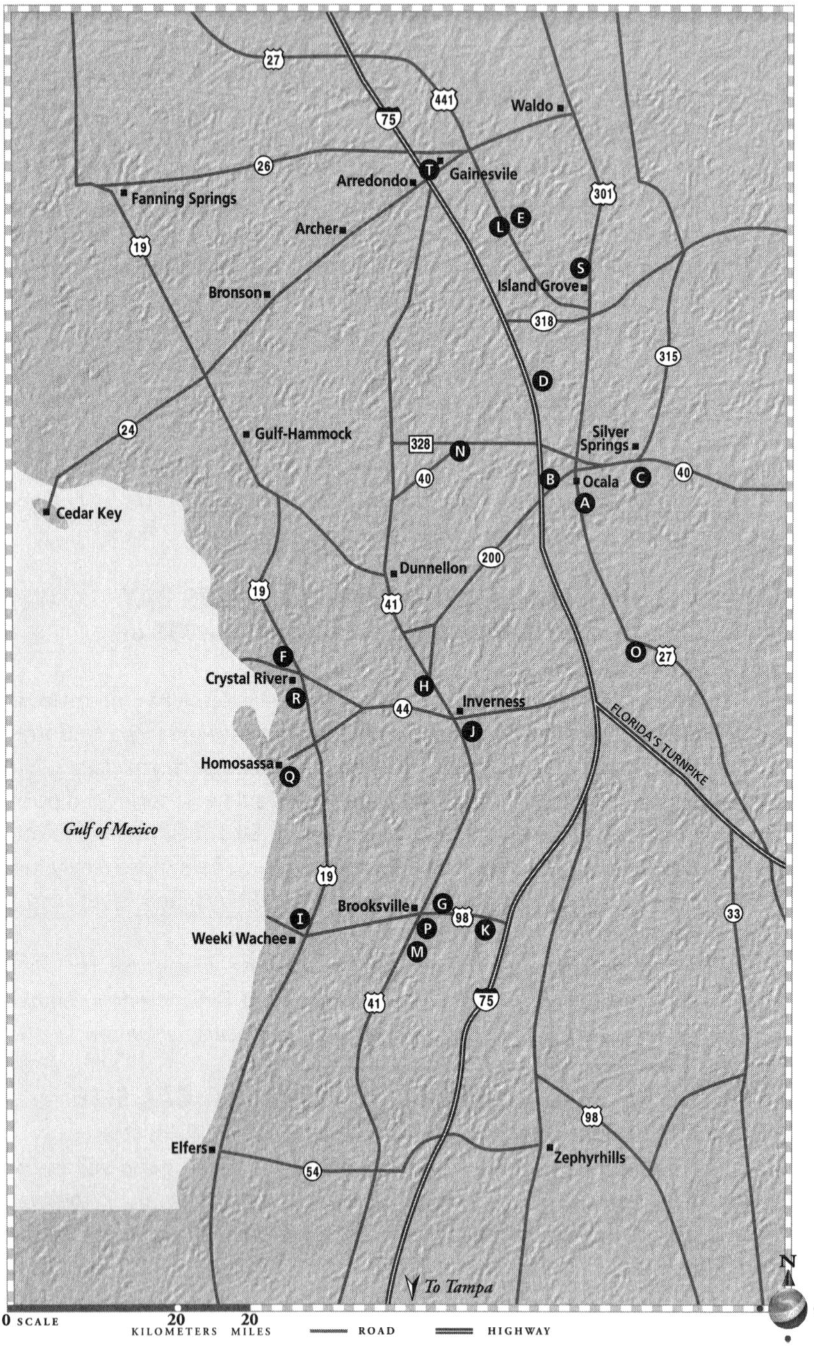

this place got its strange name, then walk down 232 steps to the bottom of a 120-foot deep, 500-wide sinkhole, observing the state's geologic past as you descend.

***Details:*** *From N.W. 43rd Street, turn west on N.W. 53rd Avenue (SR 232) and drive about a mile to the site. Open daily 9–5, until sunset Sat and Sun in summer. (30 minutes)*

## ★★★ KANAPAHA BOTANICAL GARDENS

**47 SW 58th Dr., Gainesville, 352/372-4981**

Spring begins in February in this flowery garden that enhanced a naturally pleasing landscape by introducing rare and unusual plants from around the world, including giant snake arums, bamboos, lotuses, and a collection of carnivorous plants. Butterfly and hummingbird gardens, tiny "vest-pocket" specialty gardens, and a sunken garden planted in a natural sinkhole are special attractions.

***Details:*** *Located on the north side of SR 24 (S.W. Archer Road), a mile west of I-75, Exit 75. Open Mon–Wed, Fri–Sun 9–5. Admission: $3 adults, $2 children. (1 hour)*

---

### SIGHTS

- Ⓐ Appleton Museum of Art
- Ⓐ Don Garlits Museum of Drag Racing
- Ⓑ Emergency One
- Ⓒ Florida's Silver Springs
- Ⓓ Marjorie Kinnan Rawlings State Historic Site
- Ⓔ Paynes Prairie State Preserve
- Ⓕ The Power Place
- Ⓖ Rogers' Christmas House & Village
- Ⓗ Ted Williams Museum and Hitters Hall of Fame
- Ⓘ Weeki Wachee Springs/Buccaneer Bay
- Ⓙ Wild Bill's Airboat Tours

### FOOD

- Ⓖ Blueberry Patch Tea Room
- Ⓐ Carmichael's Restaurant
- Ⓐ Kotobuki
- Ⓚ Papa Joe's Italian Restaurant
- Ⓛ Wild Flowers Cafe
- Ⓜ Ye Olde Fireside Inn

### LODGING

- Ⓝ Heritage Country Inn
- Ⓛ Herlong Mansion
- Ⓒ Seven Sisters Inn
- Ⓞ Shamrock, Thistle & Crown
- Ⓟ Verona House

### CAMPING

- Ⓠ Camp 'N' Water Outdoor Resort
- Ⓜ Camper's Holiday Travel Park
- Ⓡ Crystal Isles RV Resort
- Ⓢ Ginnie Springs Campground and Dive Resort
- Ⓒ Ocala/Silver Springs KOA
- Ⓔ Paynes Prairie State Preserve
- Ⓣ Sportsman Cove

*Note: Items with the same letter are located in the same place.*

## ★★★ MARJORIE KINNAN RAWLINGS STATE HISTORIC SITE

**U.S. 325, Cross Creek, 352/466-3672**

Whether it was reading *The Yearling* in school or seeing a screen version, generations grew up riveted to the hardscrabble story of Jody and his white-tailed deer, Flag, and the hard luck of his parents who tried to establish a Florida pioneer farm. The author's house is still here, but open to only ten visitors at a time. Wander the grounds for a look at the natural side of Florida that she poured into her Pulitzer Prize–winning novel.

**Details:** *Drive 21 miles southeast of Gainesville to Cross Creek. Farmyard, grove, and pathways open daily 8–5. Free. House tours limited to 10 (no reservations: first come, first served) Thu–Sun 10 and 11 a.m. and on the hour 1–4 p.m. Oct–July only. Admission: $2 adults, $1 children. (1–2 hours)*

## ★★★ PAYNES PRAIRIE STATE PRESERVE

**Off U.S. 441, Micanopy, 352/466-3397**

The largest cattle ranch in Spanish Florida operated here in Alachua County in the 1600s, and a century later the great naturalist William Bartram described this basin as the "great Alachua Savannah." Today this 21,000-acre preserve is among the most significant natural areas of Florida, and the wildlife Bartram observed in 1774—alligators, bison, wild horses, white-tailed deer, otter, and sandhill cranes, among others—still thrives.

**Details:** *Turn east into the Preserve off U.S. 441 just north of Micanopy. Open daily 8 a.m.–sunset. Admission: $3.25 per vehicle. (1–3 hours)*

## ★★★ ROGERS' CHRISTMAS HOUSE & VILLAGE

**103 S. Saxon Ave., Brooksville, 352/796-2415**

Over the past 40 years this year-round Christmas venture has become a Florida institution. Busloads of tourists come to stroll among the azaleas and the dogwood trees and to visit the five early-1900s homes that are filled with decorated trees, lights, ornaments, limited-edition items, toys, dolls, gourmet foods, and collectibles of all sorts. Rogers' Christmas House and Village is quite a charming place, which may be why so many people visit here to buy Christmas decorations in July.

**Details:** *Just east of U.S. 41, on the north side of East Liberty*

David J. Wilson

*Street in Brooksville's north end. Open every day but Christmas(!), 9:30–5. Free. (1–2 hours)*

### ★★★ WILD BILL'S AIRBOAT TOURS
**SR 44, Inverness, 352/726-6060**

One of the best ways to tour Florida's shallow waterways is by air boat, a noisy craft that can skim through swamp grass and across deep water in search of wildlife that often eludes the casual observer. Wild Bill MacKay's explorations of the wild Withlacoochee River provide excellent opportunties for spotting alligators, wild boar, wild turkeys, ospreys, eagles, otters, deer—the whole range of wildlife that inhabits this region.

MacKay's flat-bottomed boats do make noise, but less than most because they have special gearing, multibladed propellers, and mufflers. The hour-long tour includes a tram ride through a small animal park and a 45-minute airboat ride. Customized airboat tours may be arranged.

***Details:*** *From I-75 take Exit 66 and drive about nine miles west on SR 44. Open Mon–Sat 10–5, Sun 11–5. Last airboat trips, 4 p.m. Admission: $11.95 adults, $7.95 children. (1–1½ hours)*

## ★★ EMERGENCY ONE

**1601 S.W. 347th Ave., Ocala, 352/854-3524**

For an up-close look at how emergency vehicles are made, take a 45-minute tour through this plant that manufactures pumpers, rescue vehicles, ambulances, and aircraft-rescue fire-fighting equipment. Guides take you from the body plant through the paint facility and into the delivery center, from where finished vehicles are shipped to their purchasers. You can watch as old trucks are recycled into new ones, and witness fire-truck pump tests.

***Details:*** *From I-75 take Exit 69, drive east on SR 40 to S.W. 33rd Avenue, turn south to S.W. Seventh Street, and turn west to S.W. 37th Avenue. Open Mon–Fri 8:30–3. Admission: $6 adults, children free, $4 seniors. (1 hour)*

## ★★ FLORIDA MUSEUM OF NATURAL HISTORY

**S.W. 34th St. at Hull Rd., Gainesville, 352/846-2000, www.flmnh.ufl.edu**

This museum is a work in progress, with several important exhibits due to open between now and 2001, but it is nevertheless worth a visit because it is home to more than 19 million specimens and artifacts connected with Florida's natural history. Current exhibits include impressive displays of huge shark jaws and other bones from Florida's seas of 40 million years ago, and a Panhandle display entered through a simulated limestone cave like the Florida Caverns near Marianna. Planned exhibits include a mangrove forest and its attendant wildlife, a Calusa Indian midden and village, fossil horses, and a long list of others that will detail Florida's natural and human history.

***Details:*** *From I-75 take Exit 75, drive east on SR 24 (Archer Road), turn left on N.W. 34th Street and right at the first intersection. Open Mon–Sat 10–5, Sun 1–5. Free. (1–1½ hours)*

## ★★ THE POWER PLACE

**15760 W. Power Line St., Crystal River, 352/563-4490**

At one of the nation's largest nuclear power plants, visitors can obtain a rather good background knowledge of how electrical power systems were developed; examine the contributions of Benjamin Franklin, Thomas Edison, and nuclear physicist Enrico Fermi; and explore the future, where fusion, fuel cells, coal gasification, and solar cells are the key energy watchwords. And there's some cool hands-on stuff!

***Details:*** *Located at Florida Power Corporation's Crystal River energy complex, about four miles west of U.S. 19. Open Mon–Fri 9:30–4. Free. (1 hour)*

### ★★ SAMUEL P. HARN MUSEUM OF ART

**S.W. 34th St. at Hull Rd., Gainesville, 352/392-9826, www.arts.ufl.edu/harn**

The University of Florida has several impressive structures, but the Harn museum is one of the most striking, with a light, airy feeling that makes it seem bigger than it is. Inside, the collections range from artifacts of various cultures of North and South America to modern art of the sort that can make gallery visitors wonder just what the judges were thinking. Visiting exhibits of modern work are always part of the display.

***Details:*** *From I-75 take Exit 75, drive east on SR 24 (Archer Road), turn left on N.W. 34th Street and right at the first intersection. Open Tue–Fri 11–5, Sat 10–5, Sun 1–5. Free. (1–1½ hours)*

## FITNESS AND RECREATION

Rolling countryside dominates the relatively small cities and towns in this area of the state. An abundance of outdoor activities, from horse and trail rides offered by numerous horse farms and stables in the Ocala area, to long hikes in the forests and preserves, to canoeing and airboat riding on its lakes and rivers, await your attention.

For swimmers not afraid to get up close with large sea creatures, a highlight of any winter journey must be a close encounter with the gentle, lumbering manatees that live in the warm waters of the **Crystal River** at King's Bay. Several guides and dive shops—ask anywhere in Crystal River or phone the Citrus County Tourist Development Council, 800/587-6667 or 352/527-5223—provide the means of getting to the river where you can merely observe them or show your adventurous spirit and don the gear needed to swim with these blubbery creatures. If you'd rather just watch, drive south on U.S. 19 to **Homosassa Springs State Wildlife Park**, 9225 W. Fish Bowl Dr., Homosassa, 352/628-2311, where you can walk to an underwater viewing area of the Spring of 10,000 Fish. It's more sightseeing than recreation, but it's a way to see manatees up close without getting into a wet suit.

Hiking trails of all descriptions crisscross the area. In relatively small parks such as the 6,500-acre **San Felasco Hammock State Preserve** (off of SR 232 four miles northwest of Gainesville, 352/336-2008) or the even larger **Paynes Prairie State Preserve** (U.S. 441, Micanopy, 352/466-3307), there are relatively easy walks through the longleaf pine hammocks and around the edges of the marshes, limestone outcroppings, and sinkholes. Hikers mix with bicyclists and horseback riders on the 17-mile **Gainesville-Hawthorn State Trail**, 352/336-2135, which runs from Gainesville's Boulware Springs Park through the Paynes Prairie Preserve to the Lockloosa Wildlife Management Area, following an 1850s railroad track.

In the huge, 383,224-acre **Ocala National Forest**, 352/625-2520, on both sides of SR 40 east of Ocala, you can hike for days on end. Spend two or three of them on the 68-mile stretch of the 1,300-mile Florida Trail that runs straight through the forest's mix of sand, slash, and longleaf pine. Go fishing, rent a horse, or go boating on any of the forest's innumerable lakes.

Sparkling, spring-fed Lake Holathikaha looks as good today as it must have to soldiers fighting the Second Seminole Indian War in 1835, when Fort Cooper was built at its edge. Now visitors to **Fort Cooper State Park**, on SR 39 two miles southeast of Inverness, 352/726-0315, can walk self-guided trails through the hardwood hammocks and sandhill wildlife communities. Canoes and paddleboats may be rented lakeside. **O'Leno State Park**, 904/454-1853, on U.S. 441 six miles north of High Springs, where the 1930s Civilian Conservation Corps bridge still spans the Santa Fe River, offers swimming, camping, hiking and horseback trails, and fishing. Canoes and bicycles are available for rent. **Ichetucknee Springs State Park**, 904/497-2511, off SR 47 and SR 238 four miles northwest of Fort White, encloses a series of springs that release 233 million gallons of water daily to form the crystal-clear, six-mile-long Ichetucknee River, which empties into the Santa Fe River. Here, too, is an abundance of wildlife, hiking trails, canoeing, and tubing. Tubers should use the south entrance of the park, where a free shuttle operates May 1 through Labor Day. Otherwise, it can be a long, humid hike back upriver. Nearby, the **Canoe Outpost of High Springs**, U.S. 441 at the Santa Fe River Bridge, 904/454-2050, www.riverise.com/canoe.htm, can outfit both canoeists and divers.

Aside from the two top-rated courses at **World Woods Golf Club** near Brooksville, 352/796-5500, golfers may head to the highly regarded courses at **Silverthorn Country Club**, 352/799-2600, or **The Dunes Golf Club at Seville**, 800/232-1363 or 352/596-7888, both also near Brooksville. If time permits near Ocala, tee off at **Golden Ocala Golf &**

**Country Club**, 352/622-2245, a course widely known for eight holes that are replicas of the world's most famous golf holes.

## FOOD

Gainesville's college students tend to opt for volume over quality, but visitors will find excellent Italian selections at **Amelia's**, 235 S. Main St., 352/373-1919, and a variety of selections at somewhat higher prices two blocks away at **Steve's Cafe Americain**, 12 W. University Ave., 352/377-9337, where regional cuisine dominates the menu. For breakfast, lunch, or dinner, the food is gourmet Caribbean whether you eat inside or on the patio at moderately priced **Emiliano's Bakery and Cafe**, 7 S.E. First Ave., 352/375-7381.

In Ocala, your reward for finding **Kotobuki**, 2463 S.W. 27th Ave., in Shady Oaks Plaza at SR 200, 352/237-3900, will be a first-rate Japanese meal with or without sushi. For more traditional food for breakfast, lunch, or dinner, try the pleasant, much-honored **Carmichael's Restaurant**, 3105 N.E. Silver Springs Blvd. Driving toward Gainesville or Paynes Prairie State Preserve, don't miss **Wild Flowers Cafe**, 201 N.E. U.S. 441, Micanopy, 352/466-4330, for reasonably priced selections in an appealing antiques village.

Brooksville has a surprisingly large selection of good restaurants. Try the moderately priced **Ye Olde Fireside Inn**, 1175 S. Broad St., 352/796-0293; or a local favorite, **Papa Joe's Italian Restaurant**, 6244 Spring Lake Hwy., 352/799-3904. For sandwiches, soups, and typical American fare, stop in at the lovable old house on the hill that for more than 30 years has been the **Blueberry Patch Tea Room**, 414 E. Liberty St., 352/796-6005.

## LODGING

Ocala and Gainesville are filled with chain lodgings (Ocala has a motel/restaurant row on SR 200 at Exit 68, I-75), but there are some special lodgings to consider, too. About 25 miles southeast of Ocala, near Weirsdale, it's worth searching out the moderately priced but intriguing **Shamrock, Thistle & Crown**, 12971 S.E. CR 42, Ocala, 800/425-2763 or 352/821-1887, www.bbonline.com/fl/shamrock, an old country hilltop home. In Ocala, turn in at the Victorian mansion that was judged "Florida's Best Restoration," the **Seven Sisters Inn**, 820 S.E. Fort King St., 800/250-3496 or 352/867-1170, a high-end B&B, with gourmet breakfasts, afternoon tea, and candlelight dinners. **Heritage Country Inn**, 14343 W. U.S. 40, 352/489-0023, is more moderately priced, and its six luxuriously furnished rooms feature private baths with whirlpools. The magnificent **Herlong Mansion** bed-and-breakfast, 402 N.E.

## CEDAR KEY

*Travelers who drive southwest from Gainesville as far as SR 24 goes will drive off the edge of Florida into a land that time forgot, and it isn't about dinosaurs. It's about Cedar Key, and the history of this small place is a sobering lesson in the ephemeral nature of the world we see around us, because the promoters of the 1880s and 1890s would be astonished to learn that Cedar Key was left behind as Florida grew into the twentieth century.*

*A hundred years ago, officials of this little town of islands were sure it would be one of Florida's dominant cities. The cross-state railroad's western terminus was here. The backbone of the prosperous economy was the pencil industry. Both Eagle and Everhard-Faber built factories on neighboring keys amid an abundance of southern red cedars. The railway brought tourists to see the self-described "Venice of America," and Florida's second-largest city boasted of the best backcountry of all seaports in Florida. But things went terribly wrong.*

*Tampa's deep-water port was rediscovered, and it was much closer to Caribbean ports. Then someone noticed that the cedar forests had disappeared, and when an unnamed hurricane in 1896 nearly wiped the town off the map, Eagle and Everhard-Faber went away too. Over the next half-century, sporadic efforts to revive the economy failed. Then, not very many years ago, travelers began to discover this truly unspoiled Florida, a place stuck out in the Gulf of Mexico, virtually ignored by the twentieth century.*

*Before you get into the most historic district of the town, stop in at the* ***Cedar Key State Museum****, 12231 S.W. 166 Ct., 352/543-5350, which offers a comprehensive exhibit on the history of Cedar Key, as well as artifacts from its past and information on the flora and fauna to be found in the area. It's open Thursday through Monday, 9–5; admission $1. A plaque outside the museum notes that in 1867 naturalist John Muir ended his 1,000-mile walk from Ohio in Cedar Key, a trek recorded in his journal,* A Thousand Mile Walk to the Gulf. *Even for today's visitor, every street in this area of town, many of which are graded gravel, is worth exploring to view the sometimes modest, sometimes spectacular coastal residences. Newer ones are on stilts as high as 19 feet.*

*Second Street is both the main historic street and the chief shopping street, with restaurants, the historic Island Hotel, and excellent gift, craft, and art showplaces such as the* ***Ibis Gallery****, Second and D Sts., 352/543-6111,* *and the **Cedar Key Arts Center**, on Second St. east of C St., 352/543-5906. The **Cedar Key Historical Society Museum**, diagonally across the street from the Ibis Gallery, 352/543-5549, has photographic displays of the town's history, plus a collection of artifacts dating back to when Seminole and Timucuan Indians populated the area. You can pick up a self-guided walking-tour brochure here. The museum keeps short hours, usually 11–5, sometimes 2–5; admission $1. At water's edge, Dock Street is home to more galleries, restaurants, and the town's fishing pier.*

*Twice a year, special festivals draw people in from all over the Southeast. In April the annual Sidewalk Arts Festival is known not just for its wonderful setting but also for the quality of the artists who attend. On the third weekend of October, the annual Seafood Festival also draws visitors from distant parts of the state. The **Cedar Key Area Chamber of Commerce**, 352/543-5600, is the source for dates and more detailed information.*

*Choose wisely, and you can make dining on Cedar Key a special memory of your visit to the historic islands. For fine food in a historic setting, try the Fish in Paper or the Artichokes Atsena Otie in the dining room at the **Island Hotel**, northeast corner of Second and B Sts., 800/432-4640 or 352/543-5111. For a slightly less expensive menu, try the crab, shrimp, and sherry cream sauce of the Grouper Charpentier or other specialties at the **Island Room Restaurant** at Cedar Cove, 10 Second St., 352/543-6520, which draws consistent praise from both visitors and locals. For a sunset view over the Gulf of Mexico, get a window table at the second-story **Brown Pelican**, on Dock St. at the pier, 352/543-5428. Strange as it may seem, Cedar Key also offers Southwestern cuisine that lures islanders to the cramped blue cinder-block building that houses the **Blue Desert Cafe**, on the west side of SR 24 just south of Miller Island Rd., 352/543-9111.*

*If you stay over, numerous moderately priced hotels can be found along SR 24 after you leave the mainland. The best places to stay and soak up the ambience of the islands on which the town sits may be the **Island Hotel**, corner of Second and B Sts., 800/432-4640 or 352/543-5111, ishotel@gnv.fdt.net, with its thick, 1859-vintage seashell tabby walls, and the **Cedar Key Bed & Breakfast**, a rambling 1880 guest house that serves memorable breakfasts before you begin gliding on the porch or tree swings.*

Cholokka Blvd., Micanopy (I-75, Exit 73 east), 800/437-5664 or 352/466-3322, www.afn.org/~herlong, with its ghost and second-story porch swing, puts visitors into another era, though all 12 rooms have modern facilities. In Gainesville, two historic downtown B&B inns—**Magnolia Plantation**, 309 S.W. Seventh St., 352/375-6653, www.magnoliabnb.com, and **Sweetwater Branch Inn**, 625 E. University Ave., 800/595-7760 or 352/373-6760, www.sweetwaterinn.com—are restored 1880s residences that may make you forget, temporarily, that you're in a bustling university town.

If you've read about those homes your grandfather or great-grandfather ordered from Sears and Roebuck, here's your chance to find out what they were like. The two-story, Dutch colonial–style **Verona House**, 201 S. Main St., Brooksville, 800/355-6717 or 352/796-4001, VERONABB@gate.net, came to town in two boxcars in 1925 with 76 pages of instructions. As a bed-and-breakfast, it has four nicely furnished, intimate, and moderately priced guest rooms. Elsewhere in the Brooksville area, especially along U.S. 41 and at the exits from I-75, the chain motels abound.

## CAMPING

A few campgrounds are particularly convenient for visiting Ocala or Gainesville. **Ocala/Silver Springs KOA**, 3200 S.W. 38th Ave., Ocala, 800/562-7798 or 352/237-2138, offers quiet in a wooded setting dominated by live oaks and magnolia trees. Even quieter are the rental cabins next to a duck pond. Out of town, **Sportsman Cove**, P.O. Box 107, McIntosh (on Orange Lake, eight blocks east of U.S. 441 on F Avenue), 352/591-1435, offers 30 grassy sites for RVs or tents. Nearby, the **Paynes Prairie State Preserve**, Route 2, Box 41 (located 10 miles south of Gainesville on U.S. 441—see Sightseeing Highlights), Micanopy, 904/466-3397, offers 57 limited-service sites.

West of Gainesville is the **Ginnie Springs Campground and Dive Resort**, 7300 N.E. Ginnie Springs Rd., 904/454-2202, which offers relatively primitive sites. This a scuba-oriented campground, with camp and dive packages available to explore the nine natural springs along the camp's 2.5-mile section of the Santa Fe River.

Near Brooksville, **Camper's Holiday Travel Park**, 2092 Culbreath Rd., 352/796-3707, offers 62 RV sites with full hookups on an 18-acre lake at the edge of a standard mobile-home park—no tents, motorcycles, or mopeds, however. In Homosassa, the **Camp 'N' Water Outdoor Resort**, 11465 W. Priest Lane, 352/628-2000, has 81 riverside sites with full hookups, and cabins for those tired of living on rubber and air.

The **Crystal Isles RV Resort**, 11419 W. Fort Island Tr., Crystal River, 888/783-6763 or 352/795-3774, is a huge place with more than 250 sites on the canal that leads to the Crystal River. Aside from excellent pull-through sites and full hookups, the camp offers a large number of recreational activities plus a hot tub.

## SHOPPING

Nothing particularly extraordinary awaits you at **Oaks Mall** (6419 Newberry Rd., Gainesville, 352/331-4411) or in the 90 stores in Ocala's **Paddock Mall**, so for a special shopping day, go to **Micanopy**, Florida's oldest inland town. This small place is lined with some of the state's best antiques shops, catering to every possible taste. Start at any one of the shops and wander both sides of the town's only through street. Not far away, the even smaller town of **McIntosh** also appeals to antiques hunters.

**Alachua County Farmers Market**, at the southeast corner of U.S. 441 and N.W. 34th St., Gainesville, 352/392-1845, ext. 416, is a small, old-fashioned farmers' gathering, with growers selling out of the backs of their pickups or from makeshift tables. It claims to be the only such market in the state and guarantees that what you buy is locally grown. It's open only Thursday and Saturday mornings. One of the largest standard flea markets in north central Florida is the **Waldo Farmers and Flea Market** on U.S. 301 a mile north of the town of Waldo, 352/468-2255. About 800 vendors sell their goods on Saturdays and Sundays between 7:30 a.m. and 4 p.m.

## Scenic Route: Horse Country

*If not for the sabal palms, you might be forgiven for guessing you were in Kentucky as you drive through the pretty Ocala countryside. Suddenly, Florida's horizontal plain is upset by an area of deeply rolling hills, ranch homes, black or white board fences, and oval tracks. Florida's horse country has tall pines and mineral springs, but it is distinguished by the live oaks draped with Spanish moss. Farms are scattered throughout the area, but they're concentrated along this scenic drive down CR 475, just south of Ocala.*

*From I-75, take Exit 67 (Don Garlits Museum of Drag Racing is immediately southeast of this exit), turn right for about a quarter mile, then turn left (north) onto CR 475, a two-lane roadway. Within a mile you're driving up and down steep hills. Dirt and sod training ovals are visible on both sides of the road, while the low ranch houses themselves are often at the end of long, dirt driveways. Some properties are fenced in white, some in black. A sign on your right identifies a property where 1953 Preakness and Belmont winner Native Dancer served at stud.*

*Stay on CR 475 for about 11 miles, until you reach Paddock Mall (now you know how it got its name) or College Road (SR 200). Turn left and either rejoin I-75 or continue southwest on SR 200 to continue your drive through horse country.*

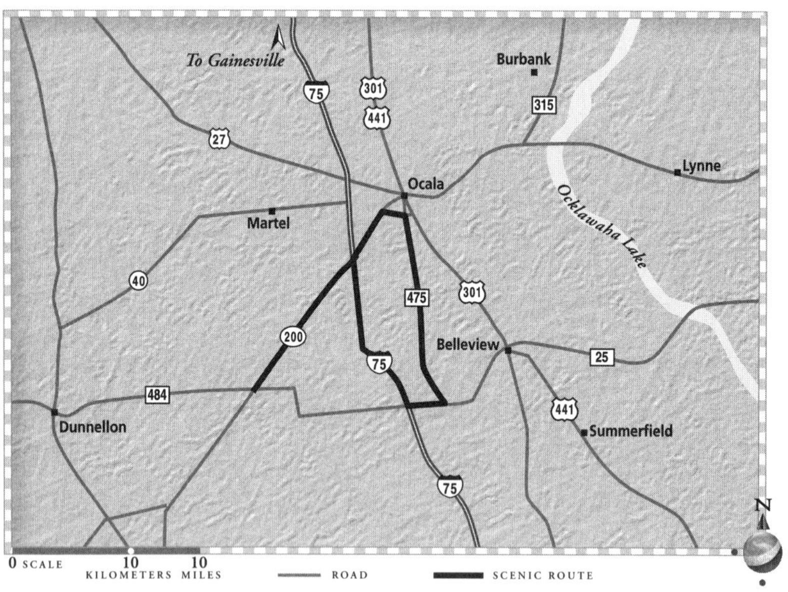

# 15
# TALLAHASSEE AND APALACHICOLA

It's not really a mystery, but somehow it is still rather sad that this lovely area of Florida is one of the least visited. There are no theme parks here, just a lush, rolling countryside covered with glorious pine forests and ubiquitous live oaks hung with Spanish moss—and touches of the truly subtropical vegetation that doesn't take firm hold until you are 75 miles south.

Florida is a state in the South, but much of it, populated by northern transplants, is not a Southern state. The region around Tallahassee is the state's true Southern face. Highways tunnel darkly through live oak forests, and some of the once-magnificent plantations live again as gracious monuments to a bygone era. It wasn't always glorious, of course. Behind the magnificence are remnants of slave quarters, and a walk through Tallahassee's historic Greenwood or Old City cemeteries illustrates that inequalities lasted beyond death.

The city is built on history. In 1539 Spanish conquistador Hernando de Soto spent his first Christmas in the New World near the plot now occupied by the Capitol, but it was not until nearly 300 years later that Tallahassee was chosen as Florida's capital city, a compromise between competing claims from Pensacola and St. Augustine. Tallahassee was a lawless place, every bit as wild as more famous towns in the West. But those are storybook days.

Tallahassee today teems with the youth of two major universities, but you'll find the town keeps a Southern pace. As you visit this gracious city or head toward the fine beaches of the Gulf of Mexico and the picturesque

# DOWNTOWN TALLAHASSEE

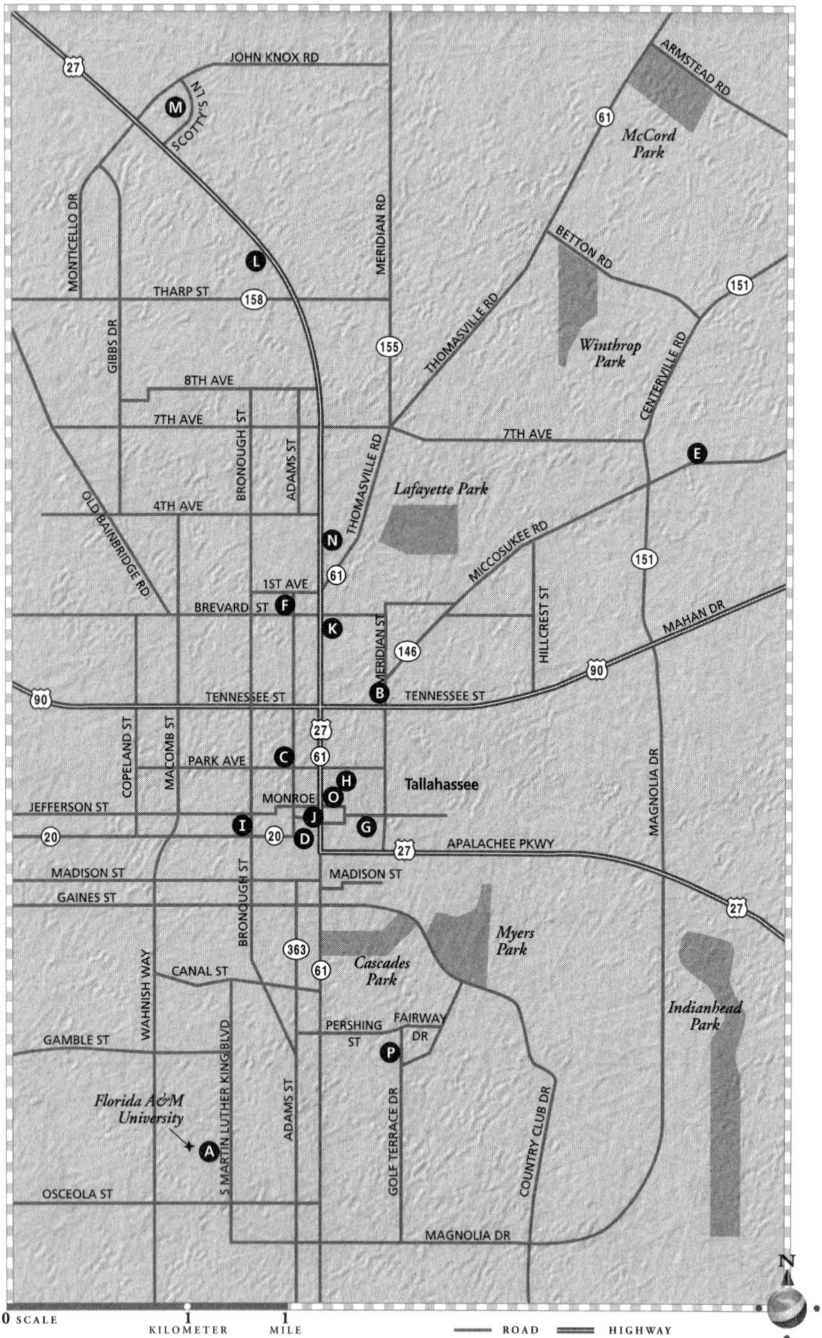

oyster town of Apalachicola, slow down just a bit. Near its northern border, this is Florida's Deep South. You can *amble* here.

## A PERFECT DAY IN TALLAHASSEE

Rise early and cruise the canopied roadways that give Tallahassee a special flavor under dappled morning sunlight, then stop for breakfast at a neighborhood café. Stick with nature for a while by way of a visit to the glorious Alfred B. Maclay State Gardens before heading into the city center for a grand perspective on the capital city by visiting the Capitol's 22nd-story observation deck. The panoramic views are stunning, especially now that you realize there's a city underneath all that foliage. The Old Capitol next door exudes the charm state capitols should have, and you may agree that you're in a rather beguiling city after you take a walking tour of the historic district. On your way south to Apalachicola, Florida's oyster capital, you can peer through the glass bottom of a boat at the mastodon bones far beneath the clear waters of Wakulla Springs. Plan to arrive in Apalachicola before sunset, and find a window table at Caroline's on the Apalachicola River.

## SIGHTSEEING HIGHLIGHTS

### ★★★★ ALFRED B. MACLAY STATE GARDENS

**U.S. 319, Tallahassee, 850/487-4556**

In an area of Florida known for lovely lakes and gardens, this park stands out. It is particularly enchanting if you can visit in the aromatic

---

**SIGHTS**

- Ⓐ Black Archives Research Center & Museum
- Ⓑ Brokaw McDougall House
- Ⓒ First Presbyterian Church
- Ⓓ Florida Capitol
- Ⓔ Goodwood Plantation
- Ⓕ Governor's Mansion

**SIGHTS** *(continued)*

- Ⓖ John G. Riley House Museum of African-American History and Culture
- Ⓗ Knott House Museum
- Ⓘ Museum of Florida History
- Ⓙ Old Capitol
- Ⓚ Tours with a Southern Accent

**FOOD**

- Ⓛ Barnacle Bill's
- Ⓜ Silver Slipper
- Ⓝ Chez Pierre

**LODGING**

- Ⓞ Governor's Inn
- Ⓟ The Riedel House

springtime, when the azaleas, camellias, and Oriental magnolias are in bloom, but it's delightful any time of year. The park began as the gardens of a New York financier when he built his southern estate in 1923. In addition to blooming gardens, the park is filled with native plants, through which nature trails wind toward the shores of a beautiful small lake. The restored living and dining rooms of the Maclay House serve as a center not only for tours but also for information about camellias.

***Details:*** *Park open daily 8–dusk. Gardens open daily 9–5. House open Jan–Apr 9–5. Admission: $3.25 per private vehicle, $1 if on foot or bicycle. Garden/house admission (Jan–Apr): $3 adults, $1.50 children; rest of the year, free. (1–2 hours)*

## ★★★★ EDWARD BALL WAKULLA SPRINGS STATE PARK

**SR 61 and SR 267 junction, Wakulla, 850/922-3632**

Ponce de León was convinced he'd found the Fountain of Youth when he heard about these springs, which Native Americans claimed had curative powers. Freshwater Wakulla Spring, one of the world's largest (averaging 576 million gallons daily) and deepest (more than 300 feet), indeed was considered special by the Seminoles, even if they didn't believe in eternal youth. The Indians valued the hardwood uplands as well as the abundance of wildlife. If you're a birder, you'll be smitten by this 2,850-acre park. If you're into hiking and biking, the trails here are long but seem too short. Snorkeling and swimming are allowed only in a designated area near the head spring. The spring is a repository for mastodon bones, which you can see along with the marine plants through the glass bottoms of boats that cruise the springs. River cruises of about 30 minutes take you close to the wildlife along the spring run.

***Details:*** *Located 14 miles south of Tallahassee. Open daily 8–dusk. Admission: $3.25 per vehicle. River or glass-bottom boat cruise, $4.50 adults, $2.25 children. (2–3 hours)*

## ★★★★ FLORIDA CAPITOL

**Southeast corner of Pensacola and Duval Streets, Tallahassee, 800/628-2866**

One of five highrise Capitols in the United States and, sadly, an eyesore in this otherwise rather gracious southern city, Florida's Capitol is still worth visiting. Aside from the hourly, 45-minute-long guided tours through legislative chambers, the reason is the panoramic view from the 22nd-floor observatory and art gallery. If you didn't fly in over Tallahassee, the view from here will confirm the fact that this is a city largely hidden under a forest, although the higher landmarks are visible. The Visitors Information Center, located off the lobby, is an excellent information source. If you ask, someone will hand you a walking guide to downtown and a driving-tour guide that specializes in canopied roads.

***Details:*** *Open Mon–Fri 8–5, Sat–Sun 9–3. Free. Self-guided walking- and driving-tour maps are free. (Capitol: 1–1 1/2 hours)*

## ★★★★ OLD CAPITOL

**S. Monroe Street at Apalachee Parkway, Tallahassee, 850/487-1902**

You may be forgiven for thinking it odd that it took the uninspiring tower next door to keep Florida's Capitol in Tallahassee, given the obvious charm of this 1845 building, which has been restored to its 1902 appearance. But it is a fact. For a century, Tallahassee held off several attempts to move the Capitol elsewhere. The 1978 dedication of the New Capitol seems to have stopped such efforts. But the Old Capitol is worth every step of a self-guided tour. When you're in the rotunda, look straight up at the stained-glass dome. Outside, you'll already have noted the red candy-striped awnings. A wonderful staircase allows you to reach the governor's suite and House and Senate chambers. The building is a museum now, exhibiting mastodon bones and weaponry and agricultural implements that played important roles in the state's long history.

***Details:*** *Open Mon–Fri 9–4:30, Sat 10–4:30, Sun–holidays noon–4:30. Free. (1 hour)*

## ★★★★ TALLAHASSEE ANTIQUE CAR MUSEUM

**3550A Mahan Dr., Tallahassee, 850/942-0137, www.tacm.com**

If you have a sneaking admiration for gutsy Preston Tucker, whose technologically advanced automobile challenged the big automakers after World War II, you'll spend a lot of time around the metallic green 1948 Tucker Torpedo, the fifth of the 51 cars produced with independent suspension, a pop-out windscreen, padded dash, all-around disk brakes, swiveling headlamp, and other features that put this car ahead of its time. The car you're looking at was used in the Francis Ford Coppola film *Tucker: A Man and His Dream*, which starred Jeff Bridges. But don't stop. Here is the original Batmobile

# GREATER TALLAHASSEE

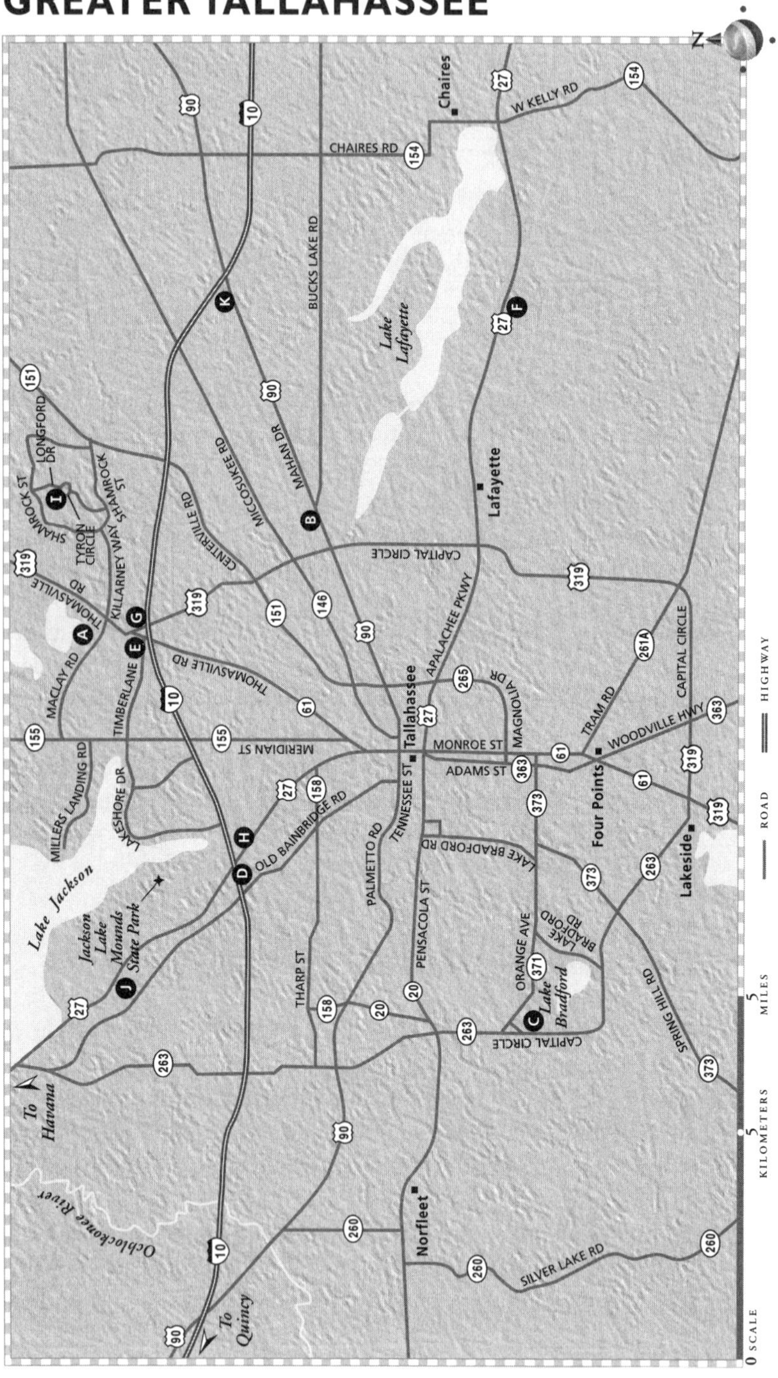

from *Batman Returns*, over there Abraham Lincoln's hearse, a 1909 Hupmobile, and more than 75 other rare cars.

***Details:*** *Open Mon–Sat 10–5, Sun noon–5. Admission: $7.50 adults, $4 children. (1–2 hours)*

## ★★★★ TALLAHASSEE MUSEUM OF HISTORY AND NATURAL SCIENCE

**3945 Museum Dr., Tallahassee, 850/576-1636**

Immerse yourself in Florida's natural and human history in this pleasant museum, which emphasizes the story of the Big Bend area (the local designation of this area of the state, where the Gulf of Mexico coast curves from vertical to horizontal, so to speak). A long and winding trail leads through 52 acres of old fields and cypress swamp and forests. Bring a picnic and take the time to explore an authentic 1880s farmstead, the museum's main feature, and don't miss the one-room schoolhouse, gristmill, caboose, church, or the antebellum home of George Washington's great-grandniece, Princess Catherine Murat. The display of regional architecture may be the best in the state.

***Details:*** *Open Mon–Sat 9–5, Sun 12:30–5. Admission: $6 adults, $4 children. (2–4 hours)*

## ★★★★ TOURS WITH A SOUTHERN ACCENT

**Welcome Center, Monroe and Brevard Streets, Tallahassee, 888/756-0045 or 850/513-1000**

You won't be sorry if you take time to explore Tallahassee close-up by foot or in a small van. The Welcome Center will lend you a cassette to guide you around the historic district, or you can arrange for guided walking or van tours titled Historic Tallahassee, Plantations, Antiques, Pre-Columbian & Spanish Colonial, and several others

### SIGHTS

- **A** Alfred B. Maclay State Gardens
- **B** Tallahassee Antique Car Museum
- **C** Tallahassee Museum of History and Natural Science

### FOOD

- **D** Monroe Street Grill
- **E** Mustard Seed
- **F** Nino—A Restaurant
- **G** Scales & Tails

### LODGING

- **H** Cabot Lodge North
- **I** Killearn Golf Country Club and Inn

### CAMPING

- **J** Big Oak RV Park
- **K** Tallahassee RV Park

***Details:*** *Open Mon–Sat 9–5. Free cassette guide requires deposit. Guided historic-district tours available, $20. Historic Tallahassee van tours depart at 10 a.m. and 2 p.m., $20. Similar tours available through Historic Tallahassee Walking Tours, 850/509-4199, www.christopher.org/tallahassee/tours, departing from The Capitol West Plaza Mon–Sat at 10 a.m. and 1 and 3 p.m. for $6 adults, $4 children. Horse-drawn carriage tours Sat 9–2, depart from Ponce de León Park, $15. This organization also offers van group tours.*

### ★★★ BLACK ARCHIVES RESEARCH CENTER & MUSEUM

**Between Gaines Street and Orange Avenue, Florida A&M University Campus, Tallahassee, 850/599-3020**

With a half-million historic documents plus a range of artifacts, photographs, artwork, oral history tapes, rare maps, and a 500-piece Ethiopian cross collection, this 1907 Carnegie Library building on historically African American Florida A&M University's campus is one of the nation's largest repositories of African American cultural history. Exhibits detail slave life and treatment and give a good sense of how the Underground Railway operated, smuggling slaves to the North before and during the Civil War.

***Details:*** *Open Mon–Fri 9–4. Visitor parking permits may be obtained from campus police on Wahnish Way. Free. (1–2 hours)*

### ★★★ BROKAW-MCDOUGALL HOUSE

**329 N. Meridian St., Tallahassee, 850/488-3901**

One of the area's finest antebellum homes, this 1856 Classical Revival structure was originally built on the town's outskirts as a residence for prosperous livery-stable owner Peres Bonney Brokaw. Because Brokaw family members lived in the house until 1973, it underwent few alterations during its time as a residence. Impressive 14-foot ceilings are complete with the plaster moldings and medallions common to the times, and the large pocket doors between rooms hint at the massive lumber used to build the place. Take in the lovely formal gardens, shaded by 150-year-old live oaks. They are particularly enchanting when the camellias are in bloom January through March.

***Details:*** *Open Mon–Fri 8–5. Tours are self-guided. Free. (30 minutes–1 hour)*

### ★★★ FIRST PRESBYTERIAN CHURCH

**102 N. Adams St., Tallahassee, 850/222-4504**

Built from 1835 to 1838, this is the city's oldest church, distinguished not only by its white spire but also by its history of accepting slaves as members, even without their masters' consent. Slaves did have to sit in galleries separate from the white congregation, however.

***Details:** Open daylight hours. Free. (30 minutes)*

## ★★★ JOHN G. RILEY HOUSE MUSEUM OF AFRICAN-AMERICAN HISTORY AND CULTURE

**419 E. Jefferson St., Tallahassee, 850/681-7881**

John Riley was born a slave in 1857 (he died in 1954) but defied the laws of the time and educated himself to the point that he became principal of Tallahassee's first public high school for African Americans. He built this house for his family in 1890 in what was a thriving African American neighborhood. It is a work in progress today, under continuing renovation and in the process of adding to its collections dedicated to African American history and culture in North Florida.

***Details:** Open Mon, Wed, Fri, 10–4. Free. (30 minutes–1 hour)*

## ★★★ KNOTT HOUSE MUSEUM

**301 E. Park Ave., Tallahassee, 850/922-2459**

This 1840s house is the "house that rhymes"—poems are quite literally attached to its Victorian-era furnishings. Luella Knott, whose husband, William, was a state politician, wrote verses about various pieces of furniture and tied her poems to the subject matter with satin ribbons. The Knott house is a time capsule of Tallahassee history, possibly built by free African American builder George Proctor well before the Civil War. After the war's end, a Union general read the Emancipation Proclamation from its steps. The house is fully furnished with either original or period pieces as the Knotts had it in the 1930s. On the tour, linger in the kitchen because, unless you're about 110 years old, you'll be fascinated by the vintage electric appliances.

***Details:** Open for guided tours Sept–July, Wed–Fri 1–4, Sat 10–4. Admission: $3 adults, $1.50 children, $7 family. (30 minutes–1 hour)*

## ★★★ MUSEUM OF FLORIDA HISTORY

**R. A. Gray Building, 500 S. Bronough St., Tallahassee, 850/488-1484**

This is a concept rather than a museum, because technically this official state museum includes the Old Capitol, the Union Bank, the

Knott House, and Mission San Luis de Apalachee. But while you're here in the R. A. Gray Building, you'll probably be impressed by a giant, nine-foot-high mastodon skeleton and a frighteningly large ancient armadillo from the Pleistocene era. The museum also has a collection of Spanish galleon treasure and a mock-up Confederate Civil War campsite (Tallahassee was the only southern city not occupied by Union troops), plus displays of quilts, cigar-box labels, farm equipment, and other items that were part of frontier life in Florida.

**Details:** *Open Mon–Fri 9–4:30, Sat 10–4:30, Sun, noon–4:30. Free. (30 minutes–1 1/2 hours)*

## ★★ BEACH AT ST. JOSEPH PENINSULA STATE PARK

**Route C30, Port St. Joe, 850/227-1327**

There are beaches, and then there are beaches. What makes this one special are the enormous, towering dunes along miles of gorgeous sand. If you want to explore this 2,516-acre island park further, take to the 10 miles of wilderness trails. It's difficult to imagine a more perfect spot for sunbathers, swimmers, walkers, and cyclists.

**Details:** *Take U.S. 98 to CR 30. Open daily 8:30–dusk. Admission: $3.25 car, $1 walkers and cyclists. (2 hours minimum)*

## ★★ CONSTITUTION CONVENTION STATE MUSEUM

**U.S. 98, Port St. Joe, 850/229-8029**

The boomtown of St. Joseph, created in 1835 to compete with Apalachicola as a trading port city, was the site of Florida's first State Constitution Convention. The museum commemorates the work of the 86 territorial delegates who worked for Florida's admission to the Union. Talking models provide an animated conclusion to your visit.

**Details:** *Open Thu–Mon, 9–noon and 1–5. Admission: $1. (30 minutes)*

## ★★ GOODWOOD PLANTATION

**1600 Miccosukee Rd., Tallahassee, 850/877-4202**

Be prepared to see a work in progress here, as renovation continues on the frescoed ceilings and lattico kitchen of this gracious 1840s home. The gardens still offer an enchanting setting for teas and small social receptions, activities the house has known throughout its history.

**Details:** *Open Tue–Sat 10–4. Free. (30 minutes)*

### ★★ GOVERNOR'S MANSION

**700 N. Adams St., Tallahassee, 850/488-4661**

Florida's governors still live in this Federal-style mansion patterned after Andrew Jackson's Tennessee estate, The Hermitage. State rooms feature antique furnishings and gifts from foreign dignitaries.

***Details:*** *Tours available during the legislative session Mar–May and during the Dec holiday season only, 10–noon. Free.*

### ★★ JOHN GORRIE STATE MUSEUM

**46 Sixth St., Apalachicola, 850/653-9347**

Scholars have argued plausibly that without the fruits of Dr. Gorrie's invention, the southern tier of the United States might have stayed an economic backwater. Certainly, air-conditioning led to the rapid expansion of Houston, Phoenix, and Florida's burgeoning cities. This small museum, Gorrie's house, has a replica of Gorrie's ice machine, a large ice chamber with a fan, devised because so many Apalachicolans were dying of yellow fever in the 1840s and '50s and he felt compelled to find a way to cool their rooms. The modern refrigeration and air-conditioning industries trace their lineage back to this good doctor.

***Details:*** *Open Mon, Thu–Sun 9–5. Admission: $1 adults and children over six. (30 minutes–1 hour)*

## FITNESS AND RECREATION

You can't ride on Florida's oldest railroad any more, but put on your skates or jogging shoes, or rent a bicycle or a horse to traverse its path via the 16-mile **Tallahassee-St. Marks Historic Railroad State Trail**, 1022 DeSoto Park Dr., off Woodville Hwy. (SR 363), 850/922-6007. For a memorable hike on the beach, go to **St. George Island State Park** at Eastpoint, 850/927-2111, about 10 miles southeast of Apalachicola. You'll see least terns, black skimmers, snowy plovers, and other shorebirds, and you can stroll the boardwalks that carry you over the swamp, and mount observation platforms. But there's a wonderful surprise waiting for you. Suddenly, as you round a corner of beach, you'll see Florida's listing lighthouse. The 70-foot-tall, 1852 Cape St. George Lighthouse tilts 7 degrees toward the Gulf of Mexico, more than the leaning Tower of Pisa's 5.5 degrees. Hurricanes have nearly killed it, but there's a restoration effort under way.

If you've ever wondered whether there really is a Sopchoppy River, head for **Apalachicola National Forest**, 850/926-3561, Florida's largest, with 565,000 acres laced with hiking trails (including a portion of the Florida National Scenic

Trail) to take you through hardwood hammocks, pine flatwoods, swamp rivers, wilderness areas, lakes, and streams. You can rent a canoe and paddle slowly down the Sopchoppy and Lower Ochlockonee Rivers, watching for red cockeyed woodpeckers or southern bald eagles as you go.

## FOOD

In Tallahassee, settle in at the moderate, unpretentious **Mustard Tree**, 1415 Timberlane Rd. (at I-10 and Thomasville Rd.), 850/893-8733, which emphasizes pleasing presentations of its "sophisticated" seafood. Or try the Florida amberjack or grouper indoors or out at **Barnacle Bill's**, 1830 N. Monroe St., 850/385-8734, a local hangout. A huge salad bar and well-regarded steaks and prime ribs are the draw at **Monroe Street Grill**, 2900 N. Monroe St., 850/386-1027, and the family that likes seafood will find pleasure at the oyster bar/pub called **Scales & Tails**, 2741 Capital Cir. N.E., 850/385-9993. The more expensive **Nino–A Restaurant**, 6497 Apalachee Pkwy., 850/878-8141, offers more intimate candlelight dining, with choices ranging from Bavarian specialties to memorable Florida seafood. Higher priced still, and considered a landmark restaurant, is the **Silver Slipper**, 531 Scotty's Lane, 850/386-9366, with its consistently award-winning steak and Greek and seafood specialties.

The nearby Gulf of Mexico just dares travelers not to try some fresh seafood, so if you're in Apalachicola and in the mood, try the local selections at **Caroline's Dining On The River**, 123 Water St., 850/653-8139, a fairly elegant place that offers a panoramic vista of the Apalachicola River. The moderately priced restaurant in **The Gibson Inn**, on U.S. 98 at the west end of the bridge at Market St. and Ave. C, 850/653-2191, is another good choice. For classic Southern cooking, few restaurants are better than **The Ball Room** at the Wakulla Springs Lodge, 1 Springs Dr., in Wakulla Springs State Park, 850/224-5950. It's time for fried oysters from Apalachicola Bay, quail, and softshell crab.

In Havana, north of the capital city along U.S. 27, stop in at **The Nicholson Farmhouse Restaurant**, an early-1800s family homestead serving grilled steak, chicken, shrimp, and fish. If you're on the road to Georgia, try **Chez Pierre**, 1215 Thomasville Rd., 850/222-0936, known for the French bistro atmosphere it has instilled in an old Southern home.

## LODGING

There is a wide range of both ordinary overnight accommodations and some particularly charming lodgings, variously set along the white-sand beaches or among the stands of pine and live oak trees that dominate this section of Florida. If you don't want to stay in one of the chain lodgings that line the I-10 exits and Monroe Street, try some of these.

If you're willing to stay a few miles north of the capital, you'll find some special accommodations. Check in at the **McFarlin House B&B Inn**, 305 E. King St., Quincy, 850/875-2526, www.gadcom.net/~mcfarlin, if you would like to stay in a particularly ornate Victorian building that features pressed ceilings, hand-carved woodwork and mantles, and a wonderful wraparound porch. Nearby, the **Allison House Inn**, 215 N. Madison St., Quincy, 888/904-2511 or 850/875-2511, is more like an English country manor, a double-parlored house furnished with antiques from the British Isles, built in 1843 for Governor A. K. Allison. **Palmer Place**, 625 W. Palmer Mill Rd., Monticello, 850/997-5519, is a restored antebellum residence in a more rural setting. The hosts think it fitting to offer gracious Southern hospitality in one of the state's oldest cities. Just a block from the town's antique and art district, **Historic Havana House**, 301 E. Sixth Ave., Havana, 850/539-5611, a 1907 home with 12-foot ceilings, has just two rooms, but you're likely to remember either the queen-sized cherry canopy bed or the king-sized wicker bed as you sip early morning coffee on the porch.

In Tallahassee, stop in at **The Riedel House**, 1412 Fairway Dr., 850/222-8569, a white-brick 1937 Georgian-style house with an acre of woodland. Inside, there's an upper-story art gallery of works by innkeeper Carolyn Riedel. **Cabot Lodge North**, 2735 N. Monroe St., 850/386-8880, is a reasonably priced two-story motel, while the **Governor's Inn**, 209 S. Adams St., 800/342-7717 or 850/681-6855, is a somewhat more expensive, small, gracious, downtown hotel with an old mahogany bar, pine-paneled lobby, and rooms filled with antiques. If you fancy the resort life, try the **Killearn Golf and Country Club and Inn**, 100 Tyron Cir., 850/893-2186, which, for rather reasonable rates, puts you in the woods near a well-known golf course and in rooms with plush furnishings and wide balconies.

Apalachicola's special lodging is the historic **Gibson Inn**, Market St. and Ave. C (west end of the U.S. 98 bridge), 850/653-2191 with its 30 moderate-to-expensive Victorian-accented rooms that take you back to the 1907 era in which it was built. And there is the **Rancho Inn**, 340 U.S. 98, 850/653-9435, a moderately priced 32-room motel. Still south of the capital city, find the **Wakulla Springs Lodge**, 1 Spring Dr., Wakulla Springs, 850/224-5950, and book one of the 27 rooms in this historic Spanish-style inn with Tennessee marble floors, heavy ceiling beams, and massive doors beneath its decorative arches.

# TALLAHASSEE/APALACHICOLA REGION

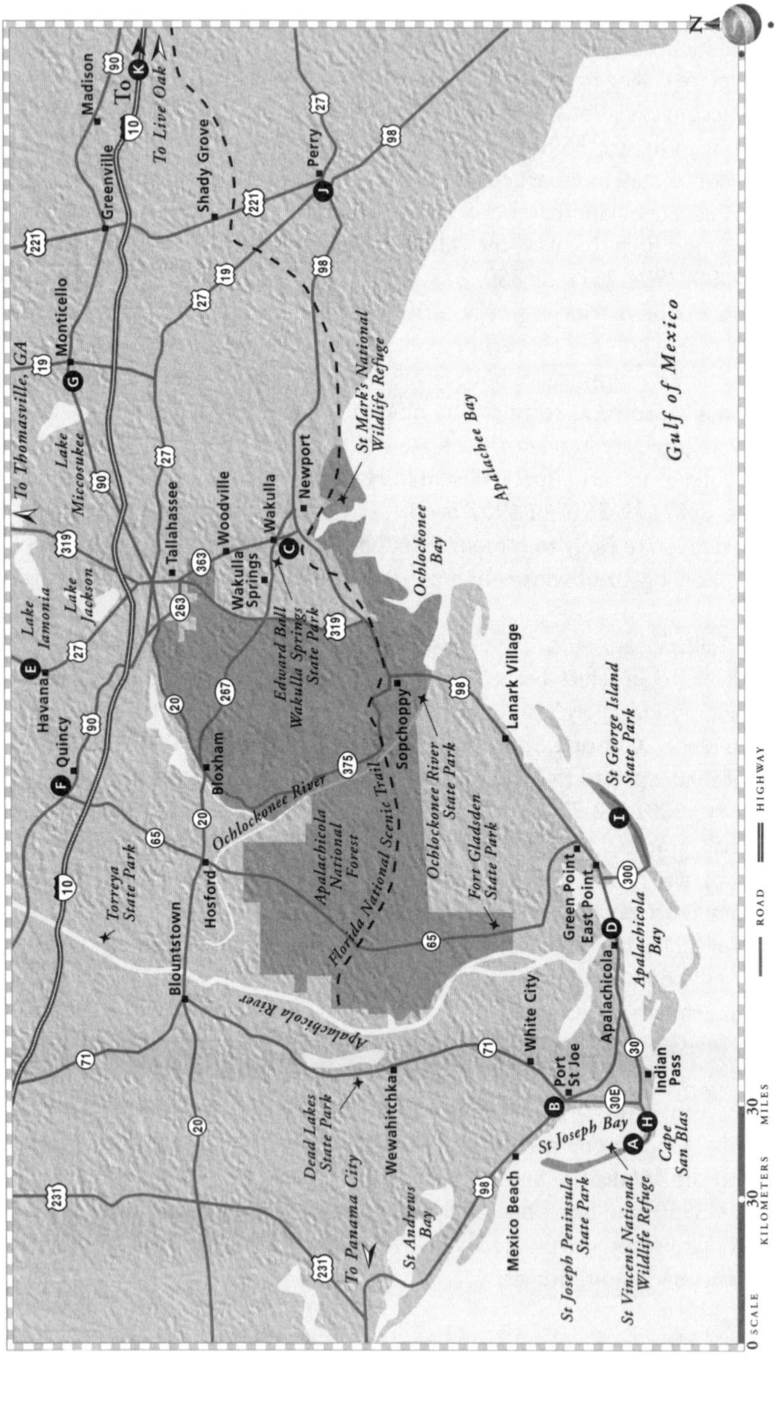

## CAMPING

Camping among northern Florida's pines is a pleasant experience any time, except perhaps in the rather cool months of January and February. Good sites are easy to find near Tallahassee as well as near the Gulf near Apalachicola. On Tallahassee's east side, **Tallahassee RV Park**, 6504 Mahan Dr. (I-10 at Exit 31A, U.S. 90), 850/878-7641, offers long pull-throughs, lighted and paved roads, full hookups, and a thoroughly country setting just 10 minutes from the Capitol. **Big Oak RV Park**, 4024 N. Monroe St. (I-10, Exit 29), 850/562-4660, offers 55 shady RV sites complete with full hookups, laundry, and showers.

A special experience among shorebirds, trail boardwalks, and hiking trails awaits campers on St. George Island, one of the prettiest examples of a Gulf of Mexico barrier island. **St. George Island State Park**, on U.S. 98 on St. George Island, 850/927-2111, offers 60 RV sites with full hookups and tent sites, but there's no food store, so arrive prepared. Not too far away, on the Gulf in Port St. Joe, is the **Cape San Blas Camping Resort**, CR 30 at Cape San Blas, 850/229-6800, which offers 44 rustic beachfront tent and RV sites, electrical and water hookups, and cabins to rent.

If you're driving U.S. 19 south of Tallahassee, you might stop in the small town of Perry, where a mile south of the city limits you'll find **Southern Oaks**, a relatively new campground with large, shaded pull-throughs with full hookups, tent sites, hiking trails, and a hot tub. Travelers along I-10 about 80 miles east of Tallahassee can hum Stephen Foster tunes at the **Spirit of Suwannee Music Park**, 3076 95th Dr., Live Oak, 904/364-2998, on the banks of the Suwanee River. The campground, seven miles north of the town, near I-10, Exit 129, has full hookups, pull-through sites, and an array of recreational activities.

---

### SIGHTS

- Ⓐ Beach at St. Joseph Peninsula State Park
- Ⓑ Constitution Convention State Museum
- Ⓒ Edward Ball Wakulla Springs State Park
- Ⓓ John Gorrie State Museum

### FOOD

- Ⓒ The Ball Room

### FOOD *(continued)*

- Ⓓ Caroline's Dining on the River
- Ⓓ The Gibson Inn
- Ⓔ The Nicholson Farmhouse Restaurant

### LODGING

- Ⓕ Allison House Inn
- Ⓓ Gibson Inn
- Ⓔ Historic Havana House
- Ⓕ McFarlin House B & B Inn

### LODGING *(continued)*

- Ⓖ Palmer Place
- Ⓓ Rancho Inn
- Ⓒ Wakulla Springs Lodge

### CAMPING

- Ⓗ Cape San Blas Camping Resort
- Ⓘ St. George Island State Park
- Ⓙ Southern Oaks
- Ⓚ Spirit of Suwannee Music Park

*Note: Items with the same letter are located in the same place.*

## Scenic Route: The Canopy Roads

*Your romantic side will be richly rewarded if you traverse Tallahassee's thoroughly enchanting canopy roads and lanes. Miles of roadways in and beyond the city have over the years been covered by canopies of huge live oaks dripping with Spanish moss. The canopy roads fan out from the city center to the north and east. One is* ***Old St. Augustine Rd.****, to which you gain access by turning south (right) as you leave town on the Apalachee Parkway (U.S. 27). Another is* ***Old Bainbridge Road****, leading northwest from Brevard Street out of the city, crossing underneath I-10 and eventually combining with* ***Capital Circle*** *N.W. near Lake Jackson. And* ***Meridian Road*** *(SR 155) runs due north after you turn left onto it when leaving town via Thomasville Road (U.S. 319).*

*But the best ride may be to take a round-trip route by leaving town to the northeast along the lovely* ***Miccosukee Road*** *(SR 146) from Brevard Street for about 14 miles, until you reach* ***Roberts Road*** *(SR 154). Turn north (left), take the sharp bend to the west as it cuts south of* ***Little Roberts Pond****, then watch for the intersection of* ***SR 151****. Turn southwest (left), and you're on* ***Centerville Road*** *(SR 151). Before you cross over I-10, in the* ***Moccasin Gap*** *vicinity, you'll see historic* ***Bradley's Country Store*** *on your right. In about 10 miles, Centerville Road will reconnect with* ***Miccosukee Road****, and you're back in Tallahassee.*

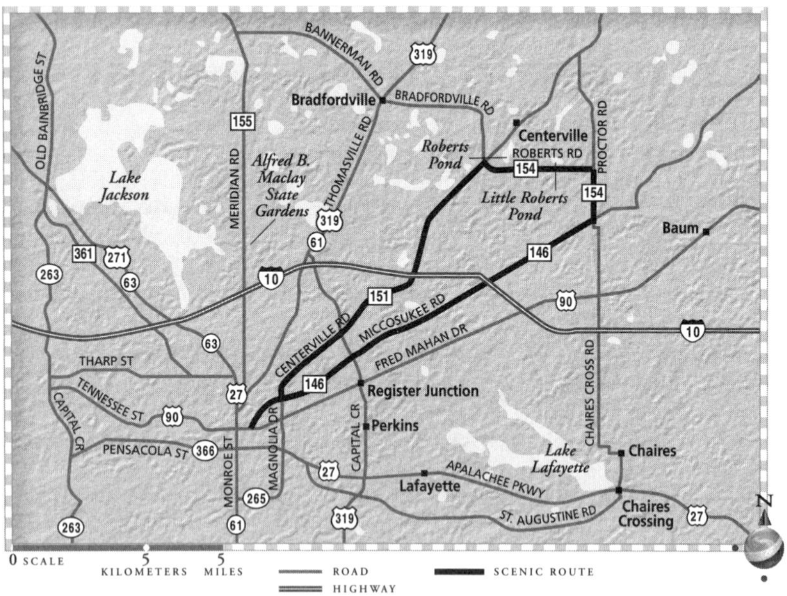

# 16
# THE PANHANDLE

Nicknamed "The Panhandle" because of its shape, the elongated northwest corner of Florida is a coastal paradise that hugs the Gulf of Mexico. Its beaches are the Panhandle's star attraction. Fine, pure quartz–crystal sand edges the shoreline like miles of white satin trimming the truly emerald waters, and dramatic sand dunes seem strategically placed for photography and sunset walks.

But every bit as appealing is its easy Southern charm and refreshingly slow pace. In fact, the Panhandle is more like Dixie than like the rest of Florida, leading some to call it the "Redneck Riviera." Diners are as likely to find grits, sausage gravy, or fried green tomatoes on menus as they are new and exotic fresh seafood dishes. There's little glitz here among the largely unspoiled beaches, low rolling hills, historic plantations, and wildlife refuge areas.

That's not to say there's a dearth of souvenir and T-shirt shops in such party areas as Panama City Beach. But you'll find plenty of quieter shoreline along the Gulf Islands National Seashore, where lovers can walk or kids can play their most raucous beach games without tripping over crowds of people.

The Panhandle is primarily a summer destination—this isn't the subtropics. Some businesses are open only seasonally and attraction hours may vary. Winters can be cool and sunny or damp and chilly, but off-season rates can make this area especially desirable, putting a beach vacation within financial reach of just about everybody.

# PANHANDLE

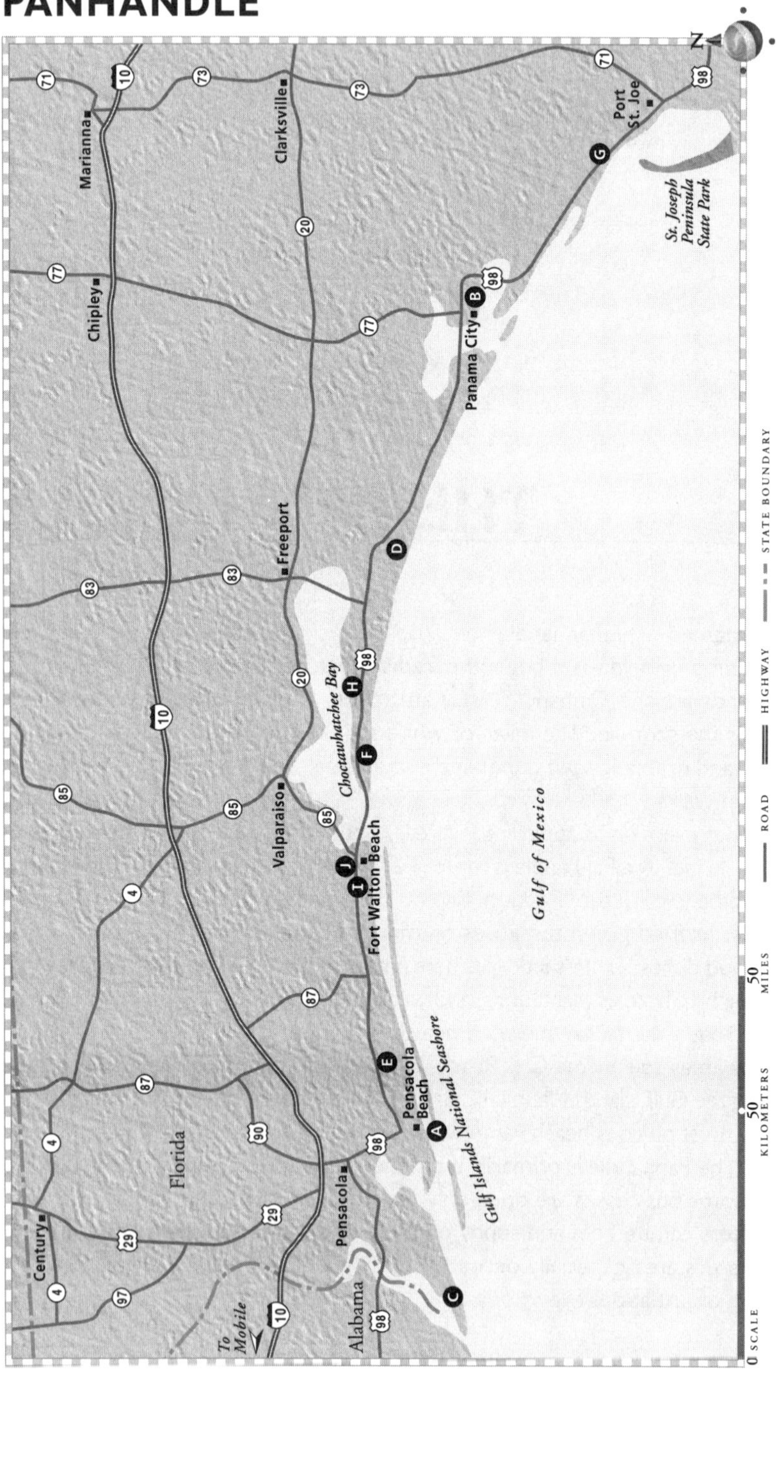

Marianna
Clarksville
Chipley
Freeport
Panama City
Port St. Joe
St. Joseph Peninsula State Park
Choctawhatchee Bay
Valparaiso
Fort Walton Beach
Gulf of Mexico
Pensacola Beach
Gulf Islands National Seashore
Pensacola
Century
Florida
Alabama
To Mobile
N
0 SCALE
50 KILOMETERS
50 MILES
ROAD
HIGHWAY
STATE BOUNDARY

# A PERFECT DAY IN THE FLORIDA PANHANDLE

Stop at a grocery, pack a cooler of cold drinks and some lunch, and get out on the water in the Destin/Fort Walton Beach area, where the Panhandle stretches as thin as a skinny cat in the sun. A huge charter-boat fleet awaits, ready to scour the sea for a record-breaking catch. If you prefer to be your own captain for the day, rent a pontoon boat and spend the day cruising the bayous, swimming in sparkling Choctawhatchee Bay, and fishing in Destin, the "World's Luckiest Fishing Village." If you're a diver or snorkeler, explore the living aquariums offshore. Natural history buffs will enjoy the artifacts and exhibits at the Indian Mound Museum. And those who prefer to do their nature hunting along the beach will find one of the state's best shelling destinations. When sunset rolls around, find yourself trekking through the dunes and sea grass, taking perfect pictures and leaving footprints that will be gone by morning.

---

## SIGHTS

- Ⓐ Fort Pickens
- Ⓑ Miracle Strip Park and Shipwreck Island
- Ⓒ Perdido Key State Recreation Area
- Ⓑ St. Andrews State Recreation Area
- Ⓓ Seaside
- Ⓔ The Zoo

## FOOD

- Ⓑ Angelo's Steak Pit
- Ⓓ Bud & Alley's
- Ⓐ Chan's Florida Cuisine
- Ⓐ Chan's Market Cafe
- Ⓕ Destin Diner
- Ⓕ Elephant Walk
- Ⓒ Flora-Bama Lounge
- Ⓐ Flounder's Chowder and Ale House
- Ⓑ Hamilton's

## FOOD *(continued)*

- Ⓑ Mako's Dockside Restaurant
- Ⓓ Modica Market
- Ⓖ The Oyster Bar
- Ⓐ Sand Bar

## LODGING

- Ⓐ Beachside Resort
- Ⓐ Best Western Pensacola Beach
- Ⓑ Boardwalk Beach Resort
- Ⓖ Driftwood Inn
- Ⓐ Gulf Aire Hotel
- Ⓗ A Highlands House Bed and Breakfast
- Ⓓ Josephine's French Country Inn
- Ⓑ Marriott's Bay Point Resort

## LODGING *(continued)*

- Ⓘ Ramada Plaza Beach Resort
- Ⓕ Sandestin
- Ⓙ Sea Isle Motel
- Ⓑ Sea Witch
- Ⓑ Sunset Inn

## CAMPING

- Ⓒ Big Lagoon State Recreation Area
- Ⓕ Camping on the Gulf Holiday Travel Resort
- Ⓕ Destin RV Resort
- Ⓗ Emerald Coast RV Resort
- Ⓓ Panama City Beach KOA
- Ⓑ St. Andrew State Recreation Area

*Note: Items with the same letter are located in the same place.*

## SIGHTSEEING HIGHLIGHTS

### ★★★★ SEASIDE

**Seaside Visitor Information Center, P.O. Box 4730, Seaside, FL, 32459, 800/277-8696, 850/231-4224 or 850-231-2228, www.seasidefl.com**

Before there was TV, before there were malls and suburbs and interstate highways, neighbors congregated downtown, passing the time of day, visiting at the grocer's, watching the goings-on from a porch or café. This very special planned community, created in the 1980s, was the set for the widely acclaimed 1998 Jim Carrey movie *The Truman Show*, and no wonder.

In addition to recreating the physical features of a lovely Southern resort town, the developers have somehow managed to capture a way of life all but vanished elsewhere. Miami builder/developer Robert Davis envisioned the 80-acre tract as an idyllic family beachside resort, embodying the pleasures of a small-town lifestyle, where everything would be within walking distance of home and where porch-sitting and visiting with neighbors were every bit as important as working or sunbathing.

Pastel cottages have white picket fences, deep-roof overhangs, and porch swings for extended sitting, savoring the Gulf breezes and sensual pleasures of life by the sea. Perfectly maintained public footpaths between the homes delight visitors with their tranquil, time-tunnel ambience. And while the residential neighborhoods are serene, there's a quiet hum to Seaside's downtown. Each building has shops opening onto a covered arcade. The central square is surrounded by brick and cobblestone streets that lead to restaurants, shopping, and pretty beach pavilions on gently contoured dunes.

Most of the cottages and bungalows are available for rent a good portion of the year, but if rates seem prohibitive, just drive in for the day. If Wally and the Beaver are fondly entrenched in your memory bank, you'll love this pretty little village.

***Details:*** *From Panama City, take U.S. 98 north to CR 30-A.*

### ★★★★ ST. ANDREWS STATE RECREATION AREA

**Thomas Dr., Panama City Beach, 850/233-5140**

Out of 600 beaches considered, the University of Maryland's Laboratory of Coastal Research named St. Andrews the best in the country for its spectacular shoreline, windswept dunes, and marshes teeming with wildlife. Jetties extend almost a half-mile into the Gulf, offering romantic views, great fishing, and a man-made reef that provides a safe, shallow play area for small children. Camping facilities, showers, restrooms, picnic areas, a reconstructed turpentine still, and a playground (nice combination!), cover more than 1,000 acres of beachfront. Make every effort to take the ferry from here to secluded Shell Island, a prime hunting ground for shell collectors and beach scavengers. This is the Florida you came to see.

***Details:*** *Take U-shaped Thomas Drive, at the traffic light behind Alvin's Island Department Store, to southernmost point. Open daily 8–sunset. Admission: $4 car.*

### ★★★ NATIONAL MUSEUM OF NAVAL AVIATION

**U.S. Naval Air Station, 1750 Radford Blvd., Pensacola, 800/327-5002 or 904/453-6289, www.naval-air.org**

Pensacola's U.S. Naval Air Station is a center for electronic warfare and cartographic training. Huge skylighted areas in the museum hold more than 100 aircraft, from the earliest flimsy flying machines to famous WWII fighters like the Corsair and Hellcat, to the four Blue Angel Skyhawks suspended in diamond flight formation overhead. An IMAX theater puts you in the cockpit in *The Magic of Flight.*

***Details:*** *Open daily 9–5. Museum: free. IMAX tickets: $4.50. (2 hours)*

### ★★★ PERDIDO KEY STATE RECREATION AREA

**Gulf Beach Hwy., Perdido Key, 850/492-4660 or 850/492-1595, www.dep.state.fl.us/parks**

Perdido Key is one of Florida's best beaches. Unspoiled and uncrowded, the soft white sand has plenty of room for quiet sunbathing, casting a fishing line, Frisbee throwing, or a game of beach ball. Amenities include picnic shelters, restrooms, and shower facilities. There are a few honky-tonk bars, T-shirt shops, high-rise condos, and stylish vacation residences, despite the relative isolation.

***Details:*** *Follow SR 292 southwest from Pensacola. (2 hours minimum)*

### ★★ MIRACLE STRIP PARK AND SHIPWRECK ISLAND

**12000 Front Beach Rd., Panama City Beach, 800/538-7395 or 850/234-5810**

These sister parks offer plenty of good family recreation. Miracle Strip

# PENSACOLA AREA

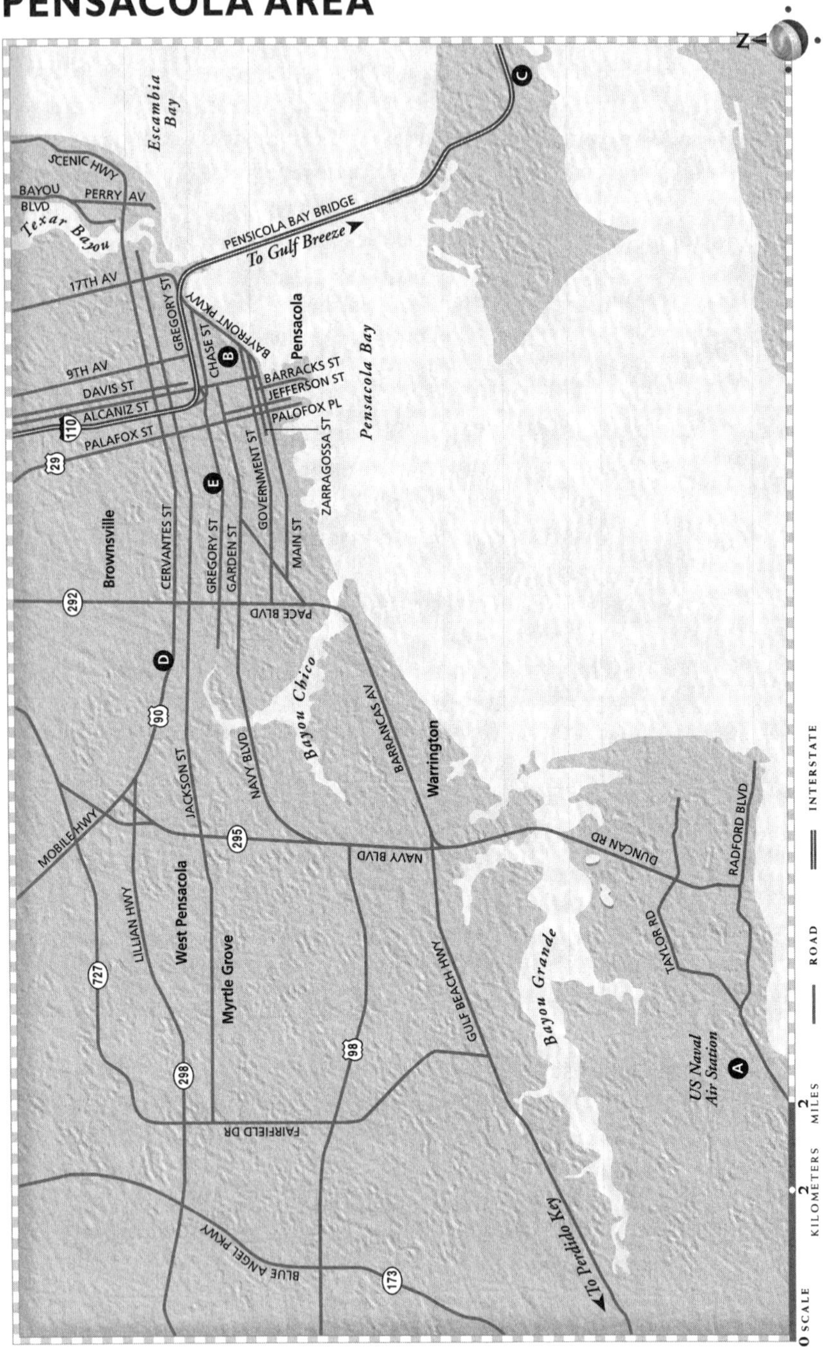

has more than 30 rides and roller coasters, including the 65-foot-high Starliner coaster; shocker-themes like Dante's Inferno, a Haunted Castle Ride, Dungeon Ride, and Hilda's Hotel of Horrors; plus the usual carnival-type midway and arcade games. More daring souls will love Shipwreck Island's 35-mph Speed Slide and 370-foot white-water tube, but there are a few gentler attractions for the timid.

***Details:*** *Hours vary seasonally. Miracle Strip admission: $15 over 33" tall, under 33" free, for armband to ride all; or $3 general admission and $2.50 per ride; Shipwreck Island admission: $18 over 50" tall, $15 under 50", under 33", free. Combo ticket, $25. (3 hours minimum)*

## ★★ PENSACOLA HISTORIC DISTRICT AND HISTORIC PENSACOLA VILLAGE

**Downtown Bayfront, Pensacola, 850/444-8905**

Pensacola is an old harbor town with a historic waterfront area that resembles New Orleans' fabled French Quarter. The streets are lined with restored homes, museums, shops, galleries, and restaurants, some of them more than 200 years old, and there's an interesting cemetery with some 3,000 graves of local settlers. You can explore much of the area at no cost, envisioning an era of Spanish explorers, seafaring men, Victorian ladies, and Creole culture.

Historic Pensacola Village, a complex of nineteenth-century buildings, offers guided tours of some of its restored structures, including the Charles Lavallé House, a Creole cottage built in 1810, and the 1804 Julee Cottage, owned early on by a free African American woman.

***Details:*** *Historic village tours Tue–Sat 10–4. Admission: $5.50 adults, $2.25 children, $4.50 seniors. (1–2 hours)*

## ★★ THE ZOO

**5701 Gulf Breeze Pkwy., Gulf Breeze, 850/932-2229**

This visitor-friendly zoo features lush botanical gardens and more

---

### SIGHTS

- Ⓐ National Museum of Naval Aviation
- Ⓑ Pensacola Historic District and Historic Pensacola Village

### FOOD

- Ⓒ Boy on a Dolphin Restaurant
- Ⓓ Mesquite Charlie's

### LODGING

- Ⓔ Pensacola Victorian Bed & Breakfast

than 700 wild and rare animals, including a good number and assortment of big cats. The safari train ride through 30 acres of pristine wildlife preserve is a good deal. You can get a close look at the free-roaming animals, including rhinos, alligators, pigmy hippos, llamas, deer, and antelope, which seem strangely unaffected by the train going by. Then stroll along an elevated boardwalk just 10 feet above the native brush creatures that live in this natural habitat. If you hold out a piece of carrot or apple in the petting area, you may feel the long, purple tongue of a giraffe caressing your outstretched palm, but you'll have to be content just watching the antics of the powerful western lowland gorillas from afar.

***Details:*** *On U.S. 98, 14 miles east of Gulf Breeze. Open daily 9–5 summer, 9–4 winter. Admission: $9.75 adults, $5.75 children, $8.75 seniors. (2–3 hours)*

### ★ FORT PICKENS

**Fort Pickens Rd., Pensacola Beach, 850/934-2635**

Built in 1829–1834 of more than 21 million bricks, this Union fort was never captured by the Confederacy during the Civil War. Walk around the 10-foot-deep moat to the officers' quarters, which later housed Apache prisoners including the fort's most famous resident, Geronimo, then take a good look at what's left of the corner of the fort after an 1899 fire reached a magazine holding four tons of black powder and blew debris over a 1.5-mile area.

***Details:*** *Open daily Apr–Oct 9:30–5. Admission: $4 vehicle. (1½ hours)*

## FITNESS AND RECREATION

The clear, green waters of the Panhandle are the open-water equivalent of a fully stocked pond. Sportfishing is a passion, and boat charters are readily available, both on the rivers and in the Gulf. Other popular water activities include parasailing, Jet Skiing, snorkeling, windsurfing, and waterskiing. Several state-designated canoe trails are easily accessible, with waters ranging from narrow, twisting rapids and shoals to clear, placid, spring-fed streams. For information on canoe trails, call the **Florida Department of Natural Resources**, 850/487-4784.

Snorkeling and diving are especially popular in Panama City Beach. A half-dozen major shipwrecks and artificial reefs lie off the coast, where warm Gulf waters encourage the rapid growth of marine life. Daily diving, snorkeling, and dolphin-encounter trips leave from the **Hydrospace Dive Shop**, 888/874-3483 or 850/234-3063; a good information source is the **Panama City Marine Institute**, 800/722-3224.

An excellent spot for fishing is the **Dan Russell Municipal Pier**, at 1,642 feet the longest in Florida and on the Gulf of Mexico. **St. Andrews State Recreation Area**, 850/233-5140, a great family area, has both woodland and beach areas, nature trails, marshes, biking, hiking, camping, a playground, swimming, and fishing. A passenger ferry (seasonal) leaves here for uninhabited Shell Island. Swimmers beware, however—ocean currents can be strong here. You'll also find plenty of fishing charters in Destin, the "World's Luckiest Fishing Village," which holds five saltwater world records.

Golf courses on the Panhandle border countless lakes and streams, wide bays, crystal-clear rivers, and the Gulf of Mexico. Players love the Arnold Palmer–designed Audubon Sanctuary Course at **Lost Key Golf Club**, Perdido Key, 800/351-8266 or 850/492-3084. Panama City Beach boasts two noteworthy championship layouts at **Bay Point**, 850/235-6909, and a par-72 plus a nine-hole executive course at **Holiday Golf Club**, 850/234-1800.

In Pensacola, soccer fans flock to the **Pensacola Soccer Complex**, 800/939-4625. The **Pensacola Greyhound Track**, 850/455-8595, offers racing with pari-mutuel betting. In Panama City Beach, the dogs run March through September at **Ebro Greyhound Track**, 850/535-4048; off-season brings satellite wagering on greyhounds, horses, and jai alai from other venues.

In Panama City Beach, the **Hidden Lagoon Super Race Track**, 850/233-1825, has single- and double-seat go-carts so parents can drive younger children on the looping .9-mile track. Beside it, the **Hidden Lagoon Super Golf**, 850/234-9289, offers two mini-golf courses around a central lagoon stocked with fish.

## FOOD

Reasonably priced mesquite-broiled steaks and jumbo shrimp are strong draws at **Mesquite Charlie's**, 5901 N. "W" St., Pensacola, 850/434-0498. On Pensacola Beach you can dine indoors or out at the **Boy on a Dolphin Restaurant**, 400 Pensacola Beach Blvd., 850/932-7954, overlooking Santa Rosa Sound—it's casual, the Greek salad is legendary, and there's live jazz outdoors on weekends.

At **Flounder's Chowder and Ale House**, 800 Quietwater Beach Rd., 850/932-2003, the signature attraction is fresh, charbroiled seafood. The waterfront deck at the **Sand Bar**, 500 Quietwater Beach Rd., 850/934-6318, is a great place to get a pound of u-peel-'em shrimp or a sandwich and play some pool or darts while you take in the view. Try the cheese grits for breakfast at **Chan's Market Cafe**, 16 Via de Luna, 850/932-8454, a winner for family dining and blue-plate specials at lunch and dinner. For gourmet meals and an impressive wine list, visit **Chan's Florida Cuisine**, 2½ Via de Luna, 850/932-3525, directly on the Gulf; downstairs has live entertainment on weekends.

For all-around fine dining on Perdido Key, including respectable steaks and seafood, seek out **The Oyster Bar**, 13700 River Rd., 850/492-0192. A quirkier, barefoot, beach-bar ambience prevails at the **Flora-Bama Lounge**, 17401 Perdido Key Dr., 850/492-0116.

For an elegant, unforgettable meal, make dinner reservations at **Elephant Walk** in the Sandestin Resort, 5500 U.S. 98 E., Destin, 800/277-0800 or 850/267-8000, with a menu of superb offerings from several continents. The impressive bungalow overlooking the ocean holds many of the treasures collected by wealthy tea-plantation owner John Whiley of Ceylon in his travels to such exotic places as Egypt, Africa, India, and Nepal.

But you're hungry *now?* Come as you are for 24-hour breakfasts and diner-style meals to the shiny silver **Destin Diner**, U.S. 98 at Airport Rd., Destin, 850/654-5843.

In Seaside, pet the cats that loll about outside the gazebo at **Bud & Alley's** on Cinderella Cir., 850/231-5900, which offers fresh, local daily specials and live jazz entertainment on the weekends. At the international **Modica Market** in Central Square, 850/231-1214, the walls of this old-style grocery store are lined with shelves. They have a good selection of old-fashioned penny candy, and a few sidewalk tables where you can have deli sandwiches, gourmet muffins, and cappuccino.

Around Panama City Beach, most places are casual and family-friendly. Along U.S. 98A, visit **Mako's Dockside Restaurant**, 5550 N. Lagoon Dr. and Thomas Dr., 850/230-4848, where you can watch the boats pull in at Capt. Anderson's Marina to unload your dinner. **Angelo's Steak Pit**, 9527 Front Beach Rd., 850/234-2531, is known for its hickory-broiled beef; and **Hamilton's**, on Thomas Dr. overlooking Grand Lagoon, 850/234-1255, has a killer Louisiana gumbo, mesquite-grilled seafood and meats, and lots of windows for watching the sunset.

## LODGING

Pensacola Beach has a good variety of lodging options. The **Beachside Resort**, 14 Via de Luna Dr., 800/232-2416 or 850/932-5331, has kitchenettes and a kiddie pool. The **Best Western Pensacola Beach**, 16 Via de

## FLORIDA CAVERNS STATE PARK

*Most Florida visitors wouldn't guess that the state is home to some of the country's most amazing caves. Yet it's true. Drive north on U.S. 231 from Panama City Beach and continue north on SR 167 to Marianna, then another three miles north to* ***Florida Caverns State Park****, 3345 Caverns Rd., 850/482-1228 or 850/482-9598. The beauty of Florida's only publicly accessible limestone caverns rivals that of Mammoth Cave and Carlsbad Caverns.*

*Guided tours wind through a lighted underground cave with many fragile limestone formations—stalagmites, stalactites, soda straws, columns, rimstone pools, flowstones, and draperies. The formations were formed over tens of thousands of years, and continue to grow at the rate of only an inch or so per century. The cave trails, lighting and passages were all constructed by the Civilian Conservation Corps between 1938 and 1942.*

*The Florida Cavern itself is the only cave open for public touring. Keep your voice down if you see any of the endangered gray bats that live in some of the caves—bats hibernate during the winter months, and will expend valuable energy that they need to survive if they are awakened.*

*While the caverns are the focal point of the park's 1,300 scenic acres, nature trails, swimming, hiking, picnicking, camping, and fishing are also available. It's a wild area for walking, with a wide variety of animals and plants, including magnolias, flowering dogwood trees, and all types of wildflowers. If you listen and step carefully, you'll likely see woodpeckers, owls, turtles, alligators, and beavers. Equestrian facilities are nearby if you want to ride the trails, and inexpensive canoe rentals are available for paddling the 50-mile Chipola River. Those who enjoy golf can play the* ***Florida Caverns Golf Course****, 850/482-4257. The park is open daily from 8 a.m.–dusk; admission is $3.25 per vehicle, and a cave tour will set you back only another $4 for adults and $2 for kids.*

*For a comfortable night's sleep among antique furnishings and southern hospitality, stay at the* ***Hinson House****, located a short distance from the park at 4338 Lafayette St., Marianna, 800/531-4786 or 850/526-1500.*

Luna, 800/934-3301 or 850/934-3300, too, is a good value, with moderate rack rates and a free continental breakfast. The **Gulf Aire Motel,** 21 Via de Luna, 850/932-2319, offers clean, modest rooms, with a private beachfront and barbecue grills. For peace and quiet, stay at **A Highlands House Bed and Breakfast**, 4193 W. Scenic SR 30A, Santa Rosa Beach, 850/267-0110. A good choice near downtown Pensacola's Historic District is the **Pensacola Victorian Bed & Breakfast**, 203 W. Gregory St., 800/370-8354 or 850/434-2818.

The **Sea Isle Motel** on Fort Walton Beach, 1214 U.S. 98 E., 850/243-5563, is inexpensive, and has microwaves, refrigerators, and a free breakfast. Moderately priced and conveniently located, the **Ramada Plaza Beach Resort**, 1500 Miracle Strip Pkwy. S.E., 850/243-9161, has a glorious, golden lobby, fine dining, and a friendly lounge and oyster bar. For a more luxurious stay, reserve a few nights at the **Sandestin** resort community, 5500 U.S. 98 E., Destin, 800/277-0800 or 850/267-8150, which has 45 holes of golf along the Choctawhatchee Bay. In Seaside, if money's no problem and you're traveling without children, you'll long remember a stay at **Josephine's French Country Inn,** 101 Seaside Ave., 800/848-1840 or 850/231-1940, a gracious, family-run B&B with an award-winning dining room.

*From March to Easter, Panama City Beach throws one of the biggest Spring Break parties in Florida, so plan accordingly.*

On Panama City Beach, **Marriott's Bay Point Resort**, 4200 Marriott Dr., 800/874-7105 or 850/234-3307, has all the bells and whistles, including golf, tennis, water sports, a marina, deep-sea fishing, children's programs, and a natural lagoon on St. Andrews Bay. Budget watchers will appreciate the **Sunset Inn**, 8109 Surf Dr., 850/234-7370, on the Gulf side, with nice one- and two-room apartments with kitchenettes and a large pool. The family-oriented **Sea Witch**, 21905 Front Beach Rd., 800/322-4571 or 850/234-5722, on the quieter end of the beach, is another good bet.

Four hotels linked by an 1,800-foot Gulf-front beach boardwalk make up the **Boardwalk Beach Resort**, 9450 S. Thomas Dr., Panama City Beach, 800/224-4853 or 850/234-3484. It offers children's activities, four pools, Jet Skiing, parasailing, and a popular beach bar. The Howard Johnson Resort Hotel, Beachwalk, Gulfwalk, and Sheraton Four Points offer accommodations from efficiencies to suites.

Further east along the coast, the **Driftwood Inn**, 2015 U.S. 98,

## DEFUNIAK SPRINGS

*An hour north of Panama City Beach (U.S. 98 W. to 331 N.) is DeFuniak Springs, a delightful Victorian town clustered around a circular, spring-fed freshwater lake. DeFuniak Springs was the winter home of the New York Chautauqua, a cultural, educational, and religious program of the late 1880s through early 1920s that attracted thousands of visitors to the area. Homes built at that time employed elaborate architectural details, like turrets, double verandahs, gingerbread trim, fluted columns, and window dormers, all of which you can see on a walk around Lake DeFuniak on Circle Drive.*

*The old* ***Walton-DeFuniak Library*** *houses many rare books dating to its earliest days (circa 1886), as well as a collection of medieval armor and artifacts. You can see the* ***Chautauqua Hall of Brotherhood*** *or the 1882* ***L&N Depot****, built in 1882, where as many as 4,000 passengers a day arrived by rail. Across from the Depot on Baldwin Avenue, do some antiques shopping at* ***Big Store Antiques****, if you can catch it open, and keep an eye out for the beautiful stained-glass windows in the sanctuary and chapel of the* ***First United Methodist Church****. If you call ahead, the Walton County Chamber of Commerce, 850/892-3191, will send a walking-tour guide with background on lakeside homes with names like Idlewild, Dream Cottage, and Pansy Cottage, built for Florida Chautauqua presidents and other city fathers.*

*You can see the area's finest grapes being made into wine, take a free tour of the facility, and taste the award-winning wines at Florida's largest winery,* ***Chautauqua Vineyards****, 1330 Freeport Rd., 850/892-5887. Later, for a meal or snack amid plenty of nostalgic decor and memorabilia, look for the striped awnings over the* ***Busy Bee Cafe****, 35 S. Seventh St., 850/892-6700, or try some fried catfish or the buffet dinner at* ***McLain's Family Steakhouse****, 622 Hugh Adams Rd., 850/892-2402.*

*If you'd like to dine in luxury and spend the night, you'll sleep tight at the* ***Hotel DeFuniak****, 400 E. Nelson St., 850/892-4383, a small, deluxe, 1920 hotel with an exceptional dining room. For pleasant B&B lodging, try the late-1800s* ***Sunbright Manor****, 606 Live Oak Ave., 850/892-0656, former home of Florida Governor Sidney J. Catts.*

Mexico Beach, 850/648-5126, offers rooms, beachfront cottages, and Old Florida–style two-bedroom houses. It's quiet, convenient, and comfortable for families, and accepts pets.

## CAMPING

A wonderful feature of camping in the Panhandle is the likely diversity within a single campground. Many offer forested beachfront sites, giving campers shady respite from the sun's heat.

In the far southwestern corner of the state, on CR 292A southwest of Pensacola, **Big Lagoon State Recreation Area**, 12301 Gulf Beach Hwy., 850/492-1595, Perdido Key, has 75 sites for RVs or tents, with cable-TV hookups, RV storage, a pool and rec room, swimming, and fishing. Numerous birds and animals live on the beaches and in the salt marsh, and an observation tower provides a panoramic view across the Intracoastal Waterway. On Santa Rosa Beach, just south of U.S. 98, the **Emerald Coast RV Resort**, 7525 W. Scenic Hwy. 30A, 800/232-2478 or 850/267-2808, has pull-throughs, paved pads, full hookups, cable and phone hookups, bike rentals, and mini-golf but takes no tents or pop-ups.

In Destin, the **Camping on the Gulf Holiday Travel Park**, 10005 W. Emerald Coast Pkwy., 850/837-6334, has 250 beachfront or grassy, shaded sites for tents or pull-throughs with full hookups. An even better value for families is the **Destin RV Resort**, 150 Regions Way, 850/837-9345, with 172 sites for tents or RVs, pull-through sites near the beach, and a heated swimming pool.

The **Panama City Beach KOA,** 8800 Thomas Dr., 800/562-2483 or 850/234-5731, has tent and pull-through sites, paved pads, patios and tables, full hookups, and beach and boat access. Full-facility or primitive camping is allowed in **St. Andrews State Recreation Area** off SR 392, 850/233-5140. The 1,260-acre park has two fishing piers, jetties, picnic sites, a nature trail and boat ramp, showers, and a concession stand.

## NIGHTLIFE

Fans of dinner theater may enjoy a night out at **Seville Dinner Theater**, 241 E. Garden St., Pensacola, 850/469-1111, which offers buffet dining and shows from Broadway plays to mystery theater or late-night cabarets. For a casual night of dancing and listening to reggae bands under the stars, go to **Flounder's Chowder and Ale House** on Pensacola Beach, 850/932-2003, which has outdoor benches and tables surrounding a natural sand floor.

In Fort Walton Beach, call about performances of the **Okaloosa Symphony Orchestra**, 850/244-3308, or the **OWCC Stage Crafters Community Theater**, 850/243-1101.

There's an active nightlife scene around Panama City Beach, where younger revelers swarm the **Club La Vela**, 850/234-3866, a 15,000-square-foot monstrosity with dozens of bars, 14 dance floors, and a poolside party area that holds hundreds. Also huge, and hugely popular with twenty-somethings, is the **Spinnaker**, 850/234-7882, a beach club with poolside contests and live entertainment. Country-western bands perform at the **Playhouse Lounge**, 850/234-7373. For fine country-style music and comedy entertainment suitable for families, the **Ocean Opry**, 850/234-5464, offers nightly shows and matinees.

# APPENDIX

Consider this appendix your travel tool box. Use it along with the material in the Planning Your Trip chapter to craft the trip you want. Here are the tools you'll find inside:

1. **Planning Map.** Make copies of this map and plot out various trip possibilities. Once you've decided on your route, you can write it on the original map and refer to it as you're traveling.

2. **Mileage Chart.** This chart shows the driving distances (in miles) between various destinations throughout Florida. Use it in conjunction with the Planning Map.

3. **Special Interest Tours.** If you'd like to plan a trip around a certain theme—such as nature, sports, or art—one of these tours may work for you.

4. **Calendar of Events.** Here you'll find a month-by-month listing of major area events.

5. **Resources.** This guide lists various regional chambers of commerce and visitors bureaus, state offices, bed-and-breakfast registries, and other useful sources of information.

# PLANNING MAP: FLORIDA

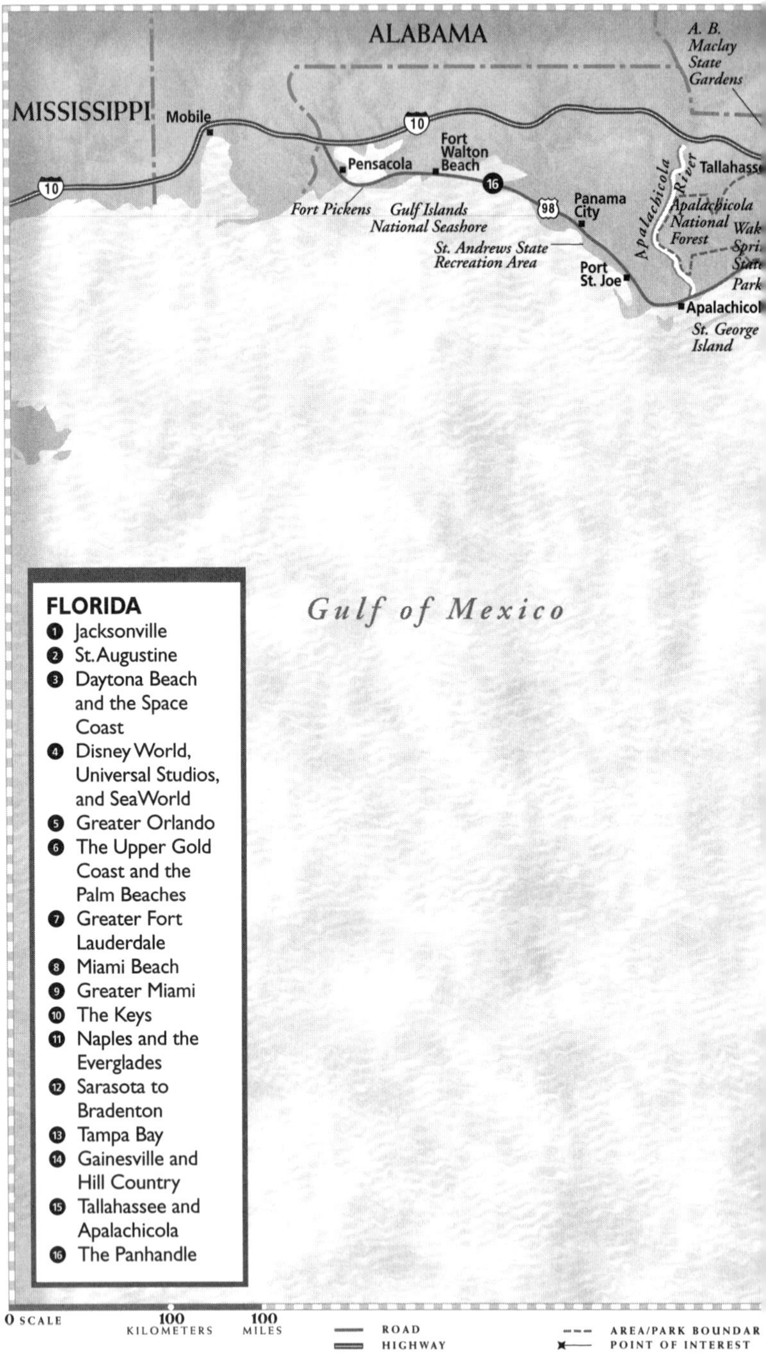

You have permission to photocopy this map.

## FLORIDA MILEAGE CHART

| | Jacksonville | St. Augustine | Daytona Beach | Orlando | Melbourne | Stuart | West Palm Beach | Fort Lauderdale | Miami | Key West | Naples | Sarasota | Tampa | Lakeland | Ocala | Gainesville | Tallahassee | Panama City |
|---|---|---|---|---|---|---|---|---|---|---|---|---|---|---|---|---|---|---|
| **St. Augustine** | 43 | | | | | | | | | | | | | | | | | |
| **Daytona Beach** | 89 | 53 | | | | | | | | | | | | | | | | |
| **Orlando** | 134 | 98 | 54 | | | | | | | | | | | | | | | |
| **Melbourne** | 174 | 137 | 86 | 67 | | | | | | | | | | | | | | |
| **Stuart** | 237 | 200 | 149 | 129 | 63 | | | | | | | | | | | | | |
| **West Palm Beach** | 274 | 238 | 187 | 166 | 101 | 38 | | | | | | | | | | | | |
| **Fort Lauderdale** | 306 | 281 | 229 | 209 | 144 | 80 | 43 | | | | | | | | | | | |
| **Miami** | 338 | 302 | 251 | 228 | 165 | 102 | 64 | 22 | | | | | | | | | | |
| **Key West** | 493 | 456 | 405 | 371 | 319 | 256 | 219 | 177 | 155 | | | | | | | | | |
| **Naples** | 319 | 285 | 241 | 187 | 201 | 163 | 147 | 105 | 107 | 236 | | | | | | | | |
| **Sarasota** | 236 | 227 | 181 | 127 | 171 | 161 | 174 | 201 | 211 | 341 | 105 | | | | | | | |
| **Tampa** | 188 | 177 | 139 | 85 | 129 | 160 | 193 | 234 | 145 | 387 | 156 | 53 | | | | | | |
| **Lakeland** | 180 | 152 | 108 | 54 | 98 | 133 | 168 | 210 | 220 | 363 | 143 | 74 | 32 | | | | | |
| **Ocala** | 95 | 83 | 76 | 55 | 138 | 196 | 233 | 276 | 294 | 436 | 229 | 142 | 93 | 87 | | | | |
| **Gainesville** | 69 | 73 | 98 | 109 | 175 | 233 | 269 | 312 | 331 | 474 | 264 | 177 | 128 | 121 | 37 | | | |
| **Tallahassee** | 163 | 196 | 234 | 242 | 307 | 365 | 401 | 444 | 463 | 606 | 389 | 285 | 239 | 247 | 170 | 144 | | |
| **Panama City** | 260 | 292 | 331 | 334 | 399 | 457 | 493 | 536 | 555 | 698 | 481 | 377 | 331 | 339 | 262 | 236 | 97 | |
| **Pensacola** | 354 | 386 | 425 | 428 | 493 | 550 | 587 | 630 | 649 | 792 | 575 | 471 | 425 | 433 | 356 | 330 | 191 | 103 |

# SPECIAL INTEREST TOURS

With *Florida Travel•Smart* you can plan a trip of any length—a one-day excursion, a getaway weekend, or a three-week vacation—around any special interest. To get you started, the following pages contain six tours geared toward a variety of interests. For more information, refer to the chapters listed—chapter names are bolded and chapter numbers appear inside black bullets. You can follow a suggested itinerary in its entirety, or shorten, lengthen, or combine parts of each, depending on your starting and ending points.

Discuss alternative routes and schedules with your travel companions—it's a great way to have fun, even before you leave home. And remember: Don't hesitate to change your itinerary once you're on the road. Careful study and planning ahead of time will help you make informed decisions as you go, but spontaneity is the extra ingredient that will make your trip memorable.

# THE ENDLESS BEACH TOUR

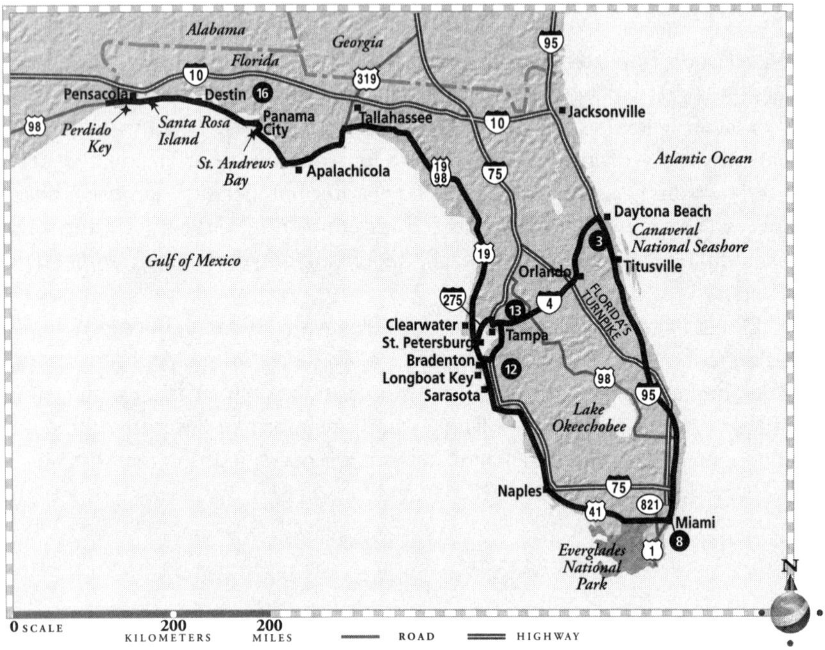


You can't quite walk the beach all the way around Florida (because of swamps and mangrove forests), but some of the world's best beaches are here, especially along the Gulf of Mexico coastline.

❸ **Daytona Beach and the Space Coast** (Daytona Beach, Canaveral National Seashore, New Smyrna Beach, Cocoa Beach)
❽ **Miami Beach** (South Beach, Lummus Park, Haulover Beach, North Shore)
⓬ **Sarasota to Bradenton** (Longboat Key, Lido Key, Bradenton Beach, Holmes Beach, Palm Island Resort)
⓭ **Tampa Bay** (Caladesi Island, Sand Key, Clearwater Beach, Pass-a-Grille Beach, Fort DeSoto)
⓰ **The Panhandle** (Seaside, St. Andrews State Recreation Area, Perdido Key, Panama City Beach, Mexico Beach, Santa Rosa Beach, Destin)

Time needed: 2 weeks—or as long as the sunscreen lasts

# FAMILY FUN TOUR

Florida is packed with family-oriented attractions. Here are some of the best

❹ **Disney World, Universal Studios, and SeaWorld** (Magic Kingdom, Epcot, Animal Kingdom, MGM Studios, Wet 'n' Wild, Universal Studios, Islands of Adventure, SeaWorld)

❺ **Greater Orlando** (Water Mania, Gatorland, Katie's Wekiva River Landing, Ripley's Believe It or Not, Jungleland, Cypress Gardens, airboat rides, Central Florida Zoological Park, Green Meadows Petting Farm)

❾ **Greater Miami** (MetroZoo, Miami Seaquarium, Everglades Alligator Farm, Miami Museum of Science and Space Transit Planetarium, Parrot Jungle and Gardens, Venetian Pool, Monkey Jungle)

⓭ **Tampa Bay** (Busch Gardens, Adventure Island Water Park, Great Explorations Museum, Florida Aquarium, Lowry Park Zoo, Museum of Science and Industry)

Time needed: 2 weeks

# PARKS AND GARDENS TOUR

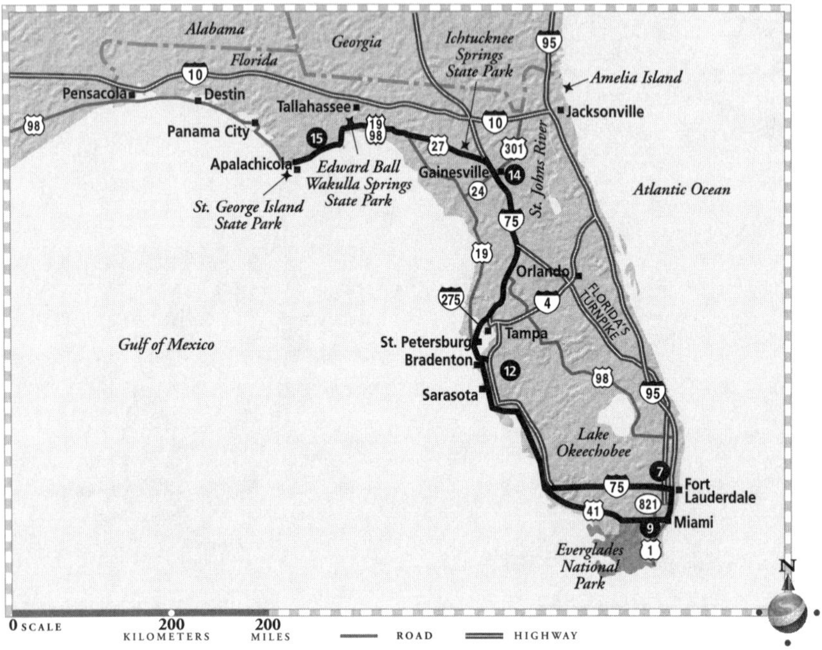


Florida's subtropical flora is the star on this tour.

- ❼ **Greater Fort Lauderdale** (Flamingo Gardens and Arboretum, Anne Kolb Nature Center, Hugh Taylor Birch State Recreation Area, John U. Lloyd Beach State Recreation Area)
- ❾ **Greater Miami** (Fairchild Tropical Garden, Vizcaya Museum and Gardens, Parrot Jungle and Gardens)
- ⓬ **Sarasota to Bradenton** (Marie Selby Botanical Gardens, Myakka River State Park, Sarasota Jungle Gardens, Historic Spanish Point)
- ⓮ **Gainesville and Hill Country** (Kanapaha Botanical Gardens, Paynes Prairie State Preserve, Ichetucknee Springs State Park)
- ⓯ **Tallahassee and Apalachicola** (Alfred B. Maclay State Gardens, Edward Ball Wakulla Springs State Park, St. George Island State Park)

Time needed: 10 days

# ARTS AND MUSIC TOUR

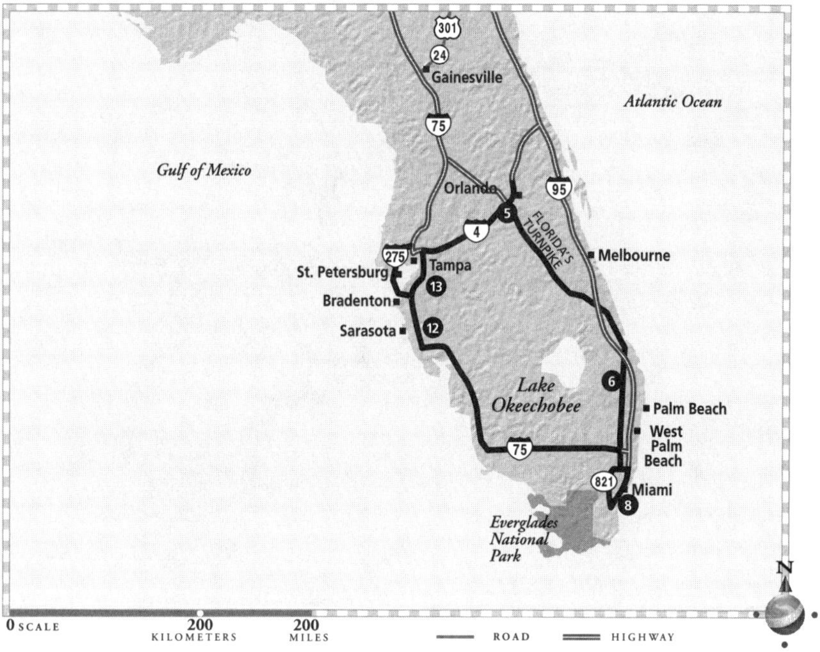


Florida as a cultural haven? You bet. The state is now home to some of the finest art museums, musical organizations, and performing groups.

❺ **Greater Orlando** (Charles Hosmer Morse Museum of American Art, Albin Polasek Museum, opera, theater, ballet, chamber music)

❻ **Upper Gold Coast and the Palm Beaches** (Norton Museum of Art, The Henry Morrison Flagler Museum, Society of the Four Arts, Hibel Museum of Art, Bethesda-by-the-Sea, chamber music, theater)

❽ **Miami Beach** (Art Deco Welcome Center, Bass Museum of Art, The Wolfsonian Foundation Gallery, orchestra, ballet, opera, theater)

⓬ **Sarasota to Bradenton** (John and Mable Ringling Museum of Art, professional theater, dinner theater, orchestra, ballet, opera, chamber music)

⓭ **Tampa Bay** (Salvador Dalí Museum, Florida International Museum, Museum of Fine Arts, Tampa Museum of Art, theater, symphony, ballet)

Time needed: 10 days

# FLORIDA CRACKER TOUR

There was Florida before Disney, and there are still pockets of old, nineteenth-century Florida dotted around the state. Here you can get a taste of life before paving and air-conditioning.

⓫ **Naples and the Everglades** (Corkscrew Swamp Sanctuary, Everglades Excursions, Wooten's, Big Cypress Gallery)

⓬ **Sarasota to Bradenton** (Gamble Plantation State Historic Site, Sarasota Jungle Gardens)

⓮ **Gainesville and Hill Country** (Cedar Key, Brooksville, Marjorie Kinnan Rawlings State Historic Site, Micanopy, McIntosh)

⓯ **Tallahassee and Apalachicola** (Brokaw-McDougall House, First Presbyterian Church, Goodwood Plantation, John G. Riley House Museum, Knott House Museum, John Gorrie State Museum)

⓰ **The Panhandle** (Historic Pensacola Village, Perdido Key)

Time needed: 7 days

# DETERMINED GOLFERS TOUR

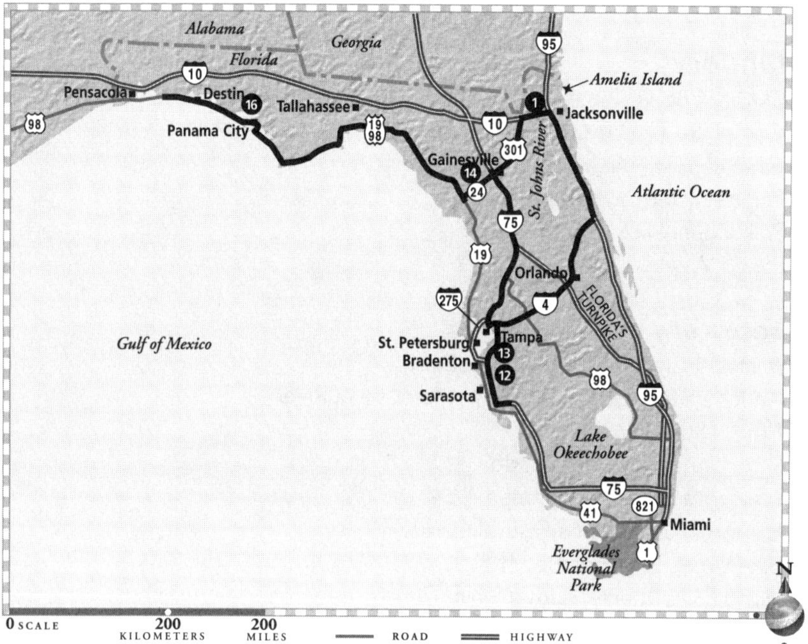


Florida is home to about 1,200 courses, including some of the most challenging you'll find anywhere.

❶ **Jacksonville** (Marriott at Sawgrass Resort courses, Amelia Island courses, Eagle Harbor, Queen's Harbour, The Ravines)

⓬ **Sarasota to Bradenton** (Legacy Golf Club, University Park Country Club, Pelican Pointe Golf Club, Riverwood Golf Club, Bobcat Trail Golf Club)

⓭ **Tampa Bay** (Westin Innisbrook Resort's Copperhead and four other courses, Saddlebrook Resort's two Arnold Palmer courses)

⓮ **Gainesville and Hill Country** (World Woods Golf Club, Golden Ocala Golf & Country Club, Silverthorn Country Club, The Dunes Golf Club at Seville)

⓰ **Panhandle** (Sandestin Resort, Marriott's Bay Point Resort, Florida Caverns Golf Course)

Time needed: There isn't enough time.

# CALENDAR OF EVENTS

## *January*

Outback Bowl, Tampa
CompUSA Florida Citrus Bowl, Orlando
Orange Bowl, Miami
Epiphany, Tarpon Springs
Polk County Fair, Winter Haven
Speed Weeks, Daytona

## *February*

Arts and Crafts Festival, Mount Dora
Antique and Classic Boat Show, Homosassa River
Florida State Fair, Tampa
Silver Spurs Rodeo, Orlando
Gasparilla Pirate Fest, Tampa
Bay Area Renaissance Festival, Largo
Bike Week, Daytona Beach
Florida Strawberry Festival, Plant City

## *March*

St. George Island Chili Cookoff and Auction, Apalachicola
Florida Irish Festival, Casselberry
New RiverFest, Fort Lauderdale
Winter Equestrian Festival, Tampa
Lakeland, Orange Cup Regatta
Carnaval Miami
Florida Strawberry Festival, Plant City
Antique Boat Festival, Mount Dora
Winter Park Sidewalk Arts Festival, Central Park in Winter Park

## *April*

Lakeland, Sun 'n' Fun EAA Fly-In
American Stage In The Park, St. Petersburg
St. Anthony's Tampa Bay Triathlon, St. Petersburg
Sun 'n' Fun Festival, Clearwater
Tarpon Springs Arts & Crafts Festival, Spring Bayou
Antique Auto Show, Mount Dora
Sailing Regatta, Mount Dora

Sidewalk Art Festival, Cedar Key
Spring Boat Show, Bahia Mar Yachting Center, Fort Lauderdale

## May

Isle of Eight Flags Shrimp Festival, Fernandina Beach
Sidewalk Art Show, Mount Dora
Great Sunrise Balloon Race and Exposition, Lake Wales Airport
Shell Air & Sea Show, Fort Lauderdale Beach
Fishing Rodeo, Pompano Beach
Florida Folk Festival, Stephen Foster State Folk Culture Center, White Springs
Sweet Corn Festival, Zellwood

## June

Music Festival, Sarasota
Goombay Festival, Miami/Bahamas
Juneteenth, St. Petersburg
Florida Philharmonic Summer Music Festival, Fort Lauderdale
Official State Play, *The Cross and Sword*, St. Augustine

## July

Pepsi 400 Race at International Speedway, Daytona Beach
Blue Angels Air Show, Pensacola Beach
Celebrate America, Clearwater
Kingfish Tournament, Fernandina Beach
Hemingway Days Festival, Key West
Tropical Agricultural Fiesta, Homestead

## August

Annual Sportfish Tournament, Fort Walton/Destin
Shark's Tooth and Seafood Festival, Venice Fishing Pier
Summerfest, Riverside Park, Vero Beach
Shakespeare Festival, Hollywood

## September

Founders Day, Menendez Landing, St. Augustine
Senior PGA Tour Emerald Coast Classic, The Moors Golf Club, Milton
Florida Birding Festival, Shell Key
Seafood Festival, Pensacola

## October

Halloween Horror Nights, Universal Studios, Orlando
NSRA Southeast Street Rod Nationals, Tampa
Seafood Festival, Cedar Key
NASCAR Winston Cup Series, Daytona International Speedway, Daytona
Biketoberfest, Daytona Beach
Jazz Holiday, Coachman Park, Clearwater
Fishing Rodeo, Destin
Boggy Bayou Mullet Festival, Niceville
John's Pass Seafood Festival, John's Pass Village, Madeira Beach

## November

Florida Seafood Festival, Apalachicola
Mum Festival, Cypress Gardens
Withlacoochee Bluegrass Festival, Dunnellon
Turkey Run, Daytona Beach
Apalachicola Seafood Festival
Poinsettia Festival, Cypress Gardens

## December

Poinsettia Festival, Cypress Gardens
Nights of Lights Festival, St. Augustine
Festival of Lights, Lake City
Holiday Celebration, Walt Disney World, Lake Buena Vista
Lighted Boat Parade, The Pier, St. Petersburg
New Year's Eve Street Party, Church Street Station, Orlando

# RESOURCES

Alachua County Visitors and Convention Bureau, 352/374-5231, www.co.alachua.fl.us/~acvacb

Amelia Island Tourist Development Council, 800/226-3542, www.goflorida.com/amelia_island

Central Florida Visitors and Convention Bureau, 800/828-7655, www.cfdc.org/tourism

Clearwater Office of Tourist Development, 888/425-3279, www.VisitClearwaterFlorida.com

Cocoa Beach Convention and Visitors Bureau, 321/459-2200, www.iu.net/cocoa.beach/chamber

Daytona Beach Area Convention & Visitors Bureau, 800/854-1234 or 904/255-0415, www.daytonabeach-tourism.com

Emerald Coast Convention and Visitors Bureau, 850/651-7131 or 800/332-3319, www.destin-fwb.com

Florida Keys Visitor Center, 800/822-1088 or 305/451-1414, www.floridakeys.org

Florida's Space Coast Office of Tourism, 800/872-1969, www.space-coast.com

Greater Miami Convention and Visitors Bureau, 800/283-2707 or 305/539-3000, www.miamiandbeaches.com

Greater Fort Lauderdale Convention and Visitors Bureau, 800/227-8669, www.sunny.org

Greater Sanford Chamber of Commerce, 407/332-2212, www.sanfordchamber.com

Hernando County Tourist Development Council, 800/601-4580, www.co.hernando.fl.us/tourdev/

Jacksonville and the Beaches Convention and Visitors Bureau, 800/733-2668

Key West Chamber of Commerce, 800/527-8539 or 305/294-2587

Key West Information Center, 800/222-5148 or 305/292-5000, www.keywestinfo.com

Kissimmee/St. Cloud Convention and Visitors Bureau, 800/327-9159 or 407/847-5000, www.floridakiss.com

Lake County Convention and Visitors Bureau, 800/798-1071 or 352/429-3673, www.lakecountyfl.com

Lee Island Coast Visitors and Convention Bureau, 800/237-6444 or 941/533-4743, www.LeeIslandCoast.com

Marco Island and the Everglades Convention and Visitors Bureau, 800/788-6272 or 941/394-7549, www.marco-island-florida.com
Miami Beach Latin Chamber of Commerce, 305/674-1231, www.miamibch-tourist.com
Naples Area Tourism Bureau, 800/605-7878 or 941/262-2712, www.naples-online.com
Orlando/Orange County Convention & Visitors Bureau, 800/554-1529 or 800/551-0181, www.goflorida.com/orlando or www.go2orlando.com
Palm Beach County Convention and Visitors Bureau, 561/471-3995
Panama City Beach Convention and Visitors Bureau, 800/722-3224 or 850/233-6503, www.panamacitybeachfl.com
Pensacola Convention and Visitor Center, 800/874-1234 or 850/434-1234, www.visitpensacola.com
Sanibel and Captiva Islands Chamber of Commerce, 941/472-1080, www.sanibel-captiva.org
Sarasota Convention and Visitors Bureau, 800/522-9779 or 941/957-1877, www.cvb.sarasota.fl.us.com
Seminole County Convention and Visitors Bureau, 800/800-7832, www.co.seminole.fl.us/visit
South Walton Tourist Development Council, 800/822-6877, www.beachesofsouthwalton.com
St. Augustine and St. Johns County Visitor Information, 800/653-2489 or 904/825-1000
St. Johns County Visitors and Convention Bureau, 800/653-2489, www.oldcity.com
St. Petersburg/Clearwater Convention and Visitors Bureau, 800/345-6710 or 727/464-7200, www.stpete-clearwater.com
Tallahassee Area Convention and Visitors Bureau, 800/628-2866 or 850/413-9200, www.co.leon.fl.us/visitors/index.htm
Tampa/Hillsborough Convention and Visitors Association, 800/448-2672 or 813/223-1111, www.thcva.com
Tropical Everglades Visitor Center, 800/388-9669 or 305/245-9180

# INDEX

# Map Index

Loren J. Wilson

## ABOUT THE AUTHORS

David and Rose Wilson took far different routes to Florida but discovered individually, then together, that the subtropical flatland really is home.

Rose has written extensively about Florida, the American Southwest, Alaska, and Canada for AAA Auto Club South's *Going Places* magazine. Her work has also appeared in travel publications and newspapers on both sides of the Mississippi.

David is managing editor of the Tampa Bay business magazine *Maddux Report*. His newspaper and magazine career has extended from Montana and Idaho to New Jersey and Florida. His travel writing has appeared in *Tampa Bay Life*, the *Sun Times of Canada*, *Coastal Living*, and newspapers across the United States.

The Wilsons try to find paths less traveled and share their discoveries with travelers who want to take home more than memories of Florida's clean air, salt breezes, and exotic wildlife. On warm January days, when they see a Minnesota license plate go by, they still find it difficult not to turn to each other and say, "What a gorgeous day—and we live here."